Essentials of Child Development and Personality

Essentials of Child Development and Personality

Paul Henry Mussen
UNIVERSITY OF CALIFORNIA, BERKELEY

John Janeway Conger
UNIVERSITY OF COLORADO SCHOOL OF MEDICINE

Jerome Kagan
HARVARD UNIVERSITY

With the assistance of Diana Steen

HARPER & ROW, PUBLISHERS, New York
Cambridge, Hagerstown, Philadelphia, San Francisco,
London, Mexico City, São Paulo, Sydney

1817

Photo credits: Page 4, Sweezy, Stock, Boston; 6, Leonard, Woodfin Camp; 10, Hoops, DeWys; 14, Hoban, DPI; 21, Laping, DPI; 29, Bernheim, Woodfin Camp; 33, Dunn, DPI; 42, Schuyler, Stock, Boston; 54, Hammid, Rapho/Photo Researchers; 64, Miller, Magnum; 66, DeWys; 73, Hardy, Woodfin Camp; 77, Dunn, DPI; 91, Dunn, DPI; 95, Dunn, DPI; 100, Nero, DPI; 106, Roos, DPI; 113, Heron, Woodfin Camp; 117, Moon, Stock, Boston; 120, Gatewood, Stock, Boston; 125, Kliewe, Jeroboam; 130, Dunn, DPI; 142, Betty Moore; 146, Lejeune, Stock, Boston; 155, Lejeune, Stock, Boston; 156, © Frostie, Woodfin Camp; 164, Shelton, Monk-meyer; 167, Ursillo, DeWys; 172, Kliewe, Jeroboam; 174, Vine, DeWys; 180, Johnson, DeWys; 190, Johnson, Woodfin Camp; 193, DeWys; 195, Hamlin, Stock, Boston; 202, Shelton, DPI; 206, Charles Gatewood; 210, Hamlin, Stock, Boston; 214, Raynor, DeWys; 221, Mannheim, DPI; 226, Mezey, DPI; 229, Tress, Woodfin Camp; 235, Kliewe, Jeroboam; 245, Sidney, Monkmeyer; 251, Sidney, Monkmeyer; 261, Vivienne, DPI; 271, Silverman, DeWys; 275, Heron, Monk-meyer; 278, Faller, Monkmeyer; 284, Adelman, Magnum; 290, Erwitt, Magnum; 291, Erwitt, Magnum; 302, Conklin, Monkmeyer; 307, DeWys; 309, Ursillo, DeWys; 311, Schmidt, DPI; 322, Sydney, DeWys; 329, Gordon, DPI; 334, Marmaras, Woodfin Camp; 348, Harrison, Stock, Boston; 352, Kaplan, DPI; 354, Haas, DeWys; 360, Payne, Jeroboam; 361, Conklin, Monk-meyer; 370, George Gardner; 379, Wolinsky, Stock, Boston; 389, Prelutsky, Stock, Boston; 394, Lebo, Jeroboam; 402, Gellerose, Stock, Boston.

Sponsoring Editor: George A. Middendorf
Project Editor: Holly Detgen
Designer: Rita Naughton
Senior Production Manager: Kewal K. Sharma
Photo Researcher: Myra Schachne
Compositor: Ruttle, Shaw & Wetherill, Inc.
Printer and Binder: Halliday Lithograph Corporation
Art Studio: Vantage Art Inc.
Marginal Cartoons: Elaine Vogt
Cover Photo: Bill Longcore

Essentials of Child Development and Personality

Library of Congress Cataloging in Publication Data

Mussen, Paul Henry.
    Essentials of child development and personality.

    Bibliography: p.
    Includes indexes.
    1. Child psychology. 2. Personality. I. Conger, John Janeway, joint author. II. Kagan, Jerome, joint author. III. Title.
BF721.M884   155.4′18   79-19041
ISBN 0-06-044704-4

Contents

Preface

Essentials of Child Development and Personality, like the fifth edition of Mussen, Conger, and Kagan's *Child Development and Personality,* published in 1979, is designed to present a well-balanced, up-to-date, and comprehensive view of human development from birth through adolescence. Recent research on the many complex factors influencing biological, cognitive, personality, and social development at each stage of development is stressed. Topics of special social and theoretical interest currently include: effects of poverty and discrimination on cognitive functioning and personality development; child abuse; effects of divorce and problems of the single-parent family; consequences of institutionalization; effectiveness of intervention strategies with disadvantaged children; assessment of day-care programs; alternative child-rearing practices; television as a socializing agent; school failure and learning disabilities; changing sex roles and sexual identity; adolescent sexuality and teenage pregnancy; vocational problems of adolescence and youth; drug use and delinquency; and changing social and cultural conditions in relation to personality development, values, and the social behavior of adolescents.

The structure and organization of the present volume differ from those of the fifth edition of *Child Development and Personality* in several important respects. Although the present book is shorter, it still contains a comprehensive and authoritative review of the basic issues, facts, and theories of human development. The reduction in size has not been achieved by omitting important information. Rather we have selected from the many studies available only exemplary investigations that contribute significant information, and we have condensed and simplified complex technical discussions of research procedures.

The present book adheres much more strictly than the fifth edition to a chronological approach. Many instructors and students believe that this organization presents a more integrated view of the child's status at each major phase of development. Consequently, individual parts are devoted to prenatal development, infancy, the preschool years, middle childhood, and adolescence.

To communicate a deeper understanding and a more immediate and direct feeling of what children are like at various ages, we have included many specific accounts of reactions and capabilities at each age, illustrating these with both everyday examples and normative data. Boxes have been used in each chapter to highlight especially interesting theoretical, applied, or research issues. Each chapter concludes with a summary of critical points.

The book reflects the remarkable progress that has been made in the study of child development during the last decade, both in depth and breadth of knowledge. Our fondest hope is that the book will stimulate students to use their curiosity and will teach them to make better judgments about developmental psychology, a field that will undoubtedly continue to gain in intellectual excitement and practical importance in the future.

We gratefully acknowledge the assistance of many others in preparation of this book. The greatest indebtedness is to Diana Steen, who assumed primary responsibility for the organization and writing of the text. Professors Harriet V. Agster, Hillsborough Community College; James Booth, Philadelphia Community College; Patricia Crane, San Antonio College; Margaret Lloyd, Suffolk University; Dennis Thompson, Georgia State University; Kathleen Van Hover, Potomac, Maryland; Ross Vasta, State University of New York; Hilda Welch, Portland Community College; and Mary Jo Williams, San Jacinto College read all or parts of earlier versions of the manuscript and made many valuable criticisms and contributions.

Paul Henry Mussen
John Janeway Conger
Jerome Kagan

Essentials of Child Development and Personality

Chapter 1

Introduction

*D*EBORAH AND JAMES are two 8-year-olds with very different personalities. One is friendly and outgoing; the other is shy and retiring. Both tend to be generous and altruistic. One gets frustrated and cries very easily; the other seems to be bothered by little. Both children are bright and do well in school. One child is well coordinated and does well in athletics, and the other finds sports difficult.

How do these differences develop? Are they produced mainly by genetic or other biological factors or by environmental forces, personal experiences, and relationships? Which environmental factors are most important in influencing different characteristics?

It is the task of developmental psychologists to study the origins of behavior and changes in behavior over time and attempt not only to describe these changes but also to discover what determines them. A developmental psychologist looking at the home environment of each child discussed above would find some similarities and some differences. Both children live in an urban setting. One has two brothers; the other is an only child. One lives with both parents; the other is being reared in a single-parent home. In one home discipline is rather strict and controlled; in the other it is more flexible. Certainly each child's particular genetic heritage is unique, although they may resemble each other in some ways. The genetic differences may account for the differences in body size and shape and in athletic ability.

One child is well coordinated and does well in athletics, and the other finds sports difficult.

The changes in behavior that are of interest to developmental psychologists range from basic physical and motor advances such as creeping and walking, to changes in **cognitive** abilities, such as becoming able to remember or to reason, and changes in personality, such as becoming consistently more or less aggressive or independent. Notice that these changes last for a reasonable period of time; they are not temporary and transient.

All of the above changes are called developments, and usually they result in behavior that is "better" — that is, more adaptive, healthier, more complex, more stable, or more efficient. However, there are some negative changes that are also regarded as developments — for instance, the development of bad habits, delinquent behavior, or mental illness.

The first goals of developmental psychology are the description, measurement, and explanation of changes that appear to be universal, that appear to occur in all children in all cultures. For example, developmental psychologists have observed that children all over the world utter their first words at about 12 months of age and walk alone at about 13 months. Also, most children begin to show anxiety in the presence of strangers sometime between the ages of 8 and 12 months. Why? Developmental psychologists assume that some interaction of maturation and experience is responsible for these universal phenomena of growth.

In addition to these universal changes, developmental psychologists are interested in explaining individual differences in behavior. For example, many 8-month-olds are closely attached to their mothers and become anxious and cry when their mothers leave them, but others do not. Most 4-year-olds can repeat a ten-word sentence immediately after it is spoken; other children cannot do so until they are 6. Developmental psychologists attempt to determine what accounts for these individual differences in development.

Furthermore, a child's behavior may vary from one situation to another. Why do children cling to their mothers in a strange room but move about freely in a familiar setting? Why are some frustrated 5-year-olds aggressive with strangers but cooperative with friends? These situational differences in behavior are also part of the study of children's development.

Finally, the developmental psychologist is concerned with explaining deviant behavior, such as **autism,** drug addiction, delinquency, and mental deficiency. Some of these maladjustments may be due to biological factors, others may be caused by certain environmental stresses or by a combination of both. If the developmental causes of these abnormalities are discovered, it may be possible to prevent some of them. For example, it has been discovered that if a pregnant woman contracts rubella, or German measles, the baby she is carrying is likely to be mentally and physically defective and a little more likely to become autistic. Innoculating women against rubella would reduce the incidence of these problems. Similarly, children's emotional maladjustments are frequently the result of adverse experiences in the family and the social environment. If we knew specifically what these damaging experiences were and the ages at which they were most likely to occur, it might be possible to intervene and thus to prevent the child's maladjustments.

The range of topics studied by developmental psychologists has grown enormously during the last few decades. Age-old issues—for example, the question of how parental practices influence the child's personality—have been investigated more thoroughly. At the same time, many previously unexplored areas—such as the cognitive capabilities of the newborn—have become the subjects of research. Then, too, many developmental psychologists are concerned with social problems, and so they focus their attention on understanding problems such as juvenile delinquency, school failure, maladjustment, drug abuse, adolescent pregnancy, and emotional disturbance.

A sampling of topics to be discussed in this book illustrates the range of recent research in developmental psychology: Does the health of a mother during pregnancy affect her unborn child's potential? What kinds of stimuli and events are most likely to attract an infant's attention? What are the cognitive (perceptual, thinking, reasoning) capacities of infants? Is there a universal sequence of steps, or stages, in intellectual development? If there is, can we speed up the progress through these stages by special training? Why do kindergarten children from minority groups in ghetto

areas score lower on the standard tests of intelligence and language than do middle-class white children the same age? Are hereditary factors important in the formation of traits such as independence? What are the effects, if any, of growing up in a single-parent home? What kinds of experiences foster the development of cooperative behavior? Are the influences of friends and classmates as powerful as those of parents in shaping adolescent behavior? These are a few of the many specific questions that we will be discussing.

THEORETICAL ISSUES

In addition to the practical applications of developmental child psychology — the "How to's" of toilet training or discipline, for example — there are theoretical concerns. That is, there are questions about the fundamental nature of children and of human development. Major theorists, such as Freud and Piaget, have made vastly different assumptions about these philosophical issues. We will briefly examine five such issues.

1. The Goals of Development

One theoretical issue involves the question of whether the child is developing toward some ideal goal. That is, should we think of the psychological development of a child as representing progress toward a "most mature" level of functioning? Or should development be thought of simply as a series of changes, without assuming that there is some final goal? Theorists differ in their point of view on this question.

2. Nature Versus Nurture

One of the best-known controversies in developmental psychology concerns the relative effects of environmental factors and of biological forces on behavior. Put more simply, this is the **nature**-versus-**nurture,** or heredity-versus-environment, issue, and we shall return to it in our discussions of various topics, such as motor development, cognition, personality, and intelligence.

All development depends on *both* biological and environmental factors, but the biological factors are relatively more important in the determination of some characteristics, while environment and experience have greater impact on others. For example, nature makes a greater contribution to the color of hair and the age when walking occurs. On the other hand, nurture (the environment and experience) is more important for other characteristics, such as the tendency toward generosity, which appears to be very little influenced by biological factors — at least in human beings. But most complex characteristics such as intellectual ability or aggressive tendencies are the products of complex interactions between biological and environmental forces. It is difficult to separate or assess accurately the relative contributions of the two types of determinants. The relevant question is *how* heredity and environment interact to produce these qualities rather than *how much* heredity and environment individually contribute.

3. The Child's Activity or Passivity

A third controversial issue revolves around the question of whether the child is naturally *active* or *passive* with respect to the world of people and objects. Is the child a passive product of experience — of what happens in the environment — or does the child actively select and influence the experiences she undergoes?

4. Continuity Versus Discontinuity in Development

Some theorists assume that the course of development is continuous, with changes and progress toward maturity taking place gradually, so that the curve of behavioral development shows a smooth, upward movement like this:

Other theorists feel that the course of development is segmented, or divided into stages, and that development advances through a series of rather abrupt changes. In each stage, new abilities, ways of thinking, and responding appear; a complex pattern of related characteristics or responses occur together and may be conveniently grouped. Each stage is characterized by distinct ways of functioning, and no stage can be skipped. In this view, every child goes through the same stages in the same order; a child cannot achieve a later stage without going through the earlier ones. The stage theorist's curve of development is more like a series of steps, and could be represented in this way:

5. Stability of Characteristics over Time

What about the stability or constancy of characteristics or abilities over time? For example, is a lively, talkative baby apt to be a lively, talkative adolescent? Is a child who is relatively intelligent likely to maintain his or her relative standing in intelligence over a long period? Can we make accurate predictions of later dependency behavior from infants' responses and characteristics? It appears that there are no fixed answers to these questions. Rather the answer varies with the particular characteristic and with the age and sex of the individual. For example, infant intelligence tests, administered before the age of 18 months, do *not* accurately predict IQ in later childhood, but IQ tests given in middle childhood *are* reasonably good predictors of adolescent and adult scores (see pp. 191 and 260).

HISTORICAL PERSPECTIVES

Contemporary Western culture is "child-centered." Almost everyone seems to be interested in the development and welfare of children. But such has not always been the case, and the ways children are treated vary from place to place and from one era to another. For example, during the early seventeenth century in Europe, many infants of affluent families were taken to a "wet nurse" for most of the day, and by the age of 10, many youngsters lived in the homes of strangers where they worked as apprentices. But by 1700 there was a marked change in attitudes toward children. Mothers were encouraged to spend more time with their babies and to assume more responsibility for their children's morality.

Philosophers and Child Psychology

Along with these new concepts of child rearing came a speculative literature dealing with child psychology and development. Many philosophers wrote about the nature of the child: Some saw the child as naturally good,

Some Contrasting Early Views of Education

Almost all major philosophers of the seventeenth and eighteenth centuries formed theories about the nature of childhood, the child's mind and development, and education. Each philosopher also offered advice to parents and teachers. John Locke, writing at the end of the seventeenth century, believed that children should be trained through rewards and punishment from the very earliest months onward; he was, in effect, a learning theorist. In contrast, Rousseau, writing in the middle of the eighteenth century, believed that the child was by nature an active explorer who had enormous potentialities that would be actualized if adults did not interfere too much.

The contrasting points of view of these philosophers are evident in the following quotations from their major works:

> *Rewards* . . . and *Punishments* must be proposed to Children, if we intend to work upon them. The Mistake . . . is, that those that are generally made use of, are *ill chosen.* . . . *Esteem* and *Disgrace* are, of all others, the most powerful incentives to the Mind. . . . If you can once get into Children a love of Credit, and an apprehension of Shame and Disgrace, you have put into them the true Principle, which will constantly work, and incline them to the right. . . . If therefore the Father *caress and commend them, when they do well; shew a cold and neglectful Countenance to them upon doing ill;* And this accompanied by a like Carriage of the Mother, and all others that are about them, it will in a little Time make them sensible of the Difference; and this if constantly observed, I doubt not but will of itself work more than Threats or blows.

> From John Locke's *Some thoughts concerning education* (4th ed., enlarged). London: Churchill, pp. 54–66, 101–108, 118–121. The first edition was published in 1693.

Rousseau, on the other hand, held a different view:

> Leave childhood to ripen in your children. . . . It is the child's individual bent, which must be thoroughly known before we can choose the fittest moral training. Every mind has its own form, in accordance with which it must be controlled; and the success of the pains taken depends largely on the fact that he is controlled in this way and no other. Oh, wise man, take time to observe nature; watch your scholar well before you say a word to him; first leave the germ of his character free to show itself, do not constrain him in anything, the better to see him as he really is.

> From Jean Jacques Rousseau, *Emile, or on education* (translated by Barbara Foxley). London: Dent, 1911. The first French edition was published in 1762; the first English edition in 1763.

others as naturally evil. The British philosopher John Locke saw the child's mind as a *tabula rasa*—Latin for "blank slate"—receptive to all kinds of learning, good or bad. That is, he believed that the child's development was determined by education and, more specifically, by the rewards and punishments provided by the environment. On the other hand, Jean Jacques Rousseau, a French philosopher of the eighteenth century, believed that children were born with an innate moral sense and that even without adult supervision and instruction, the child would develop into a moral and psychologically healthy adult unless corrupted by society.

The Beginnings of Scientific Child Psychology

The publication of Charles Darwin's great work on the evolution of plants and animals, *On the Origin of Species* (1859), was probably the single most vital force in the establishment of child psychology as a scientific discipline. Darwin's ideas emphasized the study of origins and the method of looking into the past to understand the present. It followed, then, that understanding children could lead to a better understanding of adults.

A further step in the scientific direction was the systematic study of large groups of children, which began toward the end of the nineteenth century. One pioneer was G. Stanley Hall, first president of the American Psychological Association, who devised the questionnaire as a method of scientific study. He used large numbers of children and attempted to determine the relationships among personality characteristics, adjustment problems, and background experiences. Hall's work, which continued into the twentieth century, marks the beginning of systematic child study in the United States. Although by modern standards his work cannot be considered controlled or highly objective, it represented distinct methodological advances over earlier approaches.

CONTEMPORARY CHILD PSYCHOLOGY AS A SCIENTIFIC DISCIPLINE

Early child psychologists dealt almost exclusively with age trends. They wanted to know, "What happens in the course of child development? When do these events occur?" They described and measured changes in physical, motor, and cognitive responses. Research was devoted largely to detailed analyses of the sequences of steps involved in children's acquiring various skills—such as walking, manipulating objects, and talking—and determining the ages at which children attain these capabilities.

But a mature scientific discipline has goals that go beyond description and measurement. Developmental psychologists, for example, are now interested in studying the hows and whys of changes in behavior, and thus gaining the ability to predict changes. That is, scientific explanation involves the specification of cause-and-effect, or antecedent-consequent, relationships. One must identify the antecedents (determining factors) that lead to certain outcomes or consequences—in the case of developmental psychology, to changes in behavior. In doing this, one gains the ability to predict events, one of the main advantages of scientific theory.

For example, researchers in the area of personality development attempt to discover the factors that lead to the development of characteristics such as high **achievement motivation,** aggression, and cooperation in nursery school children. For example, why is it that one child sets high standards for herself and another child does not? Similarly, why is one child aggressive in her play, hitting and pushing the other children, while another child is more orderly? What factors in the environment foster such behavior? If such questions were answered, then scientists might predict which children would be highly achievement-motivated or which children would be likely to get into trouble in adolescence. Moreover, they could suggest to interested parents how to provide the conditions that encourage high achievement motivation and inhibition of aggression. Or if there were a theory to explain why some children do not learn well in school, we could predict school failures before they occur and might be able to take more effective steps to reduce or eliminate such failures.

THEORIES OF PSYCHOLOGICAL DEVELOPMENT

Three theoretical approaches have dominated the field of developmental psychology—that of Piaget, that of Freud, and that of the learning theorists. We will review each of them, noting the areas in which they have exerted the greatest influences.

The Theory of Jean Piaget

For Jean Piaget, a twentieth-century Swiss psychologist, the developing child goes through a sequence of progressively more complex intellectual skills. Piaget derived his theories from extensive, detailed observations of children's spontaneous behavior as well as their responses to questions and problems he posed to them (see Figure 1.1). He stimulated interest in **maturational** stages of development and in the importance of cognition for

Figure 1.1 Jean Piaget observing children. (deBraine, Black Star.)

many aspects of behavior. In addition, one of Piaget's contributions to the field of child psychology was that he supported the idea that the child was active. The child is *not* a passive recipient whose beliefs, thoughts, and ways of approaching problems are primarily the result of what he or she is taught directly.

In Piaget's view, children continually try to make sense of their world by dealing actively with objects and people, and developmental changes are viewed as products of the child's activity — curiosity, searching, problem solving, and imposing structure and meaning on the environment. Children move from the level of primitive motor coordinations toward several ideal goals, including the following abilities: (1) to reason abstractly; (2) to think about hypothetical situations in a logical way; and (3) to organize mental actions or rules, which Piaget calls **operations,** into complex, higher-order cognitive structures.

Construction and Invention. According to Piaget, children use the processes of construction and invention. That is, they actively try to make sense of their experiences and to understand what is going on; in doing this they construct and invent ideas and behaviors that they have never seen. For example, the typical 7-year-old understands that a set of sticks of different lengths or a set of cups of different diameters can be arranged in a series according to their length or diameter. The typical 5-year-old does not understand this, yet by the age of 7 she will, even though she may not have seen this arrangement previously or been told about it by any adult.

The Acquisition of Operations. The central concept in Piaget's theory of intellectual growth is the operation (5). An operation is a special kind of mental routine that transforms information for some purpose and is reversible; that is, the child can perform its opposite action. Squaring the number 8 in order to get 64 is part of an operation, and we can perform the reverse operation and extract the square root of 64 in order to obtain 8. The knowledge that we can break a circular piece of clay into two semicircular pieces and combine the two semicircles into the same circular whole is also an operation. Understanding that the amount of water in a glass does not change when we transfer it to a container of a different shape is also an operation, for we know we can restore the original state of affairs by pouring the water back into its original glass. This operation is called "conservation of volume" (see Figure 1.2).

According to Piaget, the acquisition of operations is the heart of intellectual growth. He believes that the child passes through a series of stages, acquiring different classes of operations at each stage, and gradually arrives at the most mature stage during adolescence. The two major mechanisms that allow the child to move from one stage to the next are **assimilation** and **accommodation**. Assimilation is the incorporation of a new

Figure 1.2 Conservation of volume. (Shelton, Monkmeyer.)

object or idea into an idea or scheme the child already has. That is, the child applies old ideas and old habits to new objects. Accommodation is the tendency to adjust to a new object, to change one's behavior to fit the new object. Both assimilation and accommodation are discussed in Chapter 3, pp. 104–105.

Sequential Developmental Stages. As we shall see later, Piaget believes that there are four major stages of intellectual development: **sensorimotor** (0 to 18 months), **preoperational** (18 months to age 7), **concrete operations** (age 7 to 12), and, finally, **formal operations** (age 12 onward). The stages are continuous, and each later stage is built upon, or is a derivative of, the earlier ones. That is, every new ability is added to what exists, and there is always some relationship between the child's newly acquired abilities and beliefs and all of his or her past.

Since Piaget's theory and data are so central to the discussion of cognitive development, we shall present them in greater detail later on, along with a detailed critique of Piagetian theory (see Chapter 8).

**Freud and
Psychoanalytic
Theory**

Sigmund Freud (Figure 1.3), the founder of **psychoanalysis,** had interests that were quite different from Piaget's. He focused on sexual and aggressive drives and on understanding psychopathological (mentally disordered) conditions, including the role of unconscious motives, needs, and

fears. In Freud's views on development and on the goals of maturity, he emphasized emotional maturity as the goal, while Piaget emphasized reasoning. Moreover, Piaget was primarily concerned with *similarities* in the growth of *thought,* while Freud was preoccupied with *differences* in the *wishes, feelings,* and *fears* of children. Clearly, the two theorists were trying to understand different facets of human development.

Another difference between Freud and Piaget is that Freud saw children as more passive, helpless in the face of powerful biological and social forces over which they have little control. These forces include instinctual energy, which is biological in origin, and the child's social experiences, especially those that are part of family life. All children, Freud believed, develop sexual and hostile feelings toward their parents, which lead to conflict, anxiety, and, in some instances, neurosis.

Biological Energy. Freud believed that every individual is born with a fixed amount of biological energy that is the source of all basic drives and that underlies his or her future behavior, motives, and thoughts. The three sources of energy—or instincts—are (1) sexuality (sometimes called **libido**), (2) the life-preserving drives of hunger and pain, and (3) aggression—the last associated with a "death instinct" (1).

Freud believed that the amount of energy is fixed but can be channeled in different ways. It may be invested (Freud's term is *cathected*) in people, actions, thoughts, and objects. Infants are not capable of investing energy; they only possess energy. Infants are born with only one psychological structure, the **id,** a storehouse for instinctual energy. As they grow and invest energy in people and things, they gradually develop two additional psychological structures, the **ego** and **superego.** Conflicts among these three psychological structures can cause anxiety in later life.

Psychoanalytic Developmental Stages. Like Piaget, Freud believed that an individual passes through a number of distinct stages in the course of becoming mature. Freud's stages are centered on different parts of the body, depending on where the child invests most of his or her energy. For example, in the first year of life, the infant is said to be in the **oral stage.** The mouth and oral activities (feeding, biting, spitting up) are cathected (invested) with energy and supply the greatest pleasures. During the second and third years, the **anal stage,** the child experiences sensory gratification by elimination and stimulation of the rectal area. The genitals become the primary source of pleasure during the fourth and fifth years, the **phallic stage.** Finally, in adolescence, love objects become cathected (that is, the person enters into a sexually gratifying love relationship) and mature genitals are the primary source of pleasure; this is the **genital stage.**

Psychoanalytic theory maintains that the child's development can be inhibited as a result of adverse experiences that block progress toward emotional maturity. The child can become **fixated** (that is, may resist moving on to the next stage) if he or she receives either too much or too little pleasure during a certain stage of development. For example, Freud suggested that either insufficient or excessive pleasure during the oral stage might lead to enduring problems and adult symptoms such as alcoholism, depression, or excessive optimism or pessimism. **Fixation** at the anal stage was said to result in miserliness, compulsivity, aggression, and passive resistance, and fixation at the phallic stage is manifested in pompousness, narcissism, and boastfulness.

Validity of Freudian Theory. Some of Freud's basic ideas and concepts are widely accepted as valid and have been fully integrated into the wider body of psychological and psychiatric thinking. Included are the ideas that unconscious motives and ideas can influence action and thought, that early experience influences some aspects of later personality, and that children have wishes and desires that make them anxious and lead to defenses.

In other respects, however, psychoanalytic theory is inadequate to explain many of the phenomena with which it is concerned. Remember that these concepts are only hypothetical. In fact, a drawback of Freud's theory is that scientists have been unable to measure "psychological energy," and this lack of empirical support is one of the major reasons for the decreased influence in recent years of some aspects of psychoanalytic theory. For example, there is virtually no evidence to support the hypothesis that satisfaction or frustration during the oral or anal stages produces fixations that, in turn, lead to the formation of certain symptoms as the theory had predicted. Alcoholism, depression, optimism, compulsivity, and narcissism are complex patterns of behavior and have not been scientifically explained on the basis of frustration during an early stage of development.

Learning Theory

Learning theory concentrates on overt behavior rather than on the child's problem solving and thinking (as does Piaget) or on the child's wishes and feelings (as does Freud). In learning theory the powers of the environment and experience are stressed, rather than biological maturity itself. Changes in habits and beliefs are viewed as resulting from (1) imitation of models and (2) variations in patterns of rewards and punishments. In other words, the child learns by watching and imitating others. She also learns new patterns of behavior because certain behaviors are rewarded and others punished. The child may learn, for example, that it is permissible for her to touch the radio dials but not the television dials. There are no stages of development in learning theory and there is no stress on progression toward any particular goal, for there is no "ideal" adult in learning theory.

What Is Learning? Learning is the process by which behavior is modified as a result of experience (2). Of course, it is important to remember

Figure 1.3 Sigmund Freud. (Photo Trends.)

that not all behavior is learned. There are some basic responses that are innate (present from birth), such as swallowing, opening and closing the eyes, shuddering in response to a bitter taste, and grasping when pressure is applied to the palm. The concept of learning applies to the acquisition of totally new responses and to improvements or changes in the frequency of a behavior already learned. Thus, learning to play tennis requires the acquisition of a totally new set of motor coordinations, and improving one's tennis game involves changing behaviors already learned. On the other hand, learning to cry in order to attract attention involves changing the frequency of displaying an innate, "natural" response of crying.

Learning can occur almost as soon as children are born. For example, a 3-day-old newborn will learn to turn her head in the direction of the sound of a bell if she is "conditioned." That is, the infant lies on her back in a crib, and a bell is sounded on the right side of her head. If she does not turn her head to the right when the bell sounds, the experimenter lightly touches the corner of her mouth on the right side in order to facilitate the infant's turning in that direction. When she turns, she is allowed to suck on a bottle containing milk. Eventually she will turn her head in the direction of the bell without someone's stimulating the corner of her mouth. She has learned an association between the stimulus of the bell and the response of turning her head to the right.

The stimuli and responses involved in learning are of many different kinds. People who learn to respond to a stoplight by applying a foot to the brake of their car have established an association between a visual stimulus (the light) and a motor response (braking). The sight of a mother's face or the sound of her voice are also stimuli, as are internal events like thoughts, feelings, and bodily sensations. Each of these stimuli can be associated with responses, which can also be of many kinds. They can be motor acts like talking, walking, or hitting a baseball, or physiological responses like sweating or changes in heart rate.

Learning can be complex, but there are some simple forms of learning that we can look at to establish some of the basic principles of learning. Let's first take a look at classical and operant conditioning.

Classical and Operant Conditioning. The most common, and perhaps the most basic, category of learning involves the establishment of an association between an external stimulus and a response (see Figure 1.4). In **classical conditioning,** a **reflex response,** such as blinking in response to a very bright light, is associated with a previously neutral stimulus. For example, a person can be conditioned to blink at the sound of a bell if a bright light is presented frequently just after a bell sounds. The bright light causes the person to blink reflexively; eventually the person comes to associate the sound of a bell with the bright light and so blinks at the sound of the bell.

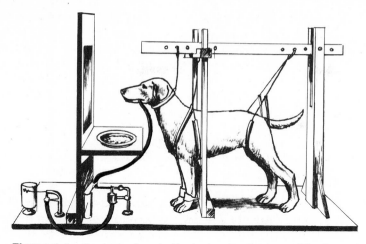

Figure 1.4 Pavlov's dog. In Pavlov's classical conditioning experiments, the dogs heard a buzzer and then received food, and they salivated. (The apparatus for the experiment involved a tube attached to the dog's salivary gland, which collected any saliva secreted by the gland, and the number of drops from the tube was recorded on a revolving drum outside the chamber.) After several "trials" in which the buzzer was paired with food, the sound of the buzzer alone produced salivation. At this point, conditioning is said to have occurred. (After R. M. Yerkes & S. Morgulis. The method of Pavlov in animal behavior. *Psychological Bulletin*, 1909, *6* (8), 257–273.)

Examples of classical conditioning in infants are observed often in natural settings. For example, within a few weeks after birth, the infant's sucking reflex, an innate (unconditioned) response to a nipple in the mouth, is readily conditioned to previously neutral stimuli, such as the sight, smell, and sound of the mother as she prepares to feed the infant. These stimuli become capable of eliciting sucking.

In what is called **operant conditioning,** a person acquires a new association between a stimulus and a learned response (one that is not a reflex). In essence, this technique involves rewarding appropriate responses whenever they happen to occur. In this procedure, something the subject does brings a reward. For example, a child might press a lever, causing candies to fall out of a slot. The response—pressing a lever—operates to bring about the reward; it is instrumental in bringing the reward; hence the terms *instrumental conditioning,* or *operant conditioning.*

In some learning situations, the experimenter, teacher, or parent may simply wait for a response to occur and then, by reinforcing it, increase the frequency of its occurrence. For example, if a baby's smiles, vocalizations, or approaches to the mother are frequently followed by rewards—such as being picked up or cuddled—the frequency of these responses will in-

Gradually, the child can be reinforced for closer and closer approximations of the desired responses, and eventually she will grip the racquet properly and swing it well.

crease strikingly. If a young child is rewarded with hugs after helping a friend, the frequency of his or her helping behavior will rise.

In other operant conditioning situations, the experimenter does not wait for a chance occurrence of the response but deliberately makes the response occur and then rewards it. For example, a little girl who is learning to play tennis can be assisted by a teacher who positions the child's hands properly on the racquet, molding her palm and fingers into a good grip and guiding the child's first swings. The teacher can "shape" more effective grip and swing responses—even though the child initially performs them poorly—by rewarding (for example, praising) responses that are approximations of good grips and good swings while disregarding poor responses. Gradually, the child can be reinforced for closer and closer approximations of the desired responses, and eventually she will grip the racquet properly and swing it well.

Drives and Motivation in Learning Theory. Learning by means of operant conditioning occurs when the learner is given some reward or reinforcement whenever he makes a correct response to a stimulus (see Figure 1.5). The notion of reward implies some prized goal, and the term *mo-*

Figure 1.5 Behavior that is followed by a reward is more likely to be repeated in the future. (LeGwin, Frederic Lewis.)

tivation refers to the forces—including biological drives such as hunger, thirst, and pain—that provoke a child to seek a particular goal. The young child's needs are fulfilled largely by means of adults. These adults thus acquire "reward value" for the child. That is, the child learns to want the presence and the nurturance of these special adults because they are associated with gratification of the child's needs. According to social-learning theorists, the need for approval and affection from adults readily becomes a general motive for a child's behavior.

Observational Learning. Not all learning depends on conditioning. Many human behaviors—perhaps most—are acquired by observing the responses of someone else (a model) and imitating them—**observational learning.** Cognitive processes, such as forming mental images, are probably involved when children learn new patterns of behavior through obser-

Learned Helplessness

Some fascinating recent research demonstrates that some young children can learn feelings of helplessness that hamper them in future efforts to achieve goals. In the original research, dogs were given shocks while strapped into a harness so that they could not escape. The next day they were placed in a different situation, without a harness, so that they could escape the painful shock by jumping over a low barrier to the other side of the room. Ordinarily, dogs readily learn this way of escaping from shock. But the dogs who had experienced inescapable shock previously did not try to make these escape responses when they had an opportunity to do so. Apparently, they had given up and accepted the inevitability of shock. It was as though they had learned that it was futile to try to escape, so they did nothing; they had learned a sense of helplessness.

In another experiment, 8-week-old human infants learned to move their heads frequently when these movements produced an interesting "show," the rotation of a brightly painted mobile hanging over their cribs. Rotation of the mobile was controlled by the infants in this way: Their heads rested on pressure-sensitive pillows and by simply moving their heads slightly, the infants activated the mechanism that rotated the mobile. A control group of infants saw the interesting rotating mobile, but it turned on its own—the infants had no control over it.

Later, both the experimental and the control infants were exposed to mobiles whose rotation they could control by moving their heads. Those who had previously been in control of the mobile's turning made this response frequently and the number of head movements in this group increased continually throughout the period of the experiment. In contrast, the infants who had no previous experience of controlling the mobile made no efforts to exercise control even when they had the opportunity to do so. Apparently this group felt helpless and made no attempt to assert any control over this aspect of their environment.

vation. By observing others, the child forms a mental idea of how new behavior patterns are performed, and on later occasions this idea serves as a guide to his behavior. Observational learning and learning by conditioning, either classical or operational, supplement each other. In many instances of learning complex responses, it is necessary to combine instruction and demonstrations with reward. For example, you would not expect anyone to learn to drive a car solely through trial-and-error procedures. Practice and instruction are both necessary.

Learning Mechanisms: Generalization and Discrimination. Two important—and related—principles of learning theory are stimulus **generalization** and **discrimination.** Let us first consider an example of generalization. If a hungry child has learned to go to the refrigerator for a snack in his own home, it is likely that if he becomes hungry in his grandmother's home he will also go to the refrigerator. Similarly, when a child has been trained to avoid a particular hot radiator or stove, he will also tend to avoid other radiators or stoves in other situations. Children learn to respond in one way to a particular cue or stimulus, and then they respond in similar ways to similar stimuli—they have generalized their responses. At first, they may judge similarity simply by appearance; later, as they get older, and language becomes more important to them, they can judge similarity by verbal labels. For example, if a child learns that the word "dog" refers to a large German shepherd as well as to a tiny toy Pekingese, then the child will generalize and respond to both animals in similar ways—patting them, expecting them to bark, and so on.

Initially, generalization is likely to be extensive. But through the process of discrimination, the child is more selective in responding to a particular label. The child who has learned to attach the label "dog" to the family pet is apt at first to extend this label to all four-footed animals. Thus, the first cow or horse encountered is likely to be called a dog. Gradually, however, the extent of the generalization will decrease until finally it is (correctly) limited only to dogs. This learned correction to overgeneralization is called discrimination (4), and is based on the elimination, or **extinction,** of incorrectly generalized responses.

Extinction. The fact that a response is learned does not mean that it will always remain strong. Each time the response is not rewarded, the association between the stimulus and the response becomes weaker, and eventually the stimulus may fail to elicit the response. When this happens, we say that the response has undergone extinction. Consider a child who throws temper tantrums to get what he wants. In this case, the parents' giving in to the tantrum is the reward, or reinforcement. If the parents stopped rewarding the tantrums, the child would eventually stop this behavior; it would have undergone extinction.

The child who has learned to attach the label "dog" to the family pet is apt at first to extend this label to all four-footed animals.

Critique of Learning Theory. The main difficulty with the learning-theory approach to child development is that it is inadequate as an explanation of spontaneous changes in beliefs, abilities, and behaviors that cannot easily be attributed to either conditioning or observation of a model. For example, why would a 10-year-old boy who has been continually rewarded for obedience at home suddenly become disobedient toward his parents? Similarly, the spontaneous solution of a problem or the emergence of a creative idea is difficult for a learning theorist to explain, and learning theory cannot adequately account for the appearance of language or novel ways of thinking and reasoning.

Summary of the Three Theories

All three major theoretical views—Piaget, Freud, and learning theory—have something important to contribute to our understanding of development. Since the theories concentrate on different aspects of the child, they are not actually as contradictory as they may appear on the surface.

This book has no single theoretical orientation because the authors believe that no current theory is sufficient to explain all the important phenomena of development. Hence, in the remainder of this book we will borrow from all theories, attempting to integrate their contributions into a more complete picture of the developing child. Certainly aspects of the child's behavior can be changed as a result of conditioning, exposure to models, and administration of rewards and punishments. But the child's development is affected not only by what others do to her. On the contrary, the child is continually active in selecting and interpreting experiences that alter her beliefs and behavior. Many of the child's goals will depend on the environment in which she lives, even though sexuality, love, mastery, hostility, and the avoidance of anxiety and pain are universal motives. Thus it is through a combination of several theories of development that we shall examine the developing child.

RESEARCH METHODS

Controlled observation and objective measurement are fundamental features of all scientific research. The scientist's observations must be as free as possible from subjective bias, and the element of control is, as you shall see, essential. Otherwise the observer (experimenter) might reach an erroneous conclusion, attributing an effect to the wrong cause.

Like other scientists, developmental psychologists use specialized techniques of measurement, appropriate to their research methods, and standard units of measurement whenever possible. When this is not possible, the units that are used must still be carefully defined so that they can be applied by others. Instruments potentially provide the most objective, and hence desirable, methods of recording natural phenomena. Moreover, the degree to which observations can be quantified (translated into numbers) is often a good index of the maturity of a science.

Psychologists can now record the reactivity of muscles, heart, and brain in a variety of environmental settings. But many psychological experiments do not lend themselves well to measurement by instruments. It would be difficult, for example, to measure attachment or dependency with instruments. In psychology, however, there are increasingly objective methods of making naturalistic observations. There are better controlled, "situational" methods of observing parent-child interactions and children's behavior, and there are improved methods of measuring the infant's behavior, perceptions, and attention. In general, during the last few years there have been marked advancements in many research techniques.

Experimental and Nonexperimental Methods

Suppose you want to know the effect competition has on children's performance on an arithmetic test. Perhaps you have hypothesized that competition will improve their performance. How might you test whether your hypothesis is valid? Observing children in classrooms in which competition is stressed and children in classrooms in which competition is not stressed might seem to be one method. But how do you know that the differences in performance are due to competition (or the lack of it) rather than to differences in the skills of the students or teachers in each classroom? A better, more controlled way of determining the effect would be to design an experiment to test your hypothesis (see Figure 1.6).

In most sciences—including psychology—the experiment is the most

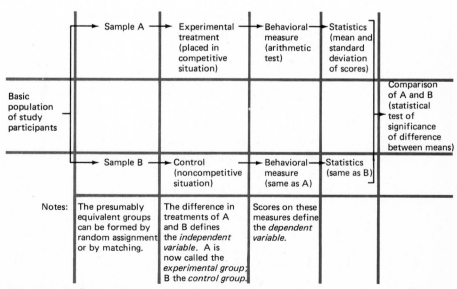

Figure 1.6 Schematic drawing of an experiment.

popular and desirable kind of observation because it permits the most direct test of a hypothesis. In its simplest form, an experiment is designed to confirm or disprove a hypothesis about how a change in one variable, the **independent variable** (in this case it is competition), affects another variable, the **dependent variable.** In this case, the dependent variable, or the one that you expect to change, is performance.

In conducting experiments, investigators do not wait for changes to occur "naturally"; rather, they try to produce these changes in systematic and controlled ways. All but one of the variables are held constant, and the experimenter manipulates that variable systematically. The experiment you might design to test performance on an arithmetic test would have two groups of children, matched (equated) on variables that might affect performance, such as intelligence, arithmetic ability, and health. One group, called the experimental group, would be tested in a competitive situation. For example, the children might be told that the student getting the highest grade would get a prize. In the control group, no such competitive situation would be created. Both groups would then be given the same arithmetic test, and the difference between the performances of the two groups would be measured. We can be fairly certain that the differences in performance (the dependent variable) would be due to the independent variable, competition, since all other factors have supposedly been controlled by the experimenter.

This simple example makes clear the unique advantage of the experimental method—namely, the direct demonstration of antecedent-consequent relationships, the precise and accurate assessment of the effects of the experimental treatment. Without the use of experimental procedures, we cannot be sure which factor or factors are determining a particular result.

There are many problems in psychology for which the experimental method is simply not appropriate or feasible. For example, suppose a hypothesis deals with the relationship between lack of parental affection early in life and later learning deficits. Obviously, parents will not reject their children simply for purposes of an experiment, so the problem must be investigated in other ways. One possible approach would involve interviews with parents of 10-year-olds to gather information about their early relationships with their children. On the basis of these interviews, the investigator could then select a group of children who had been deprived of affection and a control group who had received adequate emotional support in the early years. The two groups should be equated as closely as possible in intelligence, sex, health, and socioeconomic status. Then the school performance of the two groups could be compared to determine whether there is, in fact, a relationship between early deprivation and later learning difficulties. The study would not be an experiment in the usual sense because the experimenter did not manipulate the independent variable, early emotional deprivation. However, the study would be

Ethical Issues in Research

Developmental psychologists do research with human beings, and this entails many ethical issues and responsibilities. The researcher's primary obligation is to safeguard the welfare, dignity, and rights of all participants in research, children and adults alike. Some of the ethical dilemmas encountered in developmental research are easy to solve, but others are more subtle.

To help psychologists in making ethical decisions, professional organizations such as the American Psychological Association and the Society for Research in Child Development have formulated some broad ethical principles for conducting research with children. Of course, ethical problems cannot be solved simply by applying a set of rules; investigators must continually weigh the advantages and potential contributions of research against the disadvantages that may be involved in conducting it.

The following is a sample of principles formulated by a committee of the Society for Research in Child Development.

1. No matter how young the child, he has rights that supersede the rights of the investigator. The investigator should measure each operation he proposes in terms of the child's rights, and before proceeding he should obtain the approval of a committee of [the investigator's] peers. . . .

5. The investigator should respect the child's freedom to choose to participate in research or not, as well as to discontinue participation at any time. . . .

6. The informed consent of parents or of those who act *in loco parentis* (e.g., teachers, superintendents of institutions) similarly should be obtained, preferably in writing. Informed consent requires that the parent or other responsible adult be told all features of the research that may affect his willingness to allow the child to participate. . . . Not only should the right of the responsible adult to refuse consent be respected, but he should be given the opportunity to refuse without penalty. . . .

9. The investigator uses no research operation that may harm the child either physically or psychologically. Psychological harm, to be sure, is difficult to define; nevertheless, its definition remains the responsibility of the investigator. When the investigator is in doubt about the possible harmful effects of the research operations, he seeks consultation from others. When harm seems possible, he is obligated to find other means of obtaining the information or to abandon the research.

as close to the ideal of an experiment as would be possible under the circumstances; indeed, such investigations are sometimes called *natural experiments.*

Longitudinal Approaches and Cross-Sectional Approaches

There are two contrasting broad approaches to the study of children — **longitudinal** and **cross-sectional.** In the longitudinal approach, the same group of children is observed repeatedly over an extended period of time, sometimes for a decade or longer. This approach is especially valuable when the investigator wants to discover whether characteristics such as intelligence, aggressiveness, dependency, or behavior problems are stable over long periods of time or subject to fluctuations.

Although the longitudinal method is generally expensive, time-consuming, and difficult to use, there are many key problems in developmental psychology that require longitudinal investigation. Are scores on intelligence tests (IQs) stable over time or are they likely to fluctuate? Do symptoms of emotional disturbance that appear in childhood tend to persist into adolescence and adulthood? Do all children progress through the same sequence of steps or stages in learning their native language? These and many other questions cannot be answered without longitudinal data.

In the second and more common method, the cross-sectional approach, the investigator selects a group of children at one age period, or different groups of children at different ages, and the observations are made at one time. For example, the growth of reasoning ability can be studied with the cross-sectional method by selecting a group of ten children at each of six ages — 2, 4, 6, 8, 10, and 12 years — and comparing the average performances of the six groups on reasoning tests. It would take an investigator using the longitudinal method ten years to do a similar study of the development of reasoning, for she would have to measure the same group of 60 children at 2-year intervals from 2 to 12 years of age and assess the average 2-year growth in reasoning ability.

The short-term longitudinal approach combines some of the advantages of both longitudinal and cross-sectional methods. Groups of children of overlapping ages are tested periodically. Thus, one group might be tested annually at ages 5, 6, and 7, while another group would be tested at 7, 8, and 9. The two groups provide longitudinal data about performance at five ages, even though the study takes only three years. Moreover, both groups are tested at age 7, so the different groups may be compared at the same age.

Cross-Cultural Studies

In recent years there have been many studies comparing the members of different cultures. These **cross-cultural** studies are valuable in discovering new facts about the influences of broad social factors on personality characteristics or cognitive abilities. For example, cross-cultural studies might investigate the effects of family organization, occupational and economic activities, social-class membership, child-rearing techniques, and life

styles. Cross-cultural studies can confirm or disprove so-called universal trends in development. For example, adolescence is often seen as a period of "storm and stress" in Western cultures—particularly the United States. However, many years ago Margaret Mead showed that in some cultures—Samoa, for instance, adolescence is a relaxed and happy time (3). But "universals" of development are sometimes confirmed by cross-cultural evidence. As we mentioned earlier, children all over the world first produce very abbreviated (telegraphic) statements that communicate only very limited meanings or intentions, such as naming objects ("that doll") or stating a relationship between an action and its object ("hit ball").

Cross-cultural studies also extend the range of observations and thus permit conclusions that could not be derived from the study of a single culture. For example, it would be difficult to test the effects of various patterns of child care—such as communal child rearing and multiple mothering—on children's personality characteristics if we studied only an American sample of children, because such arrangements are relatively rare in the United States. But we can observe children raised on Israeli kibbutzim (collective farms where communal child care is characteristic) and compare their behavior with that of children brought up in nuclear families (a unit composed of parents and siblings).

Are there universal principles of cognitive or personality development? Do all children advance through the same sequence of intellectual stages, as Piaget suggests? Such questions can be answered only by means of extensive cross-cultural research. Moreover, cross-cultural studies serve as a valuable antidote to tendencies to overgeneralize the results of studies of American children and help make us aware of our own cultural biases in evaluating developmental phenomena.

SUMMARY

1. Developmental psychologists are interested in changes that occur with age, attempting not only to describe and measure these changes but also to discover what determines them.

2. Developmental psychology is concerned with both practical applications and theoretical issues, such as (a) the goals of development; (b) nature versus nurture (the effects of heredity versus environment); (c) continuity versus discontinuity in development; and (d) the stability of characteristics over time.

3. There are three major theoretical approaches to the field of developmental psychology: the theory of Jean Piaget, Freud's psychoanalytic theory, and learning theory.

4. Piaget holds that children actively try to make sense of their environment and that they move through four stages of development in reasoning: sensorimotor (0 to 18 months), preoperational (18 months to age 7), concrete operations (age 7 to 12), and formal operations (age 12 onward). The two major mechanisms that allow the child to move from one stage to the next are assimilation and accommodation.

5. Freud holds that children's personalities are shaped by powerful biological and social forces over which they have little control. Freud's theory of development is based on four stages of emotional maturity: the oral stage, the anal stage, the phallic stage, and the genital stage.

6. In learning theory the powers of the environment and experience are stressed. Learning theorists propose two fundamental mechanisms of behavior change: (a) conditioning (rewards and punishments), and (b) observation and imitation of models.

7. The study of child development has become more systematic and scientific during the twentieth century as researchers attempt to specify the causes of changes in behavior. A typical study involves a hypothesis that states a possible effect of one variable (the independent variable) on another (the dependent variable).

8. When age is the independent variable in an experiment, one can use either a longitudinal approach, investigating the same subjects at dif-

ferent ages, or a cross-sectional approach, comparing subjects of different ages. Cross-cultural studies also extend the range of observations and thus permit conclusions that could not be derived from the study of a single culture.

Suggested Readings

Bandura, A. *Social learning theory.* Englewood Cliffs, N.J.: Prentice-Hall, 1977.

Kessen, W. *The child.* New York: Wiley, 1965.

Langer, J. *Theories of development.* New York: Holt, Rinehart and Winston, 1969.

Vasta, R. *Studying children: An introduction to research methods.* San Francisco: Freeman, 1979.

Part One
The Prenatal Period

Chapter 2

Genetic and Prenatal Factors in Development

*I*F YOU HAVE never been a parent, perhaps you think that all babies are alike. They are basically squirming, crying, damp little creatures that must be fed and changed on demand. But ask three sets of parents of brand new babies about their infants and it is quite possible that you will get three detailed and varied answers describing the infants' moods, sleeping habits, eating habits, and more.

It is true that there are differences in the behavior of infants. One baby may be constantly fussy and irritable, while another is usually quiet and good-natured. And, of course, individual differences generally become more evident as a child grows older.

There are five commonly acknowledged factors that influence the behavior of the developing child and hence are responsible for the individual variations that differentiate one person from another. These are (1) genetically determined biological variables; (2) nongenetic biological variables (for example, lack of oxygen during the birth process, malnutrition); (3) the child's past learning; (4) his or her immediate social psychological environment (parents, siblings, peers, and teachers); and (5) the general social and cultural environment in which the child develops.

While each of the five factors can be described as being either biological or environmental, it is impossible to ever completely separate one from the other four. For example, a child with minimal brain damage who receives special training and learning aids may to a large extent be able to overcome the handicap, while a child with an intact brain who is not given educational training may fail to develop the full extent of her mental powers. But who is to say precisely how much a particular effect is due to brain capacity and how much is due to environment?

This chapter will deal with our current knowledge of human genetics (particularly as it affects behavior) and with factors affecting the course of prenatal development and the birth process. For purposes of organization, genetic and environmental factors will be discussed separately, but remember that all factors *interact* to produce the final behavioral effect.

Ask three sets of parents of brand new babies about their infants and it is quite possible that you will get three detailed answers.

BEGINNINGS OF LIFE

We all know the story of the birds and the bees, but just exactly how do two cells meet to form a new life? First of all, the two cells that meet are not just any cells: They are cells specialized for the purpose of reproduction. The male cell is a **sperm** cell; the female cell is an **ovum,** or egg. The life of each individual begins when a sperm cell from the father penetrates the wall of an ovum from the mother. The fertilized ovum divides and subdivides until thousands of cells have been produced. Gradually, as the process continues, the resulting cells begin to assume special functions, as parts of the nervous, skeletal, muscular, and circulatory systems. The gradually expanding ball of cells begins to take shape, as the beginnings of head, eyes, trunk, arms, and legs appear. Approximately 9 months after fertilization, a new individual is ready for birth.

**HEREDITARY
TRANSMISSION**

Life begins at conception. But what of the forces that, throughout the individual's existence, will influence her development? When do they begin? The answer, again, is at conception. For at the moment that the tiny tadpole-shaped sperm penetrates the wall of the ovum, it releases 23 minute particles called **chromosomes.** At approximately the same time, the nucleus, the inner core of the ovum, breaks up, releasing 23 chromosomes of its own. Thus the fertilized ovum has 46 chromosomes.

This process is of great interest to us, because it has been established through painstaking research that these chromosomes, which are further subdivided into even smaller particles called **genes,** are the carriers of the child's heredity. (There are about one million genes in a human cell or, on the average, about 20,000 genes per chromosome.) All the child's biological heritage from the father and mother is contained in these 46 chromosomes.

**What Is
Transmitted?**

What is biological inheritance? If the father has cultivated an interest in opera, does that mean his child will have a love of opera?

Scientists have established the fact that genes and chromosomes are responsible for the child's biological heritage, but what is included in this package? Just what is the biological inheritance? For example, if the father has cultivated an interest in opera, does that mean his child will have a love of opera? Or if a mother has developed an interest in mathematics, will her child inherit this interest? The answer is no. In contrast, the color of a person's eyes, the potential to be tall or short, large-boned or delicate, redheaded or blond *are* biologically transmitted. As we shall see, such behavioral characteristics as being active or passive, quick to respond or slow and deliberate, highly intelligent or less intelligent may also be influenced by—but not exclusively determined by—heredity.

The reproductive cells are made up of chromosomes and genes that contain the biological heritage the individual will pass on to future generations, and the makeup of these cells is determined before the father or mother is born. There are only a few circumstances under which the genes may change or be inactivated. Direct radiation—for instance, from X-rays or atomic blasts—is one of the conditions. But generally, changes in the rest of the body do not affect the genetic characteristics of the germ cells. Thus any skills acquired during life will not be included in the genetic package to be passed on to one's offspring, and so the genes that a well-educated man of 40 possesses are no different from those that he possessed as an untutored youth of 17.

Genes and DNA. How does genetic information get transmitted? What genetic element is able to reproduce the parent's characteristics? It was not until the 1940s that scientists could answer this question, for that is when they discovered that the chemical component of critical importance in genetic transmission is deoxyribonucleic acid **(DNA).** Although the existence of DNA had been known for many years, its importance was

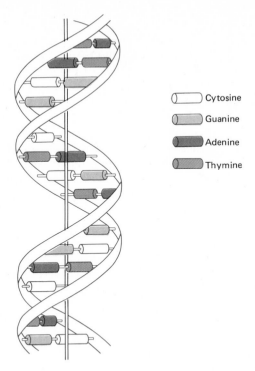

Cytosine

Guanine

Adenine

Thymine

Figure 2.1 The DNA molecule. Alternating sugar and phosphate molecules form the legs of the ladder. The rungs are made up of four chemically distinct bases that are always paired in a special way; so by knowing the order of these bases in one strand, we can determine the order in the other. It is only the permutations of the four bases that are variable. (From L. F. Whaley. *Understanding inherited disorders*. St. Louis: The C. V. Mosby Company, 1974. By permission.)

overlooked because its chemical structure appeared too simple to explain hereditary variability. DNA is composed of two molecular chains coiled around each other to form a double-stranded helix (spiral). Perhaps the simplest way to visualize this is to imagine a long rubber ladder twisted around its long axis (see Figure 2.1).

Replication of DNA. The crucial importance of DNA is that it controls the duplication of the genetic material in the fertilized egg. DNA reproduces itself by splitting the "ladder" right down the middle. The two new "ladders" that result are chemically identical to the original. During development, this process repeats itself over and over; consequently, the genetic information is the same in every cell of the body.

DNA, then, is the active element in the division that takes place in the

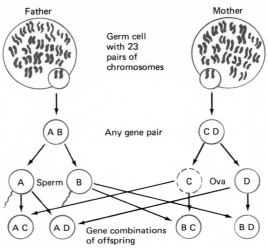

Figure 2.2 Schematic diagram showing possible gene combinations of off-spring resulting from gene pairs of parents.

fertilized ovum. When the fertilized ovum reproduces itself, the chromosomes (made up of DNA) double. Then the cell itself divides down the center. Each of the new cells contains 46 chromosomes, as did the original cell (see Figure 2.2). Even in the completed human being, when the myriad cells of the body have taken on their special functions as tissue, bone, blood, and muscle, each cell still contains a replica of the original 46 chromosomes of the fertilized ovum.

The Mechanisms of Hereditary Transmission

One of the things that must have been puzzling in prescientific days was why two children of the same parents could be so different physically. How could a first-born child be short and stout, while the second-born was long and lean? The answer lies in the mechanics of hereditary transmission.

If each child received all of both parents' genes, we could not explain individual genetic differences between siblings, as all brothers and sisters would then have identical heredities. The fact, however, is that each child inherits only half of each parent's genes. Moreover, each child in a family inherits a different combination of his mother's and father's genes. Thus individual differences between them become not only possible but inevitable.

Germ Cells. Individual differences are due to the fact that the adult organism contains not one, but two kinds of cells: **body cells,** which make up bones, nerves, muscles, and organs, and **germ cells,** from which the sperm and ova are derived. Throughout most of their history, the germ cells develop just as the body cells do. But prior to their division into recognizable sperm or ova, the pattern changes. Their reproductive process results ultimately in cells whose nuclei each contain only half the number in the original cell. This is accomplished by two successive cell divisions during which one cell (the parent cell) with 46 chromosomes becomes four germ cells, each with 23 chromosomes. Because each final sperm or ovum contains only half the chromosomes of the original cell, we can see one reason that children of the same parents are not exactly alike.

Is Identity Possible? We have seen how it is possible for individuals in the same family to be different in their genetic makeup. But is there a chance that a couple could produce two siblings (not twins) who were identical? The answer is no, for no two germ cells (sperm and ovum) contain exactly the same genetic makeup. The 46 chromosomes that divide to form the germ cells do not divide each time in the same way, with one combination going to one sperm or ovum and the rest to the other; the division is random. There are about 20,000 genes per chromosome, and it is extremely unlikely that all 46 chromosomes will divide the same way twice. In other words, the way one pair of chromosomes separates does not influence the way another pair separates.

Sex Determination

Of the 23 pairs of chromosomes, one pair is called the **sex chromosomes** and is responsible for determining the sex of the child. In the normal female, both members of this pair are large in size and are called the **X chromosomes.** In the normal male, one member of the pair is an X chromosome; the second member is smaller in size and is called the **Y chromosome** (see Figure 2.3). Thus, the body cells of males (except for sperm cells) contain one X and one Y chromosome. One-half of the sperm cells of the male contain an X chromosome; the remaining half contain a Y chromosome. When a female ovum, containing an X chromosome, unites during conception with a sperm containing a Y chromosome, a male child is produced. When an ovum unites with a sperm carrying an X chromosome, a female child develops. Since one-half of the sperm cells contain X and one-half Y chromosomes, theoretically the odds are 50–50 that a boy or girl will be conceived. There is actually a slight excess of male over female births, and this may mean that Y sperm are more likely than X sperm to unite with the nucleus of the ovum (26).

DETERMINING THE EXTENT OF GENETIC INFLUENCES

Determining the extent to which genes influence body structure and function is often a difficult task. Investigating genetic influences on personality or behavior is even more difficult. Further, the task of determining the extent of genetic influence is compounded by the interaction of many

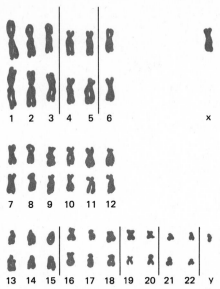

Figure 2.3 Chromosomes of the human male, magnified. Note that each pair of chromosomes differs in size and shape. In the male, the twenty-third pair is composed one X and one Y chromosome. A female would have 2 X chromosomes and no Y. (Courtesy of Dr. Theodore Puck.)

other variables, such as environment and diet, that affect the same facets of the individual.

Obviously, the logical way to deal with a problem involving so many variables is to design an experiment in which one factor is varied while the others are held constant. But since all human beings are unique, carrying out such an experiment to solve this problem is not possible.

The closest we can come to finding two identical human beings is in the case of **identical twins,** who develop from a division of a single fertilized egg. But even then their biological makeup may be slightly different at birth, because of, say, differences in intrauterine blood flow. It is because of difficulties such as these that psychology is still in its infancy compared with other sciences. Human beings simply do not conform to universal principles of identity as, for example, a carbon molecule does.

Still, since twins provide one possibility for approaching the problem of genetic versus environmental effects, many studies have been done investigating the similarities and differences between identical twins. Also, it is fortunate that intelligent assumptions can be made concerning the relative influences of heredity and environment on at least some characteristics. For example, suppose a child fails a reading-readiness test of the

type given prior to admission to the first grade in school. If the child is suffering from cerebral sclerosis, a form of mental deficiency due to the presence of two specific recessive genes, then the child's failure could in large part reasonably be attributed to heredity. If, on the other hand, the child does not show evidence of specific biological deficiency but has lived an isolated mountain life with illiterate parents, and later with proper training passes the test, environment would seem to be the primary determinant of his original failure.

Beyond determining whether certain characteristics are due primarily to genetic or environmental influence, there remains the question of *how* the genes are able to exert their influence. It is not sufficient to know that height is inherited. At some point we must learn how to determine whether the genes affect height or weight through influencing hormonal action, through direct action on bone or muscle, through a combination of these actions, or in some other way. It is not until we have answers to specific questions such as these that we can begin to explore what it means to say that a characteristic is inherited. We do know that no motive, behavior, or emotion is ever inherited as such. What may be inherited is the ability to manufacture and use certain hormones, and these differences in hormone production and use in the body may lead to certain behaviors, but no child is ever *born* happy or sad. In addition, environmental factors always interact with the genetic makeup to affect behavior.

Results of Human Genetic Research

As mentioned previously, one of the most commonly used methods for determining the extent of genetic or environmental factors is to study twins. Because identical twins come closest to being the same biologically, we can control for the effects of heredity in studying the causes of individual differences. In contrast, **fraternal twins,** who develop from two eggs but are born at the same time, share environments that are as similar as those of identical twins, yet their genetic makeup is as different as that of other siblings, permitting us, at least to some extent, to control for the effects of environment. A few studies have been done comparing identical twins reared apart with fraternal twins reared together. If the identical twins still resemble each other more closely than fraternal twins, it may be concluded that genetic factors are playing an important role.

In the next sections we shall look at specific results of many studies, particularly twin studies, on the influence of genetic makeup on various characteristics.

Physical Features

An individual's physical features depend heavily on heredity. Eye color, the shape of a nose, and the curliness of one's hair are typically determined by genes. Genetic factors play a major role in such characteristics as height and weight, although environmental influences such as nutrition and disease are also important.

Mental Defects and Retardation

What part does heredity play in cases of mental retardation? There are several genetically determined disorders that lead to gross defects or deterioration in intelligence.

One inherited syndrome for which the physiological processes have been worked out in detail is called phenylketonuria or **PKU** (2). Children with this disease lack an enzyme that is necessary for normal metabolic functioning. In the absence of this enzyme, a toxic chemical accumulates in the body and leads to damage to the nervous system and mental retardation (29). However, we are fortunate in that the effects of some diseases such as PKU can now be alleviated through a special diet. In fact, a routine check of newborns can reveal the presence or absence of this inherited syndrome, and any newborn with the disease is immediately placed on the special diet. Such infants then develop normally, without mental retardation. In most states it is mandatory to test for PKU at birth and the test is free. Thus, just because a disease is inherited does not mean that it is incurable.

There are several abnormalities known to be due to chromosomal defects or abnormalities. As we have seen, of the 23 pairs of chromosomes, one pair is composed of the sex chromosomes, which determine the sex of the child. The other 22 pairs are called **autosomes** (chromosomes other than the X or Y sex chromosomes). There are mental defects traceable to abnormalities in either of these two kinds of chromosomes. For example, one fairly common disorder due to an abnormality in the autosomes is called **Down's syndrome,** or mongolism. Children with this disorder are born with an Oriental cast to their facial appearance, and may have eye, heart, and other developmental defects. Most have IQs in the 25 to 45 range, though a few have IQs as high as 70. Generally, they are cheerful, have a faculty for mimicry, and enjoy music. The genetic basis of this defect is the presence of an extra chromosome, most likely in pair number 21 of the 22 pairs of autosomes.

Aberrant numbers of sex chromosomes may also produce defects in either males or females. **Turner's syndrome,** usually caused by the absence of one X chromosome, afflicts girls, and alters the normal puberty cycle. Girls with this syndrome normally do not develop secondary sex characteristics, but this condition can be treated by the continued administration of estrogen beginning at puberty. The estrogen brings about feminine body development and menstruation, although the girl remains sterile. Intelligence is typically normal, and gender identity remains unaffected (23).

The male counterpart to Turner's syndrome is **Klinefelter's syndrome.** In this disorder, which results from an excess number of X chromosomes in males (e.g., XXY, XXXY, and so on, rather than the normal XY), secondary masculine characteristics fail to develop at puberty, and there may be breast enlargement. Administration of androgen (male hormone) promotes development of male secondary sex characteristics, but the boy remains sterile. In contrast to girls with Turner's syndrome, boys with Klinefelter's syndrome are more likely to have behavioral problems and retarded intellectual development (23).

Mental Disorders The role of genetic factors in the development of mental disorders has been a source of considerable controversy. There is clear evidence that some rather rare forms of mental disorder (such as Huntington's chorea, a degenerative disorder of the nervous system that usually begins in adulthood) result from specific genetic defects.

There has been considerably less agreement, however, regarding the role of genetic influences in serious psychological disorders, such as **schizophrenia** and the **affective disorders.** Some experts have tended to view them as largely of genetic origin, while others have attributed them to environmental influences. Why has there been so little agreement about the origins of these disorders, especially until recently? One reason is that unless we are able to isolate the specific genetic mechanism by which a disorder (or vulnerability to a disorder) is transmitted (e.g., a single dominant gene in Huntington's chorea), or to identify the biochemical processes involved (e.g., the enzyme deficiency of PKU), we must rely primarily on statistical studies that indicate how frequently the disorders occur among family members.

Determining whether the occurrence is due to psychological or genetic factors is not an easy task. For example, suppose a study shows that there have been numerous cases of severe depression among the various members of a certain family for several generations. Does this fact alone draw us to the conclusion that the disorder is inherited? A look at the environment may suggest otherwise. If the family has for many years tried to survive by farming on a barren, rocky piece of land, the depression may be due less to a genetic predisposition than to environmental factors. Nevertheless, recent research indicates that genetic factors play a significant role in at least some mental disorders. The studies of schizophrenia discussed below are examples of such research.

Schizophrenia. What does it mean to be schizophrenic? One way to describe the disease is that it probably comes closest to the average person's idea of what it means to be "crazy." Schizophrenia, characterized by severe defects in logical thinking and emotional responsiveness, is the most common form of functional psychosis. It accounts for the occupancy of more hospital beds in the United States than any other form of illness, mental or physical.

That schizophrenia is linked in some way to genetic influence is clear: A number of different studies have shown that there is a tendency for the disease to occur more frequently in some families than in others. In particular, schizophrenia occurs more frequently in the children of schizophrenics than in their nieces and nephews. More critically, from the point of view of separating genetic from environmental influences, several well-controlled investigations have found that if one identical twin has schizophrenia, the chances are almost 1 out of 2 that the other twin will also develop this disorder. But in the case of fraternal twins, the chances of the other twin also developing schizophrenia are less than 1 in 10 (16). It is generally assumed that there are few significant environmental differences between identical and fraternal twins—that is, the effect of the environment is relatively the same for both twins—but since the genetic makeup differs for fraternal twins, this study suggests that genetic factors play a role in schizophrenia. Studies of identical twins reared apart also suggest that genetic factors play a role in a significant percentage of cases of schizophrenia, although the number of cases to date is too small to be conclusive (5).

A thorough study in Denmark involved two groups of adults—one group who had become schizophrenic and the other a control group (nonschizophrenic). Both groups had been adopted early in life, and the two groups were matched for age, sex, age at adoption, and socioeconomic status of the adopting family. Because there are extensive records in Denmark, the biological relatives (parents, siblings, and half-siblings) were known, and thus the incidence of schizophrenia could be studied among both the biological and the adoptive relatives of the schizophrenic and nonschizophrenic adults.

There was no significant difference in the prevalence of schizophrenic disorders among the adoptive relatives of the two groups. However, schizophrenia was almost six times higher among the biological relatives (11 percent) of those who had become schizophrenic than among their adoptive relatives (about 2 percent), while in the control group there were no significant differences in the incidence of schizophrenia between biological and adoptive relatives (5, 16).

Does this mean that if your great-aunt Susie had schizophrenia or if your identical twin developed the disease that your fate is sealed? The answer is no. In fact, most individuals who have close biological relatives with schizophrenia do not themselves become schizophrenic — only about 11 percent do.

There are many reasons for this. Perhaps most important is the fact that identical twins are the only individuals who have the same genetic makeup. Consequently, there is no way of saying that you have the particular genetic variable that affected your relative. Schizophrenia, in fact, may be **polygenic** — that is, requiring the presence of a complex combination of interacting genes to be manifested (16, 26). Also, what may be passed on genetically may be simply an increased vulnerability to schizophrenia. In other words, given an individual's susceptibility to psychological stress coupled with a particular set of environmental conditions, he may develop a mental disorder. But without being subjected to these conditions, the individual may never develop schizophrenia. Quite possibly, all these factors will ultimately prove to play a part as the efforts to understand and treat this most baffling of all mental disorders continue.

Depression. Another mental disorder thought to be connected in some way to genetic factors is **depression.** The term "depression" does not refer here to those occasional days when you feel blue because nothing is going right. Staying up all night to study for an exam, then failing the exam, *and* having your best friend announce plans to transfer to a school 1000 miles away are identifiable causes for feeling low. More serious problems, such as the death of a friend or relative, may result in a prolonged condition of what is commonly called depression. But the disorder referred to in this discussion is the product of no specific psychological or social factors. In at least some of these cases, genetic factors, working through biochemical processes, appear to play a significant role. Family ties similar to those found for schizophrenia have been discovered, though once again the genetic link by no means implies that having a depressed relative is a sure sign that you too will be affected with the disorder.

In the case of certain kinds of depressive disorders in which genetic influences appear clearest, many close relatives of afflicted individuals — even identical twins — do *not* develop the disorder, suggesting that here, too, psychological stress or its absence may play an important role. There are also individuals who develop depressive disorders in the apparent absence of family histories of disturbance. In this connection, it is interesting to note that stress itself has been found to produce measurable changes in the levels of certain chemicals in the brain similar to those found in patients with depressive illness (9, 19).

Personality Characteristics

Determining the genetic basis for disorders such as mental retardation, schizophrenia, or depression may not be an easy task, but it is certainly easier than figuring out why Mary talks so much while Gail says very little. Mental disorders cover a wide range of behavior, but the severe disorders are more easily identified and classified than the less severe. "Normal" personality traits, which vary widely among different individuals, are even harder to classify and study. It is the uniqueness of people that makes personality traits so hard to identify and measure.

Are personality traits handed down from one generation to another as are certain tendencies toward some severe mental disorders? Finding the answer is no easy matter, for personality qualities are strongly influenced by environmental factors. Being an only child or the youngest of nine children, for example, can certainly have different effects on one's personality no matter what genetic makeup one has. Even such factors as growing up on the streets of a city or having access to acres of wooded hills can affect the development of personality traits. Still, researchers are making progress in isolating certain personality variables, particularly ones involving a person's general temperament. Among these variables are **introversion-extraversion** and personal tempo.

Introversion-Extraversion. Imagine yourself in a crowded airport waiting room. Would you prefer to be talking to those around you or sitting quietly, reading a magazine? If you generally choose to talk to people, you can probably be classified as a *social extravert*. If you are usually content to keep to yourself and simply observe those around you, you can probably be classified as a *social introvert*. Of course, no one fits into either category all the time, but generally most people can be classified as consistently either more introverted *or* extraverted. Recently an attempt has been made to determine whether this tendency comes under genetic influence.

As in the cases discussed previously, in which the issue was to try to measure the relative effects of genetic versus environmental variables, these studies of personality variables have centered on twins. Again the assumption is that if identical twins show a closer relationship than do fraternal twins or siblings, all of whom have more or less the same environment, then genetic influence is important. Indeed, in one study of sets of adolescent twins of very different ethnic backgrounds, identical twins showed more similarity in degrees of social introversion than did fraternal twins, suggesting that the personality trait of introversion-extraversion is genetically influenced (13).

Personal Tempo. A less well-known personality variable but nonetheless one that differs significantly from one person to another is **personal tempo.** Some people seem to respond and do things quickly; others are more deliberate and measured in their actions. For example, when subjects are seated at a table and asked to knock on the table at a speed that is "natural" for them, they knock at different speeds. Similarly, when they are asked at which of a variety of speeds the ticking of a metronome seems just right, individual differences emerge. In one study in which both these measures were combined, identical twins showed the greatest similarity, and fraternal twins and siblings were next. Nonrelated individuals showed the least similarity (26).

Infant Studies. At the beginning of this chapter we noted that infants display different behavior patterns from the moment of birth. Granted that the effects of the birth experience itself may differ (e.g., effects of drugs or other trauma), what other factors might account for the infants' behavior differences? There may be something in their genetic composition that influences behavior.

Once again we turn to studies of twins, and several studies suggest that the dispositions of infants are at least partially under genetic control. For example, identical twins are more alike than fraternal twins in the tendency to smile and show fear of strangers (10). Another study looked at newborns from the same national background, and the results suggest that personality traits are partially controlled by genes. It was found that Chinese-American newborns are both less irritable and easier to console when upset than Caucasian American newborns (11). Such evidence also suggests that tendencies to be inhibited (in contrast to having a more active and spontaneous disposition) may be under partial genetic control.

In general, the results suggest that it is more likely that genetic influences are strongest on such basic "temperamental" characteristics as personal tempo, inhibition versus spontaneity, soberness versus exuberance, and social introversion versus social extraversion. On the other hand, genetic influences appear far less on characteristics highly dependent on learning and social experience (e.g., ethical and social values, objectivity). We must remember, however, that an inherited behavioral tendency can frequently be overridden by the environmental surroundings. People who are by nature shy can be helped to become more assertive, and even the most naturally exuberant and outgoing person can become more hesitant or withdrawn under certain stressful or oppressive conditions.

Intelligence

Aside from dispositional traits, another area of interest in the realm of "nature versus nurture" is intelligence. While it is true that there is usually a high correlation between the intelligence levels of children and their parents or other relatives (as measured by IQ tests), it is almost impossible to consider separately the effects of genetic variables from those of the environment. For example, parents whose genetic endowment led to higher intellect may also have provided their offspring with other advantages related to intellectual ability: good health, a stimulating home environment, superior educational opportunity. Thus to isolate the potential genetic contributions, a way must be found to control for the potential effects of such other variables.

Adoptive Parents. One way to separate the genetic and environmental effects acting on intelligence is to look at the correlation between IQ scores of parents and their adopted children and see if it differs significantly from the relation between IQ scores of parents and their genetic offspring. Indeed, the difference is significant in many cases. In only a small number of the adopted-child cases were IQ scores of parent and child alike, though there was a significantly high relationship between scores of the adopted children and their biological parents. An even higher correlation between parent and child scores was found for those children who were raised by their biological parents, where the effects of heredity and environment were combined (20).

Twin Studies. Identical twins showed a higher correlation between IQ scores than did fraternal twins, and fraternal twins showed a higher correlation than did siblings who were not twins (see Figure 2.4). Again, of significance here is that fraternal twins are actually no more closely genetically related than are siblings, since they result from two ova and two sperm, but it is likely that environmental conditions are more similar for fraternal twins than for siblings. Thus environmental as well as genetic factors have important effects on a child's level of intellectual performance, as we shall see in our discussion of cognitive development (see Chapter 8, pp. 261-266).

PRENATAL DEVELOPMENT

Up to this point we have been considering mainly the effects of genetic variables versus environmental factors, but we have looked at only the **postnatal** (after-birth) environment of the individual. It is a rather curious fact that while we recognize that life begins at conception, we reckon a person's age from the moment of birth. We seem to be saying that the

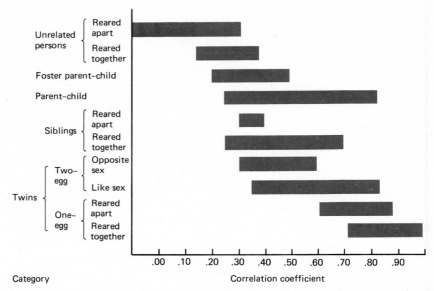

Figure 2.4 Genetic relationships and IQ. Shown here are the ranges of correlation coefficients in IQ between people of various relationships, based on the results of 52 studies. The correlation between the IQ of one person and another clearly increases with genetic similarity. (From L. Erlenmeyer-Kimling & L. F. Jarvik. Genetics and intelligence: A research review. *Science*, 1963, *142*, 1477–1479. Copyright 1963 by the American Association for the Advancement of Science. By permission.)

events in a person's life prior to birth are of little importance in determining the future course of his development. This attitude is especially likely to apply to our conceptions of psychological development. And yet the environment in which the unborn child grows can be of tremendous importance in influencing later patterns of growth, not only physically but psychologically as well.

In the following sections we shall explore a normal period of **prenatal** development. We shall see what happens when an egg and sperm combine and what the normal prenatal environmental conditions are.

How Conception Occurs

As we have already mentioned, conception occurs when a sperm from the male pierces the cell wall of an ovum, or egg, from the female. The nucleus of the sperm (containing 23 chromosomes) and the nucleus of the ovum (also containing 23 chromosomes) fuse and form one new cell. The fertilized ovum begins to grow immediately. The 23 chromosomes from the sperm and the 23 chromosomes from the ovum line up. Each chromosome then splits in half lengthwise, yielding 46 pairs of chromosomes. The process of development has now begun. In a scant 24–36-hour time period, the sperm has united with the ovum, and this union has already produced a unit of two new cells — a process of doubling that is constantly repeated as development continues.

The process of development from conception to birth is usually divided into three phases. The first phase, called the period of the ovum, lasts from fertilization until the time that the fertilized egg is firmly implanted in the wall of the uterus. This process typically takes about 10 to 14 days. The second phase, from 2 to 8 weeks, is called the period of the **embryo.** This period is characterized by a differentiation of all the major organs that will be present in the newborn baby. The last phase, from 8 weeks until delivery (normally 40 weeks), is called the period of the **fetus** and is characterized by growth of the organs of the organism.

The Period of the Ovum

The process of fertilization takes place in the tube leading from the ovary (which produced the egg) to the uterus. The fertilized ovum continues to double its cells during its journey to the uterus, where it will become implanted. By the time the fertilized ovum reaches the uterus, it is about the size of a pinhead and has several dozen cells. After about 10 to 14 days, the fertilized ovum has extended tendrils that burrow into the receptive mucous membrane of the uterus. At this time, the period of the ovum comes to an end, and the second phase of prenatal development, the period of the embryo, begins. The new individual has ceased to be an independent, free-floating organism and has established a dependent relationship with the mother.

The Period of the Embryo

Once the growing egg has firmly implanted itself in the uterine wall, it begins to grow rapidly. From a tiny mass of cells soon forms a recognizable embryo.

The inner part of the fertilized egg forms three distinct layers. These three layers develop into the various organs and coverings that make up the human body. The outermost layer of the embryo (the **ectoderm**) develops into the outermost layers of the body — the skin, hair, and nails — as well as the nervous system. The second layer of the embryo (the **mesoderm**) quite naturally develops into parts of the body that are more internal: the inner skin layer, the muscles, skeleton, and circulatory system. Finally, the third layer (the **endoderm**) develops into the innermost parts of the body, for example, the entire lining of the gastrointestinal tract and the lungs, liver, pancreas, and other organs.

The outer layers of cells of the fertilized egg function to protect and support the growing embryo within. These cells divide to form two surrounding layers of membrane (the **chorion** and **amnion**) that enclose the embryo. They form the **amniotic sac,** which is filled with a watery fluid (amniotic fluid) that acts as a buffer to protect the embryo from physical

Steps in Prenatal Development

1 week	Fertilized ovum descends through Fallopian tube toward uterus.
2 weeks	Embryo has attached itself to uterine lining and is developing rapidly.
3 weeks	Embryo has begun to take some shape; head and tail regions discernible. Primitive heart begins to beat.
4 weeks	Beginnings of mouth region, gastrointestinal tract, and liver. Heart is developing rapidly, and head and brain regions are becoming more clearly differentiated.
6 weeks	Hands and feet begin developing, but arms are still too short and stubby to meet. Liver is now producing blood cells.
8 weeks	Embryo is now about 1 inch long. Face, mouth, eyes, and ears have begun taking on fairly defined form. Development of muscle and cartilage has begun.
12 weeks	Fetus is about 3 inches long. It has definitely begun to resemble a human being, though the head is disproportionately large. Face now has babylike profile. Eyelids and nails have begun to form, and sex can be distinguished easily. Nervous system still very primitive.
16 weeks	Fetus is about 4½ inches long. The mother may be able to feel the fetus' movements. Extremities, head, and internal organs are developing rapidly. Body proportions are becoming more babylike.
5 months	Pregnancy half completed. Fetus is now about 6 inches and is able to hear and move about quite freely. Hands and feet are already complete.
6 months	Fetus is about 10 inches long. Eyes are now completely formed, and taste buds appear on tongue. Fetus is now capable of inhaling and exhaling and of making a thin crying noise, should he or she be born prematurely.
7 months to birth	An important age. The fetus has now reached the "zone of viability" (having a chance to live if born prematurely). Fetus is physiologically capable of distinguishing basic tastes and odors. Pain sensitivity appears to be relatively absent. Breathing ability is

	still shallow and irregular, and sucking and swallowing ability are weak.
7 months	During this period, the fetus becomes increasingly ready for independent life outside the womb. Muscle tone increases; movement becomes sustained and positive; and breathing, swallowing, sucking, and hunger cry all become strong. Visual and auditory reactions are firmly established.

shocks experienced by the mother (see Figure 2.5). In addition, in what is one of the most critical steps in the developmental process, these cells form the **umbilical cord,** the link that binds mother and baby from 2–8 weeks after conception until birth. All nutrients for the developing child pass through the umbilical cord, filtered first by the **placenta,** the section of the uterine wall where the uterus and the membrane surrounding the embryo are joined. In a similar manner, waste products (such as carbon dioxide) from the infant flow into the placenta to be filtered out by the mother's circulatory system.

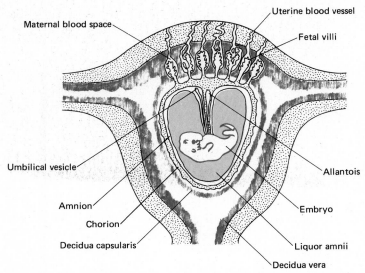

Figure 2.5 Diagram representing the relationship between the uterus, the membrane, and the embryo during early pregnancy. (From L. Carmichael. Origins and prenatal growth of behavior. In C. Murchinson, Ed., *A handbook of child psychology,* 2nd ed. Worcester: Clark University Press, 1933. P. 50. By Permission.)

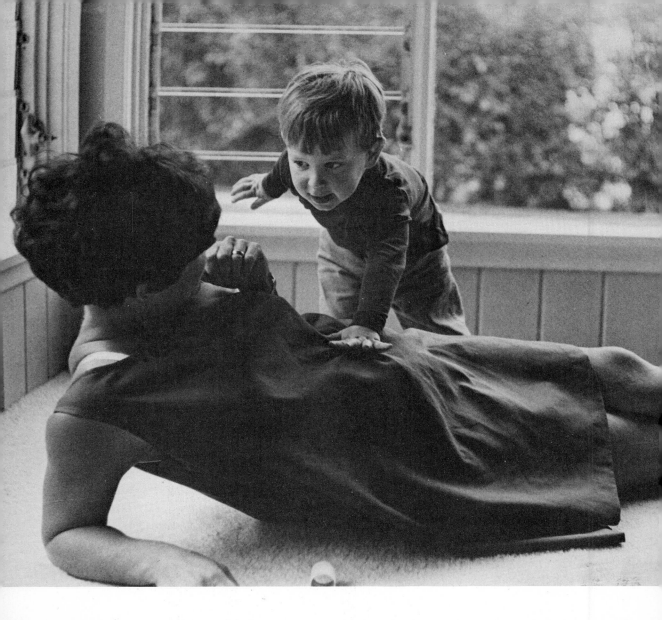

Obviously this biological link between mother and child is an important one. It can both protect and harm the unborn child, because through the placenta passes all the nutritional input for the baby and certain harmful substances, if ingested or produced by the mother, as well. Knowledge of this two-way effect enables a pregnant woman to be conscientious about what goes into her body. We shall examine some specific effects in more detail later in this chapter.

Development of the embryo is extremely rapid. Only 21 days after con-

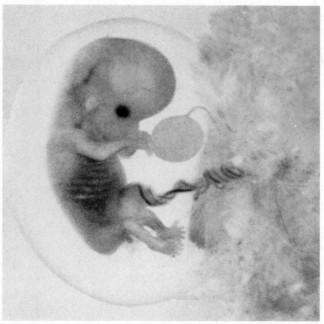

Figure 2.6   The human embryo at 5 weeks. The eye is seen as a dark-rimmed circle. (From R. Rugh & L. B. Shettles. *From conception to birth: The drama of life's beginnings.* New York: Harper & Row, 1971. By permission.)

ception a primitive heart has already developed and begun to beat (12). By 4 weeks the embryo is becoming well developed and the head and brain regions are becoming more clearly differentiated (see Figure 2.6). The most important process that takes place during the first 8 weeks of development is the growth of the nervous system. Because these first 8 weeks are so important in developing this system of the body, any complications of pregnancy encountered during this period can have a devastating effect on the child. For example, if the mother should contract German measles during this period, the child is more likely to suffer brain damage than if the mother should have this illness during the last 8 weeks of pregnancy (18).

The Period of the Fetus

After two months, the developing embryo is referred to as a fetus. During this third period of prenatal development, the various body systems that were sketchily laid out during the embryonic stage become quite well developed and begin to function.

Motor responses appear and become more complex (see Figure 2.7).

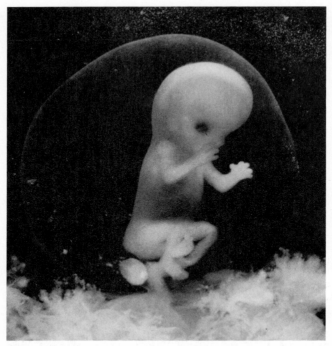

Figure 2.7 The human embryo at 10 weeks. Hands and fingers are now clear. (From R. Rugh & L. B. Shettles. *From conception to birth: The drama of life's beginnings.* New York: Harper & Row, 1971. By permission.)

For example, the fetus can respond to touch by flexing the trunk and extending the head (1). Although the nervous system is still incomplete, it too continues to develop rapidly. By the end of 16 weeks, the mother can feel the fetus' movements. At this point the fetus is about 4½ inches in length and is becoming more human-looking (see Figure 2.8).

The fetal age of 28 weeks (roughly 6½ months) is important. It generally marks the line between the ability to live if born and the probability that the infant would not survive. By this age, the child's nervous, circulatory, and other body systems have developed to a point at which they stand a chance of being able to function adequately outside the uterus. Of course, babies born this prematurely need special care but, as we shall discuss later, have surprisingly strong abilities to survive.

The Last Three Months. While a baby born after 28 weeks can survive, each additional week that the fetus remains within the mother's uterus increases the likelihood of his or her survival and normal development.

Figure 2.8 Sixteen-week-old human fetus. (From R. Rugh & L. B. Shettles. *From conception to birth: The drama of life's beginnings.* New York: Harper & Row, 1971. By permission.)

PRENATAL ENVIRONMENTAL INFLUENCES

The course of development described above is typical of a normal pregnancy, but there are occasional variations—some major, some minor. Recent research suggests that the mother's physical and emotional status, and consequently the prenatal environment she provides, may exert important influences on the course of fetal development and the subsequent health and adjustment of the child. In the sections that follow, we shall cover some of the factors found to be significant in prenatal development.

Age of Mother

"Women who are of prime child-bearing age" is a phrase that may set your teeth on edge, particularly if you are a woman, because of its connotation that women function more or less as "baby machines." However, according to statistics, the age range of 20–35 years is safer for a woman to have a child than if she is outside this range. While the whole process of pregnancy and birth has become much safer in recent years through modern developments in medical science, being younger or older than the twenties or early thirties introduces certain risks.

For example, adolescent mothers face a greater risk of **toxemia** (a

Preventing Birth Defects

Although the great majority of babies are born healthy and normal, the prospective mother will want to do everything possible to ensure that this will be the case with her baby. The following recommendations, based on research findings, can help to minimize the risk of birth defects:

1. It is best not to begin having children before age 18 and to complete the process before age 40. Although many younger and older women have perfectly healthy babies, the risks to mother and child are greater in these age groups.
2. Although the risks are not as great for older fathers as mothers, it is probably still best for the father to have his children before age 45.
3. Genetic counseling should be sought beforehand if either the prospective mother or father has reason to believe there is a hereditary disorder in the family. They are likely to find that their fears are groundless, but, if not, they can be advised of appropriate steps to take.
4. Good prenatal health care is essential and can avoid many possible difficulties for both mother and child. The lack of readily available health services for many prospective mothers in this country can properly be labeled a national scandal.
5. All prospective mothers need a well-balanced diet—one rich in proteins, vitamins, and minerals, and having sufficient calories.
6. A woman who is pregnant, or could possibly be pregnant, should not take any drugs that are not absolutely essential, and then only after consultation with her physician. This includes not only prescription drugs but also nonprescription medications, such as sleeping pills, reducing aids, laxatives, and allergy pills. It also means cigarettes, marijuana or other psychoactive drugs, and alcohol, except perhaps for an occasional, very weak drink. Potential dangers to the baby are especially great during the first 3 months.
7. Environmental dangers should also be carefully avoided, including X-rays, insecticides, pesticides, and other chemicals; undercooked meat or cat litter (which can lead to toxoplasmosis or other diseases); and communicable diseases.
8. In particular, no woman should become pregnant unless she is

sure she has had rubella (German measles) or has been effectively immunized against it.

9. Expert obstetrical care in a well-equipped hospital should be available to prevent or readily respond to emergencies. In addition, the fewer medications during labor and delivery, the better.

10. Pregnancies should be spaced at least 2 years apart, especially among younger mothers.

V. Agpar & J. Beck. *Is my baby all right?* New York: Pocket Books, 1974.

L. O. Lubchenco. *The high risk infant.* Philadelphia: Saunders, 1976.

disorder of unknown origin involving high blood pressure, excessive weight gain, and retention of fluid in the tissues), anemia (a deficiency of red blood cells and iron), labor complications, and premature birth (7). Women who deliver their first infant when they are 35 or over are also more likely than younger women to experience illnesses during pregnancy and longer and more difficult labor, and to have a baby with a chromosomal abnormality. The probability of Down's syndrome, for example, increases rapidly as the woman gets older, reaching the proportion of one birth in every 80 between the ages of 40 and 44, and one in 40 at age 45 or older (see p. 44). They are also more likely to have underweight babies or stillborn babies (18). The older the woman, the greater the likelihood that these problems will arise, but the absolute incidence of serious complications is nevertheless relatively small.

Maternal Nutrition The old adage that a pregnant woman should "eat for two" is not true for quantity of food, but quality is essential. Excessive weight gain is not healthy for a pregnant woman, but eating a balanced diet is necessary for the health of both mother and child. One of the most important elements of a balanced diet is sufficient protein. Babies born to mothers on a chronically low-protein diet are more vulnerable to serious diseases. In addition, there is evidence that children of severely undernourished mothers may have somewhat impaired mental powers.

For example, in eastern Guatemala, the residents of two small villages received nourishing supplemental diets for several years, while the residents of two similar (control) villages received soda pop supplements instead (17). Not only did newborn infant death and illness go down, and birth weight up, in the nourished villages, but children from these villages scored somewhat better on mental tests, especially vocabulary scores, at the end of 7 years. In short, it seems likely that severe maternal malnutrition may impair the child's optimal intellectual development, in addition to having adverse effects on physical development.

Drugs

No one would ever think of dissolving a powerful adult dose of medicine and adding the solution to an infant's bottle. But why are so many pregnant women seemingly oblivious to the dangers of taking drugs during

How to Eat Sensibly for Two

A good diet during pregnancy, as well as in the years before pregnancy, is essential. If the mother is malnourished, her child will also be. Malnourished mothers are more likely to have miscarriages or premature infants, and their children are more likely to have birth defects. Malnutrition may result from poverty, but it may also stem from myths or too much dieting. Pregnancy is not a time for strict dieting *or* obesity.

A woman should gain about 20 percent of her initial weight during pregnancy, or about 20–25 pounds, depending on whether the future mother is tall and large-boned or short and small-boned. This generally means eating about 2300 calories daily, although quality and balance of food is as important as quantity.

According to the National Research Council's committee on maternal nutrition, a prospective mother's daily diet should include:

Milk — 3 to 4 cups
Meat, fish, poultry, cheese, or eggs — at least two servings totaling 6 ounces after cooking
Vegetables and fruits — six servings, including one dark-green or deep-yellow vegetable and one or two servings of citrus fruit or tomato
Whole-grain cereals and enriched bread — five servings, including potato, rice, noodles, or macaroni if desired
Fats and sweets — to complete total calorie requirements
Vitamin D supplement, if milk is not fortified and if prescribed by the doctor

Because the growing fetus uses about one-third of its mother's iron to form its own blood, an iron supplement is usually advisable; other minerals and vitamins may be added by the doctor.

pregnancy? A fetus is fragile—its body systems are not fully developed—and it may be affected by even a small amount of some drugs. Many women think nothing of altering their body chemistry through drugs, whether for the purpose of treating a cold, for regulating hormones or other body functions, or simply to change a mood, as with tranquilizers.

One of the most publicized tragedies of links between drugs and birth defects involved a drug called thalidomide, but many other drugs are now suspected of producing birth defects in babies. Narcotics, steroids, some antibiotics, and even excessive doses of some vitamins are a few of the drugs believed to endanger the health of the developing child (1). Tobacco, too, has adverse effects on the fetus. For example, low birth weight and smaller and shorter bones are more common among infants born to smoking mothers than among the infants of nonsmoking mothers (18). Drugs given to relieve pain during childbirth may also have adverse effects on the baby's development, in proportion to the extent they are taken (3).

A tragic consequence of rising drug use and its effects on newborns is the increasing number of addicted fetuses and newborns. The newborn child of a heroin addict, for example, suffers serious withdrawal symptoms after birth. Symptoms of heroin withdrawal may sometimes last as long as 6 months, and include irritability, tremors, convulsions, vomiting, high-pitched crying, and respiratory distress (14).

Fetal Alcohol Syndrome

Just as the idea of indiscriminately giving drugs to a newborn baby is abhorrent, so too is the thought of giving an alcoholic drink to an infant. Yet, again, many pregnant women fail to consider the effects of liquor on the developing infant. As many as 6000 infants a year are born with what is called **fetal alcohol syndrome** (21), a disorder produced by a mother's chronic heavy drinking. Current research suggests the risk rate of this syndrome is about 2 percent if the mother drinks more than 2.3 ounces of hard liquor daily (22). Symptoms of the fetal alcohol syndrome include severe retardation of intrauterine growth, premature birth, microcephaly (an abnormally small head), and a variety of deformities, including congenital eye and ear problems, heart defects, extra fingers and toes, and disturbed sleep patterns (15, 22).

Radiation

Radiation is another factor that may have severe effects on the unborn child. X-rays during the period of time between fertilization and the time the ovum implants in the uterus almost always cause destruction of the ovum; the greatest danger of malformations comes between the second and sixth weeks after conception (1). Perhaps the most frightening possibility of X-ray damage is to the genes of the child, producing mutations whose effects may not be felt for generations. Consequently, avoiding X-rays is the best advice for any woman who is pregnant or possibly could be pregnant.

Maternal Diseases and Disorders During Pregnancy

Some diseases that strike the mother during pregnancy can easily affect the health of the unborn child. **Rubella** (German measles) is one of these. The child may be born with heart malformations, deafness, blindness, or mental retardation. Other viral diseases, such as chicken pox and hepatitis, are particularly dangerous to the fetus early in pregnancy. Toxoplasmosis is an infection that may result from contact with cats or from eating undercooked red meat. Toxoplasmosis is usually a mild disease in adults but may have serious consequences for an unborn infant. About 20 percent of the infants whose mothers had the disease during pregnancy are born with mental defects such as mental retardation, eye damage, and hearing loss.

Syphilis is another disease that can affect the unborn child, though fortunately the placenta has a natural barrier against the syphilitic organisms (called spirochetes) until after the fourth or fifth month of pregnancy (18). Consequently, if treatment of the syphilitic mother is begun early in pregnancy, the child may not suffer from the disease. Otherwise, the disease may induce abortion or miscarriage, or if the child survives, he or she may be born weak, deformed, or mentally deficient. In some cases these symptoms are not evident until several years later.

Toxemia, a disorder of unknown cause that affects about 5 percent of the pregnant women in the United States, is characterized by high blood pressure, rapid and excessive weight gain, and retention of fluid in the tissues. Fortunately, prompt treatment usually ends the danger. However, if the disorder continues to progress, it can lead to convulsions and coma, resulting in death in about 13 percent of mothers and about 50 percent of their unborn infants (18). Children whose mothers had significant toxemia during pregnancy run an increased risk of lowered intelligence (14).

Rh Disease. Until recently, probably no cause of birth defects caused more parental concern than Rh problems (18). The term **Rh factor** stands for a chemical factor present in the blood of approximately 85 percent of people, although there are racial and ethnic variations. In itself, the presence or absence of this chemical factor makes no difference in a person's health. But when an Rh-positive man is married to an Rh-negative woman (about 1 chance in 9), there can sometimes be adverse consequences for their offspring. If their baby has Rh-positive blood, the mother's blood may form antibodies against the "foreign" positive Rh factor. Then there is a danger during the next pregnancy, for the antibodies in the mother's blood will attack the Rh-positive blood of the unborn infant. Such destruction can be limited, resulting only in mild anemia, or extensive, resulting in cerebral palsy, deafness, mental retardation, or even death.

Fortunately, a preventive control for the Rh problem has been developed. The blood of the newborn infant is tested immediately after birth (by a blood sample from the umbilical cord). If an Rh-positive child has been born to an Rh-negative mother, the mother is given a vaccine to seek out and destroy the baby's Rh-positive blood cells before the mother's body begins producing antibodies against the Rh-positive factor. Thus the red cells of any subsequent children will not be attacked, because the blood of the mother was never allowed to develop the antibodies.

Maternal Emotional States and Attitudes. Diseases and readily identifiable biological properties are not the only maternal factors that can affect the health of an unborn child. A pregnant woman's emotional state can also influence fetal reactions and developments.

Emotional changes such as stress, for example, are known to produce changes in the body chemistry, because they activate the autonomic nervous system, causing the endocrine glands to liberate certain chemicals into the bloodstream. These changes may be irritating to the fetus. One study noted that movements of fetuses increased several hundred percent while their mothers were undergoing emotional stress. If the mother's emotional upset lasted several weeks, fetal activity continued at an exaggerated level throughout the entire period. When these upsets were brief, heightened irritability usually lasted several hours. Prolonged maternal emotional stress during pregnancy—whether from marital difficulties, negative attitudes toward having a child, or catastrophic life events—may have enduring consequences for the child (25). Infants born to upset, unhappy mothers are more likely to have low birth weights; to be hyperactive, irritable, squirming; and to manifest difficulties such as irregular eating, excessive bowel movements, gas pains, sleep disturbances, excessive crying, and unusual needs to be held. It is ironic that the woman least prepared to cope with the problems brought on by having a baby must also deal with the increased difficulties brought on by her emotional distress during pregnancy.

THE BIRTH PROCESS AND ITS CONSEQUENCES

The dramatic process of birth is one that can have lasting effects on the child. Whether or not the stress associated with a normal delivery has later psychological consequences is debatable, but certainly purely biological problems such as lack of oxygen (called **anoxia**) or extreme pressure on the head can affect the later development of the child.

The most common effects of oxygen-deprived babies involve motor functions. The child may show a paralysis of the legs or the arms, a tremor of the face or fingers, or an inability to use his vocal muscles. In the latter case, he may have difficulty learning to speak. The general term **cerebral palsy** describes a variety of motor defects associated with damage to the brain cells, possibly as a result of lack of oxygen during the birth process.

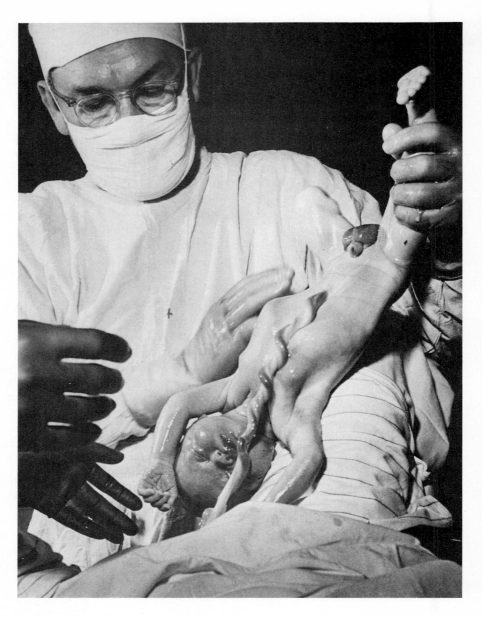

It is estimated that about 30 percent of the cases of cerebral palsy involve problems occurring during birth or immediately afterward (18).

If a baby is slow to breathe, nerve cells in the brain may be deprived of sufficient oxygen (30). Although children who suffer a mild oxygen deficit

Mortality Rates

Prenatal, neonatal, and infant (under 1-year-old) death rates, as well as maternal death rates, have all declined markedly in recent years. For example, as may be seen below, the U.S. newborn death rate (per 1000 live births) declined from 28.8 as recently as 1940 to 10.9 in 1976; in the same period the maternal death rate declined from 37.6 to only 1.2. Nevertheless, much greater improvement is possible. Many other less affluent countries than our own have significantly lower rates of infant and maternal mortality. Within our own country, rates are far higher for blacks, Native Americans, and other minorities, and for the poor. As the Children's Defense Fund observes, such statistics demonstrate that "inadequate and unequal provision of health care services to children and pregnant women in this country results in the unnecessary deaths of thousands of children. . . . The statistics are a national scandal." (Children's Defense Fund of the Washington Research Project. *Doctors and Dollars Are Not Enough: How to Improve Health Services for Children and Their Families.* Washington, D.C.: Children's Defense Fund, 1976.)

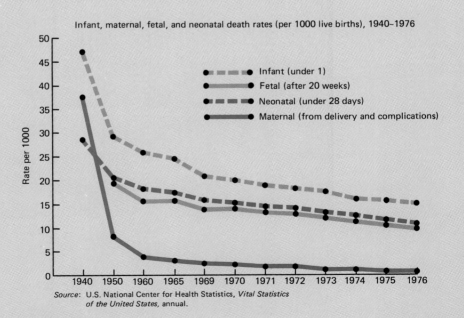

Infant, maternal, fetal, and neonatal death rates (per 1000 live births), 1940–1976

Infant (under 1)
Fetal (after 20 weeks)
Neonatal (under 28 days)
Maternal (from delivery and complications)

Source: U.S. National Center for Health Statistics, *Vital Statistics of the United States,* annual.

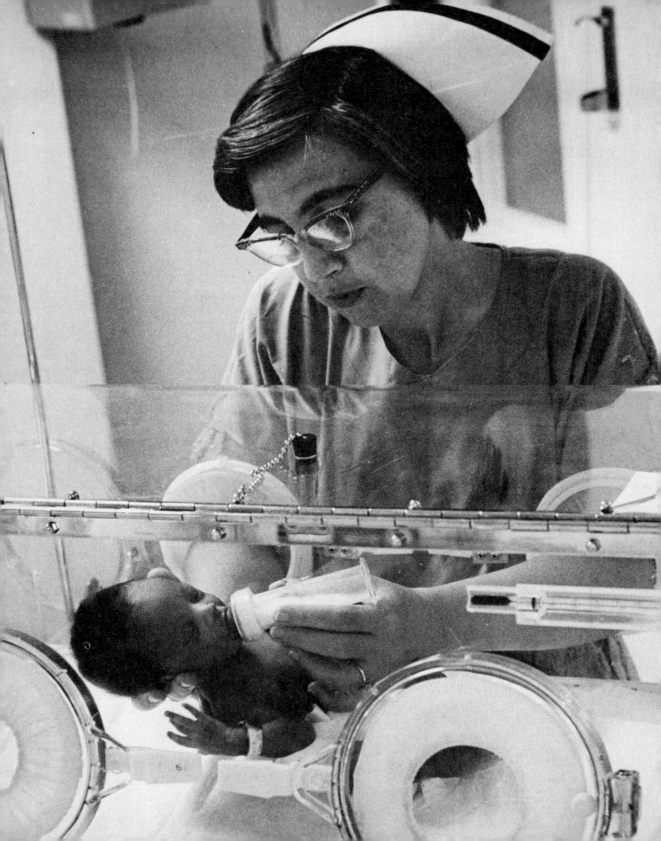

at birth may be slower to develop, by age 7 or 8 differences between normal and mildly anoxic children are greatly minimized and their IQ scores are equal, although anoxic children appear to have somewhat more difficulty in copying designs and are still more distractible (4, 8). In brief, the differences between mildly anoxic and normal children become smaller with age, and there is presently no firm evidence of serious and permanent intellectual damage, especially if they grow up in supportive homes.

Prematurity

Earlier we noted that 28 weeks is a critical time for a fetus, since it generally marks the line between survival and nonsurvival if birth occurs early. In most cases, infants with **gestation** periods of less than 26 weeks ("extreme **prematurity**") and generally weighing less than 4½ pounds (about 1 percent of all births) have little chance of survival. In contrast, those who are only slightly premature (34–38 weeks), if they are of appropriate weight for their gestational age, resemble full-term babies in many but not all ways; they are generally healthy but are less mature and more vulnerable to illness, gain weight more slowly, and must be monitored carefully (18).

Considerable progress has been made in recent years in caring for "intermediate-term" infants, babies who are more than slightly premature but not extremely premature. Their gestational ages range between 30 and 33 weeks, and they are of at least average weight for their age—around 3.3 pounds or more at 30 weeks, and 4.4 pounds or more at 33 weeks. With the recent institution of intensive, highly specialized care in technologically sophisticated "premature nurseries" in university medical centers and major community hospitals, many more premature babies have survived and have gone on to develop normally (27).

Neonatal mortality risk is a function both of gestational age and birth weight (although, of course, the two factors generally tend to go together). An infant who is significantly premature and low in birth weight even for her gestational age faces a more serious risk than an infant of the same gestational age whose birth weight is age-appropriate.

In general, risks appear to be highest for the small minority of prematures weighing less than 3.3 pounds at birth. Current findings suggest, however, that even for many of these babies, intensive, expert care can reduce the incidence of handicaps substantially. Several recent studies conducted at "premature centers" providing skilled, specialized care have found that 85 percent or more of these infants developed normally (18).

Many of the neurological problems that can occur in low-birth-weight children may not be apparent in the first months of life. Some possible disabilities, such as cerebral palsy, major defects in vision or hearing, or significant mental retardation may be discerned in the first year, but others, including below average IQ (see Figure 2.9), perceptual disorders,

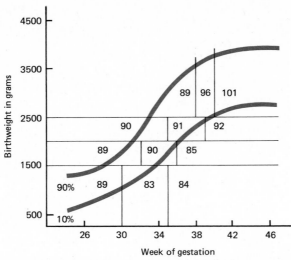

Figure 2.9 IQ according to birth weight and gestational age groups. (Adapted by L. Lubchenco from G. Wiener. The relationship of birth weight and length of gestation to intellectual development at ages 8 to 10 years. *Journal of Pediatrics,* 1970, *76,* 694–699. By permission.)

learning problems, and behavioral symptoms (such as restlessness and hyperactivity), may not become apparent until after school entrance.

The environment of babies born prematurely is particularly important, for these children often need special care to stay healthy. In the long run, infants born into loving, nurturing homes with competent care usually suffer little from the effects of moderate prematurity, but infants born into less nurturing homes with poor living conditions are far more likely to have both physical and psychological problems.

Postmaturity

Being born too early is not the only risk involved with time of birth. Some babies are born late (**postmaturity**), and these postterm infants may suffer from a variety of symptoms. Their appetite may be lacking, they may show various signs of **fetal distress,** and there may be some neurological disorder. For instance, one study found that 28 percent of children with cerebral palsy were significantly postterm (28).

There are several possible reasons for the greater risk sustained by postterm babies, including greater likelihood of difficult delivery, less resistance of the baby to birth stress, inadequate prenatal nutrition in the last stages before birth, and various congenital anomalies and defects that themselves tend to delay birth (18). Like premature infants, markedly postterm babies also require expert specialized care.

THE RELATION OF SEX AND SOCIAL CLASS TO INFANT VULNERABILITY

Women have traditionally been considered more delicate and fragile than men, but in terms of the health of newborns, more boys than girls are born with serious abnormalities, apparently because boys are more vulnerable to anoxia, prematurity, and maternal infection. It is not clear why nature has been so harsh on young males, although it has been speculated that genetic differences are involved, or that the mother may develop an immunological reaction to male tissue, and this reaction affects her fetus adversely (24).

Even socioeconomic class has been associated with differences in the health of pregnant women and their babies; problems associated with pregnancy and delivery are 3 to 4 times more frequent among lower-class families than among middle-class families. This may be accounted for by factors such as an impoverished environment (involving greater likelihood of maternal malnutrition and poorer health, and greater exposure to disease), parental ignorance about child care, and failure to seek professional help.

An example of the interaction between biological and environmental factors is reflected in the fact that problems before or just after birth are more likely to produce lasting psychological effects on the child over a period of 6 or 7 years among poor families than among affluent ones. The reasons for this are not entirely clear, but we do know that improper care of infants is more frequent among uneducated lower-class mothers, especially in the case of infants with low birth weights (6). And we also know that appropriate intellectual and social stimulation (which might help to compensate for any residual problems) may be lacking or at least less in lower-class homes (18).

Fortunately, less than 7 percent of all babies born in this country experience any of the problems discussed in this chapter. Most infants begin life well within the normal range. In addition, infants are surprisingly adaptable, and many children apparently recover from early handicaps due either to prematurity or anoxia.

A case study is illustrative. One infant, born with his heart stopped, initially suffered serious anoxia. Within several hours after birth the baby began to show convulsions, which lasted for several days. The father, who was a doctor, was concerned that the child would be permanently brain-damaged and mentally retarded. However, the convulsions stopped after a few days, and when the baby was examined at 8 months of age his psychological development appeared within normal limits. There is an enormous potential for recovery in the newborn, and it is difficult to predict later behavior from the reactivity shown during the first few days of life (2).

SUMMARY

1. The developing child's behavior results from many different influences—genetic, biological, psychological, and social. All these forces

interact, and it is often difficult to determine how much each contributes to a particular behavior.

2. Life begins when the sperm cell from the father penetrates the wall of an ovum, or egg, from the mother. At this moment, 23 chromosomes from each parent combine: all the child's biological heritage is contained in these 46 chromosomes.

3. Each chromosome is made up of about 20,000 smaller particles called genes. The genes contain a complex chemical substance, deoxyribonucleic acid, or DNA, which is responsible for the action of the genes.

4. Each sperm or ovum contains only 23 chromosomes—half the number of the original parent cell. Because of this, children of the same parents are not exactly alike.

5. In attempting to study the effects of genetic influences, researchers often compare identical twins, who share the same heredity, with nonidentical, or fraternal, twins, whose heredity is as different as any other two siblings. The assumption is that if identical twins are more similar in a particular characteristic (e.g., intelligence, extraversion) than nonidentical twins, genetic factors play a role in determining the characteristic.

6. A number of genetically determined disorders leading to mental retardation have been identified, including phenylketonuria, or PKU, Down's syndrome, Turner's syndrome, and Klinefelter's syndrome.

7. Genetic factors have also been shown to play a part in the development of a number of serious mental disorders, including schizophrenia and severe depression. In both of these disorders, however, a majority of even the close relatives of these patients do not develop the disorder, for a variety of genetic and psychological reasons.

8. The role of genetic influences on the development of personality characteristics is more difficult to investigate, but it appears that genetic factors may play some part in the development of such basic "temperamental" characteristics as personal tempo, inhibition versus spontaneity, soberness versus exuberance, and introversion versus extraversion. Genetic factors also appear to play a significant role in intelligence.

9. In the course of prenatal development, the individual goes through three successive phases: the period of the ovum, the period of the embryo, and the period of the fetus.

10. Prenatal environmental influences can significantly affect the individu-

al's development. These influences include the age of the mother, maternal nutrition, drugs, X-rays, maternal diseases and disorders, and the mother's emotional state.

11. Anoxia (lack of oxygen), excessive use of drugs, and physical injury during the birth process may also affect the baby's development adversely, either temporarily or over a prolonged period, depending largely on the degree of disruption caused.

12. Prematurity may also affect physical and psychological development. The more premature the infant is, and the less he or she weighs, the greater is the likelihood of physical or mental impairment. Postmaturity (excessively delayed birth) may also constitute a danger to the fetus.

13. More boys than girls are born with serious abnormalities, and problems associated with pregnancy and delivery are 3 to 4 times more frequent among lower-class than among middle-class families. Still, less than 7 percent of *all* babies born in the United States experience *any* of the problems discussed in this chapter.

Suggested Readings

Annis, L. F. *The child before birth.* Ithaca, N.Y.: Cornell University Press, 1978.

Apgar, V., & Beck, J. *Is my baby all right?* New York: Pocket Books, 1974.

Hendin, D., & Marks, J. *The genetic connection.* New York: New American Library (Signet), 1979.

Montagu, A. *Life before birth* (rev. ed.) New York: New American Library (Signet), 1977.

Nilsson, L. *A child is born.* New York: Dell (Delacorte Press), 1977.

Stern, C. *Principles of human genetics* (3rd ed). San Francisco: Freeman, 1973.

Part Two
The First Two Years

Chapter 3

Biological Roots of Behavior in the First Year

*D*O YOU consider 12 months to be a long time? How different was your perception of the world 12 months ago? Have you grown physically? Has your behavior changed?

Twelve months does not seem to most of us to be a very long period of time. Admittedly, in any given year, there are routine changes and happenings, and indeed, some changes may be more significant than others, but essentially we live from year to year without feeling that any 12-month period has been of crucial importance to changing our perception of the world. But the first 12 months of life after birth are full of more changes, both in physical growth and in behavior, than any other year in a person's life.

Obviously, the moment of birth brings enormous changes for the infant. After being in a protective, quiet, relatively unchanging environment, the infant is suddenly thrust into a world of change—changes in noise and light and experiences of hunger, heat, cold, and pain. No longer are the infant's biological needs automatically taken care of. In fact, in this new world, the infant must sometimes be subjected to the indignity of howling before his or her hunger pangs are alleviated by warm milk.

During the first year, the infant is constantly discovering more about the environment because she is developing physically. For example, a newborn infant cannot even turn over, but 12 months later she may be able to climb out of the crib or playpen. Such a skill obviously enlarges the scope of the infant's world. Coordination between senses and motor movements also improves rapidly during this time. At birth infants can only follow a moving object with their eyes. Six months later, however, they can not only visually follow a moving object with the eyes; they can successfully reach for the object. Moreover, the complexity of the infant's thought processes increases from birth to one year. The newborn infant is aware of little more than the immediate sensations of touch, temperature, pain, sound, and light. By the age of 12 months, however, the infant can remember past events and has begun to solve simple problems.

At six months, infants can not only visually follow a moving object with the eyes, they can successfully reach for the object.

WHY THE CONCERN WITH INFANCY?

In this chapter you will read detailed descriptions of the biological development of the infant. You will see month-by-month accounts of the infant's capabilities. Why, you may ask, is there such an interest in studying the development of the infant? What difference does it make whether a newborn can discriminate between a gray and a striped card? Who, besides the musically inclined parent, cares whether an infant can perceive the difference between one musical tone and another? Yet child development is of interest to many people other than parents or prospective parents. Scientists, and Western society in general, have always been interested in studying origins. When did life begin? When did our species emerge? A look at the infant is a look at our own immediate past. And

many believe—or hope—that there is an unbroken thread of continuity between the qualities of the infant and the person he or she becomes in later life.

The assumption that the infant's behavior gives us a preview of the future is widely held today. Some physicians and psychologists believe, for example, that the newborn must be united with the mother during the first few hours after birth if psychological development is to be optimal. Others have claimed that the course of the child's intellectual growth is set during the first 3 years; if the infant gets off to a bad start, the child may never be able to **actualize** his or her basic talents. However, recent studies suggest that the infant and young child have a great capacity for change, especially if environmental experiences of later childhood are different from those of infancy. As a result, it is not clear that one can always predict the motivations or conflicts of the adolescent by looking at the psychological profile of the 1-year-old.

How Shall We Study the Infant?

In studying the infant, there are essentially four areas on which we can focus. The first is body growth. How much does a baby usually grow during the first year? What is the normal range of weight increase? The second area is motor development. When can the child sit alone? When can the child stand? The third area on which we can focus is the baby's drives and emotions. Why does the baby cry? Why does the baby smile? The fourth possible area for study is the mental processes of the baby. When can a baby remember? How does a baby learn?

BODY GROWTH IN INFANCY

Obviously newborn babies look different from 1-year-old infants. One-year-olds are beginning to be more adultlike in their proportions, though they are still topheavy: One reason for the slightly grotesque appearance of the infant is that the size of the head is large in proportion to the body. The head, in fact, has attained 70 percent of its adult size by birth. During

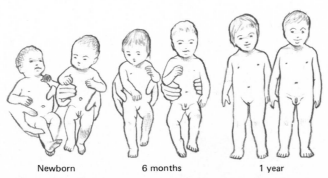

Newborn   6 months   1 year

Figure 3.1 Changes in proportion of the human body from birth to 1 year.

Infant boys have a greater proportion of muscle tissue than infant girls, and this sex difference holds true at all ages.

the first year of life, the trunk of the infant increases in length to partially counteract the topheavy look of the newborn (see Figure 3.1).

Because body size and rates of growth of newborn infants vary widely, averages or norms can give only a general picture of development. The average full-term male baby, who is slightly larger in all body dimensions than a female, is about 20 inches tall and weighs 7½ pounds at birth. But the range of "normal" birth heights and weights is large. For example, newborns from poverty-stricken environments, although similarly proportioned, tend to be smaller than those from economically more favorable environments (3). This difference is probably caused by **nutritional** differences and a different incidence of maternal infection during pregnancy.

Physical growth during gestation and early infancy is important. It is even possible that severe malnutrition during this period will have an adverse effect on the child's later intellectual capabilities by interfering with the development of brain cells.

Skeletal Development

The bones of a newborn baby are not quite "finished." Bones are formed from soft cartilage tissue that over a period of time becomes *ossified*, or hardened, into bone material, and the process of **ossification** begins during the prenatal period and continues, for some bones, until late adolescence. Infants' bones are softer, more pliable, more reactive to muscular pull and pressure, and more susceptible to deformity than those of older children and adults. Fortunately, they are less subject to breakage.

The timing and rate of ossification differs with the various bones of the body and among individuals. Some bones in the hand and wrist are completely formed by age 1 year, while the vulnerable soft spots of the skull ossify gradually and do not become completely hardened until the child is about 2 years old.

Muscle Development

Although the newborn has all the muscle fibers she will ever have, they are small, even in relation to body size. Infant boys have a greater proportion of muscle tissue than infant girls, and this sex difference holds true at all ages (9).

Sex Differences in Physical Development

There are consistent sex differences in growth patterns. Girls develop faster than boys, and this faster rate of development begins during the fetal period. The body composition of the sexes differs, with infant girls having proportionately more fat and less water than boys. Girls have less muscle tissue and are generally lighter and shorter than boys. One of the most intriguing sex differences is that the physical growth of girls is less variable than that of boys. That is, if we pick a particular quality, such as number of teeth at age 2, and examine a thousand boys and a thousand girls, the range for number of teeth would be greater for boys than for girls. There would be more boys with many teeth *and* more boys with few teeth. The range for girls would be smaller (10). In addition, girls' growth is more stable than that of boys. For example, the rate of skeletal maturity in the 2-year-old girl is a better predictor of her future rate of skeletal development than it is for the boy (1).

THE NEWBORN   What can that tiny, red-faced, wrinkled, often crying newborn you look at through the nursery window see or hear? What characteristics of the world does the newborn perceive? As we have said, the baby during the first 5 to 7 days of life is recovering from the physical ordeal of birth and is beginning to sense the world of sights, sounds, and smells that is so different from the protected environment of the uterus. Although prior to birth the infant has been deprived of a great deal of sensory stimulation, he is able to use the senses from the moment of birth. Unlike other mammals, such as puppies, who are both blind and deaf at birth, human newborns can see, hear, smell, and taste.

Somewhat surprisingly, newborns can detect the difference between two notes only one step apart in a musical scale. Newborns are also capable of sensing and differentiating the tastes sweet and salty. They will show specific sucking patterns when different substances are placed on their tongues. For example, when a sweet fluid is given every time the infant sucks, the baby will increase the sucking rate and take shorter rest periods than when no sweet substance is delivered (6). And, even during the early days of life, newborns are sensitive to various smells and quickly learn, for example, to discriminate between the odor of their mother's breast pad and that belonging to another woman (20).

Not only are the newborn's sensory capabilities surprisingly well developed; behavioral reflexes, too, are present from the moment of birth. The newborn can react to stimuli such as gentle touch or a moving light. For example, newborns only 2 hours old will follow a moving light with their eyes if the speed of the light is not too fast. In addition, these little people can flex and extend their arms and legs, smack their lips, and chew their fingers. They can grasp an object placed in the palm.

The infant goes through changes rapidly after birth, and a good illustration of the changes in the infant's nervous system is reflected in the **Moro reflex.** When newborns are startled or when their head suddenly changes position, they typically throw their arms out to the side, extend the fingers, and then bring their hands and arms back and their hands to their chests, as if embracing someone.

This reflex is common up to age 3–4 months. It then appears less frequently and by age 6 months has usually vanished altogether. Is this because the infant becomes less easily surprised as he gets older and more accustomed to the ways of the world? No, the infant can still be surprised, just as a person 25 or 50 years old can still be startled. The reason for the disappearance of the Moro reflex lies in the biological changes that occur as the brain matures. Other neural pathways, which have now matured, inhibit the Moro reflex when the infant is startled. Neurologists would view with some alarm a 10-month-old infant who was still displaying the Moro response to a change in head position or other startling event, for

The World of the Infant: A Blooming Confusion?

What is the world of the infant like? Suppose the newborn infant is in a crib in the family room. People are walking in and out, the television is on, the phone rings, brother and sister are constantly fighting with each other. Because the baby is not yet mature enough to decipher all these sights and sounds, are we to assume that the world of the baby is a "blooming, buzzing confusion"? This belief was held for many years, but recent research on the processes of attention suggests that the infant's world may actually be quieter than our own.

Human beings (both infants and adults) attend closely to only one sensory channel at a time. When you are listening intently to a bird's song, for example, you may not feel a touch, smell a flower, or see a deer. However, because adults' focus of attention shifts so rapidly, they do not always realize that they have at one time been almost totally absorbed with attending to one particular sensory input. If a bug crawls on your arm while you are listening to the bird's song, your attention shifts momentarily to the arm sensation, blocking the sound of the bird's song. Quickly, though, your attention is directed back to the bird, and you are hardly aware that you have missed a note. An insect stirs in the leaves; again, your attention shifts, but only for an instant.

In a similar manner, babies may not experience the sense of being overwhelmed by a blurry, buzzing world, even in a busy setting, because newborns may not change their focus of attention as rapidly as older children. Thus, infants' attention to single matters protects them from a sense of bewilderment at a world they are as yet unable to understand.

Table 3.1 REFLEXES OF THE NEWBORN

EFFECTIVE STIMULUS	REFLEX
Tap upper lip sharply.	Lips protrude.
Tap bridge of nose.	Eyes close tightly.
Bright light suddenly shown to eyes.	Closure of eyelids.
Clap hands about 18 inches from infant's head.	Closure of eyelids.
Touch cornea with light piece of cotton.	Eyes close.
With baby held on back, turn face slowly to right side.	Jaw and right arm on side of face extend out; the left arm flexes.
Extend forearms at elbow.	Arms flex briskly.
Put fingers into infant's hand and press the palm.	Infant's fingers flex and enclose finger.
Press thumb against the ball of infant's foot.	Toes flex.
Scratch sole of foot starting from toes toward the heel.	Big toe bends upward and small toes spread.
Prick sole of foot with pin.	Infant's knee and foot flex.
Tickle area at corner of mouth.	Head turns toward side of stimulation.
Put index finger into mouth.	Sucks.
Hold infant in air, stomach down.	Infant attempts to lift head and extend legs.

this would suggest that there might be some deficiency or damage in the infant's central nervous system. The major reflexes of the newborn and the kinds of stimuli that release them are listed in Table 3.1 (and see Figures 3.2–3.5).

Basic Needs What are the needs of an infant? Basic physiological needs are taken care of automatically by the body systems. The needs for oxygen, temperature control, and sleep, for example, are satisfied without benefit of active participation by the infant or anyone else. But other needs, such as the need for food, must be met by a caretaker.

Sleep. Although weary new parents may think their babies are up at all times, newborn infants actually spend 80 percent of the day in sleep. It's just that sometimes part of the time awake occurs at inconvenient hours such as 2 or 5 a.m. Fortunately, the rhythms and depth of sleep change rapidly during the first year. For the first 3 or 4 weeks, the average infant takes seven or eight short naps a day, but the number is reduced to between two and four longer periods of sleep by 6 weeks of age. Night sleep also becomes less broken as the child matures. By 28 weeks of age, most children will sleep through the night, and from then until they are about 1 year old will require only two or three daytime naps (12).

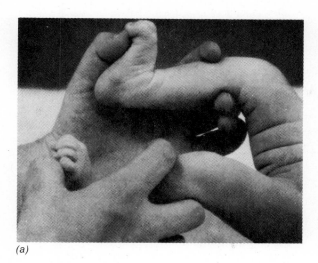

(a)

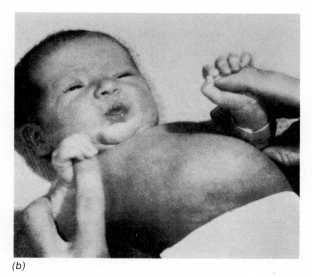

(b)

Figure 3.2 (a) Elicitation of ankle clonus. The examiner presses both thumbs against the soles of the foot; the infant's toes flex around the thumbs. (b) Testing for the palmer grasp. The examiner presses his finger into the infant's palms, and the infant's fingers flex around the examiner's finger. (From H. F. R. Prechtl. *The neurological examination of the full-term newborn infant,* 2nd ed. London: S.I.M.P. with Heinemann Medical/Philadelphia: Lippincott, 1977.)

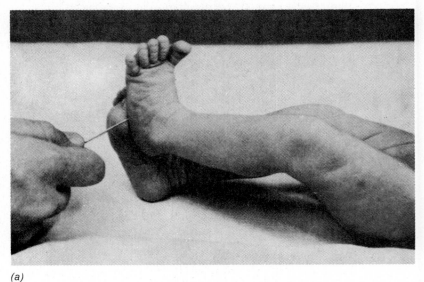

(a)

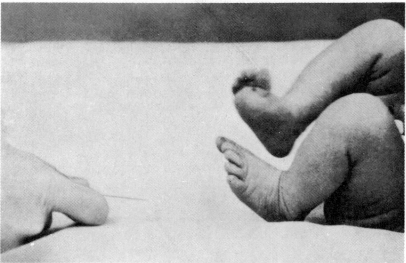

(b)

Figure 3.3 The withdrawal reflex: (*a*) Stimulation. The examiner pricks the infant's sole with a pin. (*b*) Response. The infant withdraws his foot. (From H. F. R. Prechtl. *The neurological examination of the full-term newborn infant,* 2nd ed. London: S.I.M.P. with Heinemann Medical/Philadelphia: Lippincott, 1977.)

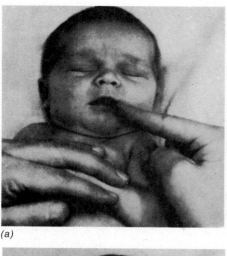
(a)

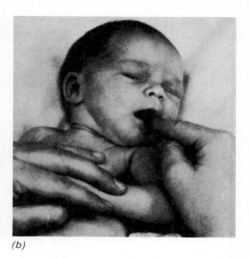
(b)

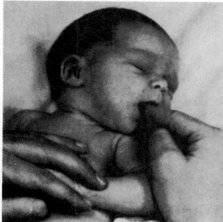
(c)

Figure 3.4 The rooting response: (*a*) Stimulation. The examiner tickles the side of the infant's mouth with a finger. (*b*) Head turning. The infant turns his head in the direction of the finger. (c) Grasping with the mouth. The infant tries to suck the stimulating finger. (From H. F. R. Prechtl. *The neurological examination of the full-term newborn infant*, 2nd ed. London: S.I.M.P. with Heinemann Medical/Philadelphia: Lippincott, 1977.)

Hunger and Thirst. While you are able to realize that sometimes you are thirsty, wanting not food but a tall, cool glass of water, and at other times you feel insatiably hungry, when nothing will satisfy your desire but solid food, it is hard to tell the difference between these two needs in young infants. Hence hunger and thirst will be discussed as one need.

From a psychological point of view, hunger and thirst in the infant are particularly important drives, for their satisfaction depends on someone else's help rather than on automatic reflex activities. If the infant's hunger and thirst are not satisfied within a reasonable period of time, tensions mount, become severe, and provoke body activity. With newborns, tension may erupt frequently, for on the average, newborns take seven or

"The Breast or the Bottle?" and Other Facts About Feeding

It may come as no surprise that there are fads in the advice given to mothers regarding the care and feeding of a baby. For example, 50 years ago a great many pediatricians told American mothers that they should feed the infant on a 4-hour cycle, and even if the baby cried before the 4 hours were up, they were not to offer the baby food. This advice was based on a small number of studies that showed it took about 4 hours for a baby's stomach to empty.

However, today most pediatricians are more permissive and advise the mother to feed the baby whenever the baby seems hungry.

It is important to realize the varied conditions under which infants have been fed throughout recorded history and therefore to be tolerant of diversity. In rural sixteenth-century France, for example, some infants whose mothers had lost their milk were suckled on goats, and, according to Montaigne, who noted this fact, these infants grew in a normal matter.

Similarly, there have been changes in the proportion of women who nurse their babies. Recently there has been an increase in the number of middle-class women who nurse their babies contrasted with the number 25 years ago. This reflects the increased celebration of "the natural" among many areas of society today and the avoidance of things artificial.

A physical benefit of breastfeeding is that mother's milk has antibodies that protect the baby against some infectious diseases early in life. And from a psychological point of view, some argue that the skin contact involved in nursing increases feelings of attachment between mother and infant. However reasonable these ideas, there is not firm proof that when other conditions of living are controlled—social class and personality of the mother, for example—bottle-fed babies are less healthy physically or less well adjusted as older children.

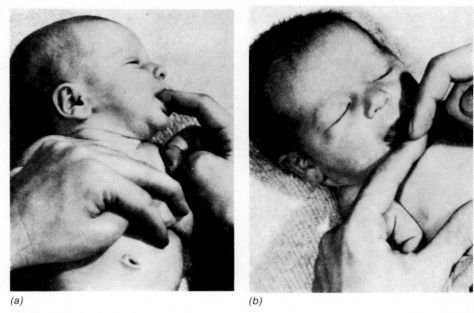

(a)   *(b)*

Figure 3.5 *(a)* Testing sucking. The infant sucks the finger placed into his mouth. *(b)* Elicitation of the jaw jerk. The examiner delivers a short, sharp tap to the chin, and the infant's chin is lifted by contraction of masseteric muscles. (From H. F. R. Prechtl. *The neurological examination of the full-term newborn infant*, 2nd ed. London: S.I.M.P. with Heinemann Medical/Philadelphia: Lippincott, 1977.)

eight feedings per day. By 4 weeks of age the number has been reduced to five or six. Within the next few weeks the number of feedings is further reduced, although total food intake does not change significantly (12). In our culture, solid foods are often introduced before the infant is 6 months of age, and by the time American children are 1 year old, they have joined the regimen of three meals a day and they have begun to show food preferences.

MATURATION

During the first year of life, motor development is largely dependent on biological **maturation,** although practice can speed up the emergence of sitting and walking. An infant is not physically capable of sitting immediately after birth. It is only when the baby has matured—has strengthened and grown—that motor coordination can occur. Once the infant is biologically ready to perform a certain function, however, perfection of the skill becomes possible. When the infant has the opportunity to practice, then

Developmental Milestones in the First Year

1 week	Moves head from side to side.
1 month	On stomach, turns head to side to permit unobstructed breathing; lifts head up briefly.
2 months	On stomach, can raise chest off surface briefly.
	Can raise head erect while held in sitting position, though head bobs up and down.
	Holds objects for a few moments.
3 months	Will swipe at an object in visual field, but typically misses.
	Likely to vocalize in response to mother's smile and talking.
4 months	Can sit supported with head erect and back steady.
	May roll from stomach to side or back.
	Can follow object with eyes across visual field.
	Can focus eyes on near and far objects.
5 months	Can reach for and grasp object; aim is now good.
	Babbles spontaneously to self and toys; uses vowel sounds and a few consonant-like sounds.
	Recognizes familiar objects.
6 months	Sits easily in high chair, grasps dangling object.
	Vocalizes pleasure and displeasure; more use of consonants.
	Transfers object from one hand to the other.
7 months	Sits alone.
	Reaches persistently for toys out of reach.
	Will pick up a second block after securing first.
8 months	Can get self into sitting position.
	Stands with help.
9 months	Stands holding furniture.
	May be able to sit down from standing position.
	Manipulates and drinks from cup.
	May crawl upstairs; can turn around.
10 months	Creeps on hands and knees.
	Side-steps along furniture.
	Walks if both hands held.
	Responds to simple words and commands (e.g., "don't touch," "give it to me").

11 months	Walks when led by one hand.
	Squats and stoops.
	May say two or three words besides mama and dada (e.g., "no," "bye-bye").
12 months	Stands by flexing knees, pushing self up from squatting position.
	Sits down smoothly.
	Crawls up and down stairs.
	Cooperates in dressing.
	Practices familiar words (e.g., "no," "baby," "bye-bye," "hi").

he may perfect the skill earlier than a child in an environment in which he cannot practice. In other words, here again we bring up the joint interaction of **nature** and **nurture** (see Chapter 2).

A nice example of the combined effect of genetic and environmental forces is in the development of speech. Almost all children in all societies begin to speak between 1 and 3 years of age. Their brains are not mature enough to permit them to speak earlier. Certainly the brain of a 3-month-old is not sufficiently developed to permit understanding and expression of language. However, the child does not automatically learn to speak when the brain is mature enough. The child must be exposed to the language of other people. Maturation does not cause a psychological function to occur; it only sets the limits on the earliest time of its appearance.

We do not possess a detailed understanding of the biological changes that permit new capabilities to emerge, but we can describe some of the milestones in the first year — the emergence of new abilities that are likely to be correlated with changes in the central nervous system. Let us consider first some of the motor behaviors that emerge during the first year.

The Maturation of Motor Development

The first times a baby sits, crawls, or stands are milestones, dates that are likely to be recorded by proud parents in the baby book. The various motor skills that emerge during the first year are among the more obvious signs of growth and development in the infant.

Such skills exemplify the pattern of maturational development. Sitting, crawling, and standing occur as a consequence of the opportunity to use the body plus biological changes — the maturation of the nervous system and the growth of bones and muscles. Generally, the baby first sits, crawls, or stands on her own, with no real "lessons," although she may have been guided by a parent. In most cases these seemingly unlearned behavior patterns improve and become better coordinated, more precise, and more accurate after practice.

The ages of the first appearance of the locomotor skills (sitting, crawling and creeping, standing and walking) given below represent *average* ages of attainment. Some children will achieve the skills earlier, some later. Slight deviation from these ages does not indicate that a child is either precocious or retarded, as there are many factors that go into the achievement of motor skills. In fact, except in some cases of obvious pathology, there is little relationship between achievement of motor skills and later intellectual abilities.

Sitting. On the average, babies are able to sit for a minute, with support, at the age of 3 or 4 months, and by 7 or 8 months, they can do it without support. Once the baby sits alone, there is rapid improvement, so that by 9 months most babies can sit independently for ten minutes or longer (11).

Creeping and Crawling. Although there are great individual differences in the ages at which infants reach the various stages of locomotion, practically all infants go through the same sequence (2). First they crawl (move with the abdomen on the floor), then creep (move on hands and knees), and sometimes creep on hands and feet. These steps in locomotion precede standing and walking.

Standing and Walking. Baby's first step does not occur without prior preparation. There is a series of preliminary achievements (pulling up, standing) that most babies go through before they are able to walk independently. Again, there is a wide range of ages at which babies attain the various stages. The average age for standing while holding on to furniture and pulling up to a standing position is between 36 and 40 weeks. The child stands alone at about 48 weeks, walks when led by one hand at 52 weeks, and walks alone, though rather awkwardly, at 13 months (11).

Sensorimotor Coordination and Reaching. As with locomotion, the development of sensorimotor coordination in infants follows a fairly standard behavioral sequence. Generally, a 1-month-old baby will stare at an attractive object but will make no attempt to grab it. By 2½ months, the infant will begin to swipe at it but will be far off target. By 4 months, an infant will raise a hand in the vicinity of the object, look alternately at the hand and the object, gradually getting closer to the object, and then perhaps touch it. By 5 or 5½ months, the infant will reach for the object and succeed in grasping it.

The development of this response, called **visually directed reaching,**

can be affected by environmental experience. Infants raised in an unstimulating environment with few objects to look at or reach for were slow to attain this response (25). Infants who were provided with attractive objects were motivated to reach for them and hence displayed the response somewhat earlier than those infants who were not stimulated.

However, providing too much stimulation too early when the child is not biologically prepared to perform may accomplish nothing, and in some cases may actually hinder normal development. For example, institutionalized infants placed in an enriched environment were more irritable and fussy than those who did not have the enriched stimulation, as if the enriching stimuli were distressing them. It is possible that the 3-week-old baby, biologically too immature to reach for the brightly colored mobile, may become more upset by the presence of the mobile than if nothing were present.

What about the interaction of nature and nurture? Both maturation of the neural and muscular systems and environmental experiences determine when a child will sit, stand, and walk. For example, a couple of twins who were kept on their backs and not allowed to practice sitting or standing until they were 9 months old became able to sit alone within several weeks (7). By that time their neural and muscular systems were capable of such an activity, and very little practice time was required. Still, other studies have shown that specific practice or teaching can speed up the appearance of walking by as much as 2½ months (28), but under no circumstances will an infant be able to walk alone at, say, 4 or 5 months, because the neural and muscular systems are simply not ready.

VOCALIZATION

One of the happiest sounds is that of a baby cooing and gurgling. During the opening weeks of life, even deaf babies with deaf parents make these sounds, though by 6 months of age these babies are normally quiet.

Babbling in infants under 6 months old usually occurs when the children are excited by something they see or hear, and often accompanies motor activity. During the second half of the first year, however, children tend to become quiet while listening to a sound. When the sound stops, they will begin to babble, apparently excited by their attempt to process the sounds. The context in which the infant is motivated to babble changes during the first year. At first the baby babbles indiscriminately. But as certain events or sights acquire more meaning for the child, they elicit more babbling than others. For example, during the first year of life, babbling increases to a human face but will decrease if the child is shown a picture of a checkerboard or a bull's-eye.

Does the environment affect babbling output? The babbling of babies up to 6 weeks old is relatively unaffected by environmental experience. However, after 10 weeks of age, the environment does have an effect. Children raised in homes in which both mother or father and child frequently vocalize to each other tend to babble more and with greater variety than infants from homes where such exchange is minimal (24).

American infants, who are spoken to 25–30 percent of the time they are awake, vocalize about 25 percent of the time they are awake.

A dramatic demonstration of the role of parental vocal play is seen in a comparison of rural Guatemalan Indian infants with those in the United States. The American infants, who are spoken to 25–30 percent of the time they are awake, vocalize about 25 percent of the time they are awake. Indian infants, who are spoken to very little because their mothers do not believe there is much value in such behavior, vocalize only about 7 percent of the time they are awake (17).

However, the fact that a baby babbles a lot does not necessarily mean that the child will be an early or prolific talker. In normal children there is no strong relation between frequency of early babbling and the time of onset or amount of speech during the second year.

A child's babbling, then, depends on both maturation (biological development) and on experience (i.e., how much the child is spoken to), just as the interaction of biological maturation and environmental experience apparently determines when the child will sit, stand, and walk. In the next section we shall explore how these two factors affect the development of **perception** and **cognition.**

PERCEPTUAL DEVELOPMENT

Although the young infant cannot reach, crawl, or talk, he or she can look, listen, touch, and smell. In studying these perceptual processes, we are most interested in noticing what it is that attracts the baby's attention, because what the baby learns will be determined by what captures his or her attention.

We can tell what babies are looking at by observing their eye movements. But for studying responsiveness to other sensory stimuli, we monitor changes in heart rate and breathing. An infant often shows a decrease in heart rate when shown a new stimulus or when a different musical tone is sounded or when experiencing a new taste, for example. This change in heart rate indicates that the infant has perceived or been surprised by something different in the environment. Eventually, the infant becomes bored with experiencing the same stimulus time after time and looks less and stops showing the change in heart rate. The absence of the decrease in heart rate after seeing the same stimulus four or five times in a row suggests that the infant now realizes that the stimulus is the same and therefore is no longer excited by it. When this happens, we say that the infant has habituated to the stimulus; **habituation** has occurred. But if a new stimulus is presented — say, a picture of a dog after repeated presentation of a face — and now the infant's heart rate decreases in response to the picture of a dog, we say that the infant has dishabituated; **dishabituation** has occurred.

Experiments show that babies are born with a natural tendency to attend to events that change. For example, infants will look at any object that moves and at stimuli with a great deal of **contour** — bull's-eyes and checkerboards — and they also listen to **intermittent** sounds, such as the snapping of fingers or tapping on a table.

In studying perception, any of the senses can be used, but we shall concentrate on the visual mode. It is the one most often studied because scientists can easily measure what children look at but have more difficulty determining what they listen to or perceive in other sense areas (see Figure 3.6).

Visual Capacities

What can babies see? Does the world pass before their eyes as a blur? The answer is no, for as you will recall from our previous discussion of the newborn, an infant 2 hours old can follow a moving light. But the muscular coordination required for very acute vision is by no means perfect at birth. The two eyes, for example, do not converge on the same stimulus at birth (26). In fact, it's common for a child under 6 months of age to have crossed or straying eyes. A newborn baby is incapable of focusing on objects closer or farther away than 8 inches, but this ability develops rapidly over the next 2 months. By 2 months of age the infant begins to focus on objects at different distances, and by 4 months the ability to focus on an object is comparable to that of an adult.

Stimulus Determinants of Attention in the Infant

If you held up two objects for an infant — one a red ball, the other a red top turning slowly — which do you think the infant would look at longer? If your guess is the turning top, you're right. The single most important criterion for gaining an infant's attention is *change*. The infant begins life, in fact, with an unlearned tendency to react to stimuli marked by change,

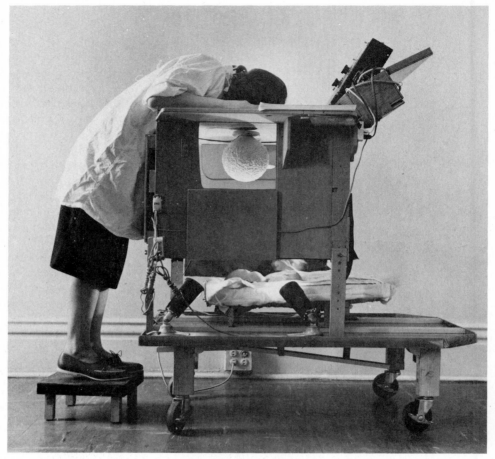

Figure 3.6 Apparatus used to study perception in infants. (David Linton.)

such as movement and contour. Even a 5-day-old baby responds to movement of objects. A baby will momentarily stop sucking on a nipple if she
sees a light beginning to move (14). The infant is also drawn to areas of
contrast created by a contour (the edge of a black line on a white background) and will focus on the area containing the most contrast. For example, if shown a black triangle on a white field, the infant's focus will
hover near the sides of the triangle, or, if shown a black vertical bar in a
white visual field, her attention will remain near that vertical stripe.

It has been suggested that young infants distribute their attention as if
they were guided by the following set of rules:

Rule 1. If awake and alert, open your eyes.

Rule 2. If you find darkness, search the environment.

Rule 3. If you find light but no edges, engage in a broad uncontrolled search of the environment.

Rule 4. If you find an edge, look near the edge and try to cross it.

Rule 5. Stay near areas that have lots of contour; scan broadly near areas of low contour and narrowly near areas of high contour (15).

Apparently, just as we are bored if the visual scene in front of us doesn't change, so too does an infant get bored; after being shown the same stimulus 10 to 15 times in a row, the infant stops looking. But show the infant a new stimulus and the infant's attention can be recaptured.

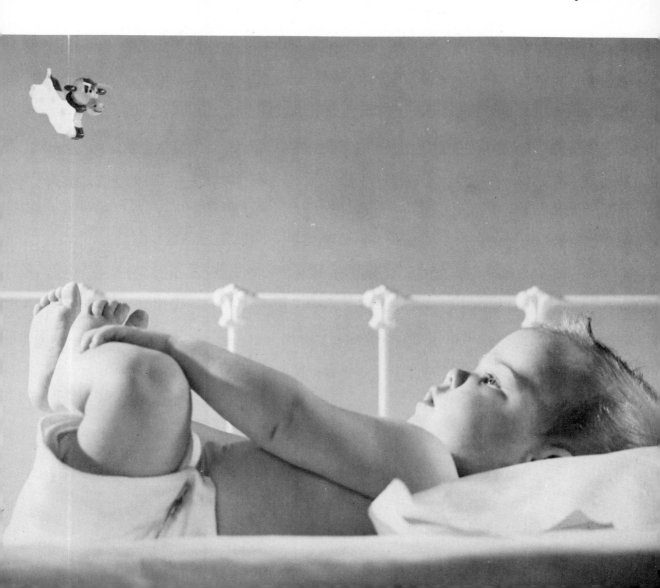

Even a change in color of the stimulus is effective, for it has been shown that infants can distinguish between colors and have color preferences. If an infant gets bored with one stimulus—let us say, a green block—then there is recovery of attention, or dishabituation (that is, the infant shows more interest) when a blue ball is shown. Infants also have color preferences and show a marked preference for the color red.

Another element that seems to attract the attention of infants is the number of elements in a visual pattern. Most infants, for example, prefer to look at a pattern of 32 small squares rather than at a pattern composed of 18 larger squares, even if the amount of contour is the same in the 32-square and 18-square stimuli (8).

Still another facet of infants' visual preferences concerns straight and curved lines. For some reason, infants look longer at curved lines than at straight ones and will look longer at a circle than a square or at the concentric pattern of a bull's-eye rather than a concentric set of squares (23) (see Figure 3.7).

Nature, then, has given the infant an unlearned tendency to pay particular attention to certain aspects of the environment, especially movement, contour, curvilinearity, and particular colors. The infant's tendency

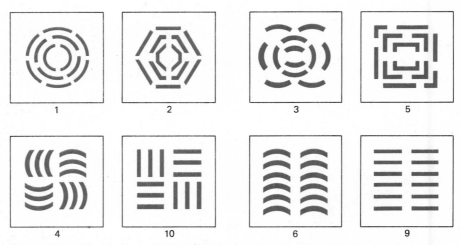

Figure 3.7 When 13-week-old infants were shown pairs of patterns composed of curves and straight-line segments, they were found to prefer forms constructed of arcs to forms constructed of straight lines, and they studied concentric patterns longer than nonconcentric ones. The numbers below each pattern refer to the relative power of that stimulus to maintain the infant's attention; stimulus 1 elicited the most attention, stimulus 10 the least. (From H. A. Ruff & H. G. Birch. Infant visual fixation. *Journal of Experimental Child Psychology*, 1974, *17*, 460–473.)

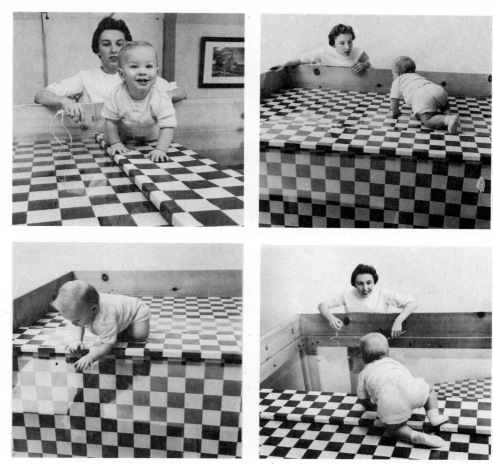

Figure 3.8 Apparatus used to study the baby's avoidance of the appearance of depth. (William Vandivert.)

to look at the mother's eyes is consistent with the findings above, for the eyes have the qualities of movement, contour, and curvilinearity.

Perception of Depth and Three Dimensions

Can infants perceive the quality of depth from birth or must they learn to perceive three dimensions? At least one study has indicated that the capacity to appreciate depth is present very early in life. To test the idea, infants were placed on a center runway that had a sheet of strong glass, thus giving the illusion of depth. The other side appeared solid; a textured pattern was placed immediately beneath the surface of the glass, giving the appearance of a tiled floor (see Figure 3.8).

Infants showed a marked preference for the "safe" side. Six-month-old infants avoided the side that appeared to have the "drop-off," or cliff.

Even if the infant's mother stood at the "deep" side of the glass and beckoned the child to cross over to her, most infants would not approach, although the heavy glass (which they were able to touch) would have made the crossing safe (13). Younger infants who could not crawl also perceived something special on the deep side, for they showed a marked decrease in heart rate (indicating attention) when placed on the deep side (4) and extended their arms only when lowered face-down to the shallow side, not the deep side. Thus it is probable that the infant is able to perceive depth from the earliest months of life.

MEANING AND DISCREPANCY

At birth, infants have limited intellectual capacities. But this is not to say that infants are devoid of mental processes. As a result of attending to and perceiving stimuli, babies create mental representations of experiences that are called **schemata** (the plural form of *schema*). A representation of knowledge is called a **schema,** an abstract representation of the original elements in the event and their relationship to each other. The infant's schema of a face, for example, is likely to emphasize a circular outline containing two circular elements representing the eyes. A nursing bottle may be represented to the infant by a general bottle shape with a nipple on the end (or, if the mother is breastfeeding the infant, by the shape, feel, and position of the mother's breast). As the baby acquires more knowledge, we say that the child is developing schemata.

Once the infant has established a schema for an event, the infant is most likely to attend to those events that are slightly different — but not extremely different — from the one that created the original schema. In our discussion of the physical aspects of objects or events that attract the attention of infants, we saw the importance of **discrepancy,** or change, throughout several of the categories. An infant gets bored, for example, with repeatedly looking at a yellow ball. But the baby's attention can be attracted again by showing a red ball or a yellow cube.

This principle of discrepancy holds in other kinds of stimuli as well, such as in hearing or taste. However, an interesting discovery is that while the infant studies a certain amount of change, he or she is less attentive to too much change. That is, if a stimulus — for example, a face or taste or smell — is different in many ways from what the baby has come to expect, the stimulus will not hold the infant's attention. The stimulus must bear some relation to what the infant already knows. It must not be very different from an existing schema. Thus, showing a baby a set of golf clubs, for which the infant has no prior schema, will not elicit much attention. But a 4-month-old infant, who probably has formed schemata for the faces of the parents, will look a long time at a picture or a sculpture of a face in which the eyes are arranged vertically rather than horizontally. The reason for the infant's increased attention is that the face is *moderately* discrepant from the schema established earlier. However, the infant will not look very

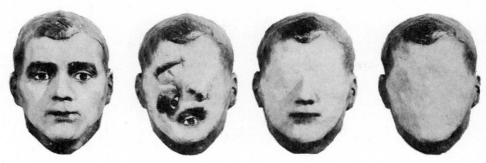

Figure 3.9   Facelike masks shown to infants from 4 to 36 months of age.

long at a face that does not contain any facial features, for a face without eyes, nose, or mouth is *markedly* discrepant from the infant's schema (see Figure 3.9).

Similarly, in the auditory mode, a moderately discrepant event holds the attention of the infant longer than an event that is extremely discrepant. For example, after listening to and eventually becoming bored with repetitions of a short segment of music, infants showed greater recovery of attention to a musical stimulus that changed either the rhythm *or* the melody than to one that changed both the rhythm and the melody (18).

THE ENHANCEMENT OF MEMORY AND THE EMERGENCE OF THOUGHT

Thus far we have suggested that the infant's pattern and duration of attention are controlled by two different factors—first, absolute physical dimensions such as contrast, color, movement, and circularity, and second, the element of discrepancy, which is based, in part, on the child's prior knowledge. But around 8–12 months of age, the infant reaches a new cognitive stage. This stage seems to involve a greater ability to (a) remember events that happened in the past, (b) hold an awareness both of a past event and the event that is happening in the present, and (c) compare the two events (or segments of knowledge) with each other in an attempt to understand their relation.

How, you may ask, do we know such things about an infant? How can we tell what a child is thinking or remembering when the child is not yet able to talk? One fact that suggests this new capacity for memory is an increase in attentiveness to certain events near the end of the first year.

Suppose a mask of a human face is presented to an infant at ages 3 months, 7 months, and 11 months. At 3 months, the infant will look for a fairly long time at the mask. It is a discrepant stimulus. The infant at 7 months, however, will spend less time looking at the mask, but at age 11 months, the amount of time the infant looks at the mask increases. What accounts for the *decrease* at 7 months and the subsequent *increase* in attentiveness at 11 months?

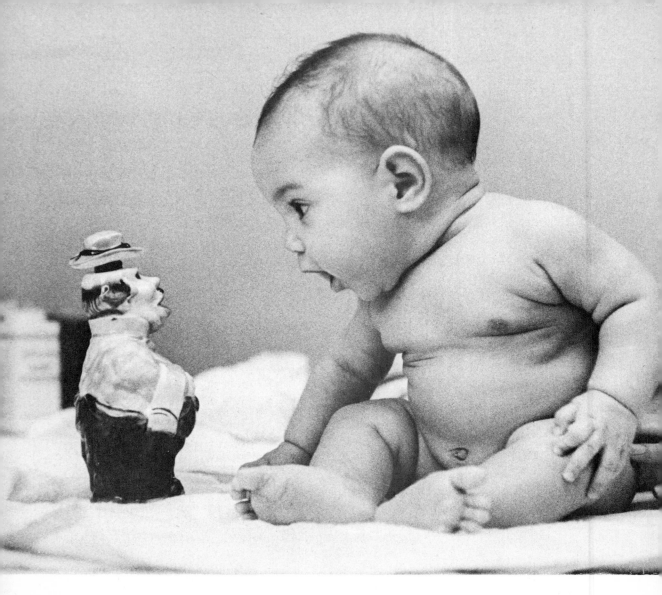

One possibility is that the older infant, while staring at the mask, remembers the familiar face of the parent and tries to figure out how the mask is related to the parent's face. Originally, at 3 months, the mask is a discrepant stimulus. Then at 7 months the mask is just another face. But at 11 months, the infant, now able to recall faces seen in the past, must ascertain whether the mask is the same as one of the faces retrieved from memory. In other words, the capacity for memory adds a new dimension to the infant's world and the stimuli in it. Obviously, such mental work takes time, and so the infant must continue to look at the mask while engaged in this mental activity.

The increase in attentiveness is not the only phenomenon emerging between 8 and 12 months of age that suggests a capacity for memory. After 7 months of age, there is a dramatic increase in signs of apprehension when the child is surprised. Infants younger than 6 months rarely show signs of fear—for example, to unfamiliar adults, a jack-in-the-box, or a mechanical dog. If infants could not remember the past and did not try to relate the past to the present, they would not fear new experiences. But "a little knowledge is a dangerous thing," for when infants become capable of retrieving the past and trying to relate past and present, they become prey to a host of new fears.

Crying, inhibition of activity, and facial expressions of fear all increase in infants older than 7 months when they are surprised or exposed to discrepant events. For example, as we shall see in the next chapter, after 8 months there is an increase in the appearance of signs of fear when the child is left alone in an unfamiliar situation—an event called **separation anxiety.**

The Growth of Memory

The ability to remember the past improves steadily during the last 4 months of the first year. As indicated earlier, we believe that the behaviors of increased attentiveness, inhibition, and distress in response to discrepant events that occur between 8 and 12 months of age are due, in part, to the ability to reach back and recall schemata from the past without any clues. Now the child can retrieve a schema related to the present experience and retain that schema in active memory while comparing it with the present in an attempt to understand the discrepancy. Fear may be a consequence of the failure to resolve the inconsistency between the discrepant event and the child's prior knowledge.

Consider an adult analogy. An airplane passenger who has been reading a book suddenly detects a discrepant or unfamiliar sound in the jet engines of the plane. She retrieves her schema for the sounds she experienced on prior trips, compares that schema with the sounds she is now hearing, and tries to relate them. She tries to resolve the discrepancy. She inhibits what she was doing and concentrates on the unusual engine sounds. If she cannot understand them, she may become apprehensive. Thus increased attentiveness, inhibition, and apprehension follow exposure to discrepancy in adults as well as infants.

It is interesting to see the difference that even 3 or 4 months can make in an infant's ability to remember. Infants a year old will hesitate a few seconds before reaching for a new toy after being shown another toy six or seven times in a row, while 6-month-old infants will reach immediately for the new toy. The 1–2 second delay, short but obvious, suggests that the older infants remember the first toy and are surprised by the new one.

In another study, infants were studied from 8 to 12 months of age. On each visit, the child had to remember the location of a toy that was hidden under one of two identical cloths. There was a delay of 1, 3, or 7 seconds

Figure 3.10 Experimental apparatus used for testing memory. A baby sitting in the mother's lap was first shown a toy. Then the toy was hidden in one of two wells in a table, and an opaque screen was lowered for a few seconds. The baby's "task" was to find the toy after the screen was raised.

between the hiding and the time when the infant was permitted to reach for the toy. Additionally, on some trials, a screen was placed between the child and the toy after the hiding so that the child was temporarily prevented from seeing the array (see Figure 3.10). There was a steady improvement in the child's ability to remember the location of the toy across the 4-month period, with and without the screen. The 8-month-olds were unable to locate the object when there was a 1-second delay and the screen was lowered during that brief interval. By 1 year, however, all the infants could find the toy when the screen was lowered for 3 seconds, and 70 percent of the infants could solve the problem when the screen was lowered for as long as 7 seconds (16) (see graph, Figure 3.11).

Thus far we have been talking about some specific cognitive abilities like perception and memory, relating the present and past. But other psychologists have emphasized other processes and abilities. Jean Piaget is the most important theorist of cognitive development in this century, and his view of intellectual development is different from our own.

Piaget's View of Intellectual Development in Infancy

Piaget believes that intellectual development passes through a series of **stages** during which the child's knowledge of the world takes different forms. During infancy, for example, the child's knowledge is contained in his motor interactions with objects. Piaget calls this knowledge sensorimotor schemes. Thus the 6-month-old's knowledge of a rattle is con-

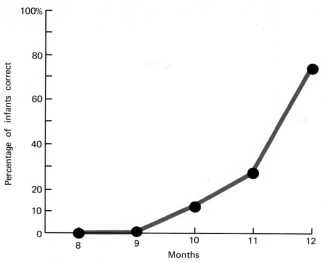

Figure 3.11   At 8 months of age none of the infants in this study could remember the location of the hidden toy when an opaque screen was lowered for 7
seconds. But by 12 months 70 percent of the infants could remember the location. (After N. Fox, J. Kagan, & S. Weiskopf. The growth of memory during infancy.
Genetic Psychology Monographs, 1979, *99*, 91–130.)

tained in the varied set of motor responses he can direct at the rattle—biting, chewing, shaking, or throwing.

During the first year and a half of life, Piaget believes that infants are
in the **sensorimotor stage** of development, and thus their intelligence is
manifested in action. When a 1-year-old wants a toy resting on a distant
blanket, he pulls the blanket toward him to obtain the object. Piaget calls
the act of pulling the blanket an *action scheme* that can be used to solve a
variety of problems.

Piaget's theory holds that the sensorimotor stage is divided into six
developmental substages covering the first 18 months of life (21). The substages are differentiated by the child's growing ability to plan his actions,
to invent new ways to respond to objects, and to separate the goals of his
action from the actual behavior used to reach the goal.

Object Permanence. Piaget has studied many facets of infant development. To give you an idea of his research, let us examine, in some detail,
the emergence of what Piaget calls **object permanence**—a major achievement of the sensorimotor stage of development.

Object permanence is the child's belief that objects continue to exist
even if they are out of sight. Piaget observed that during the first two or

three months of life children will follow an object visually until it passes out of sight and then will abandon their search for it. From 3 to 6 months, as vision and movement of arms and hands become coordinated, infants will grab for objects they can see but make no effort to reach for those they cannot see. Piaget interprets the failure to search for the hidden object to mean that children do not realize that the hidden object is still there. Infants behave as if an object out of sight had no permanence, that it no longer existed.

During the last 3 months of the first year children advance one step further. They will reach for an object that is hidden from view if they watched it being hidden. Thus, if the child sees the mother place a toy under a blanket, he or she will search for the toy there. Moreover, 10-month-old infants will show surprise if they watch an object covered by a person's hand and then note that the object is missing when the hand is removed. The fact that children are surprised by the "disappearance" suggests that they expect the object to be there; in other words, they believe in the permanence of the object (5).

In the final stage of acquiring the concept of the permanent object, children will search for objects that they have not actually seen hidden. For example, if the mother shows the child a toy fish in a box, puts the fish and box under a cover, and then removes the box without the fish, the child will search for the fish under the cover, as though she realized that it must be there. This searching behavior does not occur during the earlier stages (21).

Assimilation, Accommodation, and Equilibration. How does the baby progress from one stage of development to the next — whether we are talking about the substages of object permanence or the transition from the sensorimotor stage to the next stage of intuitive thought? In Piaget's view, the major mechanisms that allow a child to progress from one cognitive stage to the next are **assimilation, accommodation,** and **equilibration.** Assimilation is the tendency to relate a new event to an idea one already possesses. Accommodation is the tendency to change one's ideas to fit a new, initially puzzling event. Equilibration is the process by which the child finds the resolution between assimilation and accommodation.

For example, a 1-year-old sees a large balloon on the floor. Because of its size, the child assimilates that object to his schemes for heavy objects and adjusts his body and arms in preparation to pick up a heavy object. After picking up the balloon, the child realizes that it is light. This surprise forces him to accommodate to the weight of the balloon, and in the future he will prepare his body to pick up a light object when he sees a balloon. The conflict created when he unexpectedly picked up a light object while expecting a heavy object is resolved. Piaget calls this resolution *equilibration.*

Infants display a more sophisticated and more complex level of intellectual functioning than we might expect.

Although babies differ in the speed or rate at which they acquire sensorimotor behaviors, precocious development of these behaviors is not necessarily related to precocious development of vocabulary, comprehension of speech, or the ability to master arithmetic concepts. It cannot be assumed that advanced sensorimotor development at 1 year of age indicates that the child will later have superior linguistic or numerical ability. Although marked retardation in sensorimotor development at 1 year may be an early sign of retardation in the child, the psychological significance of advanced or precocious sensorimotor development is still largely a mystery.

Piaget's observations on the cognitive processes in infants, however, have stimulated other researchers to examine the quality of infant's mental activity. Results show that infants display a more sophisticated and more complex level of intellectual functioning than was expected. For example, 1-year-old infants seem to recognize similarities in objects, suggesting that they have at least an elementary idea of classes, a primitive conceptual skill. That is, a child who touches on ten different trials a different toy animal, will, if shown a new toy animal and a doll on the eleventh trial, play more with the doll than the animal. This behavior suggests that the child has become bored with the category of animals and so was interested in touching a different class of objects—dolls (22). It is somewhat surprising that as early as 1 year of age children seem to possess, or are able to generate, categories for certain classes of real objects, though obviously they don't verbally label them as such.

INDIVIDUAL DIFFERENCES IN NEWBORNS

Throughout this chapter most of our discussion has centered on describing the general course of infant development. But what about individual differences among infants? Parents notice differences between the behavior of one child and another. "Suzy was always such a quiet baby. Why does this one cry so much?" Although these individual differences are real, their causes are largely unknown. The significant question is whether these individual differences are important or lasting.

There are two reasons why individual differences may be important. First, the infant's temperament may influence the way the parents handle the child. If, for example, a child is hard to calm down, a nervous parent may become edgy and irritable, feel inadequate, and eventually resent the child. A less irritable baby, however, may elicit a more pleasant, mutually rewarding parent-child relationship. Second, it is possible that some specific qualities may push the child to develop in one particular direction. For example, a frail child may never be athletically inclined and may instead prefer to read and study. In the following we shall look at four kinds of behavioral differences among infants that parents usually notice: spontaneous motor activity, irritability, passivity, and span of attention.

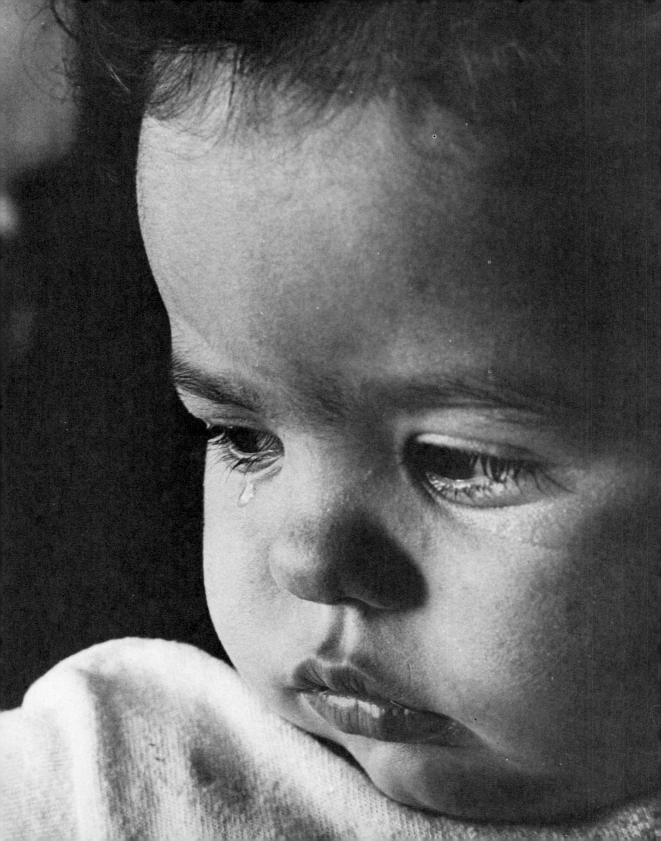

Motor Activity

Some children show frequent and vigorous thrashing of arms and legs, whereas others lie still and quiet. Some infants sleep restlessly, whereas others show minimal activity during sleep (27).

It is reasonable to assume that the child's later development might be influenced by level of activity. For example, an extremely energetic infant might be more apt to get into closets and upset dishes and, therefore, encounter more parental restriction and punishment than a less active baby. A mother who is easily irritated may be more punitive toward an active child than toward a placid one. An energetic, athletic father may be cross and irritable with a placid boy, but more accepting of an active one.

Irritability

Some infants are easily provoked to crying, whining, and fretting and are difficult to comfort. At the other extreme are infants who rarely cry and seem to have an almost infinite tolerance for frustration. One possible cause of irritability, but obviously not the only one, is precocious mental development—a tendency to note unusual situations while being unable to understand or react to them. This combination of an ability to detect the unusual while having no appropriate reaction can evoke fear and crying.

Passivity

Some children react with withdrawal, freezing, or inhibition to people or events that are unexpected or slightly frightening. Such infants are called *passive*, because they show withdrawal to an intrusion, threat, or new event. At the other extreme are infants who are likely to approach or to do something in response to a threatening or unusual event. Such infants are called *active copers*. The fact that an infant is passive does not mean that he or she will be less intelligent.

Span of Attention and Tempo of Play

Another dimension on which children differ is span of attention. One child may play with a toy for a long period of time, while another may lose interest very quickly. The first can be described as having a slow tempo; the second as having a fast tempo. Children tested as early as 4 months of age who demonstrated extremely fast or slow tempos retained that tendency at least through their second birthday. But by age 10 there were no differences between the fast-tempo and slow-tempo children on a variety of tests, suggesting that this temperamental dimension may not extend its influence indefinitely (19).

Consequences of Temperamental Profiles. A further classification of children based on individual differences involves three basic types. The *easy* child usually seems to be in a good mood, has regular sleep and bowel movements, adapts readily to new surroundings, and is not timid in new situations. The easy child is a cheerful infant who is easy to care for and love. The *difficult* child does not establish regular feeding or sleep patterns, reacts intensely to imposition or frustration, and withdraws passively from strange events or people. She seems to require a long time to adjust to anything new and is difficult to rear. The child who is *slow to warm up* is relatively inactive, withdraws from novelty, is negative in mood, and reacts with low intensity.

Of a group of infants studied in New York City, 40 percent were "easy," 10 percent were difficult, and 15 percent were slow to warm up. These children were studied from infancy to 4 years of age. Some of the infants eventually developed psychological symptoms serious enough to require psychiatric help when they were 4 or 5 years old. Many of these were classified as difficult infants. It is likely that the psychiatric problems resulted from the combination of an infant who was difficult to care for and an impatient mother whose frustration with her irritable child led to tension in the parent-child relationship.

However, when the children were school-age, there was not a strong correlation between the temperamental patterns displayed during infancy and personality or school adjustment during the school years. In sum, it appears that there is short-term stability for some temperamental qualities, but the evidence for long-term constancy is fragile at the present time. Either the influence of these temperamental traits is gone by later childhood, or the influence is extremely subtle and submerged by other factors. Finally, whether these temperamental differences are hereditary in origin or the result of environmental events during intrauterine development is a fascinating but still largely unsolved mystery.

SUMMARY

1. During the first year of life the infant experiences many changes in body growth and motor and cognitive development, although even the newborn is a perceptually capable organism with well-functioning sensory and motor systems.

2. The Moro reflex illustrates the changes in the infant's nervous system. This reflex in response to startling commonly appears until the infant is 3–4 months old and by 6 months usually has vanished altogether because of the development of other neural pathways.

3. During the first year of life, motor development is largely dependent on biological maturation, although practice can speed up the emergence of sitting and walking. Babbling, too, is a product of the interaction of biological maturation and environment.

4. The development of locomotor skills and of sensorimotor coordination follows a fairly standard behavioral sequence in almost all infants.

5. Infants attend to events that change — they are visually attracted to movement, contour, curvilinearity, and particular colors, such as red.

6. Infants create representations of experience called schemata and are drawn to events that are slightly different (discrepant) from the one that created the original schema.

7. By around 8–12 months of age the child has developed a capacity for memory, and this ability improves steadily during the last 4 months of the first year.

8. Jean Piaget holds that infants are in the sensorimotor stage of development for the first year and a half of life and that their intelligence is manifested in action. The developing child's increasing willingness to search for a hidden object illustrates the development of the Piagetian concept of object permanence, the child's belief that objects continue to exist even if they are out of sight.

9. In Piaget's view, the major mechanisms that allow a child to progress from one cognitive stage to the next are assimilation, accommodation, and equilibration.

10. Although newborns differ in spontaneous motor activity, irritability, passivity, and span of attention, these temperamental differences do not remain constant over long periods of time.

Suggested Readings

Fraiberg, S. *Insights from the blind*. New York: Basic Books, 1977.
Kagan, J. *The growth of the child*. New York: Norton, 1978.
Willemsen, E. *Understanding infancy*. San Francisco: Freeman, 1979.

Chapter 4

Social Experience and the Infant

ℰIGHT-MONTH-OLD Alice reaches and grabs when a toy is held in front of her. She coos and babbles when an adult leans over her crib; she cries when her diaper is wet. But 8-month-old John is listless and apathetic. He vocalizes very little; he rarely even cries when he is wet or hungry. Why? What makes the personalities of these two infants so different?

Some individual differences are due to biologically based temperamental characteristics. Some children simply cry more than others. But biology alone is not entirely responsible for the boldness or fearfulness that may begin to emerge during the first year. As you may recall from the preceding chapter, many physical and mental skills, such as sitting, standing, and walking, even the capacity for memory, almost invariably appear as a result of maturational factors that come with time, at least as long as the child grows up in a reasonably normal environment. But many of the infant's *personality* characteristics stem primarily from the special influence exerted by other people. In this chapter we shall examine the effects of social interaction on psychological growth during infancy.

THE INFLUENCE OF ADULTS

Adults play two important roles in the life of an infant. They are responsible for taking care of the basic needs of the infant. If the baby's diaper is wet, an adult must change it. If the infant is hungry, an adult must feed the baby. But the role of adults extends beyond these examples of actively relieving the infant of distress. As important as taking care of basic needs is providing opportunities for social interaction. For example, when an adult talks to an infant, the baby may look up, move his or her lips, and gurgle and coo. The adult is someone for the baby to talk to, look at, and play with.

There are two major results of social interaction between infants and adults. First, infants develop a special emotional relationship with the human beings who regularly care for them and interact with them — a relationship that is commonly called attachment. Secondly, social interaction promotes cognitive and social development, and influences the rate at which that development proceeds. Looking at and "talking" with adults give infants opportunities for trying out emerging cognitive and social skills. Activities such as pulling a child to a sitting or standing position, playing peekaboo, even simply pointing to and naming objects can help the child develop.

Infants develop a special emotional relationship with the human beings who regularly care for them and interact with them — a relationship that is commonly called attachment.

The quality of this interaction may vary. One child may have a highly verbal caretaker who is attentive and affectionate toward the infant, while another child's caretaker may offer only brisk, routine handling of the basic needs of the baby — simply feeding, clothing, and changing the baby. One question we shall explore is whether infants who are not played with, who are rarely talked to, are different from more normally reared infants. In other words, how do the quality and extent of the interaction affect the development of the infant?

It is important to note that in this chapter we shall often refer to the mother as the primary caretaker, but bear in mind that other people — the father, for instance — may fulfill this role.

Why Study Infant-Adult Social Interaction?

The adult's role in stimulating cognitive skills is considered very important in Western society. In less developed cultures relieving distress and promoting health are seen as the adult's most important function in connection with babies. This difference may in part be accounted for by the fact that the values are different. Cognitive skills are necessary for survival in Western society, but in those cultures in which an adult is expected to work in the fields or to pasture cattle, cognitive skills are less critical. A strong back may be deemed more essential than an inquiring mind. Thus the infinite subtleties and finesse — the strong verbal and mathematical skills — required for success in complex societies such as the United States are simply not necessary in a great many rural, agricultural societies.

Cognitive and verbal skills are generally furthered through formal education, and thus in our competitive society, in which future status and wealth may depend on education, there is an emphasis on doing well in school. There is some reason to believe — and many American parents do believe — that psychological differences among young school-age children are at least in part due to variations in how the children were treated during infancy. And because doing well in school is so important, social interaction in infancy assumes a special importance in Western society that it may not have in many other places throughout the world.

CULTURAL DIFFERENCES IN CHILD REARING

Child-rearing practices vary from culture to culture. For example, in some villages in rural Guatemala, infants spend most of their first year in a cradle in a dark hut with no toys and little playful interaction. On Israeli kibbutzim infants live with a nurse and other young children in a spacious room. In a residential nursery in Peking, infants live in a large room with 25 other children and experience a relatively regimented day. In a modern American home, an infant is often raised in a private, airy room, and receives a great deal of individual attention and toys from the moment of birth.

Why do these differences in child rearing exist? One factor that affects how children are reared is what the parents believe about the basic nature of children and their theory of how children can be molded into ideal adults. In some cultures — India, for example — parents believe that the infant is willful and must be tamed. In contrast, Americans generally view the infant as relatively helpless, a being who must be pushed, stimulated, and encouraged. You might expect that child-rearing practices in the two countries would be quite different.

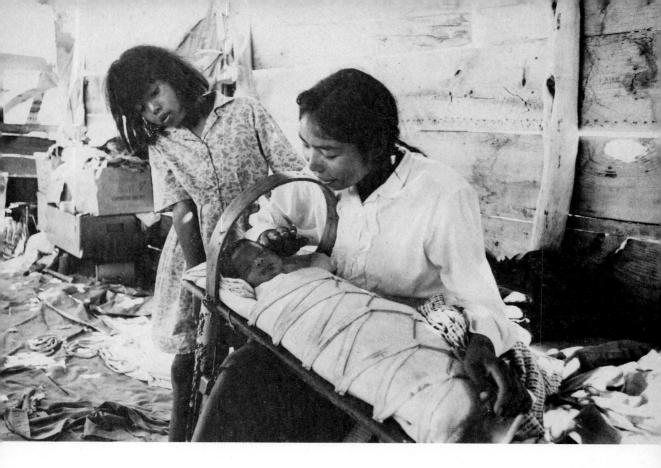

One contrast in child rearing is reflected in a study comparing Japanese and American mothering practices (4). Japanese children live and sleep in the same room with their mother and father, and the Japanese mother is always close to her infant. Consequently, Japanese mothers tend to the fretting child very quickly. In contrast, an American child is more apt to have a separate room and may fret for some time before crying is heeded. Furthermore, Japanese children are generally encouraged to be quiet; American children are more often stimulated to babble. American mothers play excitedly with and talk to their babies; Japanese mothers typically restrain their infants and talk to them less frequently.

How do these variations in mothering affect the children? There are differences between the behavior of Japanese children and American children. In general, Japanese babies are less active than American infants and much less vocal, thus implying an association between maternal practices and the infant's behavior.

Again, we see that these differences in child rearing are related to cultural differences in philosophies about the infant. An American mother is more likely to view infants as totally malleable and to see her job as one of molding her infant into an active, independent child. As a result, she feels she must stimulate the infant and teach independence and self-reliance. The Japanese mother views her infant as having some inherent disposition of his own. As a result, he is not totally malleable in the hands of the mother. Additionally, the mother views her task as making the child more dependent on her and the family rather than more independent, as is true in the United States.

Fashions change from time to time, and so do child-rearing practices, even within our own society. In 1914 women wore long skirts, and for a lady to show her ankles was considered risqué; in the 1960s women wore miniskirts. In 1914 government pamphlets advised American mothers to avoid all excessive stimulation of their children because babies had extremely sensitive nervous systems; in the 1960s government pamphlets urged mothers to allow infants as much stimulation as they wished, because that was the only way they would learn about their world. In 1914 women were told not to feed or play with the baby every time he cried, because such action would spoil him. Fifty years later the mother was told the child would feel secure if she nurtured him, and she should not be afraid of "spoiling" her baby. The 1914 pamphlet urged the mother to toilet-train her child before the first year was over and to prevent thumb-sucking and handling of the genitals. A half-century later she was told to wait until the child understood the purpose of toilet training (at least until

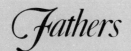

Fathers

For most of America's history, fathers have not seen themselves as playing an influential role during their child's infant years. This view is shared by fathers in most societies. Indeed, in some societies a man would be regarded as odd or at least eccentric if he spent a lot of time with his infant. However, because of the increasing equalitarian relationship between the sexes and a more positive attitude on the part of young men toward the paternal role, more young fathers in America are spending a great deal of time with their young children—feeding them, diapering them, and playing with them, and students are even taking them to class.

Most psychologists believe that this increased participation on the part of the father is beneficial to the child's development. It also enhances the father's emotional investment in his child and can strengthen the marital relationship by the fact that both parents share a common concern.

America is today less Puritan than it was in 1914, and "enjoying life" is accepted as a legitimate aim, for infants and adults alike.

the middle of the second year) and not to worry about thumbsucking or genital touching.

These changes in advice to mothers mirror the cultural changes that occurred between 1914 and 1960. America is today less Puritan than it was in 1914, and "enjoying life" is accepted as a legitimate aim, for infants and adults alike. Thus, again you can see that child-rearing practices are good indicators of the value system of a society, and changes within a culture from time to time or differences between one culture and another are reflected in the various philosophies toward children and child rearing.

In the next section we shall see that there are also differences between individual mothers or other caretakers in the ways that they interact with their young children. Such differences can affect the child's response and the nature of the relationship between caretaker and child.

DIFFERENCES BETWEEN CARETAKERS

It is not surprising that adults differ in the way they interact with infants. After all, everyone is aware of the individual differences that distinguish one adult from another. Some of your friends may be warm and affectionate, while others are more reserved and shy. It is likely that the behavior of young infants will be influenced by interaction with different kinds of adults. In one study, two groups of 10-day-old infants were cared for 24 hours a day by either Nurse A or Nurse B. Infants in the group assigned to Nurse B cried much less than they had in the newborn nursery, while the infants who were transferred to the care of Nurse A showed a much less significant decrease in crying. Sleep patterns also improved more under the care of Nurse B. Since the two groups of infants were randomly selected and thus probably very similar, the differences in behavior can be attributed to differences in care. Apparently, Nurse B was especially effective at soothing and calming her infants, perhaps because she was more sensitive to the individual needs of the infants than Nurse A (17).

As you will see below, there are many factors that affect the interaction between the baby and the caretaker. Even differences as subtle as variations in adults' speech rhythms and voice inflections can affect the baby's behavior patterns. A baby will respond to a person's speech by synchronizing body movements with the rhythm or tempo of the speech. As a person pauses for breath or accents a syllable, the infant shifts her body and moves ever so slightly—for example, raises an eyebrow or lowers a foot—much the way dancers respond to music. Being around a fast-talking, energetic person may cause the infant to be more active than when in the presence of a calmer, slower-talking person. For instance, it is possible that Nurse B had a more calming voice than Nurse A.

The interactions that occur between baby and caretaker tend to result in feelings of **attachment** between the two. Of course, this feeling of attachment may be strengthened or weakened by the nature of the interaction, and in the next section we shall explore how interactions affect that relationship.

THE CONCEPT OF INFANT ATTACHMENT

It is an undeniable fact that early in the first year of life, and certainly by 12 months, infants establish a special relationship with a small group of people, usually the ones who care for and stimulate them — who feed them, talk to and play with them, cuddle and rock them. This attachment relationship has three main characteristics. First, the child is likely to approach these people — the targets of attachment — for play or when distressed, tired, bored, hungry, afraid, or in pain. Second, the child is more easily soothed and placated by these people than by anyone else. Third, the infant shows no fear when with one of these adults. These caretakers provide a secure base or haven; the baby can explore without anxiety in strange situations when one of them is near.

By 4 to 5 months of age infants will have differentiated their caretakers from other people and will not allow just anyone to pick them up when they cry, to rock them when they are sleepy, or to feed them when they are hungry. Only a few special people have earned this privilege, and they are the people the infant is most likely to approach, smile at, and play with and least likely to fear. Infants can become attached to more than one person, and, as we shall discuss later, the attachments of infancy can be altered in both animals and human beings (9).

There are two processes believed to be responsible for the development of the infant's attachment to another person. One is the interaction that occurs between the infant and the caretaker. The infant responds to signals from the caretaker, who in turn responds to the infant's responses, each providing continuing "feedback" to the other. Baby responds by smiling and gurgling; mother laughs.

The second process that results in feelings of attachment is the association the infant makes between feelings of pleasure and relief of distress on the one hand and the presence of the target of attachment (the caretaker) on the other. That is, as the baby experiences the pleasant state that accompanies the caretaker's feeding, diapering, and warm and gentle contact, he or she is perceiving the caretaker as a stimulus. As a result of the association between the caretaker and the pleasant feelings, the caretaker comes to represent the pleasant emotional state. In the future the child will psychologically anticipate and search for the caretaker when he wants alleviation from feelings of distress (9).

Action and Reaction

We start with a basic fact. From the moment the baby is born, he acts and reacts. Some responses are spontaneous; others are reactions to needs. Some of the behaviors are necessary for survival; others are not. A newborn baby scans the environment, sucks, smiles, babbles, cries, and thrashes about. During the third and fourth months of life, the infant

begins to cling to and explore the face, fingers, and hair of the person holding him. These interactions—and the ones discussed below—all influence the attachment relationship that develops between infant and caretaker.

Looking. The human face is a natural target of interest for the infant. Eyes are circular and moving, lips move, sounds come from the mouth. In other words, the face displays several of the requirements for maintaining an infant's interest (see Chapter 3). Each face is somewhat like other faces, and thus bears a relation to the schema the infant may have developed for a face. However, there are also slight differences in each face and voice, thereby supplying the element of discrepancy that is so important in holding an infant's attention.

Vocalizing. Babbling is a second spontaneous response infants display, especially if it provokes a response from another person. Most objects do not produce a sound when the infant babbles. Mobiles and cribs do not "do something back" to the child when she vocalizes. The caretaker does. The infant babbles, the mother smiles and talks back; the infant babbles again, and the mother repeats. This interaction may continue for several minutes, with the mother's talking and facial reactions maintaining the child's babbling response.

Smiling Behavior. Smiling, like babbling, is another response the infant often directs to the caretaker. However, this mode of interaction may have different meanings for the caretaker and the infant. While an adult generally smiles as a form of social greeting or in response to some humorous event, the young infant is likely to smile after resolving some discrep-

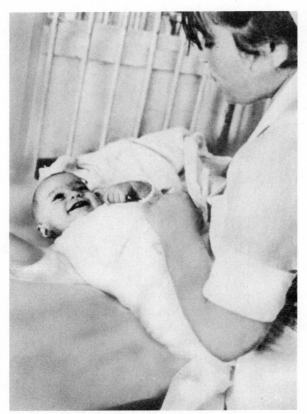

Figure 4.1 Four-month old institution infant smiling at caretaker while being dressed. (From J. L. Gewirtz. The course of infant smiling in four child-rearing environments in Israel. In B. M. Foss, Ed., *Determinants of infant behaviour*, Vol. 3. London: Methuen & Co. Ltd., 1965.)

ancy — that is, figuring out just what something is. Of course, resolution of a discrepant event for an infant is not as complex as understanding the law of thermodynamics; an infant may feel a sense of resolution from a task as simple as establishing that the form above the crib is a human face.

An infant's smile does not always signify recognition of the moderately familiar, however. Many newborn infants display smiles when they are sleeping or after a feeding before they have developed a schema for anything, and some 1-year-old babies will smile at almost anyone who smiles at them (see Figure 4.1).

Some babies smile frequently; others raised in apparently similar environments smile rarely. The difference in temperament may have biological origins. Interestingly, babies who frequently smile in response to faces during the first year are a little more likely to be cautious and **reflective** when solving a difficult perceptual problem at 10 years of age than those infants who were infrequent smilers (9).

Among the many factors that may affect the frequency of smiling behavior are age, social context, temperamental differences, and even ethnic background (see Figure 4.2). In one study, Chinese-American and Caucasian 4-month-olds smiled equally often when an unfamiliar woman talked to them, but eight months later the same Caucasian children smiled at the woman more often than did the Chinese (9). It is possible that the ethnic difference in smiling behavior at 1 year is due to child-rearing practices and interactions in the family.

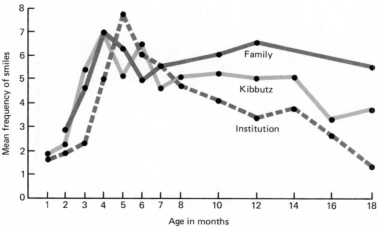

Figure 4.2 Frequency of smiling among infants raised in three different environments. (From J. L. Gewirtz. The course of infant smiling in four child-rearing environments in Israel. In B. M. Foss, Ed., *Determinants of infant behaviour*, Vol. 3. London: Methuen, & Co. Ltd., 1965.)

Effect of the Smile on the Caretaker. Those infants who smile frequently are charmers. They generally elicit a positive emotional response from their caretakers, for smiles are generally interpreted by the caretaker to mean that the baby is happy and content, and who but the caretaker is responsible for baby's feelings of satisfaction? Thus the caretaker of a smiling baby feels her work is effective, while a person whose infant smiles infrequently may begin to doubt her competence. While the baby's infrequent smiles may not really signify that the infant is happy, the smiling behavior (or lack of it) does contribute to the quality of the emotional relationship with the parent.

Distress Calls. If you have ever been subjected to the sounds of an unhappy baby during a show or concert, you may have the idea that crying is an infant's favorite activity. A baby generally cries in response to either internal distress or an unexpected or strange event. A clear example of how interaction between baby and caretaker can strengthen the attachment relationship is seen in what happens when babies cry. When crying babies are picked up, they typically relax their muscles and, when held upright, rest their head on the shoulder of the person holding them and hold her about the neck or body. Both caretaker and baby feel closer during this interaction — the baby because distress has been relieved and the caretaker because the baby has displayed affection. Responding to the infant's distress calls is thus important for both baby and caretaker, and parents need not fear that attending to their baby's needs quickly and consistently will lead to a "spoiled" child.

The Significance of Feeding for the Attachment Process

An important activity in an infant's daily routine is feeding, and thus it is natural that the infant develops an attachment for the person who relieves the pangs of hunger.

Consider what happens during a typical hunger–feeding cycle. The infant begins to feel uncomfortable, thrashes about, and cries for relief. Usually, after several minutes, the caretaker (often the mother) comes to feed the infant. She picks the infant up, cradling him in her arms, and he gradually becomes less active during the feeding. As the baby experiences the pleasurable sensation of relief from hunger and pain, he studies the mother's face. Also, the infant senses other identifying characteristics of the mother — how it feels to be held by her, how she smells, and how she sounds. These experiences, all occurring at the same time, have two consequences.

First, infants associate the comfortable, pleasant sensations of hunger relief with the many stimulus cues (visual, auditory, tactile, and olfactory) of the mother. Such an association is bound to strengthen the attachment relationship of the infant. Second, during the feeding situation, there is interaction between the mother (or other feeder) and the baby. Babies respond by scanning, babbling, smiling, and clinging to the person feeding them. Again, this interaction strengthens the attachment relation.

But while the infant's attachment to the caretaker — as well as the caretaker's attachment to the infant — may be strengthened by the feeding process, this situation alone may not be the major foundation of the infant's attachment. At least in the case of experiments with monkeys, the feeding process has been of less importance in forming the attachment than have other aspects of care.

In a series of famous experiments, infant monkeys were placed with two "mother" monkeys constructed of wire mesh (7). The monkeys were fed from a bottle attached to the "chest" of the plain wire-mesh mother. The other wire-mesh mother, from which they were not fed, differed in just one respect from the other mother — it was covered in terrycloth (see Figure 4.3). In all cases, the monkeys, when given a choice, chose to cling to the terrycloth mother and would run to it when frightened (see Figures 4.4 and 4.5). In other words, the fact that the wire mother "fed" the infant

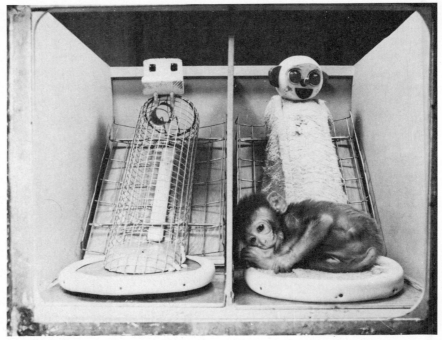

Figure 4.3 Wire and cloth mother surrogates. (From H. F. Harlow & R. R. Zimmerman. Affectional responses in the infant monkey. *Science*, 1959, *130*, 422.)

Figure 4.4 Typical response to cloth mother in the modified open-field test. (From H. F. Harlow, & R. R. Zimmerman. Affectional responses in the infant monkey. *Science*, 1959, *130*, 430.)

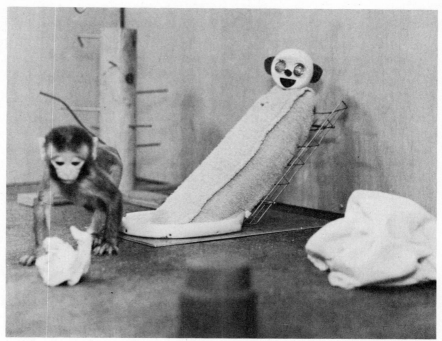

Figure 4.5 Rhesus infant, raised with a cloth surrogate mother, displaying security and exploratory behavior in a strange situation in the mother's presence. (From H. F. Harlow & M. K. Harlow. Learning to love. *American Scientist*, 1966, *54*(3), 251.)

monkeys was less important than the fact that the infant could cling to the softer mother monkey.

Apparently, then, it is not feeding alone that is responsible for the infant-caretaker attachment—there are other factors as well. Can we generalize about them?

A Tentative Explanation. It may be that infants, both animal and human, become attached to those people (or things) to whom they direct behavior—the basic responses characteristic of the species, many of them necessary for adaptation or survival. Many of these actions are present at birth or develop shortly thereafter. Among these are cuddling or clinging, for instance, or looking. Anything (or anyone) to which the infant can habitually make these responses, particularly one such as the caretaker, who reacts and responds to the infant's actions, becomes important to the infant.

Nature has supplied infant monkeys with a strong **grasping reflex,** and monkeys become attached to those objects to which they can make this response. In the jungle the young monkey clings to the hairy under-surface of the mother for several months after birth. But in an experimental situation in which another monkey is not available, the infant monkeys choose the terrycloth mother instead of the wire mother as the object of their attachment, because they can cling to it.

What of the human infant? What are its naturally strong reactions? The infant smiles, sucks, babbles, cries, scans, manipulates, and holds, among other things. In the natural course of events, the mother is often the target for these responses. The mother talks and stimulates the baby to babble; she moves her face and the child scans it; she allows the baby to play with her hair and explore her face. Equally important, the mother alleviates the child's hunger, cold, and distress, and while she is performing these care-taking acts, the infant is studying her face and form, babbling, and occa-sionally smiling. As a result of the daily repetition of these interactions in-fants become attached to their caretakers, whether the location is a city apartment, a farmhouse, or a bamboo hut in the mountains of Guatemala.

Such a scientific view of infant-caretaker attachment is not meant to detract from the concept of love for parents and family. But the usual con-cept of love is more **symbolic,** based not on ideas such as "I love mother because she feeds me," but on deeper, more enduring principles, which may be as simple as "I love Mom and Dad because they love me." That is, the child knows that the mother and father value him or her and so wants to maintain an emotionally close relationship with them. This emotion of love does not emerge until around 2 years of age, when the ability to use symbols develops.

The premise is that early infant attachment need not have a strong relation to later love relationships. It is possible for a 4-year-old boy who did not see his father until he was 3 years old to believe that his father val-ues and loves him and to have a close relationship with the father. More-over, it is possible that this emotional bond can develop without prior at-tachment to the father in infancy. Many children who are adopted after age 3 come to love their foster parents.

MATERNAL ATTACHMENT TO THE INFANT

What about the other side of the relationship? Not only does the infant become attached to the caretaker, but the caretaker feels a **reciprocal** sense of attachment to the infant. In the process of holding, feeding, touching, kissing, playing with, and talking to the infant, the caretaker may experi-ence deeply satisfying emotions and develop an emotional bond with the infant.

As with all affairs involving human beings, the relationships between caretakers and infants vary. Mothers, for example, differ in their emotional involvement with and responsiveness to their infant as well as in their sensitivity to the signals that their baby communicates to them. Some

mothers seem to possess a special ability to soothe their distressed infant easily and to anticipate upset and prevent the child from becoming extremely distressed. It may take one mother half an hour to realize that baby's distress was related to a need to burp, whereas another mother may realize immediately what the problem is. Many psychologists believe that infants with these more effective and more sensitive mothers are less irritable and are more securely attached to their caretakers.

Why are some mothers particularly sensitive to their infants and emotionally involved with them while others are not? There are, of course, many factors that affect such a complicated issue, and we can speculate on only a few such factors here.

Being sensitive to an infant's needs requires an ability to see things from the infant's point of view (2). The mother must, in effect, be able to ignore her own needs and project herself into the baby's world. Often, younger mothers are less able to respond selflessly than older mothers. Some adolescent mothers, for example, may be too immature, still too concerned with their own needs, to be able to subordinate their needs to those of their infants.

Another problem encountered by some caretakers, especially young mothers, is lack of knowledge about and experience in care of infants, which can lead to health problems during infancy. It is not surprising that the incidence of loss of appetite, weight loss, and illness during the first year of life is higher among the infants of mothers under 19 years of age, especially if they are economically disadvantaged. These young mothers who experience such problems are likely to experience less joy with their babies and therefore may have some difficulty establishing a deep and richly satisfying emotional bond with their infants. For such mothers, psychological support and education about infants would be useful.

But of course, self-preoccupation and lack of knowledge are not limited to some of the very young mothers. Older mothers may resent the infringement of child care on their activities and view the child as a burden. Other mothers, whether because of economic or family problems, may be too tired or discouraged to be responsive to the child. They may be depressed or anxious. Background factors, too, may play a part, for it is possible that some people may have experienced so little love and caring themselves that they find it difficult to give affection to their child.

However, let us not forget that no relationship can be based solely on the attributes of one partner. The relationship between parent and child is an interactive one, and often some characteristic of the child plays an important part. For example, if the child is premature and needs extra care, or if the child is chronically ill, the task of child care is more difficult and thus may cause problems in the relationship. Fortunately, many adults today regard bearing children less as a duty to be performed by all adults and more as a matter of choice. Thus, as it should be, childbearing can be reserved for those who want children and who are willing to assume the obligations involved.

THE FEARS OF INFANCY

Why does a child cry when the mother leaves the room? Some psychologists have suggested that this fear following separation from the caretaker is due to the fact that the infant has developed an attachment to the mother (or caretaker). They have also assumed that other common fears during the first 2 years of life, such as fear of strangers, also stem from the attachment relationship. But recent research suggests that the appearance of these fears might be due, in large measure, to the emergence of certain new cognitive skills that are exhibited toward the end of the first year. Differences in the intensity of these fears may be due to such factors as temperament or the nature of the mother-child relationship, but the basis for the appearance of the fears is the capacity for memory and relating past and present, as discussed in Chapter 3. In the following sections we shall explore the relation between early fears and infant attachment.

Stranger Anxiety

Alice studies the stranger 10 seconds; her face tightens, and suddenly she begins to cry.

Alice, an 8-month-old girl, is sitting in her high chair playing with her cereal. An unfamiliar woman enters the kitchen and stands facing the baby. Alice studies the stranger 10 seconds; her face tightens, and suddenly she begins to cry. It is clear that the unfamiliar woman has elicited the cry, for if the stranger leaves, the child becomes happy again. If she reappears, Alice cries again.

Alice's behavior illustrates a phenomenon called **stranger anxiety,** and typically appears first at about 6 months of age, peaks at about 8–10 months, and then gradually disappears by the time the child is 15 months old. As in all aspects of development, the extent to which stranger anxiety is shown will vary with the situation. For example, all infants when sitting on the mother's lap are less likely to show fear of strangers. Environmental experience, too, affects the display of stranger anxiety. In rural areas, where infants do not see many strangers, the fear reaction to strangers may last for a longer period of time. Even the child's rate of mental development may affect the emergence of this fear. In infants whose rate of cognitive development is relatively slow, the fear reaction often occurs a little later, perhaps at 11–12 months.

Why does this fear reaction develop, and why does it disappear after a time? To find the answer, we first go back to several ideas discussed in Chapter 3. Remember that a child forms in memory definite schemata—mental representations of events or objects. For example, a child's schema for Daddy's face may be a round form with a little hair on top and a bushy beard. Secondly, around the age of 8–12 months, the child develops the ability to compare a certain stimulus with a firmly established schema. In other words, suppose a man looks at the child. The child can look at the man's face while at the same time comparing it with the schema of round face, a little hair, and bushy beard that represents Daddy. After comparing the two, the infant decides that this face is not the familiar face of Daddy. That is, the face of this man is a moderately discrepant event. Next, the infant attempts to cope with the discrepant event and to predict the future. What will this man do? But the 8-month-old infant is not capable of answering such a question. At this age the infant possesses neither the cognitive abilities to know who this is nor the experience to be able to decide whether this man will be a friend or foe, and thus is left in a state of **uncertainty.** The infant's inability to resolve the state of uncertainty leads to signs of distress such as crying or inhibition of activity.

However, if the infant can assimilate the discrepant event or has a coping reaction—say, crawls from the room where the stranger is—then distress is unlikely to occur. In fact, children may signify their ability to deal with a strange person by smiling or laughing. By 18 months of age, when the child is more mature, she is able to make better predictions about what a stranger will do and is able to do something when uncertain. The child is much more mobile and can run to the mother or leave the room quickly. Now signs of fear such as crying or inhibition of play become much less common. The period of stranger anxiety is over.

Apprehension of Other Children

Although 8-month-old Alice showed signs of distress when an unfamiliar woman entered the room, she did not cry when an unfamiliar 8-month-old crawled into the room. Most infants do not show fear of other children until they are between 12 and 20 months of age, and this fear gradually declines, until it disappears around 30 months of age. Furthermore, the distress associated with seeing unfamiliar children is not so intense as that resulting from seeing an unfamiliar adult. For example, when an unfamiliar child (along with the child's mother) enters a room in which another child is playing while the mother sits nearby, the child rarely cries, though he or she may stop playing and retreat to the mother.

The signs of fear are less intense in response to other children than they were earlier when confronted with strange adults, because the older child is capable of making some responses in the face of uncertainty. The older child can retreat to the mother, play with toys, or actively avoid the strange child. If these coping behaviors are not available, then the child may cry, as she did with the strange adult several months earlier.

It has been found that infants in day-care centers who have early contact with other infants still display apprehension in the presence of an unfamiliar child. But the youngsters who have early and frequent contact with other children do overcome their apprehension of other children earlier than children who do not have frequent interaction with other children (see Figure 4.6).

Separation Anxiety

Alice, the 8-month-old infant, not only cries when a strange woman enters the room; she also becomes unhappy when her mother leaves the room, regardless of whether a stranger is present. This anxiety following temporary separation from the primary caretaker, called **separation anxiety,** makes its appearance at about 8–12 months of age and begins to disappear by the time the child is 24–30 months of age (2).

The intensity of separation anxiety can be influenced by many factors. For example, the child is much more likely to cry when left in an unfamiliar place than in a familiar location such as the living room of the home (16). Even the exit the mother uses can affect the intensity of the child's fear. Seeing the mother leave through an unfamiliar or rarely used door, such as a dressing-room door, will induce more crying from the infant than seeing her walk out the kitchen door. Of course, as you might expect, if a familiar person, such as the father, is present when the mother or other

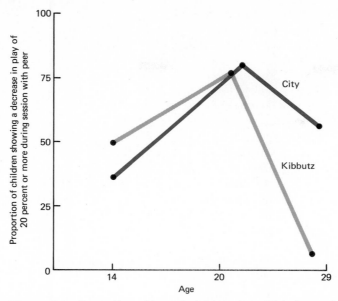

Figure 4.6   Proportion of Israeli children from kibbutz or city showing a decrease in play of 20 percent or more following an encounter with an unfamiliar peer. (After M. Zaslow. Wariness of unfamiliar peers in kibbutz and city children in Israel. Unpublished doctoral dissertation, Harvard University, 1978.)

primary caretaker leaves, the child's level of anxiety is much less intense than if the child is left alone or with a stranger.

It is also not surprising that the child's level of anxiety is less intense when there is an opportunity for her to do something about the separation. That is, a child whose mother leaves the room and closes the door behind her has little recourse other than crying for coping with distress. But when the mother leaves the door open, the infant can walk or crawl after her (15).

Crying as a response to separation, then, seems to be influenced by the child's ability to recognize that she is in an unusual situation and, at the same time, by her inability to understand why and her lack of more appropriate coping responses. Since all these processes depend on a certain level of cognitive functioning, the very young infant who is not yet capable of remembering or of generating questions does not experience separation anxiety.

Separation anxiety, like other fears, depends on cognitive abilities. Since the rate of cognitive development is, at least at first, fairly regular, being in large part due to biological maturation processes, separation fear develops at about the same age in children growing up in a variety of set-

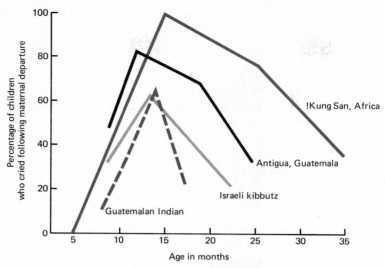

Figure 4.7 Separation anxiety in a variety of cultural settings.

tings. No matter whether contact with caretakers is continuous, as in the !Kung San infants of the Kalahari Desert in Africa, or whether the infant is away from the primary caretaker for regular and prolonged periods of time, as in China, or whether the infant experiences a mix of being with the mother or with other caretakers, as do many American infants, the distress following separation tends to emerge around the first birthday, the time when certain cognitive abilities tend to emerge (see Figure 4.7). These abilities permit the child to generate questions such as "Why is mother leaving?" and "What will happen to me?" Because the 1-year-old is unable to resolve or answer these questions, he becomes anxious. Separation anxiety vanishes when the child can resolve those questions—the child knows the mother will return or knows what to do to bring the mother back.

However, while the initial appearance of separation anxiety is similar, though not identical, for children growing up in different societies around the world, children within the same culture differ in the intensity and frequency of fear they display following separation from the primary caretaker. What causes these differences? Why does Alice scream every time her mother leaves her, while Susan only occasionally cries when her mother leaves? One possible cause is that some children are temperamentally more prone to become severely upset in uncertain situations.

Another factor affecting the intensity of separation anxiety may be the quality of the infant's attachment to the parents. Securely attached infants seem to be able to tolerate brief everyday separations from the mother from time to time, but infants who are less securely attached to their mothers are more likely to cry when their mothers leave the room.

In one observational procedure the child's behavior is used as an index of the infant's attachment to its mother. The infants are observed in an unfamiliar room during the time prior to their mother's leaving the room, during the time when the mother has left, and after the mother has returned. On the basis of the infant's behavior during the mother's absence and when she returns, children are assigned to one of three categories: Securely attached infants—about 60 percent of the group—may cry when the mother leaves but seek the mother when she returns. Avoiding children are less likely to cry when the mother leaves and do not seek the mother when she returns. Ambivalent children may cry and seek the mother when she returns but they resist physical contact with her. The avoiding and ambivalent children make up about 40 percent of the average group of 1-year-olds (1).

In short, there are three factors that influence the child's behavior following separation and the mother's return: the maturation of cognitive abilities, the child's temperament, and the nature of the parent-child relationship. As in any other area involving the behavior of human beings, infants display a wide range in intensity of separation anxiety.

The fears of infancy are similar to fears children will have later. Children are always vulnerable to new uncertainties, and whether the uncertainty is "what happens if mother leaves?" or is a later childhood fear, such as "what ghosts lurk in the darkness?," the mechanism for many fears is similar. That is, a child's level of cognitive maturity determines when he will be able to generate possibilities. For example, fear of the dark typically does not appear until 3 years of age because the 2-year-old does not try to imagine the events that might occur when night falls. In a similar manner, the child is able to overcome these fears when the level of cognitive maturity reaches a certain stage and the child is able to resolve the uncertainties.

In the next section we shall look at the effect of adults on another facet of human behavior: social responsiveness and cognitive development.

THE ROLE OF SOCIAL INTERACTION IN COGNITIVE DEVELOPMENT

Alice laughs with delight when her father plays peekaboo. She smiles and laughs when her mother talks to her. How do these activities influence Alice's development?

Most parents and psychologists believe that such playful interactions not only produce an emotional attachment but, equally important, also aid in the development of the child's cognitive abilities. An infant is surprised by events such as a face that is present one minute and the next is mysteriously gone, replaced by two hands. Even more interesting is the face suddenly reappearing. In attempting to understand the puzzling game of peekaboo, the child's mind grows. Interaction stimulates cognitive development.

Infants in institutions, lying in beds with no toys and no opportunity for playful interaction, are slower in cognitive development than home-reared children who experience more stimulating conditions (5).

But institutional life need not always be detrimental to a child's development. The effects of social interaction were examined in a study in which a group of eight institutionalized infants were cared for by one "substitute mother" 8 hours a day, 5 days a week, for 8 consecutive weeks. The substitute mother tried to give each baby as much individualized attention as possible. A control group, also consisting of eight institutionalized infants, was cared for in more routine fashion by several women. Results of tests given during and after the 8-week period showed that motor development of the two groups was apparently unaffected by

Inexpensive Toy Chest

Babies tend to grow cognitively when they are faced with problems they understand, with "tameable" surprises. This follows from Piaget's theory and from the other cognitive studies discussed in Chapter 3.

Many mothers and fathers naturally engage in cognitively stimulating games without being aware of what they're doing. For example, they play peekaboo; they hide small toys in their hands; they engage in reciprocal imitation with their infant when the child babbles or smiles.

All these games present potentially understandable challenges to the infant, and in accommodating to these challenges, the child's mind grows. Of course, what is surprising to a 6-month-old will be boring to a 1-year-old. Parents usually recognize this and automatically adjust the complexity of their play so that it is in accord with the child's cognitive level.

There is no reason to believe that expensive toys have any advantage over spoons, pie plates, blocks of wood, or even wrapping paper. Indeed, crinkly Christmas paper contains enormous potential for variation that can keep a 6-month-old baby's attention for minutes. The changing sounds of six glasses filled to six different levels with water create an inexpensive xylophone that any parent can construct. Dangling a cloth doll from a piece of string and letting a 5-month-old hit and twirl it usually elicits gurgles of delight.

the differences in care, but there were dramatic differences in social behavior.

The babies cared for by the one substitute mother showed much more social responsiveness than the control children did (14). That is, when people smiled or talked to the children, the "nurtured" infants were more likely to smile back or show some facial reaction to the adults than the children who were more routinely cared for. It is reasonable to assume that the factor responsible for the increased social responsiveness of the experimental babies was the reciprocal and playful social stimulation that occurred between child and adult.

Effects of Minimal Interaction with Caretakers

Playful interaction with adults provides the child with a greater variety of experience in muscular stimulation, vocalization, and play than the infant could get alone, and this variety stimulates cognitive growth. What about those infants who do not have opportunities for playful interaction? What aspects of caretaking are most important? Does an infant really need much besides a clean dry diaper, a bottle of milk, and a warm place to sleep? In poorly run, understaffed institutions, infants may receive no more than routine care. Seldom are they held, and rarely does anyone talk or play with them. As we would expect, children in such settings are retarded in language, less vocal, less socially responsive, and less alert to changes around them (see Figure 4.8).

Animal experiments, too, suggest that the social development of infants will be adversely affected by the lack of individualized care. A somewhat extreme example, but one that is nonetheless relevant, concerns

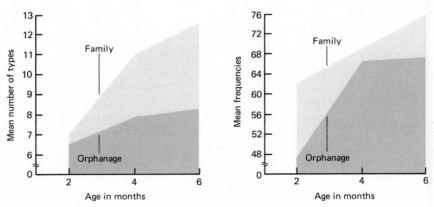

Figure 4.8 Mean frequencies of vocalizing and mean numbers of types of sound in the vocalizing of infants in home and institutions. (From A. J. Brodbeck & O. C. Irwin. The speech behavior of infants without families. *Child Development*, 1946, *17*, 149. Copyright 1946 by The Society for Research in Child Development, Inc.)

monkeys isolated from contact with other living objects for the first 6 months of life. They show extremely abnormal behavior when removed from isolation. These animals avoid all social contact, appear very fearful, clutch at themselves, and crouch (7). But fortunately the effects are not irreversible. Monkeys isolated for less than 6 months can recover a great deal of normal functioning if they are placed with infant monkeys for a period of 5 or 6 months.

The importance of contact with other living objects is seen in the experiments discussed earlier involving wire and terrycloth "mother" monkeys. While the infant monkeys raised with terrycloth mothers seem secure with them, they do not show normal social and sexual behavior when they grow up. The absence of the attentions of a living mother seriously affects their social behavior.

Human infants, of course, are rarely subjected to total isolation, but some are raised in institutions that do not conscientiously promote interaction between the infants and their caretakers. In some institutions, one person cares for seven to nine infants 8 hours a day; for the other 16 hours a day, the infants are alone except at feeding times, when an attendant heats formulas, props bottles, and changes diapers. Such infants experience little variability in their environment. There are no vocalizations from other people, and there is no reciprocal play. There is not even a close relationship between a child's crying and the reaction of the caretaker, for there is no time to respond each time a baby cries.

Before 3 to 4 months of age, there is little difference between normal home-reared babies and babies in such an institution. But after 4 months of age certain differences become evident. The institutionalized infants are listless and apathetic, showing little responsiveness to adults, toys, or other aspects of their external environment. They do not seek adults for play or for help. In other words, all the behaviors that were most likely to be learned as a result of interaction with an adult (clinging, crying in distress, approaching adults for play, and vocalization) are most clearly retarded or absent in the institutionalized children (13).

The infants in the too-quiet, restricted environment of the poorly run institutions fail to develop at a normal rate because of lack of variety in stimulation. It is the variety that is important, not the absolute level of stimulation. A child in a crowded one-room apartment encounters many sights and sounds simultaneously, while an infant in his own bedroom in a suburban home with a relatively quiet environment is presented with distinctive stimuli. A mother's voice breaking the quiet of the bedroom addressed directly to the infant will be more likely to catch his attention and teach him something than a voice yelling over a television set in a sea of noise. It is distinctive quality, not simply quantity of stimulation, that is effective in enriching an infant's intellectual development.

One study on the distinctiveness of stimulation has revealed differences between lower- and upper-middle-class mothers of 4-month-old girls (8). When the upper-middle-class mothers vocalized to their infants, they were likely to be face-to-face with them and not providing any other stimulation. They were not touching them. The mother's vocalization to the infant was very distinctive. The lower-class mother was apt to talk to her infant when she was feeding, diapering, or burping the baby. As a result, the vocalization was less distinctive, for the infant may have been focusing attention on the tactile stimuli that accompanied the diapering or burping. It is probably more than coincidence that the upper-middle-class girls produced more varied sounds than the lower-class children and showed precocious language development during the first 2 years of life.

The Influence of Good Care Outside the Home

What, then, are the ideal conditions for bringing up baby? Are we to believe that consistent care by the infant's mother is the only way? Clearly, the answer is no. It should be stressed that children growing up in institutions that provide individualized care and a rich variety of experience seem to grow in a manner similar to that of home-reared children. School-age children from the People's Republic of China raised in group-care centers from 2 or 3 months of age appeared similar to Chinese children who remained at home for the first 2 or 3 years (11). And children who grow up in well-run Russian nurseries do not develop the characteristics of children raised in inadequate institutions (3).

Infants who attend good day-care centers develop attachments to both the mother and the woman who cares for them at the center. They still show a preference for the mother when bored, tired, or distressed. Despite the fact that the day-care teacher spends as many hours with the infants as the mothers, the infants feel more secure with and are more attached to their biological mothers.

What is so special about the mother-infant relationship that makes the parent more appealing than the substitute caretaker? One reason may be that the parent is both more emotional and more unpredictable with the infant and hence is a greater source of pleasure and uncertainty. While the mother is more likely to display strong affection, she is also more likely to judge the child's development and to correct the child's responses when they deviate from her standards. For example, she may decide that her infant must begin learning good table manners early and may try to help the infant be less messy when eating.

A caretaker, on the other hand, may be conscientious and sympathetic but is less profoundly emotionally involved with the children than are the parents. Also, because she is aware of the differences in behavior of the children under her care, the caretaker is less likely to hold rigid standards for such things as cooperativeness, cleanliness, or aggression. As a result, the caretaker does not become as intense a source of uncertainty for the child as the parent, but neither does she become as frequent or intense a source of joy and excitement. The parental relationship hence is the more intense and special relationship for the infant.

Measures of cognitive functioning in children attending a day-care center—those of middle-class parents and those of working-class parents—and in children being reared at home revealed no important differences between the two. Although middle-class children scored higher on tests of language development than working-class children, and Chinese children were more inhibited and fearful than Caucasians, the day-care and home-reared children grew in a similar fashion (9).

Similar results have been found in studies of children who attend well-run, adequate day-care centers. By "adequate" we mean that one caretaker is not responsible for more than three to four infants or five to six

Mothers' Worries About Day Care

American mothers have five worries about placing their children in day care. The first is that they are afraid the infants' attachment to them will be diluted because they are not with them during most of the day. Since most mothers believe that the child will be difficult to socialize if he does not have a strong love relationship, they worry that perhaps placement in day care will produce a disobedient and unruly child.

A second fear is that the child's intellectual development will be retarded. Mothers are afraid that the child will not have a sufficiently varied set of interactions in the day-care center to guarantee that his language and curiosity will develop properly.

Third, mothers may be afraid that the child will not learn to control his anger, tantrums, and extreme dependency. The mother is not sure that the caretaker in the center will be as conscientious as she in punishing the undesirable acts at the right time.

Fourth, many parents believe that a young child can be unduly influenced by other children. Indeed, Jacob Abbott, a nineteenth-century Dr. Spock, warned mothers, "Keep children as much as possible by themselves—separate—alone." This attitude is still held by many people.

Finally, the average middle-class American mother sees herself as the effective agent in controlling the growth of her child, and she is reluctant to give that responsibility to someone else and anticipates feeling guilty for failing to honor the first duty of a mother.

toddlers and that the infants are exposed to a variety of stimulation and have an opportunity to practice new abilities as they mature. Under these conditions it appears that group care need not have hidden dangers. Children tend to develop the way they would have if they had remained at home. However, if the day-care center has too many children or too few caretakers, and does not provide variety or restricts the child's explorations, then, of course, the child's growth will be retarded, often seriously (12).

The Capacity for Recovery

Suppose that an infant is deprived of the stimulation required for learning certain social and cognitive skills during early childhood. As we have noted, the effects of environmental deficiencies — the lack of distinctive stimulation, the absence of interaction with adults, minimal opportunity to practice language and motor abilities — are evident as early as 4 to 8 months of age. The infant shows definite signs of mental retardation. But are these effects irreversible? Can a change in environment effect a change in development?

The available evidence indicates that much can be done to remedy learning deficits through a beneficial change in environment. One example is found in a study of institutionalized children living in a Lebanese institution in which personal care was minimal (6). Children from this institution who had been adopted into good homes before their second birthday, at a time when they had scored in the mentally retarded range on developmental tests, eventually attained average IQ scores. The infants who remained in the institution continued to score in the mentally retarded range.

In a similar study, a group of severely malnourished Korean girl orphans between 2 and 3 years of age were adopted by middle-class American families. Six years after admission to their foster homes the children were functioning well in elementary school; they surpassed the expected mean height and weight for Korean children, and their average IQ was 102, which was 40 points higher than the average IQ scores reported for similar Korean children returned to their original home environments (18).

Thus it appears that retardation during the first year or two of life does not necessarily doom the child to permanent incompetence, for with the proper environment, children do have amazing powers of recovery. The secret is to find the proper environment to overcome the initial handicaps in these children.

Children can and do change, and it is difficult to make predictions about adolescent and adult behavior based on behavior during the first 2 years of life, even for children growing up in normal healthy environments. Most investigators find that the infant's behaviors — fearfulness, activity, dependency, aggression, and shyness, for example — during the first 2 years of life bear little relation to the incidence of these qualities in adolescence and early adulthood (10). For example, one of the authors recently completed a study of 10-year-old first-born Caucasian children from working- and middle-class homes who had been evaluated four times during the first 27 months of life. The educational level of the family — not the child's attentiveness, activity level, or irritability as an infant — predicted the 10-year-old's IQ score and reading skill.

Most of the information gathered by psychologists to date does not provide much basis for the popular belief that the experiences of infancy create fixed behavior patterns that persist no matter what environmental circumstances follow. However, neither can we conclude that the experiences of infancy are of no consequence for later childhood. It is encouraging, however, to find that if the conditions that may have caused fearfulness and retardation during infancy are favorably changed during the years 2 to 6, dramatic changes can occur.

SUMMARY

1. Adults not only care for the basic needs of infants; they also provide opportunities for social interaction. There are two major results of this interaction: (a) the development of an attachment relationship between the infant and the adult, and (b) the promotion of cognitive and social development.

2. There are differences in child rearing from individual to individual and from culture to culture. These differences in interaction can affect the baby's behavior patterns.

3. Attachment relationships are believed to be formed as a result of two processes: (a) the interaction that occurs between the infant and the caretaker (looking, vocalizing, smiling), and (b) the association the infant makes between feelings of pleasure stemming from relief of distress and the presence of the caretaker.

4. There are three main characteristics of the attachment relationship between the infant and the caretaker: (a) the child is likely to approach these people for play or help; (b) the child is more easily soothed and placated by these people than by anyone else; and (c) the infant shows no fear when with one of these adults.

5. It is normal for infants to display certain fears during the first years of life. Three of the most common fears are unfamiliar adults, unfamiliar children, and temporary separation from the caretaker. The appearance of these fears is dependent, in part, on the maturation of cognitive abilities, and also on the child's temperament and the nature of the parent-child relationship.

6. The fears of infancy begin to decline when children become mature enough to interpret or deal with the uncertainty involved in encounters with unfamiliar people or with separation from their caretaker.

7. Playful interaction with adults provides the child with a greater variety of experience in muscular stimulation, vocalization, and play than the infant could get alone, and this variety stimulates cognitive growth. Consequently, the institutionalized infant in a monotonous and impersonal environment is likely to be cognitively and emotionally retarded.

8. Children who attend *well-run*, adequate child-care centers tend to develop the way they would have if they had remained at home. Moreover, the 2-year-old child who may have been a victim of a *depriving* environment seems to possess a substantial capacity for recovery if he or she is moved to a normal environment.

Suggested Readings

Bowlby, J. *Attachment and loss,* Vol. 1: *Attachment.* New York: Basic Books, 1969. Vol. 2: *Anxiety and anger.* New York: Basic Books, 1973.

Dunn, J. *Distress in comfort.* In the series entitled *The developing child,* edited by J. Bruner, M. Cole, and B. Lloyd. Cambridge, Mass.: Harvard University Press, 1977.

Schaffer, R. *Mothering.* In the series entitled *The developing child,* edited by J. Bruner, M. Cole, and B. Lloyd. Cambridge, Mass.: Harvard University Press, 1977.

Chapter 5

Development During the Second Year

*T*HE TWELVE-MONTH period between the ages of 1 year and 2 years is an important time for a child. During this year the child progresses from being a rather helpless infant, most of whose needs must be taken care of by an adult, to a child who has begun to achieve some measure of independence, able to take care of some of her own needs. For example, a 2-year-old child can hold a cup and drink from it, toddle around, open drawers and cabinet doors, spreading the contents over a wide area, and talk using two-word sentences to indicate dissatisfaction in not finding what she was looking for.

The emergence of new abilities during the second year is, as in the first year, the product of the combined effect of physical growth, biological maturation, and learning. The child's transition to being more independent cannot take place without the development of all three factors. For example, suppose a 2-year-old girl is able to open the cabinet where cookies are kept and help herself to a cookie. She must first have the physical capability of walking so that she can get to the cabinet door and pull it open. In addition, her brain must have reached the stage of biological maturation at

which she has the cognitive capacity of remembering (otherwise she would not be able to remember where the cookies are kept). Lastly, she must have learned, through observation or instruction, the specific fact — in this case, that cookies are kept in the cabinet next to the refrigerator.

Throughout the study of child development, it is important (and interesting) to note that there are significant individual differences. Children at this stage of development vary considerably in their physical and motor abilities, in the development of language, and in the expression of various personality traits.

Baby clothes seldom wear out, for children grow rapidly. Pants that were so cute on a child at the age of 1 are likely not to fit even six months later.

Regardless of the rate of development, this second year of learning and growth is exciting for children. As they realize their growing capabilities, they want to do things independently, without help from Mommy, Daddy, or anyone else. They like to walk alone, to try to feed and dress themselves, and to explore alone. Naturally this period of change affects parents, too. As they see their child becoming more capable, they expect the child to begin taking some responsibility for his or her actions. Thus, it is generally during the second year that parents begin the important process of **socialization.** That is, they begin to teach the child certain values important to them and/or to society.

In this chapter we shall first consider the child's physical development. Then we shall look at the fascinating process of language development and at other aspects of cognitive development during the second year. Finally, we shall discuss how parents of 1-year-olds go about the process of socializing their children, and how the personalities of young children are affected.

GENERAL PHYSICAL DEVELOPMENT

Baby clothes seldom wear out, for children grow rapidly. Pants that were so cute on a child at the age of 1 year are likely not to fit even six months later. The average infant grows about 5 inches and gains 5 to 6 pounds during the second year. Of course, this growth spurt is not as great as during the first year of life, when babies grow 8 to 9 inches and gain 14 to 15 pounds, but still the body changes during the second year are significant (23).

As with other aspects of modern life, the pace has accelerated in the last years, and American infants today gain more rapidly in height and weight than those of earlier generations. By the age of 2 years, the average child is vastly different in size and appearance from the newborn, being 33 or 34 inches tall and weighing approximately 28 pounds (22). Heights and weights at age 2 are somewhat predictable, since children who are tall and heavy for their age on their first birthday are likely to maintain their relative standing at age 2 (15).

During the second year the child's skeletal structure changes. Bones increase in size and number, and more of them become calcified. The fontanelles, or soft membrane spots in the skull, generally close (i.e., the

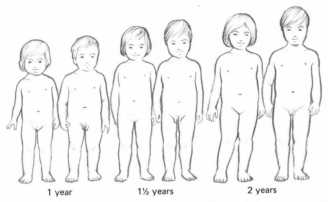

1 year   1½ years   2 years

Figure 5.1 The child's body proportions change during the second year: arms and legs increase in length faster than the trunk, and growth of the head is slow, so that the baby's body begins to look more like an adult's.

bones become hardened and fused) somewhere between the ages of 18 and 24 months, and most of the child's temporary teeth erupt during the second year (22).

Body Proportions   Although the 1-year-old is growing fast and no longer looks as topheavy as did the newborn, the head is still large in relation to the body, and the cranium is out of proportion to the size of the child's facial features. Indeed, it is primarily these differences that account for the "baby look" that still persists. But the various body parts grow at different rates during the first two years, so that gradually the baby's body begins to look more like an adult's (see Figure 5.1). For instance, the head, which was way out of proportion at birth, grows a good deal more slowly than the rest of the body and assumes more adultlike proportions. Arms and legs increase in length faster than the trunk, with arms growing faster than legs.

Muscular and Nervous Systems   The growth of the muscles and nerves is extremely important, for in these two systems lies the key to the child's coordination and ability to make finer, more precise movements. Dressing, for example, requires a number of coordinated movements, even strength. Have you ever tried to put on a sock while standing?

During the second year, muscles develop and grow, causing a great increase in strength and accounting for a greater proportion of body weight. The brain, too, becomes heavier, increasing from an average of 350 grams (3/4 pound) at birth to about 1000 grams (2.2 pounds). At age 2, the brain has reached three-quarters of its total adult weight, and the nervous system has become more complex and more highly differentiated.

Motor Development

Although some babies walk before their first birthday, most are just beginning to try walking on their own. In a sense, all the child's motor developments in the first year—crawling, sitting, creeping, standing, and walking with support—are preliminary steps toward one of the major events of the second year of life: walking. With her first steps, the child begins to gain more physical independence and the freedom to explore a rapidly expanding world. Unhappily for parents, this world is not restricted to things bright and beautiful; it may also contain hot stoves, delicate china, and household poisons.

Like earlier motor responses, walking depends primarily on physical maturation. Practice in creeping or standing plays a role, too, in that complete lack of opportunity to practice may delay the development of walking (5), but more important is the course of physical development. Increased neural development, greater muscle strength, and changed body proportions all contribute to the development of walking.

Until the child's muscles have developed sufficiently, no amount of practice can make the child walk. For example, in a twin study, one member of a pair of identical twin girls (Twin T) was given 6 weeks of daily practice sessions in stair climbing, beginning at the age of 46 weeks. Her twin sister (C) had no contact with stairs until she was 53 weeks old. At that time, she was given a brief 2-week training course. The results were not what you might expect, for Twin C climbed more rapidly and efficiently than her sister, who had been trained for a longer period of time at an earlier age (10). Clearly, until a child's neuromuscular apparatus is sufficiently mature, efforts to "teach" locomotor responses are bound to meet with failure.

The average child begins walking alone, although awkwardly and precariously, around 12 months of age (see Table 5.1), but there are marked individual differences. Some normal children begin walking as early as 10

Table 5.1 SOME SECOND-YEAR ITEMS IN BAYLEY SCALES OF PSYCHO-MOTOR DEVELOPMENT

ITEM	AGE PLACEMENT (MONTHS)
Walks alone	11.7
Throws a ball	13.3
Walks sideways	14.1
Walks backward	14.6
Walks upstairs with help	16.1
Walks downstairs with help	16.4
Tries to stand on walking board	17.8
Walks with one foot on walking board	20.6
Walks upstairs alone; marks time	25.1

Source: Reproduced from the Bayley Scales of Infant Development by permission. Copyright © by The Psychological Corporation. All rights reserved.

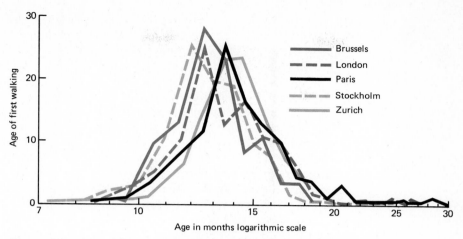

Figure 5.2 Age of first walking in five sample groups. (Reprinted from C. B. Hindley, A. M. Filliozat, G. Klackenberg, D. Nicolet-Meister, & E. A. Sand. Differences in age of walking in five European longitudinal samples. *Human Biology*, Vol. 38, No. 4, 1966. By permission of The Wayne State University Press.)

months, others not until 16 or 17 months. Despite popular opinions to the contrary, there is no strong correlation between age of walking and intelligence during the preschool or early school years. That is, a child who walks early is not necessarily more intelligent than a child who doesn't walk until later. There is also no evidence to support the assumption that heavy infants sit, stand, and walk at later ages than children who weigh less (17).

What about sex differences? Do girls walk earlier than boys, or vice versa? In a recent cross-cultural study of five European cities (Paris, London, Brussels, Stockholm, and Zürich), it was found that there were no significant sex differences in the age of onset of walking in children in any of the five cities. Nor were there any social-class differences in age of walking. But there were differences between geographical areas (see Figure 5.2). Swedish babies walked earliest, on the average, and Parisians latest. It is difficult to explain these national differences. They may be due to differences in genetic factors or in nutrition. Or it may even be that they are due to differences between French and Swedish mothers' handling or encouragement of locomotion.

What the Child Can Do: Other Motor Skills

Although walking alone is a major milestone in motor development in the second year, many other significant developments also occur during this period. By 18 months, the average child can hurl a ball, sit alone in a small chair, turn the pages of a book (usually two or three pages at a time), walk up and down stairs with help, build a tower of three blocks, and pull a toy wagon. By age 2, the child runs fairly well, can jump in place, walk a straight line (more or less), walk up and down stairs without assistance, turn the pages of a book one at a time, and pretend to feed a teddy bear or put it to bed.

Practice Makes Perfect

After a child becomes capable of basic locomotor or other motor responses, practice brings improvements. For example, in walking and stair climbing, coordination improves; waste movements are eliminated; steps become longer, straighter, and more rapid. The child's impressive advances in motor abilities during the second year seem to be accompanied by a real urge to experiment. He or she seems intent on exercising new-found skills and capabilities for the sheer pleasure of it. Testing and perfecting recently acquired motor, manual, and manipulative skills become absorbing goals.

But why do children seem to enjoy exercising these skills? It may be that a child "practices" handling an object, for example, not just from excess energy and not even just because the child wants to be able to reach effectively and grasp the particular object. In a larger sense, the child may have a basic need to deal with the environment competently—that is, a need for competence (24). The child may feel a need to conquer the environment, to interact on an effective, competent level. Motor activities such as grasping, exploring, crawling, and walking allow the child to become more active and more in control of the environment.

As we shall see later, parental reactions to the child's emerging need for competence and to manifestations of the child's newly developed skills become extremely significant factors in the process of socialization at age 2 and beyond.

Another manifestation of emerging independence is the child's growing ability to talk and communicate. In the next section we will look at this phenomenal process.

THE DEVELOPMENT OF LANGUAGE

A 1-year-old who in one rather poorly pronounced word asks for a cup of milk is likely to be praised by her excited parents more than a high-school debater who has just delivered a winning argument. The beginning of verbal communication is one of the most exciting events of the second year. The development of language comprehension and production is a sensational accomplishment—one that seems to come fairly easily and quickly to children, considering the complexity of the task. But to ask why or how this almost magical process takes place is almost like asking why a bird learns to fly. Of course, a child must be exposed to a language in order to learn it, but it is not simply through imitation that a child learns to speak. Rather, in interacting with others, children hear many well-formed sentences. From listening to adults and other children, they extract rules about the language they hear. They very quickly absorb rules of structure and begin to use them to form their own novel sentences.

Theories of Language Acquisition

What accounts for the impressive, incredibly rapid development of the child's use and understanding of language? There are no scientific answers to this question, but a variety of theoretical explanations have been proposed. None of them is adequate to explain all the phenomena of language development, however, and all the theories have been severely criticized.

According to *B. F. Skinner's theory,* language is learned like other habits, through conditioning, reward, and punishment. When a mother says, "Say cookie," any response from the child that resembles the word cookie will be reinforced immediately; other sounds will not be reinforced. Through reward and withholding of the reward, children learn to imitate their parents' words. But the creation of novel sentences by young children and the acquisition of complicated grammatical structure cannot be explained in terms of simple conditioning and reward.

Social learning theorists stress observation and imitation, even without rewards, as basic factors in language acquisition. Certainly, these factors must be important in language learning, for children cannot learn language, vocabulary, and grammatical structure unless they listen to the language in their environment. But observation and imitation in themselves cannot account for the child's early ability to generate *new* sentences.

Noam Chomsky, a distinguished linguist at the Massachusetts Institute of Technology, proposed a *biological, nativistic theory* of language development. He maintains that the ability to acquire and use language is *innate;* human beings possess a kind of built-in, prewired mental structure (an "innate schema") that enables them to absorb language as they hear it and to discover and apply language rules. Thus, they can generate appropriate grammatical sentences, including *new* ones they have not heard before. The theory is extremely difficult to prove or refute empirically. Although there is a neural basis for language development, there is no compelling evidence of any built-in language-processing mechanism. The theory has been very influential, however, because it does take into account that even very young children have some notion of grammatical structure and can use language in creative ways.

While a child's early attempts to speak are amazing, it is even more astounding that children can comprehend fairly complicated statements at a very early age. The old saying "Little pitchers have big ears" is probably based on the fact that children can understand and react to relatively complex requests, questions, negative statements, and commands long before they can produce them. Their ability to understand and inability to produce complicated sentences may be due to their inability to say some of the words, or to their ignorance of the grammatical rules necessary to express the ideas. For example, even a 1-year-old can go get her teddy bear on request, though she may not be able to say the words *teddy bear*. In this chapter, however, we will focus on the production rather than the comprehension of language, mainly because most **psycholinguistic** research focuses on the production of sentences, it being undoubtedly easier to measure what a child says than what a child comprehends.

First Words

Baby's first words are generally spoken around the time of the child's first birthday. *Mama* and *dada* are typically among the first words—not only because the child has been coached but because these are easy words to pronounce. The most frequently occurring consonants are *p, b, v, d, t, m*, and *n*, while the most common vowel sounds babies produce are *o* (as in *drop*) and *e* (as in *week*).

Not surprisingly, children usually first talk about familiar things and their functions. And, since the functions and surroundings of children are basically the same, the early vocabulary of all children tends to be similar. Typical are words designating important people, such as *mama, daddy*, and *baby*; food (for example, *juice, milk, cookie*); and body parts (*ear, eye, nose*). Children also name their clothing (*shoe, hat, sock*), animals (*dog, cat, Rex*), household items (*clock, light*), and vehicles (*boat, car, truck*).

However, though there are similarities in early vocabularies, individual differences are apparent in the types of words children learn first. Some children tend to specialize in names of objects (*ball, doggie*), while others speak names for people or words used in social interactions, such as *no, yes, want, please, stop it, go away, hi*, and *touch* (16).

A 1-year-old can put a lot of meaning into one word. The child through one word can not only name an object but can describe an action, make a request, or express surprise or an emotional state. Of course, the intended meaning is fully understood only in the context of the situation. For example, suppose a child points at a red ball on the floor and says "ball." The child may be simply calling attention to the ball, or he may be communicating surprise at finding his ball. The child's gestures and **intonations** may clarify his intentions, and adults, particularly those who know the child well, are fairly good at interpreting these clues (see Figure 5.3). Thus, if the child emphatically repeats "ball, ball" while reaching toward it, he is obviously asking for help in getting the ball.

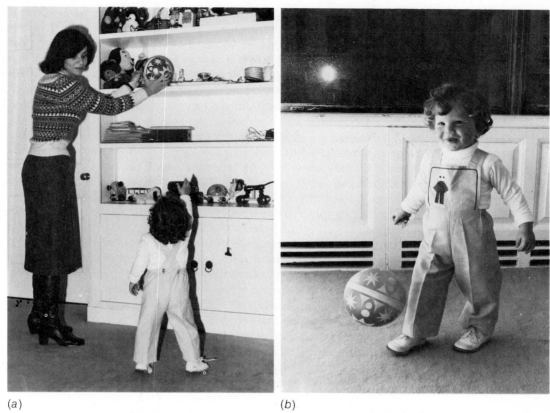

(a)   (b)

Figure 5.3 A child may express a complex idea by using only one word. Thus "ball" in one context (a) may mean "Give me the ball," and, in another context (b), "I am throwing the ball." (Howard Leiderman.)

Early Sentences It is during the second year that children make their first attempts at combining words into sentences, and here again the 1- or 1½-year-old communicates using far fewer words than an adult. "More car," for example, may mean "drive around some more." "Allgone shoe" may mean "I don't know where my other shoe is." Other two-word sentences may be simpler —"see doggie," or "where daddy," for example.

It usually takes the child a while to pick up the knack of using two-word sentences, but after several months the number of two-word combinations increases dramatically. One boy began to use two-word combinations at 19 months and spoke 14 different two-word combinations that month. Five months later the boy was using 1400 different two-word combinations (2). Clearly, at no other point in life do our vocabularies show such significant advancement.

The Structure of the Earliest Sentences

As we have seen, a child in the second year shows a remarkable ability to communicate using the barest essentials of a sentence. Early sentences are abbreviated, or **telegraphic,** versions of adult sentences made up primarily of nouns and verbs with a few adjectives. The child does not use prepositions (e.g., *in, on, under*), conjunctions (*and, but, or*), articles (*a, the*), or auxiliary verbs (*have, has, did*). Nor does the child bother with inflections — endings that indicate noun plurals or verb tenses, such as the *s* on *cats* or the *ed* on *dressed.*

Even when the child attempts to repeat a sentence after an adult, the response is telegraphic. Ask a child to say "I can see a cow," and the sentence will likely come back as "see cow" or "I see cow." The child repeats the important words, preserving the word order, but omits the unnecessary words. The child's comprehension is evident: To the child the sentence is not simply a list of words; it is a construction, composed of important and less important words.

Gradually children begin to produce longer strings of words, and their sentences become more complex and more highly structured. Sentences are not just two-word combinations; they can be analyzed into components or small units. For example, suppose a child says, "Hit ball." Then he expands the sentence: "Jeff hit ball." The child is not just stringing words together — he has added a subject to the verb and its object. He is organizing his sentence according to grammatical principles. Similarly, children express negative ideas by placing a negative word at the beginning or end of their utterance. For example, the child might say, "No sit there" after being told that he is not allowed to sit in a particular chair. The child apparently operates on these basic and universal principles even though he is composing only short, childish utterances (20).

Errors in children's early speech also indicate that they are learning grammatical rules. One type of error is overregularization, or overgeneralization, illustrated by a 2-year-old's comment that "birdies flied away." The child has learned the rule that past tenses are formed by adding *-ed,* and she has made the assumption that one "flies" today and one "flied" yesterday. Some very young children may at first learn and use a number of irregular past forms by repeating sentences their parents say, such as "kitty fell" or "mama went bye-bye." But after they learn the general rule for forming regular past tenses, they may replace these correct forms with *falled* or *goed* or *wented.*

The Development of Semantics, or Word Meaning

Around the world, across different language boundaries, children progress in linguistic competence in similar ways, suggesting that the development of **semantics** is related to general cognitive development (20). These similarities in development are called "language universals." For example, children all over the world express similar kinds of meanings in their simple two-word sentences. Moreover, children in all languages tend to omit nonessential **inflections,** which are special word endings. Another similarity at this stage is that many statements in all languages have an imperative or commanding nature: "More milk," "Sit chair," "Give papa" are all statements intended to get someone to take a certain action. Questions are not yet marked by all the characteristics of adult questions; instead, many children's questions are essentially statements spoken with the rising intonation characteristic of questions. "Mommie hat?" is an example of a child's question at this age.

One operating principle, apparently universal in linguistic development, is that word order in children's speech reflects word order in the language they hear (21). That is, in languages in which a fixed order of words in a sentence is required, children follow that order. But in languages in which the use of word endings may make a fixed order unnecessary, children may vary the order of words in sentences.

One of the earliest ideas expressed by all children in all languages is that of action. In English, action is expressed by a verb and an object, in that order, as in "throw ball." English-speaking children learn this order very early. In many other languages, such as Turkish, an inflection is required to indicate the object of the verb. Consequently, Turkish children learn to use the object inflection very early, probably because action, movement, and change are important to all children, regardless of what language they are learning. In other words, a child's linguistic accomplishments develop along with the child's growing understanding of the world and of the relationships among events and objects. What the child is able to say reflects what the child knows.

But a child is not always able to express ideas that he may, in fact, understand, in part because of his limited cognitive abilities. The forms used to express a particular meaning — say, plurals — vary from language to language. For example, the forms used to express plurals in English are relatively simple and easy to use in English (just add an s), but in the Arabic language plurals are considerably more complex. Thus English-speaking children master the art of forming plurals much earlier than do Arabic-speaking children, even though both groups of children understand the meaning of plurals at the same time.

The Child's Activity in Language Acquisition

There are many theories of how a child learns to speak, but one factor that must be stressed is the child's own activity and creativity. Young children are not always simply imitating the speech of others; they are busy exercising their skills and discovering and trying out their own sounds, words, and phrases. Novel sentences such as "Allgone shoe" or "Him a girl" are inventions, not imitations of statements children have heard previously. Children use trial and error in the production of language, trying to figure out how to make themselves understood by others. Although some of the child's progress in language is due to reinforcement or instruction by parents, much of the child's progress in language is a product of the child's own perceptual processes (4).

**COGNITIVE
DEVELOPMENT
AND
INTELLIGENCE**

Two-year-olds are on the verge of being quite capable individuals, having progressed far beyond the helpless, demanding infant stage. At age 2, they are actively acquiring skills that will extend their independence and increase their ability to cope with the world on their own.

During the second year, cognitive functioning becomes more complex, more objective, and increasingly oriented toward reality. For example, a 2-year-old, when handed a novel object such as a crayon, may begin to see uses for the object beyond the subjective experience of how the object tastes. A 2-year-old may discover that a crayon may be broken, thrown, stepped on, or used to mark on the wall as well as put in one's mouth. Two-year-olds will actively experiment in new situations, and their behavior shows definite intention. Also, they become increasingly goal-oriented, setting tasks for themselves to complete, such as piling all their toys in the center of the room.

As early as the second year, the foundation for creative play skills begins to emerge. Two-year-olds will often spend long periods stacking one block on top of another, as if learning this new skill were fascinating, absorbing all their attention and energy. In fact, they can stack three blocks one on top of another. Similarly, rolling a ball and toddling along after it to catch it may not be your idea of a good time, but it is essential that a 2-year-old learn to retrieve a ball before being able to play the more exciting game of "catch."

During the second year, children become considerably more daring. The stage from 12 to 18 months (Piaget's Stage 5 of the sensorimotor period) is one marked by experimentation (8, 18). The child is curious about objects and explores their unique features. For example, an object as simple as a button and buttonhole (if large enough for awkward little fingers) can amuse a child this age for quite some time. One-year-olds enjoy "busy boards," featuring zippers, doors that open and close, and hooks and latches, for they are eager to learn new actions.

The child in this stage is also interested in new ways of doing things. The child may discover that clay is not just to be rolled on the table — it can also be stuck on the wall, much to the caretaker's distress. Also, during this experimental stage, the child begins to use trial-and-error approaches to discover new solutions to problems. If pulling on a toy fails to move it, then the child may try another tactic, such as pushing the toy.

During the last half of the second year (Piaget's Stage 6 of the sensorimotor period), the child begins to invent solutions mentally as well as by using the trial-and-error method. That is, the child forms mental images of objects and can imagine new ways of playing with a toy. With this capacity for imagery and symbolic thought, the child can now play "pretend" games. For example, a child may offer you a flat block, urging you to "take the cookie." A toy teapot may hold imaginary tea; a cardboard box may be a little house.

Because the child can imagine actions or events before acting them out

in reality, certain events become less mysterious and confusing to the child. If mother leaves the room, for example, the child knows to follow her through the door to find her. At an earlier age, the child might just have assumed that mother was gone and the situation was hopeless, and cried in frustration. Another example of the child's ability to use symbolic images is that the child at this stage is able to "defer imitation"—that is, to reproduce a model's behavior from memory. For example, suppose a girl accompanies her father to the hair stylist. Later she may remember watching the hairdresser at work and pretend to cut her doll's hair. In the next section, we will look more closely at the process of imitation.

Imitation

Children begin to imitate the acts of others around the end of the first year or the beginning of the second. Imitation is a significant part of play, for it shows the increasing cognitive abilities of the child. An 18-month-old girl may watch her mother pick up the telephone and talk to a friend. A few minutes or hours later the child goes to the telephone and mimics that act. The child did not have to learn any new motor responses to repeat the action, for it involved only picking an object up and holding it to the face. But it was necessary for the child to get the idea for the action by watching her mother, and it was necessary for the child to be able to remember her mother talking on the phone. In other words, the child must be able to create a schema for the action and must be able to store and remember the schema.

Given that most 18-month-old children do possess the ability to create and retrieve schemata for actions witnessed earlier, we know *how* the child imitates others. What has to be explained now is *why* the child imitates the actions of others.

Sometimes the person a child is watching (called a model) serves as an incentive for further pretend play by the child. For example, suppose a 15-month-old boy has played with a set of toys but has failed to display any ''pretend'' acts. He merely put blocks in a pail and banged toys together. Now a 2-year-old girl who is somewhat familiar comes into the room. She invites the child to watch her. She gives a toy nursing bottle to a teddy bear and explains that the animal is hungry. The 15-month-old boy will not only imitate the action just modeled but may also display a wide vari-

ety of other behaviors that have no relation to the one displayed by the model. Once spurred into the imaginative realm, the child may pick up a toy telephone and pretend to talk or pour imaginary liquid into a cup and drink it. Although all these responses were not displayed by the model, they belong to a class we might call "acts displayed by others." It is as if the model's behavior serves as a reminder to the child for a class of actions seen earlier.

Still, we have not really explained why children duplicate an action they have seen and why they do not imitate *every* act they have seen. There are several possibilities.

A simple explanation, particularly for something such as early vocal imitation, is that the child wants to prolong the excitement produced by the interaction. Or the imitated act may produce interesting results. A little girl who saw her father play the piano may bang the keys herself, generating sounds that delight her.

But sometimes there are other reasons for imitating an act. If a child is unsure of, say, her ability to hold a telephone and talk on it, imitating the act may increase her confidence in her own abilities. Or, finally, a child may imitate an act in order to play the role of another person. Pretending to be her mother may give the child a sense of security, of vicarious power (see section on identification, Chapter 7).

We know *how* the child imitates others. What has to be explained now is *why* the child imitates the actions of others.

SOCIALIZATION IN THE SECOND YEAR

During the second year, children are learning about themselves and their skills. They can use language, at least in an elementary way, to communicate with others. They are intensely curious about their surroundings and move about more freely. They explore cupboards, spill paint, shuffle papers, and call for more food. In short, they are learning to take a much more active role in relation to the environment.

Most parents begin the process of **socialization** during this period. They begin to direct the child's learning of culturally appropriate behavior, values, and motives. Parents tend to concentrate training on the areas most important to them, and in most cases early socialization centers not on instructing the child positively but on the inhibition of certain activities. That is, during the second year the child learns the "do nots." "Don't tear the book." "Don't wet your pants." "Don't touch the hot stove." It is only later that parents teach the child the "do's."

Of course, parents are not the only forces of socialization during the second year. Many children are cared for by caretakers or are placed in day-care centers (see box on "Day Care").

Because the child can walk and talk, or at least can almost talk and can comprehend much, parents often assume too much. They think the child is capable of more adult behavior than a 1-year-old can handle and set standards of behavior that are too rigorous for the young child. Not realizing that the child does not yet have the cognitive capacity for understanding or remembering why certain behaviors are unacceptable, or that the child may not possess the physical ability to control constantly the muscles of the bladder, for example, the parents may experience frustration with the child's behavior. When the child continues to spill milk or wet the bed, parents often feel the child is deliberately disobeying them, while in most cases it is simply that the child is not yet mature enough—physically or mentally—to behave always in accordance with the standards set up by the parents. It is important for parents to realize that there are biological timetables of development that make certain behaviors unlikely—or at least harder—before the child reaches a certain stage.

The process of socialization during the second year is accomplished mainly through two social mechanisms. First, parents use reward and punishment—a direct means of shaping a child's behavior.

The second mechanism at work in the socialization process is a more indirect means of influencing a child's behavior. Through observing the actions of parents or older children, the child learns what behavior is acceptable and what behavior is not.

Day Care

The number of working mothers has increased tremendously in the last three decades, and it is estimated that there are currently about 7 million children of preschool age whose mothers work outside the home. This means increasing numbers of babies are cared for in day-care centers for large parts of each day.

In the past, many child-care experts have believed that separating infants from their families regularly would have adverse effects on the children, but the bulk of the recent evidence suggests that experts have been overstating the dangers. What is important is not separation itself but the *quality* of the child's day-care experiences.

Quality day-care centers provide a great deal of individual attention to each child, well-balanced meals, opportunities and facilities for exercise and recreation, learning, and constructive social interactions with other children. Consequently, children cared for at high-quality day-care centers are not impeded in social and personality development. There is some evidence that in America, children with long-term day-care experience become more spontaneous and assertive in their play, whereas in socialist countries they become more cooperative. Unfortunately, many children attend day-care centers of much lower quality than the ideal, but we do not yet know what effects this may have on their subsequent development.

Through these two processes—reward and punishment and observation—the child begins to learn the values and behavioral standards supported by the parents. In the following sections, we shall examine some of the areas of socialization on which parents concentrate with their 1-year-olds.

Socialization and Toilet Training

Progressing through the diaper stage to using a toilet is a significant step for both baby and caretaker. For the baby, using a toilet is a visible step toward independence and maturity. The caretaker, in addition to having to change diapers no longer, faces the realization that the rather helpless infant has gained new independence. Toilet training may be a major source of friction between parent and child, for the child is now expected to take some responsibility for his care and to control elimination responses.

Of course, the ease of toilet training depends on biological and cognitive maturity, as does any other part of the socialization process. The process of training a child is much easier and more likely to succeed if the child is physically able to control the muscles of the urethra and anus. Just as important is that the child understand why controlling urination and defecation is preferable to free expression of these urges. Consequently, the older a child is when toilet training is started, the shorter the time required to accomplish the goal (19).

Pediatricians and child psychologists generally agree that training should be delayed until the child is "ready" for it. The child should be able to sit up comfortably, to understand, and to communicate. In most cases this means that the child will not be able to achieve toilet training until about 18 months of age. However, there are wide cultural variations in the time of beginning toilet training.

Europeans in general tend to start training earlier than do Americans. London parents may begin as early as 4.6 months, Parisians at 7.8 months, and Stockholm parents at 12.4 months (12). Middle-class American mothers generally start the process of toilet training between 12 and 18 months of age, although one study indicated that lower-class mothers tend to start toilet training earlier (3).

Toilet Training and Personality. Perhaps no other aspect of childhood training is blamed as much for later personality factors as is toilet training. We have all heard of the classic case of the severely inhibited person who is a product of severe toilet-training practices. But what of the actual clinical data on the subject? One study indicated that premature or severe toilet training may result in *immediate* personality problems, such as bed wetting, fear of the toilet, temper tantrums, defiance, anger, and overconcern with cleanliness (13).

It is true that excessive timidity and overconformity may stem from unduly severe toilet training. If the parents are overly harsh when the child does not successfully control bowel movements, then the child becomes afraid to make any response unless he or she is certain that the response is what the parents expect. Hence the child may become inhibited, timid, and afraid to attempt responses that are not specifically approved by the parents (6).

What, then, is the recommended procedure for toilet training? In general, toilet training is likely to proceed most smoothly and be achieved with a minimum of conflict if parents encourage the gradual acquisition of

Toilet Training

Toilet training children has been a major problem in many cultures since the beginning of modern civilization. Freud emphasized the significance of it in the child's development and believed that the use of coercion in toilet training or training a child prematurely would adversely affect later adjustment. Psychologists have also devoted attention to the problem.

Children complete their toilet training at different ages, depending on their own rates of maturation, their motivation, their caretaker's training techniques, and the situation. A child who is very sensitive to being wet or dirty may be motivated to become toilet-trained earlier than a child who is less sensitive.

In the United States, most children complete their toilet training between the ages of 18 and 24 months, and many parents wait even longer before training the child because doctors advise it. Postponing toilet training until the child is 2 years of age greatly reduces the frequency of bed wetting, soiling, and constipation in early childhood. Training the child too early and putting too much emphasis on the training may make the child anxious and upset and lead to more accidents.

There are several things a parent can do to make toilet training less difficult. The child should be provided with a small potty chair, and, of course, parents should show the child how to use it. Modeling, either by the parent or an older child, can be effective in toilet training. Allowing young children to observe their older siblings going to the toilet may motivate them to learn more rapidly. In addition, clothes that are easy to remove, such as elasticized pants or clothes with large buttons or snaps, will make it easier for the child to take responsibility for undressing before using the toilet.

control. Parents must understand the difficulty of the task—substituting voluntary control for what has been from birth an involuntary, reflex process. They can help initiate the correct response by watching for signs that the child needs to relieve himself and taking the child to the bathroom immediately. If the child uses the toilet, the parent can praise the child, and both will feel a sense of satisfaction. If this is done frequently, the child will eventually learn to associate the internal cues (bowel and bladder tensions) and the external cues (being in the bathroom, removing clothes, sitting on the toilet seat) with the response of excretion.

It seems that, as with the bottle-or-breast feeding controversy, the specific toilet-training method used is not of critical significance in itself. But the method may be important in terms of its intimate connection with parent-child relationships in general. For example, a parent who is overly strict about toilet training may consistently demand too much of the child. Similarly, the parent who is warm and nurturing, yet firm, during toilet training, is likely to be the same way in other interactions.

In the next section we shall see that one of the results of the child being toilet trained is a feeling of competency or autonomy.

Autonomy

The second year of life brings an emerging sense of self in the young child. The child is more physically capable at this age, having learned to control the body functions of elimination and having increased skills in manipulation, locomotion, and exploration. All these factors contribute to the child's sense of **autonomy** and competence. According to Erikson, the sense of autonomy or self-control that the child acquires at this time may be an important determinant of an enduring sense of personal pride and good will toward others (7).

The child in this stage discovers new capabilities each day, and is eager to try out these skills. The 1-year-old wants to explore, climb, and use his own spoon, and may try to dress himself, for example. Learning to walk up and down stairs is exciting, and the child in the second year may insist on demonstrating this new ability whenever he sees steps. But while it is important for the child to try out these new skills and feel self-reliant, it is also important that the child realize that there are limits to what he can do alone—limits imposed for the well-being either of self or of others. Some stairs, for example, are off-limits; they are "For Employees Only" or lead to an upstairs bedroom.

The parents' role in this process of the child's developing a meaningful sense of autonomy is to help the child achieve some sense of independence without letting the child go beyond his or her capabilities. For example, the 1-year-old is certainly not old enough to go for a walk around the block alone, but may be permitted to wander about a fenced-in yard without constant close supervision. A child should also be given the opportunity to choose. The parent may supply the alternatives—for example, offer the child peas *or* carrots—and the child gets to make the decision.

It is very important in our culture for parents to encourage their child's independence. If the parent constantly keeps the child from exploring and investigating, the frustration may have immediate and enduring effects on personality and adjustment. But if parents are accepting and reasonably permissive, allowing the child reasonable freedom in exploration, manipulation, and investigation, then the child is likely to become self-confident, able to approach new situations without anxiety.

Aggression sometimes serves as an outlet for a child's emerging sense of self. In the next section we'll look at how aggressive responses develop and how they can be socialized.

Aggression

One-year-olds may not pack much power behind their fists, but that does not stop them from trying to get their way through aggression.

One-year-olds may not pack much power behind their fists, but that does not stop them from trying to get their way through aggression (responses intended to harm others). Aggression in childhood seems to be universal, and learning to control aggression is an important aspect of socialization in all cultures.

Why does a child develop responses that are intended to harm others? The potential for behaving aggressively may be innate, but the nature and form of aggressive expression, and its timing, depend on learning. The infant was accustomed to getting demands met by crying, and the child may learn that by adding a few kicks and punches (or substituting them), demands may be met even faster. The methods the child uses for expressing aggression are a function of what the parents and others respond to. Suppose 14-month-old Jamie finds that fighting with another child usually results in the other child giving up. Naturally, Jamie will continue to behave aggressively, since it seems to be an effective means of getting his own way.

Anger and aggression may be expressed in many ways. Lying down on the floor of a supermarket kicking and screaming is not usually included in an adult's repertoire of behavior, but for some children it works—they get a nickel for the gum machine. As a child grows older, certain aspects of the original anger responses are rewarded and thus repeated, while others are punished and eliminated. For example, a child may occasionally get his way by, say, grabbing a coloring book away from another child without his parents intervening. However, his parents may have no tolerance for another aggressive act—say, spitting on another child—and may punish him, thus reducing the possibility that he will repeat the spitting act.

Early Manifestations of Anger

During the first 2 years of life, the most common expression of anger consists of tantrums and other undirected outbursts of motor activity. The child may learn that screaming, kicking, and holding the breath are the most effective means for getting one's own way (11). It does not take long, however, for the child to learn that directed motor and language responses are also effective. That is, lying down on the floor and screaming because a friend refuses to share cookies may work some of the time, but physically grabbing a cookie away from the other child or verbally demanding a cookie is likely to be even more effective. Since aggressive behavior is more likely to be accepted and rewarded (or even encouraged) among boys, they tend to show this kind of behavior more frequently than girls (11).

What brings on angry outbursts in children? One-year-olds are frequently angered by being forced to remain on the toilet. Or they will often resist putting on shoes and socks, for example, or other restrictive clothing. Being put to bed early is another frequent source of outrage in 1-year-olds. They do not like to be told no, particularly when it means they will not be able to carry out some desirable activity. Being told to put mother's purse down is clearly frustrating to the child, particularly when there is a chance of finding candy or other goodies in her purse. At the age of 1 disagreements between playmates account for only a few of the angry outbursts.

Dealing with Anger

There are some times when a child is more irritable and more prone to aggression, and certain factors are known to contribute to the child's irritability. Visitors in the home, restless sleep or bed wetting during the previous night, colds, constipation, illness, hunger, and fatigue all bring on a certain amount of frustration for the child. Consequently, the child reacts in ways that have been successful in overcoming interference in the past—that is, with anger and aggression.

Suppose Janie is angry because she wants to play with big sister's game, which is just out of reach on a shelf. How can parents cope with the child's angry outburst at being told no? The most effective and easiest means for bringing the outburst to an end is removing the interference with the motivated activity. That is, the parents may get the game down from the shelf and allow the child to play with it. But while granting the child's desire may easily put a stop to the angry outburst, it is not always the best solution. As would be predicted on the basis of learning principles, if Janie finds that aggressive responses are rewarded—that is, get her what she wants—she will repeat them. In other words, giving the child her own way can lead to more frequent temper displays.

Another means of dealing with the problem is to remove the source of trouble—for example, the parents can move the game to a closed cabinet, hoping for an "out of sight, out of mind" effect. Diverting the child's attention or providing a substitute activity is also a way of handling the outburst. The child may find another activity equally appealing and completely forget about the forbidden game. Ignoring the outburst or imposing isolation—for example, sending the child to her room—is another method effective in bringing the outburst to an end. Generally, coax-

ing, soothing, reasoning, and scolding are effective only if used in conjunction with other methods.

Perhaps the best rule for parents to follow in controlling aggression is to set standards for the child's behavior that the child is able to achieve. Parents should be reasonably consistent in enforcing these standards but should consider the child's emotional and physical state. For example, an adult should remember that a child who is tired or does not feel well is more easily frustrated, and more temper displays are almost inevitable. But standards should not be relaxed simply for the parent's convenience or mood. Giving Janie her sister's game to play with to avoid having the child throw a fit while Aunt Ruth is visiting will not help the child learn that rules are consistent. For the child to learn self-control, it is necessary for parents themselves to exercise self-control and to be reasonably firm and consistent in controlling aggression (11).

Fears of Young Children

The 2-year-old child is still susceptible to **separation anxiety,** showing signs of anxiety and emotional upset if the mother (or primary caretaker) leaves, even temporarily. The mother's presence is, in most cases, associated with feelings of satisfaction and lack of tension. In new or strange situations, the mother's presence ordinarily reduces the insecurity and anxiety and hence enables the child to react adaptively (1). Her absence disrupts the child's usual responses and may represent a discrepancy from the child's schema for how things should be. At this age, long separations from the mother (for example, disruptions of a home) are likely to result in more drastic and enduring emotional upsets than they would have at an earlier age (9).

Separation from the mother is an important source of anxiety in the young child, but it isn't the only one. In one study it was found that in the second year fear reactions were commonly elicited primarily by noises, strange events, and falling or danger of falling. Sudden movements and flashes of light were less frightening than they were previously, but fears of animals and persons or objects associated with pain increased. Some children in the second year were afraid of the dark or of being alone, although they had not shown these fears earlier (14).

SUMMARY

1. During the second year of life, children develop many new abilities. The emergence of these abilities is the product of the combined effect of physical growth, biological maturation, and learning.

2. Physically, children gain in height and weight. Bones increase in size and number, body proportions change, and muscles and nerves develop and grow.

3. Motor development is rapid during the second year. By age 2, children

are fairly well coordinated and can walk, run, and walk up and down stairs alone.

4. Children's language skills increase rapidly during the second year, and 2-year-old children show a remarkable ability to communicate.

5. Children all over the world progress through language development in similar ways, demonstrating "language universals," or similarities in development. Thus it seems that the development of semantics is related to general cognitive development.

6. During the second year, cognitive functioning becomes more complex, more objective, and increasingly oriented toward reality. The child also develops a new capacity for imagery and symbolic thought and can imitate the actions of others.

7. The process of socialization during the second year is accomplished mainly through two social mechanisms. First, parents use reward and punishment. Second, through observation the child learns values and behavioral standards.

8. The ease of toilet training depends on biological and cognitive maturity, and it is important that the child be physiologically ready. A warm and nurturing yet firm attitude on the part of the parents can also facilitate training.

9. Because of their new capabilities and skills, children during their second year develop a growing sense of autonomy and competence. Parents can encourage their child's independence by allowing the child reasonable freedom.

10. One- and 2-year-olds sometimes display aggressive responses in order to get their own way, and learning to control aggression is an important aspect of socialization in all cultures.

11. The 1- or 2-year-old child is still susceptible to separation anxiety when the mother or primary caretaker leaves. Often the child has other fears as well, such as fear of loud noises or animals.

Suggested Readings

Chukovsky, K. *From two to five*. Berkeley: University of California Press, 1968.

Clark, H. H., & Clark, E. V. *Psychology and language: An introduction to psycholinguistics*. New York: Harcourt Brace Jovanovich, 1977.

Dale, P. *Language development structure and functions* (2nd ed.). New York: Holt, Rinehart and Winston, 1976.

Flavell, J. H. *Cognitive development*. Englewood Cliffs, N.J.: Prentice-Hall, 1977.

Garvey, C. *Play*. Cambridge, Mass.: Harvard University Press, 1978.

Schaffer, R. *Mothering*. Cambridge, Mass.: Harvard University Press, 1977.

Smith, L. *The children's doctor*. Englewood Cliffs, N.J.: Prentice-Hall, 1969.

Part Three
The Preschool Years

Chapter 6

The Preschool Years: Motor and Cognitive Development

*P*RESCHOOL CHILDREN are considerably more "grown-up" than those in the first 2 years of life. A preschool child may remark with considerable self-assurance, "But that was when I was a baby!" Indeed, by age 3, most of the persisting traces of infancy have disappeared, and the little girl or boy has begun to look, talk, think, and act more like a *child* than a *baby*.

The preschool years are exciting ones in the child's development physically, cognitively, and socially, and between the ages of 2 and 5 progress is rapid in all areas of development. In this chapter we will first examine the physical development of the preschool child. Next we will look at the fascinating process of language development and the development of cognitive functioning. Finally, we will look at conditions affecting language development and cognitive functions.

PHYSICAL GROWTH

At age 3, the average boy stands about 38 inches tall and weighs about 33 pounds. The average girl is almost as tall (37.6) and almost as heavy (32.5 pounds). The rate of growth is slower now than in infancy, and as a result of gradual increases, boys generally gain about 5½ inches in height and about 10 pounds in weight between the ages of 3 and 5. Girls' growth rates are roughly comparable, although the average boy is still slightly taller and heavier.

Children's relative height during the preschool period is a fairly good predictor of their relative adult heights. That is, tall preschool children are likely to become tall adults, and short preschoolers are likely to be relatively short adults. Nevertheless, quite a few individuals *do* shift in relative height in the intervening years; many who are short preschoolers become average or tall adults.

During the preschool period, the child's body form is also becoming more mature (see Figure 6.1). As the upper parts of the body begin to approach adult dimensions, their growth slows down, giving the lower extremities a chance to catch up. Thus, during the preschool years, head growth is slow, trunk growth is intermediate, and limb growth is rapid (29). By age 6 the child has lost the relatively large, round, and protruding stomach characteristic of the younger child.

Along with these changes in body proportions, the child's skeletal, muscular, and nervous systems are also becoming more mature. The size and number of bones in the body increase, and the bones become harder; between ages 2 and 3 development of the child's temporary teeth is usually completed. Beginning at about 4, muscles develop at a faster rate than the rest of the body, so that during the fifth year about 75 percent of the child's weight increase is due to muscular development. But a child's muscles develop differentially: Throughout this period, the larger muscles remain better developed than the small, fine muscles. Consequently, the child of this age is more skillful in activities involving large movements than those requiring more precise, finer coordination. Thus, throwing

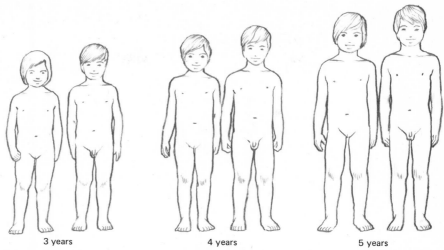

3 years   4 years   5 years

Figure 6.1 During the preschool period the child's body proportions continue to become more adultlike: head growth is slow, trunk growth is intermediate, and limb growth is rapid.

bean bags at a target is a more appropriate activity for this age group than pick-up sticks. Or children this age enjoy opportunities to run, ride a tricycle, climb, slide, or throw. Muscular development, along with such changes as deeper, slower respiration and slower heart rate, causes the child's strength and endurance to increase markedly during these years.

In addition, the nervous system grows rapidly during this period. For example, the child's brain, having reached 75 percent of its adult weight by the end of the second year, grows to 90 percent of its adult weight by age 6. **Myelinization** (development of sheaths over the nerve fibers), which has already been nearly completed in the lower portions of the body, is generally completed in the higher brain centers during the ages 3 to 6.

Psychomotor Development

The child's more mature body proportions, increased strength and coordination, and more highly developed nervous system provide the foundation for greatly increased motor skills, although learning begins to play an increasingly important role once the foundation is laid. By age 3 the child runs more smoothly, speeds up and slows down with greater ease, turns sharper corners, and negotiates sudden stops. He or she can easily go up stairs unaided, alternating feet, and jump up as much as a foot with both feet together. The child is now ready for a tricycle.

Other motor developments help to make 3-year-olds much more "social" beings; they can now wash and dry their own hands, feed themselves with a spoon with little spilling, go to the toilet, and respond to instructions. They can also build a building or tower of nine blocks; draw a circle instead of simply a straight line (though not yet a triangle); and build a bridge of three cubes.

By age 4, the child's psychomotor skills have increased still further. Unlike the 3-year-old, who usually is able merely to jump up and down, 4-year-olds are able to make moderately good running and standing broad jumps. They can also skip, though they are still unable to hop. Whereas at 2 or 3 they would merely toss or hurl a ball in an awkward, pushing fashion (with much body participation), they can now swing back a more independent arm and execute a strong, overhand throw (15).

The average 4-year-old can trace a diagonal pathway between parallel lines a centimeter apart and can at last fold a piece of paper diagonally. He is still unable to copy a diamond from a model but can draw a circle and a cross.

Preschool Children's Social Play

It used to be thought that in their earliest interactions, children tended to play parallel with others—that is, alongside but without co-operation or real interaction. Piaget maintains that preschool children are egocentric, unable to take another's point of view and insensitive to other children's wants, feelings, and ideas.

More recently, research has made it clear that children become interested in their peers during the second year of life. If a child observes another doing interesting things with a toy, she will move toward the interesting activity, observe it, and then try to use the toy herself. Children between 16 and 18 months are more likely to approach other children directly, looking at each other, smiling, and talking to each other.

By the time they enter school, children are much more skillful in social exchanges and play together in cooperative ways, influencing each other's activities. They act out fantasies, pretending to be adults, animals, or television or storybook characters. As their experiences and imagination grow, their play becomes more complex and more dramatic. Boys' fantasies generally involve more action and aggression, whereas girls' play involves more personal relationships.

At about the age of 4 years, what has been called sociodramatic play, involving several children, emerges. In this kind of play, the child's imagination is free and the child expresses his imagination more freely and in more complex ways than he did when he was younger.

Play serves many functions for children. Some of the child's play seems to be motivated by a desire for mastery. That is, in his play the child focuses on dealing competently with challenging problems. Thus the young child's active play contributes to cognitive development and helps the child understand the world. In addition, play makes children feel less helpless, providing more experiences in dealing with others' ideas and feelings (particularly in sociodramatic play), permitting them to act out in safety feelings such as frustration, aggression, hostility, and tension that it would be dangerous to express in real life. Role playing in sociodramatic play contributes to the child's developing sense of self.

Many preschool children, particularly first-borns and only children, adopt imaginary companions, either as friends or as outlets for aggression and hostility. With this companion the child can practice and develop social skills that he might otherwise develop more slowly. Imaginary companions usually disappear as children have more interactions with real playmates.

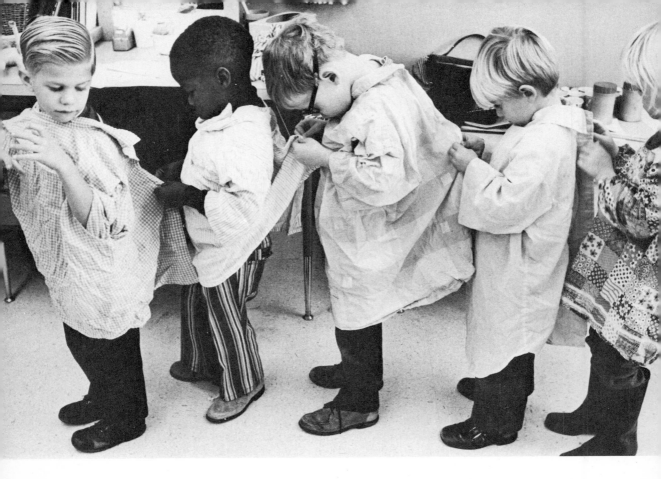

By 5 years of age, the average child has a fairly mature sense of balance, which is reflected in a more self-reliant abandon in motor behavior. While still unable to hop, he skips and jumps more smoothly. Fine movements have also become better differentiated. For example, the average 5-year-old requires only 20 seconds to take a dozen pellets and drop them into a bottle one by one.

Generally, it is not until the age of 5 years that a child can draw a recognizable picture of a human being. The 5-year-old can draw straight lines in all directions, though drawing diagonal lines is still not easy. Thus, the 5-year-old can copy squares and triangles but not diamonds (15). If this seems strange to you, try the task yourself. Although you can easily draw all three figures, no doubt you can see that the spatial arrangement of the four lines making up a diamond figure makes a diamond a bit harder to copy than a square.

Playing ball with a 5-year-old is a little more entertaining than playing ball with a 4-year-old, for 5-year-olds can throw a ball somewhat more accurately than their 4-year-old counterparts. However, it is not until about age 6 that children achieve sufficient eye-hand coordination, timing, and fine-muscle control to demonstrate any real skill in this activity.

Motor functions are not the only skills a youngster develops during the preschool years. Another step toward maturity is the development of language skills.

LANGUAGE DEVELOPMENT

"Why are you watering that plant?" "Why does it grow?" "Why is it green?" If you have ever been around a curious child who seems to do nothing but follow you around asking "why" questions, you realize just how much knowledge can be conveyed quickly through the spoken word.

A child's entry into the realm of human language admits him or her into a world of knowledge and culture. Much of what we know is handed from generation to generation primarily by means of the written or spoken word, enabling everyone to know much more than he or she could possibly learn by direct experience.

A conversation with a 2-year-old may consist of little more than two-word sentences. A 5-year-old child, on the other hand, can talk your ear off. Preschool children show remarkable gains in language development (see Figure 6.2); children in most cultures speak their first sentence when

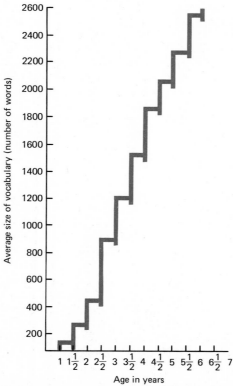

Figure 6.2 Average vocabulary size of children at various ages. The child's vocabulary increases rapidly in the years from 2 to 6.

Motor and Language Development During the Preschool Years

At the Completion of:	Motor Development	Language Development
24 months	Runs, but falls in sudden turns; can quickly alternate between sitting and standing; walks up or down stairs, one foot forward only. Feeds self.	Vocabulary of more than 50 items; begins spontaneously to generate two-word phrases that are his own creations; increase in communicative behavior and interest in language; simple declarative sentences, lacking auxiliaries (examples: "I running"; "Doll broke"); doesn't change order of words in negative phrases ("I no want by-by").
30 months	Jumps up into air with both feet; stands on one foot for about 2 seconds; takes a few steps on tiptoe; jumps from chair; can move digits independently and shows good hand and finger coordination; manipulation of objects much improved; builds tower of six cubes; attempts to hop.	Rapid increase in vocabulary, many new additions every day; average size of vocabulary, 400 words; utterances consist of at least two words (many have three or four) and have communicative intent; seems to understand everything that is said to him; intelligibility not yet very good, though there is great variation among children; frustrated if not understood by adults; utterances have characteristic child grammar—that is, they are rarely verbatim repetitions of an adult utterance.
3 years	Tiptoes 3 yards; runs smoothly with acceleration and deceleration; negotiates sharp and fast curves without difficulty; climbs stairs by alternating feet; jumps 12 inches; can pedal and steer tricycle; walks path without stepping off; jumps off floor with both feet; throws ball, but not well; uses fork and spoon with some effectiveness; helps in undressing self.	Vocabulary about 1000 words; about 80 percent of utterances are intelligible even to strangers; grammatical complexity of utterances roughly that of colloquial adult language, although mistakes still occur; does not ordinarily use many different grammatical forms in one sentence; few passive sentences; beginning use of future tense; use of negatives with auxiliary verbs ("Sally can't run"); asks questions in adult form ("Why is Mama going?")

At the Completion of:	Motor Development	Language Development
4 years	Jumps over rope; running with better form and more power; walks circle without stepping off; hops four to six steps on one foot; begins to assume adult stance in throwing; catches large ball; dresses self in part; can walk balance beam quickly and without hesitation.	Language well established; longer and more complex relative clauses used ("I saw what Ted did"); two or more ideas expressed in one sentence ("Tommy wants me to go but I don't want to"); deviations from the adult norm more evident in style than in grammar.

E. Lenneberg. *Biological foundations of language.* New York: Wiley, 1967.

they are approximately 15 to 30 months old, and by the time they are 4, most speak in well-formed sentences. Sometimes, in fact, they may express surprisingly complicated thoughts. By the age of 6, the American child has a vocabulary of between 8,000 and 14,000 words (7). This means that between the ages of 1 and 6, an average of five to eight words are added to the child's vocabulary each day—a remarkable accomplishment!

How does the child learn so much language in so short a period of time? Although the processes underlying language development are not fully understood, we do know that language development is not simply a result of reward and punishment for verbal responses or imitation of the speech of others. Rather, the child assumes an active role in comprehending and producing language. Listening to others talk, the child somehow analyzes the language he hears and discovers the rules governing that language. Of course, the motivation to learn to speak is great, for even a young child sees the value of learning to communicate with others. Through language, the child can express his emotional states and gain help in satisfying needs.

Preschool Speech Development

The language of the preschool-age child gradually becomes more complex than the **telegraphic** forms used earlier. Now the child begins to use adverbs, such as *here* and *there,* and an occasional article, such as *an,* and puts proper endings on some nouns and verbs.

However, progress is gradual. Children may use the proper **inflection** (word ending) half the time and not use it at other times. For instance, one child whose speech development was studied added the *-ing* verb ending (called the progressive form) in half the instances where it was required when she was 2½ years old, but she did not supply this ending all the time until she was almost 4 years old. Other children may not supply the progressive ending correctly in all instances until they are 5½ years old.

Though children vary in the rate at which they master adult use of grammatical forms, the order of mastery is remarkably uniform in a particular culture. For example, in one long-term study of the language development of three American children whose vocabularies were quite different, all three children mastered the -*ing* verb form, the prepositions *in* and *on*, and the plural forms of nouns before they used the regular and irregular past-tense forms of verbs correctly (6). That is, the child might say, "I going outside," (the correct -*ing* form minus the auxiliary verb *am*), but for the past tense would say "I goed outside" instead of using the correct form, "I went outside." The children did not show consistently correct use of the auxiliary verbs (such as *is, was,* and *were*) until still later.

Why is it that all children follow the same sequence of steps in learning to use their language correctly? Is it that certain forms always appear most frequently in the speech of the parents, and thus the children pick them up first because of frequent exposure? Apparently not, for in the study of the three children cited above, all three followed the same order of progression regardless of whether the -*ing* verb form or prepositions such as *in* and *on* were used frequently or infrequently by the parents. It is more likely that the order of acquisition of certain language forms is related to the child's level of cognitive functioning. That is, the child learns to use the easier forms of language first, the harder ones later.

Complex Sentences

Between 2 and 3½ years of age, children reach a further stage of development in language: They learn to construct complex sentences. Usually, they join two or more simple sentences by the conjunction *and*, as in "You snap and he comes" or "No, you have some and I have some." Other complex sentences may be formed by embedding one sentence or thought in another, usually as the object of the verb—for example, "I see you sit down." Other examples of embedded sentences are "I hope I don't hurt it" and "You think I can do it?" Complex sentences containing *wh* clauses (*what, who, where, when*) also begin to appear at this time, including "I know where it is," "When I get big I can lift you up," and "Mary sang what I like to hear" (6).

The Construction of Questions

Children's development in the use of language is also illustrated by their progressive ability to construct questions. At first, a question is simply a statement spoken with a rising **intonation** at the end—"Mommie sock?" Next, children progress to asking *wh* questions (*what, where, who, why*), using most frequently *what* and *where*. Interestingly, they can respond correctly to *where* questions, but *what* questions usually bring irrelevant answers. For example, when a mother of a child at this stage asked, "What did you hit?," her child responded, "Hit" (2).

By the age of 3, the child's grammar has become more complex and so have his questions. But the child still does not transform word order correctly ("Why John can't eat cookie?"), and *yes/no* questions are still marked simply by adding an interrogative intonation. Later stages of language development find preschool children able to properly invert word order in *yes/no* questions ("Are you going to help me?") but still unable to make the proper inversions in *wh* questions ("What you have in your mouth?" or "Why kitty can't stand up?").

We have so far looked at the child's progress in using appropriate rules of grammar. But an equally important area of interest in studying language development is the meanings children attach to their words and sentences. How does a child learn the meanings of words? In the next section we shall look at some of the progress involved in the development of **semantics** (word meaning).

The Development of Semantics or Word Meaning

The words *ball, cup, juice, cookie,* and *water* may sound simple to you, but to a beginning talker, they are magic. Just say the word, and lo and behold, someone brings a cup of orange juice. Four- and 5-year-olds, who are by now speaking in well-formed sentences, find an even greater response to learning new words. They can be more articulate in arguing about what they want or don't want to do; they can learn more about their environment.

Between the ages of 1 and 6, a child's vocabulary increases dramatically (recall the average of 5 to 8 new words learned each day). Though it has been shown that children themselves take an active role in acquiring language, parents are a major influence on a child's vocabulary. Many new words and their meanings are acquired through elaborate "naming rituals" that Western middle-class parents indulge in with their babies from the time a child first utters something that sounds like a word (26). Often a baby will initiate the game, asking, "What's dat?" The parent will then name the object, the child will try to say the word, and the parent will correct the child's attempt.

But the "name game," or direct instruction, is not the only way children learn. Apparently, simply hearing the word on a few occasions, usually in reference to an object or action or some property of an object in the environment, is sufficient for the child to acquire some sense of the word and to begin using it (6, 23). A child often surprises the parents by saying a word they have never tried to teach her.

However, though a child may use a certain word, the meaning intended by the child may be quite different from the adult meaning. Some words are not interpreted or used in the adult manner until a long time after they appear in the child's vocabulary for the first time.

Just say the word, and lo and behold, someone brings a cup of orange juice.

Overextension. Sometimes a child may apply a word to a variety of things that are similar in appearance. Some psychologists call that **overextension.** For example, the word *doggie* may be used to name cats, cows, horses, rabbits, or other four-legged animals (see Figure 6.3). The child may use a word such as *ball* to name many objects that share perceptual qualities such as shape, size, sound, texture, or movement (4, 10).

Apparently, the child at first tends to use only one or two perceptual features of an object—for example, four-leggedness or roundness—in applying the category name to an object. That is, if an object has four legs and moves, it is labeled a dog, or if it is round, it is called a ball. But by the time the child gets a little older, other features—such as size, shape, furriness, movement, and barking—must be present before the child calls the animal a dog. Children gradually narrow down the meaning of overextended definitions as they learn new words that take over parts of the definition. For instance, when the child learns the word *cow*, features such as

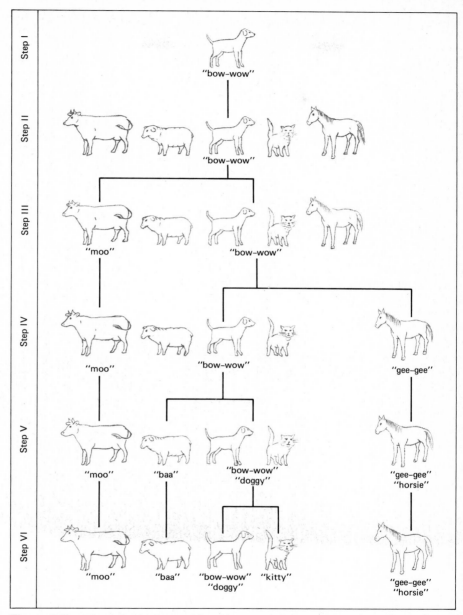

Figure 6.3 A hypothetical example of how an infant overextends at first and later restructures the meaning of the word *bow-wow*. (Adapted from E. V. Clark, What's in a word?: On the child's acquisition of semantics in his first language. In T. E. Moore, Ed., *Cognitive development and the acquisition of language.* New York: Academic Press, 1973. Pp. 65–110.)

moo sounds, large size, and hoofs are added to the criteria of four-leggedness and movement; the meaning of *cow* is thus differentiated from the meaning of *dog* (10).

Overextension of a word seldom lasts longer than a few months and often lasts very briefly. Only some of the child's words will be overextended; others seem to approximate adult usage from the beginning.

Underextension. Sometimes children make a naming error in the other direction. That is, they define some words too narrowly, or **underextend** the definition. For example, one little girl used the word *car* to refer exclusively to cars moving on the street outside but not to cars standing still or pictures of cars (3). For some children the word *kitty* may refer at first only to the family's pet cat. The child will not respond to other cats with the word *kitty*. Later, however, the child may extend the meaning of the word to include other cats. Like overextended meanings, underextensions become modified until the child's meaning matches the adult's (10).

Level of Labeling. One of the general principles found in language development is that the child learns words at an intermediate level of generality. As adults, we can label objects at several different levels of generality. A pet, for example, going from the most specific to the broadest level of generality, is "Prince," a Dalmatian, a dog, a mammal, or an animal. But a child is more likely to respond to a picture of a Dalmatian by calling it a *dog* rather than a Dalmatian or an animal. This use of an intermediate level of generality seems entirely reasonable, because adults generally name objects at this level of generality when talking with 2- or 3-year-olds, though they may use the other level when speaking with adults. Thus, a mother may speak of Fords, Plymouths, and Fiats when speaking with her friends but simply labels these vehicles *cars* when speaking to her youngster. The practicality of this level of labeling is evident for both adult and child. It is easier for the adult to refer to a car instead of naming the make, and easier for the child to learn one word than many. After all, what child needs to distinguish between Fords and Fiats? For the child, they are both large vehicles that move and take you places (1, 5).

Beyond Nouns: Verbs, Adjectives, and Conjunctions

The remarkable uniformity of the stages children go through in learning to speak has been studied for verbs, adjectives, and conjunctions as well as for nouns.

The verbs a child uses first generally refer to his or her own actions (for example, *run, throw, hit, jump*) or to actions of objects played with (for example, *go, broke, fell, move*). As with nouns, children may overextend the definitions of some verbs. A child may use the word *kick* correctly but also use it to refer to other actions in which something moves forward. If the child sees a ball rolling because it has been bumped by the front wheel of a kiddy car, the child might say that the ball has been "kicked" (4). But it is only a matter of time before the child learns more labels—that is, more verbs—to apply to different actions and thus begins to use the verb *kick* more appropriately.

There are certain verbs that children have particular trouble learning, and *ask* is one of them. Preschoolers often use and respond to the verb *ask* as if it meant the same thing as *tell*. For example, when a child in an experimental play situation was instructed to "tell Chris [another child] what to feed the doll," she answered, correctly, "A banana." However, when she was told to "ask Chris what to feed the doll," she did not ask Chris a question; instead she simply responded, "A banana." Surprisingly, it is not until they are 9 or 10 that most children will use and respond to *ask* and *tell* as adults do. This is just another example of how uniform the process of language acquisition is, for most children go through the same sequence in learning to use *ask* and *tell* correctly (8, 20).

The adjectives *big* and *little* are generally a child's first words describing space or extent of objects (6), and this contrasting pair of words is used widely by the child for quite some time. Even 4- and 5-year-olds continue to use *big* and *little* to describe something that is higher, longer, or wider than something else (28). Other adjective pairs, such as *high-low*, *long-short*, and *wide-narrow*, do not appear until later (11).

Younger preschool children are not attuned to listening for different conjunctions, such as *before* and *after*; instead they tend to interpret the order of events from the order in which the events are mentioned in a sentence. For example, in one experiment children between ages 3 and 5 were given toys and asked to use them in acting out simple stories such as these: "The boy patted the dog before he kicked the rock" (Case 1), and "Before he kicked the rock, the boy patted the dog" (Case 2). Three-year-olds clearly were following the order of mention, for they got the order correct 93 percent of the time in Case 1, but only 18 percent of the time in Case 2. By the age of 5 or 6, however, most children got the order right in both stories (9).

Children continue to make great progress in language development between ages 4 and 10, as we shall see in Chapter 8.

The Relationship Between Language and Cognition

Determining the relationship between language and cognition is similar to trying to answer the question "Which came first, the chicken or the egg?" Do the child's language skills determine the level of cognitive functioning? Or, on the other hand, do a child's cognitive capabilities determine the rate of language acquisition?

Although the relationships between language and cognition are complex, to say the least, many authorities hold that cognition directs language development rather than the reverse. Piaget and his followers, for instance, assume that language development is part of cognitive development, *reflecting* rather than *determining* levels of cognitive achievement.

They point out that thought, in the form of sensorimotor intelligence (see Chapter 3), begins to develop before language. For example, even 2-year-olds can place objects in groups, though they can't verbally label the groups or explain why they grouped the objects a certain way. That is, although they may group objects on the basis of shape, they are not capable of saying, "I put all the round ones here, and all the square ones there, or all the yellow ones here, and all the red ones there" (12).

Another fact that suggests that cognition can develop independently of language is that many deaf children who are deficient in language solve reasoning problems as well as hearing children do (13). The deaf child's cognitive development follows the same course as the hearing child's though some deaf children go through the developmental stages more slowly.

Verbal Mediation

What about the role of language in cognitive functioning *after* a child has learned to speak? It seems that once children have learned to use words, speech becomes instrumental in controlling their behavior. That is, we turn to the concept of **verbal mediation.**

For example, when an adult introduces something new that the child has never seen before and says, "Have a piece of candy," the child will react to it as she has toward other things labeled candy, taking it joyfully and popping it into her mouth. Thus, the word *candy* mediated her response: the stimulus was the actual piece of candy, and her response of reaching for it was influenced by the verbal label (*candy*) applied to the unfamiliar object.

Verbal mediation helps the child learn, remember, and solve problems. Most of us have observed young children trying to solve problems by talking to themselves, thinking out loud, using words and sentences to guide their actions: "I'll get a chair . . . then I'll stand on that box." As the children grow older, such verbal planning won't be necessary, but at ages 3 or 4 verbal mediation is a definite aid in accomplishing new tasks.

The relation between language and the usual methods of measuring cognitive functioning (intelligence tests) will be discussed later. But first let's look at the development of cognitive skills in the preschool child.

COGNITIVE DEVELOPMENT

The study of cognitive functioning during the preschool years is of special importance. The child now possesses a capacity for symbolism and language, capabilities that were just beginning to emerge during the second year. He is in what Piaget calls the **preoperational** stage and can manipulate images and symbols as well as overt actions. The child will treat a stick as if it were a candle and blow it out, or treat a block of wood as if it were a car and move it around, simultaneously making a noise like an engine. This ability to treat objects as symbolic of things is an essential characteristic of the preoperational stage (27). Consequently, cognitive

Piaget and Education

Although Piaget is not an educator, his theories and writings have had a major impact on educational philosophy and practice. The implications of Piaget's theory for educational practice, including preschool education, have been spelled out by Professor David Elkind of Tufts University.

First of all, Professor Elkind points out, Piaget maintains that the child enters school with many ideas about the physical and natural world, although these ideas are different from those of adults and are expressed in different language. The first task in educating children, then, is developing effective ways of communicating with them. For example, it is better to use actions, rather than words, in working with preschool children. *Showing* children how to make orange juice is likely to be far more effective than *telling* them how. Second, educators must help children to change their existing incomplete ideas about space, time, causality, quantity, and number, as well as help them to learn new material. Furthermore, Piaget stresses that spontaneous interactions with the environment are critical in a child's progress toward a more accurate view of the world and that children actively construct world views. In other words, it is not necessary to give a child the incentive to learn — that incentive is inherent. What is important, however, is not to dull the child's eagerness to know by using overly rigid programs that disrupt the child's own rhythm and pace of learning.

Other findings of Piaget have implications for preschool educational programs. For example, young children are egocentric, do not operate according to rules, and have not coordinated their language and thought well. Consequently, formal instruction in the sense of presenting rules is *not* an effective means of teaching young children; rather, educational materials must be concrete and related to action. For example, during juice time, children and teachers may talk about what they are doing. Children can develop ideas about numbers, quantity, and classification and learn some concepts about the physical properties of objects by asking and answering questions such as, "How many cups of juice do we need for the children today?" and "Do you want more or less juice than Jane has?" "Show and tell" also helps children coordinate their experiences with language — that is, learn to describe their experiences. At the same time, children learn to overcome their egocentrism and come to realize that another child's view of the world may be different from their own.

D. Elkind. Early childhood education: A Piagetian perspective. *The Principal*, 1971, *51*, 48–55.

growth from the preschool years through adolescence takes on an important new dimension from that of the first year or 2 years of life, and becomes more complex or sophisticated.

But although the preschool child's thought is symbolic, the symbols are not necessarily organized into firmly articulated concepts and rules. Moreover, the preoperational child has difficulty taking the point of view of another child or adult. The child cannot anticipate how an object will look from the point of view of another person or even realize that a scene he sees may look different in the eyes of another. Piaget regards the preoperational child as *egocentric* in perspective. The ability to take another's point of view or to organize symbols into firmly articulated concepts and rules will come later in development.

In studying cognitive development, it is important to remember several general principles. One is that there seem to be universal cognitive processes that appear in an orderly sequence among children growing up in any reasonably normal environment. Although certain experiences may either hasten or retard the emergence of these processes, it appears that eventually any normal human being will achieve certain cognitive capabilities, following a given order.

Another point to remember is that the measurement of a particular cognitive skill—say, reasoning—is a complicated process, and the nature of the problem on which the test of reasoning is based must be taken into account. In other words, one should not attempt to measure cognitive competences as abstract abilities independent of the information being processed; they are dependent on the nature of the problem. For example, an investigator who wants to test a child's ability to remember must decide whether to test a child's memory for pictures, words, or numbers. The three different categories may reveal quite different memory abilities —for instance, the child may remember a group of pictures more accurately than a list of numbers.

Even the content of pictures may affect the child's ability to remember. For example, one group of children was shown a set of photographs. Then they were shown pairs of photographs, composed of the original picture they had seen and a slightly transformed picture. If the original picture was of a single object—say, a television set or pocketbook—the child could easily point out the transformed picture (the difference was obvious). But if the original picture was of a scene—say, a group of similar objects such as three bicycles leaning against a rack—the child found it hard to identify which photograph she had seen earlier (25).

The development of any cognitive skill is gradual. While a child may show a certain capability early, it may be months or years before she fully uses the skill in every situation in which it might be applied. For this reason, it is often difficult to assess accurately levels of cognitive functioning.

In studying cognition, we must differentiate between units and processes. As in the study of chemistry there are units called molecules that are involved in processes like condensation or crystallizing, or in a political system there are "units" — that is, the people — who participate in processes such as voting or making laws, in cognition there are units, such as schemata or symbols, that are used in processes, such as perception (see Chapter 3).

The Units in Cognitive Activity

Preschool children are capable of using all five kinds of units in cognitive activity: **schemata, images, symbols, concepts,** and **rules.** Before discussing cognitive processes, let us review the definitions of these terms.

Schema. A schema is the mind's way of representing the most important aspects, or critical features, of an event. A schema is a little like the cartoonist's caricature of a face, for it exaggerates distinctive features. A baby, you will recall, may develop a schema for Daddy that emphasizes his beard and bald head (see Chapter 4). Your schema for the Capitol in Washington probably emphasizes the dome as its most outstanding feature. Schemata (the plural of schema) are not limited to the visual mode; a schema may be based on other sensory events, such as the smell of roses or the feel of sandpaper. What is important to remember about this cognitive unit is that a schema does not refer to an idea. While a girl may have a schema based on seeing her mother feed milk to her baby sister, she does not have a schema for the mother's kindness or nurturance. Kindness and nurturance are ideas, not physical events.

Young children have a remarkable capacity to store schemata. A group of 4-year-olds were shown 60 pictures one day, with each child looking at each picture for about 2 seconds. The next day the children were shown a group of 120 pictures. Sixty of the pictures were those seen the previous day, and 60 were new photographs. Asked to identify the pictures seen previously, the average child was correct at least 80 percent of the time (19).

Images. An image is a more detailed, elaborate, and conscious representation created from the more abstract schema. An image is more like a complete picture of a person, whereas a schema is more similar to a caricature of a person. Since conscious mental work is required to generate an image from the more abstract schema, a young infant probably has no images.

Images can help a child answer a question such as "Does an elephant have ears?" Although adults quickly say yes to the question without pausing to think, a child more often feels the need to generate a mental image to solve the problem (22).

Images can help a child answer a question such as "Does an elephant have ears?"

Symbols. While schemata and images are based on physical aspects of specific perceptual events, symbols are arbitrary ways of representing concrete events, characteristics, or qualities of objects and actions. For example, kindergarten-age children know that a "skull and crossbones" symbolizes danger, and that an octagonal sign at the end of a road symbolizes STOP. And as we saw in Chapter 5, as children grow toward the age of 2, they can treat objects in a symbolic, though rather rudimentary, way. They engage in "pretend" play, in which a flat block symbolizes a cookie, and almost any two things large and small can symbolize an adult and child. For example, a child may pretend that a tall pencil and a short one "walk" and "talk" as parent and child.

Concepts. A concept stands for, or represents, a common set of attributes among a group of schemata, images, or symbols. The concept *dog*, for example, refers to the collection of properties we call furriness, tail, four feet, elongated face, friendliness to humans, and a barking sound. *Animal, human,* and *food* are all concepts—related not to one particular event but representing a quality or set of qualities common to several events.

Rules. Rules are essentially statements about concepts. "Water is wet" or "winters are cold" are examples of rules. As children grow older, they establish new rules, and their rules get progressively more sophisticated. Stage theories of development attach particular significance to the development of rules, for certain rules of reasoning characterize more mature stages of development.

The Processes in Cognitive Activity

Cognition refers to the processes involved in (1) **perception,** (2) **memory,** (3) **reasoning,** (4) **reflection,** and (5) **insight.** Though each of these terms is no doubt somewhat familiar, the following are brief formal definitions: *Perception* is the detection, organization, and interpretation of information from both the outside world and the internal environment; *memory* is the storage and retrieval of the perceived information; *reasoning* is the use of knowledge to make inferences and draw conclusions; *reflection* is the evaluation of the quality of ideas and solutions, and *insight* is the recognition of new relationships between two or more segments of knowledge.

Cognitive Processes

Children's cognitive processes, like adults', can be divided into two types: undirected and directed.

Undirected cognition is perhaps the more mysterious of the two, referring to free associations, dreams, or reveries, including the free flow of thoughts that occur continually as the child walks home or stares out the window. Because it is difficult to study such private, undirected associations, there has not been much inquiry into this exciting and important kind of cognition.

It is far easier to study directed cognition, those processes children use when trying to solve a problem. In the following, for example, we shall look at the process of perception, and how it develops in preschool children.

In Chapter 8 we will look in more detail at some of the other cognitive processes.

Perception

Perception is the process by which children (and adults) detect, recognize, and interpret information from the barrage of physical stimulation we experience at almost all times. No one is capable of taking in every detail of a scene all the time. Just now, for example, you may have been aware only of your book and desk. You were not really perceiving those everpresent, unobtrusive background noises. You were extracting from the environment only some of the information; you were not attending to (or perceiving) all the information that was available.

The goal of perception is to understand events; to match what is sensed to some cognitive unit, whether that be a schema, image, or concept. For example, now that you are aware of those background noises, can you identify them? Do they fit in with your schemata for certain events— say, routine traffic noise, the sound of a plane passing overhead, people walking about? In addition to sounds, other events or sensations that we perceive include (1) static objects—physical things such as trees and chairs; (2) dynamic events that occur over time, such as a person getting up from a chair or one in the process of sitting down; (3) pictures; (4) symbols, such as letters, numbers, words, and speech; and (5) sensations of the body, such as an increase in heartbeat or muscle tension.

The nature of perception in preschoolers is different from that of older children. The very young child seems to represent experience by schemata; the older child often uses linguistic symbols or concepts. For example, if shown a simple abstract shape, a 1-year-old might simply notice the shape and form a schema for that shape; a 5- or 6-year-old would try to categorize the shape to some existing schema and label it with a word. The larger a child's vocabulary, the more likely he is to rely on words.

The child under 5 years seems easily distracted and has difficulty maintaining attention for a long time on a problem. A preschooler finds it difficult to listen very long to someone else talking. Also, young children may be unable to shift the focus of their attention as rapidly as older children.

Under proper environmental conditions, the greater part of the major developmental changes in cognitive functioning occur between the ages of 4 and 10 years. These changes in cognitive functioning are associated with important changes in the central nervous system, including the growth of neural tissue and changes in the electrical potentials generated by the brain. It is possible that an important reorganization of the central nervous

system occurs between 4 and 10 years of age, and this reorganization may be partly responsible for the dramatic increase in the child's capacity for sustained attention.

In the next section we shall look at the instruments often used to measure cognitive functioning—**intelligence tests.**

Intelligence Measured by Intelligence Tests

The child's progress in cognitive development during the preschool years is usually measured by standardized intelligence tests. Such tests yield a score, the IQ (intelligence quotient), which is commonly considered an index of intellectual ability. (For further discussion of IQ, see Chapter 8.) By and large, the items in these tests measure language acquisition and comprehension, immediate memory, perceptual organization, reasoning, and problem solving.

Most of these tests are heavily dependent on language. But preschool children, especially 2- and 3-year-olds, are not yet in full command of the language. Consequently, language cannot be used as the sole measure of intelligence. So how can we measure what a preschool child can do? How can we determine the level of cognitive functioning in a variety of areas?

Tests for preverbal children (infants) are made up primarily of items measuring motor skills and sensorimotor development—for example, placing pegs in a peg board, placing blocks in a form board, building towers of cubes. As children develop greater language facility, however, it becomes possible to use tests with more items involving knowledge of words, abstractions, and problem-solving processes. By the time a child is 2 or 3 years old, the tests given to measure intelligence are composed of both motor and cognitive-verbal tasks. More and more verbal items and relatively fewer tests of sensorimotor functions are included with each succeeding year throughout the preschool period. For example, the norms for the Stanford-Binet, one of the best-known intelligence tests with both verbal and performance tasks, indicate that the average 2-year-old can do the following: place simple blocks properly in a three-hole form board; identify models of common objects, such as cup, by their use; identify major parts of a doll's body; and repeat two digits.

Tests for the 4-year-old involve much more language. Test items include naming pictures that illustrate a variety of common objects; naming objects from memory; discriminating visual forms such as squares, circles, and triangles; and defining words like *ball* and *bat*. Four-year-olds must also count four objects and repeat a ten-word sentence. (Try "I saw the girl go into the store for candy." It may be easy for you, but it is unlikely that, say, a 2- or 3-year-old could repeat a sentence that long.)

Numerous factors influence scores on intelligence tests: genetic makeup, parental stimulation of intellectual achievement, cultural opportunities, and motivation to do well in school or on tests (which are made up of items that resemble school tasks). It is now generally acknowledged

The child's progress in cognitive development during the preschool years is usually measured by standardized intelligence tests.

that many tests of intelligence are biased toward the middle class: that is, the experiences and background of the middle-class child give him an advantage over the lower-class child in responding to the content of the test. One of the most significant factors is the child's language skills.

Because intelligence tests are heavily weighted with language, children who have achieved high levels of language skills tend to do well on these tests; others do not. A culturally deprived or disadvantaged preschool child is likely to be deficient in language skills, and consequently he or she may not do well in intelligence tests. For example, black children from urban ghettos are often at a disadvantage because their use of language may differ from that used in the intelligence tests. It is interesting to note that black and white babies 40 weeks of age did not differ significantly in their scores on infant intelligence tests (largely motor tasks) but that the white group scored 16 points higher, on the average, in intelligence (largely verbal) test scores at the age of 3 (21).

Since language skills are obviously an important part of the usual IQ scores, in the next section we will look at some of the conditions affecting the development of language and cognition.

CONDITIONS AFFECTING LANGUAGE AND COGNITION

What are the factors that affect the development of language and cognition? Home environment is, of course, one important influence on a child's development. So, too, are the values of the community in which children live. A child from an inner-city area may find that being physically skilled and strong is of more importance than using a proper verb form.

Because children from poor families tend to be less successful in school than children from middle-class families, special programs have been initiated during the last 15 years to try to improve the performance of lower-class children. But the goals of such programs are very broad: How does one change the conditions of the disadvantaged? Can an outside source be a substitute for a stimulating home environment?

A variety of tactics have been tried—some in one program, some in another. Sometimes the program leaders simply tried to enrich the experiences of the children by taking them to museums, circuses, or planetariums. Sometimes there was direct teaching of language, arithmetic, and problem-solving skills. In other programs there was emphasis on reasoning and exactness of language expression. Other programs based on Piagetian theory worked on improving physical coordination and children's ability to categorize, to understand relationships, and to solve cognitive problems.

How successful do you think such programs are? In general, the results suggest that while the child is in the program, scores on tests of cognitive abilities are higher than they are for children from the same social class who are not enrolled in such a program. But if the children

leave the program (or if it is terminated), the cognitive skills of the children who participated in the special intervention programs may decline to a level similar to that of children who never experienced the intervention. The effects of home environment are difficult to overcome. However, there are a few notable exceptions—principally where the program has been unusually intensive and comprehensive—and these demonstrate that with well-planned, intensive programs some changes can be effected.

One effective program began with an intensive effort directed at newborn infants (14, 17). Working in an inner-city ghetto in which there was a high prevalence of children with low IQ scores, the investigators chose forty mother-infant pairs, all of the mothers having IQs of 75 or less (the average IQ is 100). Each pair was randomly assigned to either the experimental or the control condition. The controls were given no special treatment, but the experimental subjects participated in a special program.

Specifically, each infant was assigned a teacher who would be in charge of her for the major part of the waking day, 5 days a week, for the first year of life. The teachers, whose educations varied from eighth grade to one year of college, were chosen for the job because they were fluent in the language of the parents and affectionate and had some experience with infants and young children. The majority of them lived in the same neighborhood as the children and thus shared a similar cultural background.

The teaching program, directed at improved cognitive and language skills, was implemented through structured learning experiences. The teachers were carefully instructed in planning and presenting relevant, integrated learning activities; their work was carefully guided and supervised.

The teachers worked in the child's home for the first 6 to 8 weeks, until the mother had enough confidence in the teacher to allow the child to go to a day-care center, where the major part of the teaching took place. The teachers maintained continuous contact with the parents, reporting on the child's progress and emphasizing the child's accomplishments and ability.

While the children were having stimulating and challenging learning experiences at the research center, the mothers were not being neglected. They were given job training, remedial education, and counseling. It was assumed that positive changes in the home environment would result from the mothers' having improved employment potential, increased earnings, and increased self-confidence.

This program had a significant positive effect. By the time the children entered school, the IQs of those in the experimental group who had experienced the intervention were about 25 points higher than those in the control group, a remarkable difference. Additionally, language development of the children in the experimental group was more advanced than that of the controls. Children in the experimental group mastered certain

grammatical forms at age 3½ that the control children did not learn until they were 5½ years old.

But even this highly successful program failed to affect some of the children. Thus, as the investigators said, it is important to note that while some families can be successfully helped by the remedial program, the program is not foolproof, for not all families can be helped.

Other successful attempts to help disadvantaged children of preschool age have focused on encouraging achievement motivation. In one study, 87 black preschool subjects who came from poverty-stricken families were studied. The subjects were, as usual, divided into experimental and control groups (16, 18).

The experimental subjects participated in a stimulating, concentrated program designed to promote stronger motivation toward achievement. The children also received instruction in the development of behaviors and characteristics correlated with achievement—persistence, ability to delay gratification, and interest in school materials such as books, puzzles, and pencils. In addition, the mothers of the experimental subjects met weekly with a specially trained teacher who attempted to make the mothers aware of children's motives and to encourage them to reward strivings for achievement.

The results of postprogram testing showed that the trained children were superior to the controls in tests of vocabulary, language ability, and reading readiness. Follow-up studies as much as 5 years later showed that the trained children retained their advantage, although, not surprisingly, the positive effects of the training were less marked than they had been earlier.

However, in other studies, the long-range results were less encouraging. While children in various enrichment programs generally show significant gains during the program, too often there is no lasting effect. In one investigation of three different types of preschool enrichment programs — structured, child-centered, or general enrichment — the gains acquired during all three programs disappeared by the time the children were in the second grade (24).

SUMMARY

1. Physical growth continues during the preschool period, skeletal, muscular, and nervous systems become more mature, and psychomotor skills increase.

2. Language skills improve during the preschool period. As the children's sentences become longer and more complex, some little words and word endings (inflections) are added — a few prepositions and articles, forms of the verb *to be*, plurals, and possessives. Although there are individual differences in the *rate* of acquisition of these grammatical forms, there is amazing uniformity in the *order* in which they emerge.

3. Although the child's improved verbal ability often enhances cognitive functions — such as memory, thinking, problem solving, and reasoning — cognitive processes are not completely dependent on language. For example, the cognitive development of a deaf child follows the same course as a hearing child's, though sometimes more slowly.

4. Preschool children are in what Piaget calls the preoperational stage. They are unable to organize symbols into firmly articulated concepts and rules, and they are unable to take another's point of view — that is, they are egocentric.

5. Cognitive competences are dependent on the nature of the problem. For example, a child's memory ability may differ for pictures, words, or numbers.

6. There are five kinds of units in cognitive activity: schemata, images, symbols, concepts, and rules. Similarly, there are five processes in-

volved in cognition: perception, memory, reasoning, reflection, and insight.

7. Tests of intelligence (IQ tests) measure language acquisition and comprehension, immediate memory, perceptual organization, reasoning, and problem solving. Most IQ tests are heavily dependent on language; thus, children who are deficient in language skills tend to score poorly on IQ tests.

8. Many programs have been designed to aid disadvantaged children who are deficient in language skills. While it is often difficult to overcome the effects of home environment, some well-planned, intensive programs have been successful in improving IQ scores of these children.

Suggested Readings

Cowan, P. A. *Piaget with feeling: Cognitive, social and emotional dimensions.* New York: Holt, Rinehart and Winston, 1978.

Garvey, C. *Play.* Cambridge, Mass.: Harvard University Press, 1978.

Ginzburg, H., & Opper, S. *Piaget's theory of intellectual development.* Englewood Cliffs, N.J.: Prentice-Hall, 1969.

Landreth, C. *Early childhood: Behavior and learning.* New York: Knopf, 1967.

Neisser, U. *Cognitive psychology.* Englewood Cliffs, N.J.: Prentice-Hall, 1967.

Tanner, J. M. Physical growth. In P. H. Mussen (Ed.), *Carmichael's manual of child psychology,* Vol. 1. New York: Wiley, 1970. Pp. 77–155.

Chapter 7

The Preschool Years: Personality Development

WHY IS ONE child a lamb and another a tiger? Why is one child happy-go-lucky and another fearful and shy? Each child has a unique personality—a particular pattern of characteristics and ways of thinking, feeling, relating to others, and adapting to the environment. The development of personality is affected by many factors, including genetically determined predispositions, the values of the social class or ethnic group to which the child belongs, rewards and punishments in the home, interactions with peers, and exposure to behavior and standards through the mass media. Obviously, an important part of personality development is the process of **socialization,** the process by which the individual acquires those behaviors, beliefs, standards, and motives that are valued by his family and the cultural group to which the family belongs.

During the preschool years, parents and siblings are generally the most influential agents of socialization. Of course, they are not the only ones; peers, teachers, neighbors, and the mass media also shape the child's behavior. But typically family members have the most contact with the child during this period, interacting intensely and frequently, regulating and modifying the child's behavior continually.

In this chapter we shall examine the process of socialization and its main areas of influence: **sex typing, aggression,** or aggressive behavior, **dependency, competence** and autonomy, **fear** and **anxiety,** and **conscience development.**

We shall first look at the three major ways in which socialization takes place: rewards and punishments, observation, and identification.

Children pick up more than just the behaviors reinforced by parents. They also learn through observation and through identifying with their parents.

HOW CHILDREN ARE SOCIALIZED

What do parents actually *do* in socializing a child? That is, how do they train their sons and daughters to adopt culturally approved behaviors, motives, and values? One method, of course, is the direct one of reward and punishment. Parents often use this method in training their children in behaviors such as sharing possessions with others or helping with household chores. For example, parents may reward their children for sharing toys with a friend and punish them for not sharing.

But children pick up more than just the behaviors reinforced by parents. They also learn through observation and through identifying with their parents. Beliefs and attitudes, for example, are often the outcomes of **identification** with parents.

Rewards and Punishments

From the start, parents train their children by rewarding or reinforcing certain responses and punishing others. Rewarded responses become stronger and are likely to appear frequently. Punished responses, on the other hand, are likely to become weaker and less frequently exhibited or perhaps disappear. Of course, physical punishment may also have other deleterious effects—making the child hostile, aggressive toward the punisher, and tense.

Figure 7.1 Photographs of children reproducing the aggressive behavior of the female model they observed on film. (From A. Bandura, D. Ross, & S. A. Ross. Imitation of film-mediated aggressive models. *Journal of Abnormal and Social Psychology*, 1963, 66(8). Copyright 1963 by the American Psychological Association. Reprinted by permission.)

If a 2-year-old boy finds that his parents are pleased when he kisses his teddy bear or hugs his grandmother, he may kiss the dog, his friends, or his brothers and sisters.

Observation

A child is likely to generalize a rewarded response and apply it to other situations. For example, if a 2-year-old boy finds that his parents are pleased when he kisses his teddy bear or hugs his grandmother, he may kiss the dog, his friends, or his brothers and sisters.

Reward and punishment can also be influential in a child's tendency to act independently. For example, children around the age of 2 spontaneously begin to try out their new abilities to get around and manipulate objects. If parents encourage the child's exploration of the surroundings and his or her attempts to act independently, then the child will be more likely to explore freely and with less inhibition. Later the child is more likely to act independently. If, on the other hand, parents punish or do not permit their child's early explorations and efforts to experiment with the environment, the youngster will later be less inclined to do things on her own. Similarly, parents who reward a child's dependent responses, such as crying, clinging, staying close to the parent, or asking for help unnecessarily, strengthen the child's tendency to be dependent (19).

Many of the child's behavioral responses—both positive and negative—are acquired by watching others' actions. Parents, in particular, serve as models of behavior, and much of a child's socialization is achieved when children imitate their parents' behavior. Nursery-school children often observe and adopt their parents' fears—notably fears of dogs, insects, and storms (7). Children may watch their parents' behavior with friends and learn patterns of social interaction—avoidance or friendliness, for example. Children may watch their parents preparing food and try to help in

Observational Learning and Imitation: A Classic Study

Albert Bandura, an outstanding social-learning theorist, and his associates have clearly demonstrated that observational learning is pervasive among children; children will imitate many responses they observe even if neither they nor the models observed are rewarded for their responses.

In one classic study, children were individually brought into a room where they observed an adult model hitting and kicking a large inflated Bobo doll, while making many verbal and motor responses the children had never seen or heard before. After the model left the room, the child was alone with the Bobo doll, and assistants, who could not be seen by the child, recorded the frequency of aggressive responses that duplicated the model's. A control group of children who had not observed the model were also left alone with the Bobo toy and their responses were also recorded.

In this situation, children who had observed the model imitated many of her aggressive responses accurately, while the controls reacted in different ways. Clearly, observers had learned new responses although no reinforcements were given to the model or to the viewer; these new responses had been acquired simply by vicarious learning—that is, observation.

A substantial body of research shows that a wide range of behaviors—including such socially positive actions as helping, sharing, and donating to charity—can be learned by observation. The models may be adults, peers, or actors viewed on the television screen. In general, children are more likely to emulate the behavior of models they regard as similar to themselves than models that differ from them. Thus, child models are more likely to be imitated than cartoon figures. Actions of models that bring rewards are more likely to be duplicated than punished or unrewarded responses.

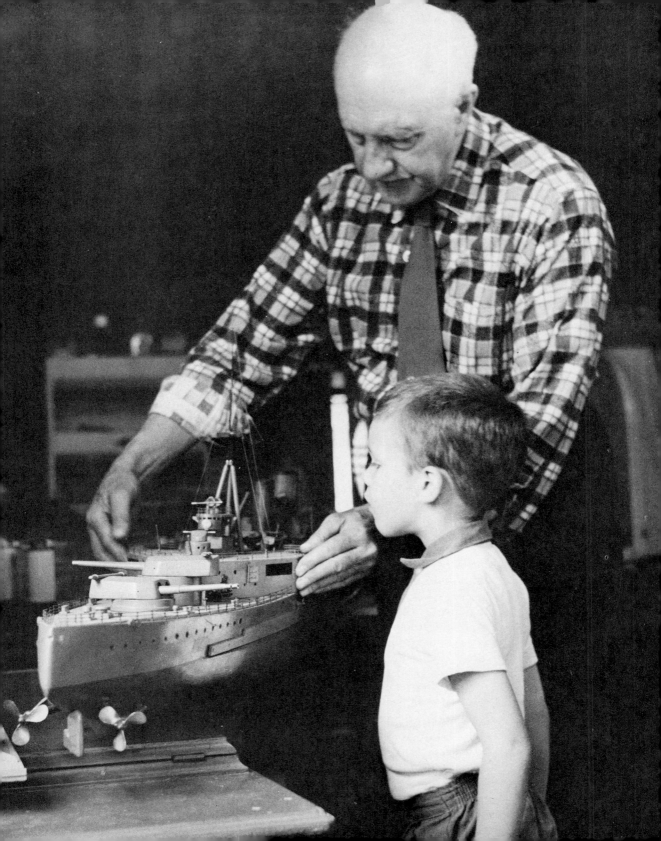

the kitchen. Or a child may see one of his parents repairing something and subsequently attempt to use a hammer.

In many cultures, boys are expected to enter their father's occupation when they grow up. From early childhood, boys in these cultures watch their father's activities as much as they can and thus gradually acquire the knowledge and skills needed for the father's work. In this situation, the process of learning through observation is combined with the father's reinforcement of correct responses and punishment of incorrect responses.

Children at nursery-school age are also likely to imitate behavior of **models** (persons) other than their parents. For example, children who observe television characters acting aggressively may imitate the aggressive actions of the television characters. Similarly, seeing television characters act in a helpful and cooperative way may lead children to be more helpful and cooperative.

Personality and social development cannot be explained simply in terms of rewards and punishment or observation of models, however. Many complex patterns of behavior are acquired without direct training or reward—without anyone's "teaching" and without the child's intending to learn. A more subtle process, called identification, is involved.

Identification

The concept of identification refers to two processes: one involves the child's belief that he or she is similar to another person and the other involves the fact that the child shares vicariously in the emotions of the other person. Both criteria must be met before we say that a child is identifying with another person. In the case of a young child, the model is most often a parent.

Identification entails more than simple learning by observation and imitation. Learning through observation does not require emotional ties with a model as identification does; a child may observe and imitate a response made by a model with whom he or she has only a casual relationship. Also, identification is a more subtle process than imitation. A 4-year-old girl may unconsciously begin to adopt the total pattern of personal attributes, motives, attitudes, and values of her mother, whereas she may consciously decide not to eat eggs simply because a friend refuses to eat them. It may take only a little effort to reverse the child's decision on eggs; responses acquired by identification, on the other hand, seem to emerge spontaneously and are relatively enduring.

Identification with a parent may be a source of security for the child, because the child may come to feel that he or she has incorporated the parent's strength and competence. The child's identification with a **nurturant** and powerful parent may be a source of pleasure and gratification, for as the child identifies with the parent, he or she shares in the parent's achievements, power, skills, and pleasures. But some parental models are inadequate, and the result of the identification process may be that the child feels anxious and insecure. A young boy who identifies with his fa-

Since children generally do resemble their parents in some physical way, it is likely that they will notice some of the special attributes they have in common with their parents.

ther will respond with the emotions of sadness and shame if the police arrest his father, because in his mind, he possesses his father's undesirable attributes. But a 5-year-old girl who identifies with her mother will feel happy and proud when her mother wins a tennis match.

What conditions are necessary for a child to identify with a parent? First, the child must perceive some similarities to the parent—particularly some special or unusual physical or psychological attributes, such as flaming red hair, a distinctive posture, or a way of walking or talking. Since children generally do resemble their parents in some physical way, it is likely that they will notice some of the special attributes they have in common with their parents.

Second, for a strong identification to develop, the parent should possess qualities that are attractive to the child. The child will identify more readily with a parent who is nurturant, warm, and loving than with one who is rejecting. Likewise, a parent who is highly competent and, in the child's view, powerful will be a more likely model for identification than a parent who seems inadequate and powerless.

What about sex? Does a girl always identify with her mother and a boy with his father? Chances are that if both parents are nurturant and competent, the child will perceive certain similarities with both parents and hence will be likely to identify somewhat with each. Typically, however, the child perceives greater similarity to the parent of the same sex, for they are more obviously alike in dress, hair style, and genital anatomy, and will therefore identify more strongly with this parent. Such identifications are frequently reinforced by others. A boy may be told he is just like his father; a girl may be told she has her mother's smile.

Children can strengthen their feelings of identification through their own behavior. That is, once the process of identification has started, the child will try to increase the similarity to the parent by adopting more of the model's behaviors and characteristics. For example, a young girl may unconsciously pick up her mother's distinctive way of talking as part of the identification process. Then, as she becomes more similar to her mother because they talk alike, her identification with her mother becomes stronger.

The three basic processes that contribute to socialization—training by reward and punishment, observation of others, and identification—are not independent. In many cases, a child does not pick up a behavior solely through reward and punishment or just by watching another person exhibit the behavior. Rather, the three processes interact and supplement each other. For example, a little girl hands her younger brother a toy he cannot reach himself; her mother hugs her. By doing this the mother is essentially using all three processes. First, she has rewarded the child's helpfulness. Second, she has served as a model for affectionate behavior (observation). Third, through her nurturance, she has increased the child's tendency to identify with her.

Sometimes learning through one process (say, observation) may conflict with what is taught through another method (say, reward and punishment). A child may be punished for saying four-letter words heard on the playground, but hearing mother or father say the same words every time the car is stopped in traffic is also likely to have an effect on the child's behavior.

In the following sections, we will look at the development of certain personality characteristics and social responses that emerge during early childhood and that change as a consequence of the socialization processes discussed above. The first area we shall discuss is that of **sex typing**.

SEX TYPING

One area in which socialization plays a major role is in the development of what is called "sex-appropriate" behavior. The use of such a term is also taboo in today's increasingly nonsexist society, and within a dynamic, technologically advanced society such as ours, the ideas of sex-appropriate behavior are themselves subject to change over time. In America, where in recent years there have been many strong and successful pressures for revision of traditional, culturally prescribed definitions of sex roles, old sex-role differentiations have been breaking down, notably in the areas of education and work. Women today are trained for and undertake tasks that ten years ago they would not have dared to attempt. Men, too, are finding that new areas of employment are opening for them. Nevertheless, there are still some well-established sex differences in activities, interests, abilities, and orientations in our own and all other cultures.

Of course, the definitions of sex-appropriate behavior differ from culture to culture. Weaving, cooking, and care of domestic animals are women's activities in some cultures; in others, they are men's. In most cultures, aggression, self-reliance, and independence are considered masculine attributes, while nurturance, obedience, and social (family and community) responsibility are feminine qualities. However, the women in a few cultures are typically aggressive and self-reliant and the men nurturant and obedient. This is true of the Tchambuli, a New Guinea tribe studied by Margaret Mead (14). She found that in this group, women were aggressive and dominating, while the men were emotionally dependent, nurturant, and sensitive. A short distance from the Tchambuli lived two other tribes with vastly different conceptions of sex-appropriate behavior: Among the Arapesh, both men and women were passive and gentle, while among the Mundugumor, high levels of hostility and suspiciousness were characteristic of both sexes. Other cultures have still different customs. In Kenya, women work in the fields, planting and harvesting, while Guatemalan Indian women usually do not participate in agricultural work because it is considered a masculine activity. In America, notions of sex-appropriate behavior vary among regions of the country and among social classes.

In our own and other cultures, certain boy-girl differences continue to

exist for preschool children. Young boys, for example, engage in more rough-and-tumble play than do girls. In the area of cognitive skills, girls seem to be more advanced in language development than boys, at least during the first 4 or 5 years. In addition, there are other responses, characteristics, and abilities considered appropriate to the individual's sex in his or her own society. *Sex typing* is the term used to refer to the process of acquiring these responses.

What accounts for children's adopting sex-appropriate behavior patterns? Sex typing may be in large part an outcome of observation and identification with the same-sex parent. That is, through identification, the child adopts that parent's behaviors and attributes, which usually are "appropriate" for his or her own sex.

There is much evidence that identification with the same-sex parent contributes to the process of sex typing. For example, young boys who are separated from their fathers for long periods of time, and therefore may have failed to form strong father identifications, have less firmly established sex-typed responses and characteristics than boys whose fathers are continually available (13). In one study, it was found that boys separated from their fathers in early life—at age 4 or earlier—were less aggressive and less involved with competitive physical-contact games than boys who grew up with fathers present. They also tended to have a feminine pattern of test scores—that is, higher verbal than mathematical abilities. The usual masculine pattern is higher mathematical than verbal scores (4).

Identification, though, is not the only process underlying sex typing. Reinforcement also plays a major role, for parents help shape sex-typed behavior directly by encouraging and rewarding sex-appropriate responses and discouraging behavior that is not considered appropriate for the child's sex.

Parental practices that encourage sex differentiation begin in infancy. Most parents still dress boys and girls differently and give them different kinds of toys to play with. The first household tasks assigned to girls in most cultures are child-care tasks, such as looking after younger children, cleaning, and helping in the kitchen, while boys are generally given things to do outside the house. As a result, in all cultures young girls are found to be significantly more nurturant and more responsible than boys. Clearly, from early childhood on, socialization emphases vary with the sex of the child being socialized.

During the nursery-school periods, parents are likely to encourage their young sons to fight back if another child shows aggression but punish the same behavior in their daughter (19). If a girl cries after losing a game, her parents are likely to accept her reaction as appropriate but may remind their sons that "boys don't cry."

Interestingly, fathers have a tendency to differ in their treatment of sons and daughters more than mothers. When teaching a child how to solve a cognitive problem, for example, fathers of sons stressed the cognitive aspects of the situation, yet fathers of daughters emphasized the interpersonal aspects of the situation. Mothers, on the other hand, were less sex-differentiating in their emphasis on cognitive achievement (3).

Some cognitively oriented psychologists, such as Lawrence Kohlberg, have maintained that sex typing is a result of the child's knowledge of being labeled "boy" or "girl." In effect, a boy says, "I am a boy; therefore I want to do boy things" (12). Kohlberg also emphasizes a different cause and effect sequence from the one discussed previously. He believes that a boy identifies with his father because he wants to be masculine, not that a boy is masculine because he identifies with his father. In other words, he sees sex typing primarily as a cognitive process rather than a product of identification or reward and punishment; he holds that identification is a result of sex typing instead of the other way around.

But while the child's being labeled "boy" or "girl" undoubtedly plays a role in sex typing, Kohlberg's theory cannot explain why some boys are highly masculine and some feminine. All boys learn that they are "boys"; therefore differences in identification and social learning must account for the differences in masculinity and be of more importance than a simple cognitive label.

As definitions of sex roles change, many parents modify their socialization practices to "keep up with the times." In fact, because socialization practices — observation, identification, and reward and punishment — play critical roles in sex typing, parents can play a critical role in shaping the definitions of sex-appropriate behavior. Girls will become more assertive if they are rewarded for assertive responses, and boys will become more nurturant if their attempts at nurturance are encouraged. And as more boys and girls act in ways that are different from the traditional stereotypes of sex-appropriate behavior, new conceptions of sex-appropriate behavior will become apparent.

Just as parents can have a significant influence on sex typing, so too can they influence their children's aggressive behavior.

AGGRESSION

Parents in all cultures must socialize their children to exert some control over their **aggression** — that is, over their desires or tendencies to harm or injure others. But attitudes toward the expression of aggressive feelings vary from culture to culture, and consequently the socialization practices of parents vary. For example, among the American Indian tribe the Harney Valley Paiute, children's expressions of aggression are severely punished; if brothers or sisters are found fighting, the older ones are whipped, and if a child strikes a parent, the parent hits back. Children are severely punished for hurting any bird or animal. In contrast, a tribe in Brazil (the Siriono) encourages its children to fight with their fists or with bows and arrows. Among the Uktu Eskimos of Hudson Bay, parents ignore aggression. As a result, most 5-year-olds in that culture seldom express anger or aggression openly.

Age is another factor that dictates differences in the way a child expresses aggression. Two- or 3-year-olds have temper tantrums and are more likely to hit, push, and kick others than older children are. Nursery-school children are both physically and verbally aggressive toward others and are more likely than older children to take another child's toys or other possessions (6).

The form and intensity of aggressive expression also depend on conditions and events in the immediate situation, as well as on personal characteristics of the child. For example, if children feel "attacked," they will react intensely. If children are feeling irritable, or if they are dealing with pent-up hostility, they may exhibit more aggressive acts.

Past experience, too, can affect the expression of aggression. A child who has been reinforced in the past for aggressive actions or who has had opportunities to observe and imitate aggressive acts is likely to be aggressive, since that seems to be a successful method for getting one's own way. There is abundant evidence that children acquire aggressive responses by observing others behaving aggressively. The child who observes his or her mother banging things around when she loses her temper is likely to imitate this behavior. In addition, aggressive models among peers may evoke aggressive behavior, as may models on television.

But some children have strong inhibitions against the expression of their aggressive impulses, either as a result of past punishments for aggressive actions or through identification. These children are not as likely as others to be aggressive.

The reasons for expressing aggression also vary. According to one popular and well-substantiated hypothesis (the **frustration-aggression hypothesis**), aggression is a common reaction to **frustration.** In the course of growing up, children inevitably encounter many frustrations (barriers that prevent the individual from obtaining a goal or satisfying a motive). Sometimes the child's self-esteem may be threatened by another child or an adult; in other instances, a child may be physically prevented from carrying out her intentions. Such events cause the child to feel frustrated. The source of frustration is often external—for example, a parent may forbid the child to do something—but sometimes the source of frustration may be internal. For instance, a 3-year-old may want to approach and pet a big furry cat but not have the courage to do so.

The frustration-aggression link can be seen in many situations. Nursery-school children make more aggressive responses (hitting, shouting, pushing, teasing) when they are confined to a small overcrowded play area where they are more frequently interfered with and frustrated (10). Children made to feel frustrated by a puzzle they cannot solve behave more aggressively than they do ordinarily, especially if they are in a permissive situation.

The intensity of reactions to frustration is influenced by many factors, which can vary from one child to another. For example, a highly dependent boy may be intensely frustrated if separated from his mother for a short time but, being quite passive, may not feel frustrated if he is dominated by another child in play. A more independent child may not mind the mother's absence at all but may be terribly frustrated if another child takes over in a game.

Even the makeup of the child's play group can affect reactions to frustration. In one study children were frustrated while they were playing with good friends. Under these circumstances, they demonstrated socially

acceptable responses to frustration, and their play became more constructive. They became more outgoing and cooperative, joining together in expressing aggression toward the experimenter (the source of their frustration), instead of taking it out on each other (21).

Learning Aggression in the Family Setting

"An eye for an eye, and a tooth for a tooth." Though aggression is a common, "natural" response to certain kinds of situations, such as frustration, whether it is expressed freely or is inhibited is a result of socialization practices. For preschool children, the most important influence is the family, and it is obvious that children *learn* to fight back, for aggressive children generally come from families in which aggression is freely expressed. In fact, when highly aggressive problem children were studied in their family situations, it was found that all members of the aggressive child's family—parents and siblings—showed more aggressive behavior than their counterparts in normal families. Moreover, the "problem" child displayed no more aggressive responses than his or her siblings did (16).

In most cases, the aggressive behavior of the problem child was a response to aversive stimuli from other family members, such as hitting, disapproving, demanding, teasing, and ignoring—all of which could be considered frustrations. The experience in the family can be illustrated by a typical exchange: A younger sister teases her older brother. From repeated experiences, the boy knows that if he yells at her, she will stop teasing. But if she teases her brother more viciously after he yells, he may react by yelling louder, and if she goes on teasing him, he may hit her.

Among highly aggressive children, aggressive responses tended to come in bursts; that is, an aggressive response was initiated and repeated several times within a short period. One reason for this pattern is that the family interactions, as we saw above, encourage aggression. For example, members of the aggressive children's families were five times as likely as members of the normal families to respond to the child's actions in ways that maintain or escalate the level of aggression, such as teasing or frustrating the child further.

Parents, too, played a role in influencing aggressive behavior. The mothers and fathers of the problem children were inconsistent in handling their children's aggressive outbursts. On the one hand, they often reinforced aggressive actions by approving, paying attention, complying with the child's wishes, or laughing at the action. On the other hand, they sometimes punished aggressive outbursts with hard spankings. While intense punishment can be effective in reducing aggressive outbursts, it must be used consistently to be effective. It seems that the parents of problem children often threatened punishment but seldom carried out their threats; by contrast, parents of nonproblem children ordinarily carried out their threats (16). The erratic use of punishment is ineffective in reducing the problem child's aggressive behavior and in fact often serves to increase the child's ongoing aggressive behavior.

As we have seen, socialization, or child-rearing, practices have a tremendous effect on a child's personality. One area of particular interest is the child's feelings of competence and autonomy; in other words, how self-reliant is the child?

DEVELOPMENT OF COMPETENCE AND AUTONOMY

Some children are anxious to try out new skills; others would rather cling to their parents and let someone else be adventurous. The behavior of most children may fall somewhere between these two groups. The differences in these children are variations in their feelings of **competence** and **autonomy.**

There are many factors that affect the development of competence and autonomy, but one of the most important is the parents' method of child rearing. In an extensive study of the relationship between children's behavior and parental child rearing, three groups of nursery-school children

Handling Temper Tantrums

Between the ages of 18 and 36 months, children inevitably encounter numberless frustrations as they strive for autonomy and independence. An 18-month-old cannot climb a ladder to reach the candy she wants; unless her mother is very sensitive to nonverbal clues, the child may have difficulty communicating her wants or needs; something she expects to happen may not happen. Experiences like these anger the child whose motor and language abilities are still very limited. And because she has not yet developed much self-control, she may react with a temper tantrum. According to clinicians, temper tantrums are almost universal in early childhood, and they are considered pathological only if they are very severe and prolonged or if they occur too frequently.

There are no real treatments for the temper tantrum because during a tantrum the child is not accessible to persuasion or reason. Yelling at the child or striking her will not help much and is likely to prolong the temper tantrum. Furthermore, the adult serves as a model and the child may imitate the model's aggressive reaction in response to difficult problems and/or frustrations.

Clinicians recommend that adults respond to their children's temper tantrums by remaining as calm as possible and by reaching out to the child and talking to her in soothing tones, which may have a calming effect. Or the child may be carried firmly but gently to another room and left there until the tantrum has passed. This is done not as punishment but simply because there is nothing else to do. Tantrums that go unrewarded tend to subside.

Simple behavior modification techniques may be effective in reducing the frequency and intensity of tantrums that are used to control adults. For example, a 20-month-old boy succeeded in keeping one of his parents in the bedroom after he was put to bed by having a temper tantrum if the parent tried to leave. His mother decided to put an end to this tantrum behavior by removing the reinforcement. The procedure was a simple one. After putting the child to bed in a friendly and relaxing way, she left the bedroom and closed the door. The boy screamed and raged but the mother did not reenter the room. After a few days, the temper behavior was extinguished. On the tenth day the child smiled as his mother left the room, and no further tantrums were reported during the next few years.

with different personality structures were studied (1). Pattern I children were the most mature and competent. They were content, independent, realistic, self-reliant, self-controlled, explorative, affiliative, and self-assertive. Pattern II children were rated as moderately self-reliant and self-controlled but relatively discontented, insecure and apprehensive, withdrawn, distrustful, and uninterested in peer affiliation. Pattern III children were the most immature. They were highly dependent, less self-controlled and less self-reliant than the children in the other two groups, and more withdrawn, tending to retreat from novel or stressful experiences.

After the children were rated, their parents were studied. The parents were rated on four dimensions of child rearing: (1) *control*, that is, their efforts to change or modify the child's behavior; (2) *maturity demands*, that is, pressures on the child to perform at the level of his or her ability intellectually, socially, or emotionally; (3) *clarity of parent-child communication* (for example, using reason or asking the child's opinions and feelings); and (4) *parental nurturance*, including both warmth (love, caretaking, and compassion) and involvement (praise and pleasure in the child's accomplishments). The "scores" of the parents of the three groups of children are shown in Figure 7.2.

The parents of mature, competent children were firm yet loving and supportive. These are classed as **authoritative parents;** they are warm parents who communicate well with their children. While they respect

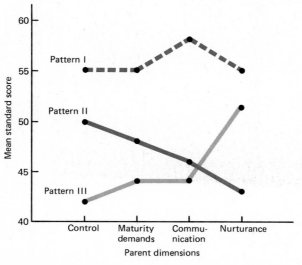

Figure 7.2   Parent dimension scores from the home-visit data for three patterns of child behavior. (From D. Baumrind. Child care practices anteceding three patterns of preschool behavior. *Genetic Psychology Monographs*, 1967, *75*, 43–88. By permission of The Journal Press.)

their youngsters' independence and decisions, at the same time they are controlling and demand mature behavior from their children. Such parents generally hold firm in their own positions, being clear and explicit about the reasons for their directives. They do a great deal of "teaching" — for example, helping the child understand that Mother does not want children playing with her guitar because it can easily be broken. Authoritative parents encourage independence in decision making; for example, they may trust the child not to open the guitar case, and they reward the child with love and approval for not bothering the guitar. These warm and nurturant yet firm parents are excellent models of competent and mature behavior.

Children who were somewhat self-reliant but relatively discontent, withdrawn, and distrustful usually had parents who used power freely and were less warm and nurturant with their children. These parents are called **authoritarian parents** (not to be confused with *authoritative,* the category discussed above). Authoritarian parents are less likely to explain parental decisions or rules and do not encourage their children to express disagreement with parental decisions (1).

The least mature children—those who were least self-reliant, explorative, and self-controlled—tended to have permissive parents. Although such parents may be warm, they make few demands for mature behavior and pay little attention to training for independence and self-reliance. This inattention to discipline is reflected in their children, who tend to appear immature and lacking in independence and self-reliance.

Thus, it is clear that authoritative parents—those who are warm and loving, yet rational, firm, and consistent in demands for mature behavior —are most effective in promoting competence and autonomy. They do not dominate their children but use reason. They give their children the opportunity for independent actions and decision making, and encourage self-assertion and responsible behavior. Because they are warm and nurturant, and explain their reasons for their standards of behavior, they serve as effective models for responsible behavior. Authoritarian and permissive parents, on the other hand, are not effective models, since they don't provide children with the knowledge and experience they need if they are to learn to act in independent, self-reliant ways.

Parental influence can be significant in still another area of development: childhood **fear** and **anxiety.** In the next section you will see that parents can have a positive effect in helping children overcome their fears, or they can have a negative influence—they can be the source of their children's fears.

FEAR AND ANXIETY

Fear and anxiety are two emotions common to all of us in one form or another. Just the mention of the words may call up a physiological or psychological response—a tightening of the stomach muscles, a sense of mental oppression. Although the nature of fear and anxiety may change with age, preschool children are by no means immune to this psychological problem.

Both fear and anxiety are basically anticipations of danger or of an unpleasant event, feeling, or reaction. While they are, of course, related emotions, there is a distinction between the two. Fear is generally considered the more specific emotion, a response to a particular real danger such as a wild animal or a fast-moving vehicle. Anxiety is "free-floating," not having a realistic, objective focus. However, it is often difficult to distinguish between fear and anxiety in a young child because the child does not differentiate between real and imagined dangers (5). To a child, the "bogey-man" in the dark may seem to be a real and present threat.

Preschool Children's Fears

Every child has fears, and some of these fears serve a very healthy function. Some of them are important in self-preservation. Being afraid of highways, fierce animals, dangerous tools, and moving automobiles, for example, can literally save a child's life. Think of what might happen to a child who is not afraid of such things. Moreover, fears may serve as a basis for learning. A child who is afraid of speeding cars will be likely to learn the rules of crossing streets safely.

While there are healthy fears, overly intense and very frequent fear reactions can interfere with the development of stable or constructive behavior. A child who constantly cries, withdraws, cringes, protests, appeals for help, or clings to parents is not on the way to competent behavior. But for most normal children, the frequency and intensity of fear reactions, such as crying, panic, and withdrawal, decrease between ages 2 and 5.

What, besides the proverbial "bogeyman," are preschool children likely to be afraid of? At first, around age 2, they are afraid of actual objects or unusual stimuli, such as strange objects, settings, or people. But as the children get older, they fear anticipated, imaginary, or supernatural dangers, such as the possibility of accidents, darkness, dreams, and ghosts. Apparently, the children's cognitive development—their increased understanding of the world and greater use of representations and symbols—influences their emotional reactions, enabling them to generate their own fears.

Intelligence does, in fact, influence the development of fears. Children with higher IQs generally have more fears than children with lower IQs. Apparently, intelligent children are able to recognize potential danger more readily than duller children, have livelier imaginations, and probably think and reflect more about dangers (9).

Childhood fears are highly unpredictable, and at all age levels, there are marked individual differences in susceptibility to fear. One child may be terribly frightened by cats; another child may love them. But even a child who is frightened of cats may not display this fear in every situation. Sometimes the child may scream, but sometimes he or she may just ignore the cat.

A year or two may bring significant changes in an individual child's fears. A child may drop some fears, only to develop others. Many new fears seem to grow out of older ones. For example, a child who had been afraid of a balloon used in administering anesthetic during an operation became fearful of all balloons and objects resembling them. Another child, frightened by a mouse running through his bedroom, began to fear all scratching sounds at night. Apparently, fears spread by the process of stimulus generalization. The child may think, "If that balloon made me feel sick and hurt, then this one will, too," or "That other scratching sound was a mouse. This sound may be one, too."

Nightmares and Sleep Disturbances

Not all childhood fears, anxieties, and troublesome feelings emerge during the child's waking state. Some may come out in nightmares or "bad dreams." Nightmares tend to reach a peak between ages 4 and 6, though many older children continue to have nightmares (11). A parent need not be overly concerned about a child's having occasional bad dreams, or even nightmares, although they indicate the presence of at least temporary anxiety and conflict in the child. However, when a child has severe or frequently recurring nightmares, an effort should be made to determine the source of the child's anxiety and relieve it. Often the content of nightmares provides some clue as to their source. For example, a child who repeatedly dreams that his father has been killed and wakes up terrified may have a deep fear of losing his father. But dream interpretation is not easy, for the child above may well be feeling the reverse: He may be feeling hostile toward his father but be repressing those feelings because admitting them to himself would be too anxiety-producing.

Sleepwalking. As a child, did you ever wake up, only to find that you were not in your bed but down the hall? Sleepwalking is another sleep disturbance that occurs more frequently among children than adults. A child who has been put to bed and has gone to sleep reappears later in the living room or is found wandering down a hall or across the lawn, eyes open, and seems at least partially to comprehend the situation. However, it is evident that the child is not really awake and alert (10). The child may be put back to bed and not remember, or only vaguely remember, the event the next morning.

Children who are generally suggestible, histrionic (dramatic in their behavior), and emotionally immature appear somewhat more likely than other children to exhibit sleepwalking. As in the case of other sleep disturbances, the seriousness of sleepwalking depends on its frequency and severity (11).

Sleepwalking behavior is often referred to as a "dissociative" state, for only a portion of the child's full stream of consciousness is operative, and she is only partially responsive to stimuli in the surroundings. It appears as though the child is responding to some need during sleepwalking—for example, looking for something about which she is concerned—or escaping from an anxiety-producing situation. Of course, the anxiety (and responding to it) disturbs sleep, but the child is protecting herself from a full awareness of this need by not wakening to full consciousness. It is in this respect that sleepwalking bears some resemblance to other "dissociative" states, such as amnesia or hypnosis.

Relationships Between Parents' and Children's Fears

Most fears are acquired. That is, children are not born with fears; they learn them. And, since the young child's most important learning occurs in the home, it is not surprising that children show a strong tendency to adopt their parents' fears. This is most clear in the cases of fears of dogs, insects, and storms (7).

Children pick up their parents' fears through the mechanisms of identification or observational learning. As you will remember, these are the same mechanisms active in socialization for values, and they are powerful tools for teaching. Childhood fears learned this way are particularly long-lasting, for the child is not likely to learn any other way of behaving toward, say, dogs, than to be afraid. If, for example, the mother is afraid of dogs, she will find it difficult to convince her son that there is nothing to fear. Consequently, the child will learn only avoidance and withdrawal responses when in the presence of dogs. Naturally, such responses are reinforced, because they reduce tension in the child by removing him from the object of his fear (the dog). Consequently, the child tends to repeat these responses and thus does not learn new, more mature reactions. For these reasons, fears that children share with their parents are particularly resistant to treatment and extinction.

Techniques of Eliminating Fears

Suppose a child is afraid of the dark. What do you think is the best method for helping the child outgrow this fear? With very young children, simply explaining that nothing mysterious or scary happens when the bedroom light is turned out is not enough, for these children may not yet have learned to associate words with their fear of the dark. It is better to couple the verbal explanation with physically encouraging the child to confront the fearful situation gradually. The parent's calming presence and gentle words of explanation serve as a reward for the child's inhibiting of the fear responses, so that new, more mature responses to the fear-provoking stimulus can be learned (7).

Mary Poppins' advice, "Just a spoonful of sugar makes the medicine go down," can be applied to fear reduction, for another method of eliminating a fear is to pair the feared stimulus with something pleasant. For example, youngsters afraid of the dark were encouraged to become active explorers in dark places where they found valuable prizes (8). Because the children looked forward to finding the prizes, this conditioning technique weakened the connections between the feared stimulus (the dark) and the anxiety and fear responses. The children were, in effect, learning new responses to the fear-eliciting stimulus. As the children grow older and better able to use language, or verbal mediators, pairing the above conditioning techniques with verbal explanations becomes more effective.

Anxiety

Like fear, anxiety may serve constructive purposes, acting as a spur to creativity, problem solution, and inventive accomplishments. Can't you recall feeling vaguely anxious at some point and reducing your feelings of

A Case of Behavior Modification

A nursery-school teacher served as a behavior therapist in the case of 4-year-old Ann, a social isolate at a university nursery school. When she first came to school she was verbal, intelligent, well coordinated, and creative; hence she readily gained the attention of the teachers. But she seldom made contact with children or responded to their attempts to play with her; she preferred to interact with adults.

As time passed Ann became more isolated and withdrawn, complaining at length about invisible sores and abrasions, speaking in such a low voice that it was difficult to understand her, and spending most of the time simply standing and looking. To stimulate Ann's interactions with other children and to reduce attention seeking from adults, the teacher began to reward her with maximum attention whenever she played with another child, and withdrew attention from her when she was isolated or attempted to interact with adults alone.

Ann's behavior was meticulously observed for 5 days before the "therapy" began and throughout the therapy period. During the 5-day "baseline" period, Ann spent a little more than 10 percent of her nursery-school time interacting with other children, and about 40 percent with adults. For at least half the time she was essentially alone, either quiet or playing by herself (see graph).

A marked change was apparent even on the first day of therapy. As the graph shows, Ann spent 60 percent of her time that day in active play with other children, while adult-child interactions, which were not rewarded, decreased to less than 20 percent. High levels of interaction with other children were maintained with little variation throughout the 6-day training period.

Then, to test the effects of reinforcement, the procedures were reversed after the sixth day of the training period. Beginning on this day, solitary pursuits and interactions with adults were rewarded by adult attention, while interactions with children were disregarded and ignored. Under these conditions, Ann's previous behavior reappeared immediately (see graph), and for the next 5 days she averaged less than 20 percent of her time in interaction with children and about 40 percent with adults.

Then a final shift was made, with adult attention and reward again contingent upon interaction with children. The change in Ann's behavior was immediate and dramatic. For the final reinforcement period of 9 days, interactions with children rose to about 60 percent of the total time in school, while interactions with adults decreased to about 25 percent.

Six days after the last reinforcements had been given and for a long time afterward, Ann's behavior was fairly stable; about 60 percent of her time was spent with children and less than 15 percent with adults. Moreover, the teacher reported that her complaining, babyish behavior disappeared, and she became a happy, confident, sociable member of the school group.

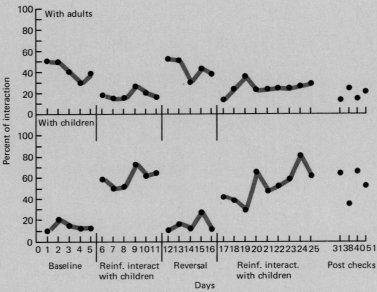

Percentages of time Ann spent in social interaction during approximately 2 hours of each morning session. (From K. Eileen Allen, Betty Hart, Joan S. Buell, Florence R. Harris, & M. M. Wolf. Effects of social reinforcement on isolate behavior of a nursery school child. *Child Development, 35,* No. 2,310. Copyright 1964 by The Society for Research in Child Development, Inc.)

anxiety by attacking their source—for example, by finishing a required paper and meeting the deadline? On the other hand, anxiety is sometimes emotionally crippling, tying the individual in knots and rendering him ineffectual and desperate.

What causes anxiety in a preschool child? Certainly there are no term papers to cause anxiety. But a preschool child may become anxious about expressing aggressive, sexual, or dependent feelings. The arrival of a new baby can be threatening to a child, or the child may become apprehensive about real or imagined rejection by parents or peers.

Behavioral Correlates of Anxiety. Anxiety affects the social behavior and the cognitive functioning of preschool children. However, it is often

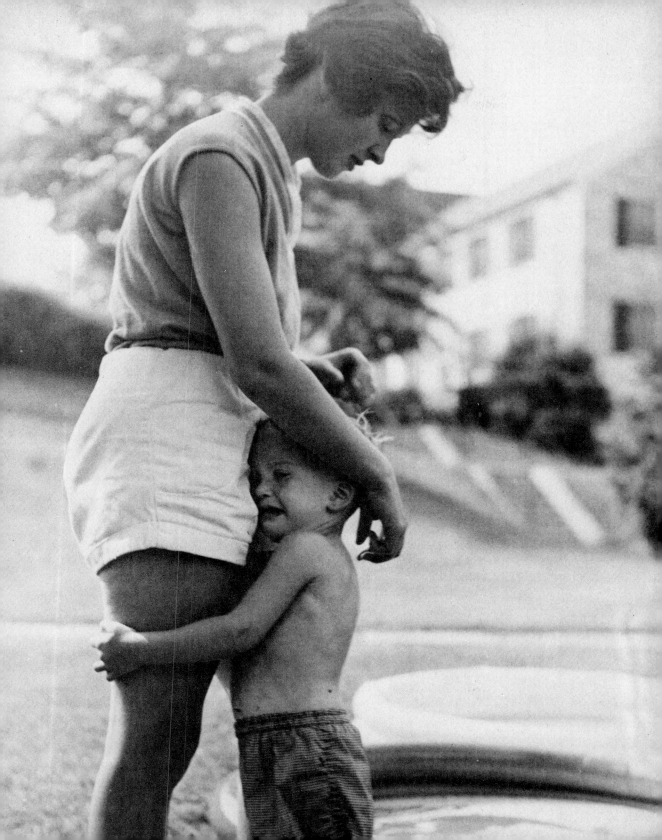

difficult to assess the degree of a preschool child's anxiety objectively, for the assessment usually depends on observations of behavior. Still, some generalizations can be made. High levels of anxiety among nursery-school children, as judged by their responses in a strange new room, were found to be associated with frequent dependency reactions. The children displayed both active (attention- and help-seeking) and passive (touching, clinging) forms of dependency (17).

Most of the studies on the effects of anxiety on cognitive functioning have used schoolchildren as their subjects, but the findings are probably applicable to nursery-school children as well. A moderate degree of anxiety may help learning if the task is simple and the correct response is one the child already knows well. But if anxiety is intense and the task to be learned is complex and difficult or involves responses the child is unable to make, then anxiety interferes with learning. Particularly susceptible to the negative effects of anxiety are verbal learning tasks and the use of abstract concepts. Highly anxious children make more irrelevant, and even interfering, responses than children low in anxiety.

Parent-Child Relations and Anxiety. Unfortunately, intense and frequent anxiety among young children often has its root in early parent-child relationships. When parents are too demanding of their child and inflict severe punishment and restrictions, when they evaluate a child's behavior and accomplishments harshly and negatively, or when they are inconsistent in their treatment of the child, the child is likely to experience anxiety. When parents abuse their children, the anxiety generated by harsh parents may turn into a genuine fear.

Child Abuse

Parents who use excessive physical force on a child are often using the child as an outlet for expression of their own deep-seated anger, feelings of frustration, and unhappiness. They are reacting to the intolerable conditions of their own lives and releasing their hostility on the child. Much remains to be learned about the factors that increase the probability that a parent will abuse a child, but it has been frequently noted that abusing parents were themselves very frequently abused or neglected as children (20). Most child-abusing parents (about 70 percent) are mothers—often teenage mothers—and their targets are usually their sons (15). Any serious stress—such as trouble in the marriage, disobedient children, inability to care for the child properly, unemployment, job dissatisfaction, or poor housing—can make the parent feel frustrated and therefore can contribute to the likelihood of child abuse. Abusing parents tend to have exaggerated and unfulfilled dependency needs, and they expect the new baby to love them. This is especially true in cases of infant abuse (children under 1 year of age). These people are typically naïve about how much care a newborn baby demands, and the stress builds up.

Abusing parents usually seem to be social isolates. They maintain very few personal friendships or relationships outside the immediate family. They also tend to impose this kind of isolation on their children, forbidding them to participate in recreation activities, such as organized parties. Consequently, the children find it difficult to establish normal friendships, and they, too, are likely to become, and remain, social isolates.

Child abuse is generally the outcome of an interactive process between the parents' treatment of the child and the child's behavior. Abusing parents are generally inconsistent in their discipline. Because of the parent's failure to establish firm guidelines, the child will not develop guidelines for his or her own behavior, and is likely to misbehave. The situation can escalate: The child misbehaves, the parent punishes, the child

Child Abuse

Drs. Henry and Ruth Kempe, of the National Center for Child Abuse in Denver, have had long experience with the detection and treatment of child abuse. They point out that once a case of child abuse has been identified, medical staff and social workers need some means of assessing the likelihood of future abuse by parents. They report that the following checklist of factors in the parents' background and behavior can predict that risk with a high degree of accuracy:

1. As a child was the parent repeatedly beaten or deprived?
2. Does the parent have a record of mental illness or criminal activities?
3. Is the parent suspected of physical abuse in the past?
4. Is the parent suffering lost self-esteem, social isolation, or depression?
5. Has the parent experienced multiple stresses, such as marital discord, divorce, debt, frequent moves, significant losses?
6. Does the parent have violent outbursts of temper?
7. Does the parent have rigid, unrealistic expectations of the child's behavior?
8. Does the parent punish the child harshly?
9. Does the parent see the child as difficult and provocative (whether or not the child is)?
10. Does the parent reject the child or have difficulty forming a bond with the child?

Ruth S. and C. Henry Kempe. *Child Abuse.* Cambridge, Mass.: Harvard University Press, 1978.

misbehaves again, and the parent will be provoked to punish the child severely, justifying the punishment by blaming the child for "driving me to it." While it is often true that the child did misbehave, the reason for the child's behavior lies with the parent's treatment of the child, so actually the parent is responsible.

Along the same lines, another factor contributing to child abuse is that the child victim of abuse is likely to become a highly aggressive individual, for physical punishment by parents is often associated with aggression in children. Therefore, again there is an escalation effect: The parents punish the child aggressively, the child responds aggressively, the parents punish the child for the aggressive response, and so on.

In addition to parents being annoyed or frustrated by the child's misbehavior or resistance to discipline, other characteristics or behaviors of the child may irritate the parents, driving them to abuse the child. Sadly, they may even resent the child's physical unattractiveness or demands for care, and may release their frustration by abusing their child. Infants with very low birth weight are frequent targets of abuse, perhaps because they cry and fuss more and require greater care (more frequent feedings and special handling) than other infants. Also, because of their poor health, these infants may have been separated from their mother for long periods immediately after birth, and thus a strong mother-child attachment, which is ordinarily a deterrent of abusive behavior, may not have been established.

Fortunately, the majority of parents are not child abusers, and their influence results in fairly normal, well-adjusted children. An important area of parental influence in the development of the preschool child's personality is that of **conscience development.**

CONSCIENCE DEVELOPMENT

The preschool years are important ones, for it is during this time that children begin to develop a conscience, or superego. By identifying with their parents and striving to be similar to them, children take on parental values, attitudes, and standards of conduct—they learn "right" and "wrong." In most cases, their parents' values and attitudes are also the rules and standards of the society and cultural group. Children apply these standards to their own conduct, feeling guilty and anxious if they do not follow them, even punishing themselves. In effect, they acquire a built-in or internal monitor that judges and regulates their behavior.

The first signs of conscience development generally become evident in the second year, when children acquire specific prohibitions against specific acts. "Don't touch the books." "Don't open the cabinet." Gradually, the child internalizes these prohibitions, and, with age, the child's conscience becomes less simplistic and encompasses more idealized standards—including not just the "do nots," but also the conceptions of what one *should* do. Not only does the child refrain from hitting her little brother; she also exhibits positive behavior—she acts in kind, considerate ways. Other behavioral manifestations of conscience development in preschool children are being honest, obeying rules and regulations, resisting temptations to lie, cheat, or steal, and considering the rights and welfare of others.

Conscience development is at least partly a function of a child's increased cognitive functioning. That is, as a child becomes capable of understanding and comprehending more, her standards of behavior are likely to change, to go beyond simple prohibitions such as "don't hit your brother." The child becomes aware of the broader applications of moral values and standards, realizing, for example, that most living things deserve to be treated kindly. But, as we shall see in the next section, a child who acknowledges these standards does not always act in accordance with them. A child's commitment to values depends on other factors, such as the strength of parental identification and the probability of experiencing guilt reactions for violations of these standards.

Many studies show that a child's adoption of parental values and standards is fostered by parental warmth and love (2). This seems reasonable for two reasons. First, we know that conscience development involves the process of parental identification, and we already know that identification is strongest when the parent-child relationship is warm and nurturant (see pp. 203–205). Thus, a child who identifies strongly with a parent will, of course, be quick to adopt the parent's standards of behavior. The second reason is that conscience development also involves fear of loss of love or approval. Obviously this factor is related to a warm, loving relationship. Most children have at least some anxiety over possible loss of love from their parents and take on the standards of their parents at least partly in order to keep that anxiety low and under control. But whether loss of love is important depends on whether there is any love there in the first place. In other words, a child who does not feel strongly loved by his parents will hardly fear withdrawal of love (2).

Clearly, the standards of parents themselves and the nature of parent-child relationships govern the strength of a child's developing conscience. Ideally, it seems that normal conscience development in the child is facilitated under the following conditions: (1) the parent's own conscience and moral standards are mature and reasonable and not overly strict, harsh, and inflexible, and (2) the child's adoption of the parent's standards is based on positive identification and modeling.

The development of conscience in children may proceed normally, but children do not always act in accordance with their moral beliefs and judgments; that is, they do not always exhibit prosocial behavior. In the next section we shall look at the factors that influence this behavior.

Prosocial Behavior

Prosocial behavior is, basically, "looking out for the other guy." These moral social actions include honesty, generosity, kindness, **altruism,** obedience to rules and regulations, resistance to temptations to cheat and

lie, and consideration of the rights and welfare of others. As you might expect, parents have a strong influence on the development of prosocial behavior. They serve as models for the child, and so if they are generous and nurturant, chances are the child will observe these qualities and adopt them.

Obviously, the mechanism of identification is influential, for the child who identifies with his parent will tend to adopt the behavior of the parent, whether that behavior is prosocial or not. "Do as I say, not as I do" is not an effective philosophy for parents trying to encourage prosocial behavior in their children. As one study showed, generous boys (those who shared many of the candies they had won in a game with friends) perceived their fathers as much more generous, sympathetic, compassionate, and nurturant than did boys who were unwilling to share their winnings. Thus, we can infer that warmth and nurturance encourage strong identifications and consequently adoption of the parents' generosity and sympathy (18).

Modeling is also effective in encouraging altruistic (helping) behavior, and the most effective models are warm and nurturant adults who are themselves altruistic. Children who were exposed to a nurturant adult who demonstrated helping behavior both symbolically (with a miniature reproduction of a scene) as well as realistically—that is, she actually helped another person in front of the children—showed a dramatic increase in helping behavior. In this experiment, after the children were exposed to helping behavior, they were taken individually to a nearby house to visit a mother and her baby. While there, they had an opportunity to help the mother by picking up a basket of spools that had spilled, or by retrieving toys the baby had dropped out of the crib. Eighty-four percent of the children who had observed a nurturant adult helped the mother, whereas only 24 percent of them had helped in similar incidents before the training. Children who had trained only in the symbolic sense—that is, they had used miniature scenes but had not seen the model demonstrate "live" altruism—showed increased altruism *only* in the miniature situations; the effects did not generalize to pictured situations or to real behavioral incidents (22).

SUMMARY

1. During a child's preschool years, the family members—parents and siblings—are generally the most influential agents of socialization, though there are other agents of socialization such as peers, teachers, and the media.

2. Children are socialized in three ways: training by rewards and punishments; observation of others; and identification. These three processes interact and supplement one another.

3. Socialization is important in the process of sex typing—the development of what is considered sex-appropriate behavior. Sex typing varies from one culture to another.

4. Aggression is another target of socialization responses, and the form and intensity of aggressive expression vary with age and culture. Aggressive children often come from families or cultures where aggression is freely expressed. According to the frustration-aggression theory, children are more likely to express aggression when they have been frustrated in some way.

5. A child's feelings of competence and autonomy are strongly affected by the parents' method of child rearing. Authoritative parents—that is, those who are firm yet loving and supportive—are most effective in promoting competence and autonomy.

6. Conscience development during the preschool years ranges from specific prohibitions against specific acts to more idealized standards of behavior such as being honest or obeying rules.

7. All preschool children have a tendency toward certain fears and anxieties, though there are of course marked individual differences. Children fear anticipated, imaginary, or supernatural dangers.

8. The prosocial (altruistic) behavior of preschool children is affected by parental models. Parents who are generous and show altruism tend to have children who are generous.

Suggested Readings

Erikson, E. H. *Childhood and society.* New York: Norton, 1950.

Kagan, J. *The growth of the child.* New York: Norton, 1978.

Lamb, M. E. *Social and personality development.* New York: Holt, Rinehart, and Winston, 1978.

Lynn, D. B. *The father: His role in child development.* Monterey, Calif.: Brooks/Cole, 1979.

Maccoby, E., & Jacklin, C. *The psychology of sex differences.* Stanford, Calif.: Stanford University Press, 1974.

Mussen, P., & Eisenberg-Berg, N. *The roots of caring, sharing, and helping: The development of prosocial behavior in children.* San Francisco: Freeman, 1977.

Part Four
Middle Childhood

Chapter 8

Physical and Intellectual Development in Middle Childhood

*T*HINK OF a child you know who is 6 years old. Now think of one who is 12. Chances are that you will have noticed many differences between the two children, in terms of both their physical development and their mental abilities. The 6-year-old, while certainly not a baby, is clearly a child, a naïve first-grader with much still to be learned and experienced. By the age of 12 however, the child has grown considerably both physically and mentally. In fact, in some ways a 12-year-old may seem to be more similar to an adult than to a child.

The 6-year-old, for example, rarely engages in "cognitive" games such as checkers or chess. Nor does the 6-year-old have a clear picture of how attractive or talented he or she is; that is, 6-year-olds have little idea of their rank among peers, while 12-year-olds are acutely aware of their relative standings on issues such as attractiveness or talent. Six-year-olds are not as likely as 12-year-olds to consider the intent behind another's actions. For example, a 6-year-old boy would probably react to a physical shove with anger, while a 12-year-old boy might try to determine if the person *accidentally* pushed him before getting angry. The basis for most of these differences is that the 12-year-old *thinks* more than the 6-year-old.

In this chapter we shall look at what happens during middle childhood (ages 6 to 12), first looking briefly at physical growth and development, and then concentrating on the child's intellectual and cognitive development. We will discuss the various cognitive processes and the way these change as the child develops, including a discussion of Piaget's theory of cognitive development. Then we will turn our attention to the concept of **intelligence** and intelligence (IQ) tests.

PHYSICAL GROWTH FACTORS DURING MIDDLE CHILDHOOD

General Trends in Physical Development

By the time their children are 6 years old, discouraged parents can breathe a small sigh of relief, for their children will not outgrow clothes quite so rapidly. Physical growth, which has been proceeding at a remarkably fast pace, has begun to slow down. The average boy of this age in America stands about 3 feet 9 inches tall and weighs about 46 pounds. The average 6-year-old girl is slightly shorter (about 3 feet 8 inches) and lighter (about 42 pounds). By age 6, the average boy has attained about 65 percent of his eventual adult height, the average girl about 69 percent. By age 12, boys and girls are almost as tall as they ever will be—boys have attained 86 percent of their adult height and girls have reached 93 percent (7, 15).

For most of middle childhood, growth in both boys and girls tends to be steady and regular, with boys remaining slightly taller and heavier. Beginning at about age 10, however, the so-called adolescent growth spurt begins in girls, but does not begin in boys till about age 12 (see pp. 333–339, Chapter 11). The result—as any children's dancing school instructor can testify—is that by age 11 girls tend to be taller than boys, and they remain so until about age 14, when boys again become—and remain—tal-

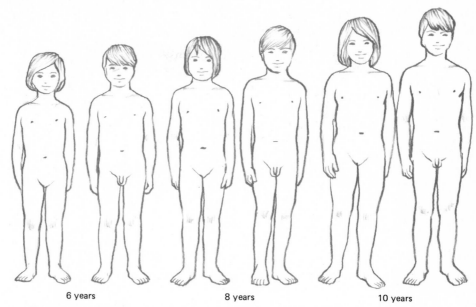

6 years   8 years   10 years

Figure 8.1 Body proportions change during middle childhood.

ler. Until about 11 years of age, boys tend to weigh slightly more than girls, but from 11 to 15, girls weigh slightly more (see Figure 8.1) (15).

Compared with infants and younger children, the school-age child's body proportions are much more like those of an adult. For example, whereas the child's head comprises one-quarter of its total body length at birth, by age 6 it is only one-sixth (in adulthood, it is one-eighth). Most of the child's changes in body proportions during middle childhood result from continued lengthening of the arms and legs.

At the same time, other less visible changes are taking place. Because of deposits of various mineral salts, especially calcium phosphate, the 12-year-old's bones are harder, but easier to break, than the 6-year-old's. At about 6 children usually lose their baby teeth, but by 12 they have most of their permanent ones. With advancing age from 6 to 12, blood pressure increases and pulse rate decreases.

No doubt when you were a child, you were told to eat your dinner so that you would grow "big and strong." It's true that during this age period growing children need more to eat and, indeed, they begin to eat more than they did at earlier ages. And as a result, they grow. Muscle tissue increases and they grow stronger. As earlier, there are still sex differences in proportion of fat and muscle tissue, with boys having more muscle mass and girls a greater proportion of body fat (15).

Although the various aspects of growth (that is, rates of development in height, weight, bone hardening, and so on) are generally correlated with one another, not all children develop in the same way or at the same rates, giving us those individual differences that make a group of people interesting. Some children grow relatively more in height, others in weight, producing variations in general body type such as "tall and slender" or "short and stocky."

Motor Development

During the middle childhood years, the child makes steady progress in physical strength and motor skills. Adult running patterns have begun to be established by age 6, although a 12-year-old can sprint more than twice as fast as a 6-year-old. A 6-year-old, unlike a younger child, is effective in catching a ball, but his or her movements tend to be rather slow and jerky; by age 12, the child's movements tend to be smooth, accurate, and well co-ordinated (3, 15). Similar steady progress takes place in throwing, jumping, and fine motor development. A 7-year-old may begin to ride a two-wheeled bicycle, but not very far; by age 8, he can ride unaided, and with considerable skill. A 7-year-old can draw a diamond neatly and form most letters. An 8-year-old can draw a house, showing a fair amount of skill.

The child's steady growth in physical strength and motor skills during middle childhood, combined with similar growth in cognitive ability, opens exciting new worlds—physically, socially, and intellectually.

COGNITIVE ACTIVITIES

Tracing the course of the child's intellectual and cognitive development during middle childhood is indeed fascinating. As you will recall, cognition involves both units and processes. The units, which were discussed in Chapter 6, are schemata, images, symbols, concepts, and rules. In this chapter we shall concentrate on the cognitive processes—**perception, memory, reasoning, reflection,** and **insight.** But first let us look at an example of the developmental changes that occur in a child's use of concepts.

Developmental Changes in Concepts

If you have ever followed the growth and development of a child from ages 5 to 12, you know that the child becomes increasingly more articulate as she gets older. Of course, there are many factors that enter into this—the child's language abilities improve, for example—but one of the most important factors is that the child's use of concepts is progressing. To study changes in a child's conceptual thinking, we need to look at three different qualities of concepts. These are *validity, status,* and *accessibility* (4).

The *validity* of a concept refers to the degree to which the child's understanding of the concept agrees with that of other children. For example, a 2-year-old's concept of the word *good* is often personal and may not be

similar to that of other 2-year-olds or adults (*good* to a 2-year-old may mean someone who doesn't wet his or her pants), though by middle childhood, the meaning of the word *good* will have become similar for all children in a society. In that sense, the concept has become more valid.

The *status* of a concept refers to its degree of articulation—the clarity, stability, and exactness of its use in thinking. How consistent is the child in using a particular concept? For example, a 3-year-old's concept of size is rather murky, whereas an 8-year-old's is clearer and more exact. That is, the concept "size" has an *enhanced status*. A 2-year-old knows that fathers are larger than babies but will not be able to use the concept of relative size in other situations — say, with animals or sets of buildings. The child has not yet learned to generalize the concept of *size* to other situations; in other words, the child has not yet fully developed the status of the concept.

Accessibility refers to how available a concept is for use in thinking and the degree to which the concept can be communicated to others. The child becomes increasingly able to talk about concepts. Ask a 5-year-old boy the meaning of the concept of goodness or of number, and he often says he doesn't know, even though his behavior may indicate that he does have some comprehension of the concepts. On the other hand, a 10-year-old can easily talk about these ideas.

Not only does a child's use of the *units* of cognition (for example, concepts) become more sophisticated with age; use of the *processes* involved in cognition also improves. As noted at the beginning of this chapter, these include perception, memory, reasoning, reflection, and insight. During middle childhood, children show considerable development in all five of these processes, and, of course, the developments are interrelated. As perception improves, memory is likely to improve. Conversely, as memory improves, and the child develops a richer base of stored knowledge, his or her initial perception will improve because objects will have more meaning; the child will know more and thus be able to perceive more accurately. Similarly, the child's competence in the processes involved in manipulating the information — reasoning, evaluation (reflection), and insight — will also increase as a result of improved perceptual and memory capabilities.

As we examine development in these areas, it is important to note the context in which the child is using the particular cognitive ability. As noted earlier (see Chapter 6), a child may show a certain capability at an early age in some situations, yet not use it in other situations for quite some time. For example, the young child may be able to remember a long list of friends but not recall the places where he met each of those friends on the last occasion.

Let's look next at the cognitive processes and how they develop during middle childhood.

Process 1: Perception

As you will remember from Chapter 6, **perception** is the process by which we detect, recognize, and interpret information from the physical stimulation around us.

Young children are surprisingly good at inferring an object from very little information. Designs like those illustrated in Figure 8.2 were shown to both American children and Mayan Indian children growing up in isolated rural villages. Both groups had no trouble guessing that the top two pictures illustrated fish.

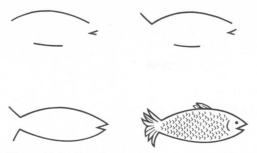

Figure 8.2 Test items shown to children who had to guess the object from its incomplete form.

Several important changes in the nature of perception occur between early childhood and adolescence. Because the child knows more about the world, he or she is able to make a more specific search, to know more about what he or she wants to or is likely to perceive. For example, a child in the woods who sees some branches move knows that animals can make branches move. Furthermore, the amount of noise or movement can help the older child make a more specific search; for example, if many branches move, an older child will look for a deer, rather than a squirrel, for he knows that deer are larger than squirrels. Hence, because the older child knows what he is looking for, perception will be faster, more efficient, and, on the whole, more accurate.

One aspect of perception that improves with age is selective attention. This is the ability to listen to a variety of sounds and perceive them separately, or to look at a number of stimuli and perceive them separately. Selective attention shows rapid development between ages 5 and 7.

Age, however, is not the only factor that affects a child's ability to perceive one stimulus separately from a group. The capability of selective attention is related, in part, to the child's expectations. For example, if a child expects a particular sound to occur, it will be easier for the child to detect that sound accurately when it does occur than if she did not expect it.

One experiment demonstrated the effects of both age and the preparation factor. In this experiment, two loudspeakers were used, one with a picture of a woman's face on the front, the other with a picture of a man's face. Each child listened to a man's voice and a woman's voice simultaneously speaking two-word phrases (for example, the man's voice might say "dog eat" while the woman's voice might say "big light"). After hearing the two voices, the child was asked to report what was said. Sometimes the child was asked for the message from the man, sometimes for the message from the woman. Older children were more capable of reporting the

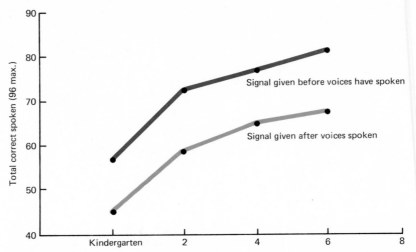

Figure 8.3 Differences in amount of message reproduced as a function of whether the child was told to attend to the voice before or after he or she heard it. (From E. E. Maccoby. Selective auditory attention in children. In L. P. Lipsitt & C. C. Spiker, Eds., *Advances in child development and behavior.* New York: Academic Press, 1967. P. 117.)

words accurately from either voice. However, all children, no matter what their age, improved considerably if they knew before hearing the two voices which one they would be asked to report (see Figure 8.3). Having a preparatory set—that is, knowing whether to listen for the man's voice or the woman's voice—was a definite advantage (16).

Further progress is made during middle childhood in the area of memory. First let us look at what memory is and how it works; then we shall examine the developmental changes that occur.

Process 2: Memory

Sometimes it seems that children delight in letting you know what a vast amount of information they can remember; at other times, their lack of memory is terribly frustrating. They can remember the way to every ice cream store in town but can't recall where they left their slippers. The development of memory during middle childhood is a fascinating process.

There are two different ways to test for information that has been registered and stored. One method is called **recall;** the other is called **recognition.** The recall method requires the child to retrieve all the requested information from storage in memory; in the recognition method the child is given information and only has to decide whether that information matches some experience that was registered in the past. For example, in the recall method, a child may be asked to tell what a shilling is or to give George Washington's birthday. Using the recognition method, the child may be asked whether a shilling is a French or British coin or whether Washington's birthday is in February or July.

As you might suspect, most of the time recognition memory is far superior to recall memory. Recalling a bit of information is a more complicated mental process than simply recognizing it. For example, a child who is asked to name all the children in her class may find the task complicated because the names of other children she knows get in the way. Also, recalling all 20 names may exhaust her. But if a list of names is given and all the child must do is decide which children on the list are in the class, then the task is much easier.

Three Kinds of Memory. Memory can be classified according to how long the information lasts. *Sensory memory* refers to the fleeting and unconscious representation that remains for less than a second after a person has looked at or heard something. *Short-term memory* refers to the awareness of information one has just perceived and usually lasts for about 30 seconds. A person uses short-term memory to recall a new telephone number long enough to dial it. *Long-term memory* refers to the permanent or nearly permanent registration of information. Names of friends or important experiences are in long-term memory.

As we have indicated earlier, there is no general memory ability. Rather, children differ in their ability to recall different kinds of information. Some are very good at remembering sentences, words, and other verbal information; others are better at remembering pictures or specific scenes. One demonstration of this principle is seen in a study of Indian children growing up in a small town in the Guatemalan highlands (24). Nine-year-old children were each given four memory tests: two involving recognition and two involving recall. Moreover, two of the tests were verbal and involved memory for sentences, while two were visual and involved three-dimensional scenes (see Figure 8.4). The results showed that children who have a good memory for visual scenes do not necessarily have a good memory for sentences.

Furthermore, cultural factors apparently have some sort of effect on memory ability, too. In one study, a group of American children and a group of Guatemalan children were shown photographs of single objects or scenes. Then the children were shown the original photograph paired with one of three transformations—either an object was added to the scene, the perspective of the photograph was changed, or the objects or their parts were rearranged. The American children were better at recognizing additions or perspective changes than rearrangements, while the Guatemalan children recognized all three—addition, perspective changes, and rearrangements—equally well (21). These results imply that it is dif-

(a)

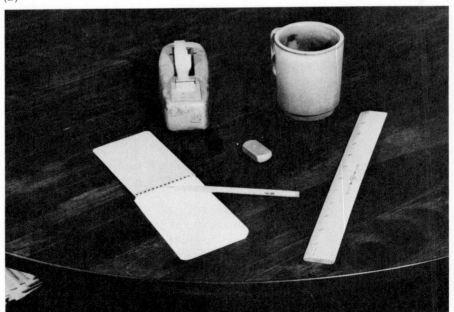

(b)

Figure 8.4 Examples of the kinds of photographs used to test memory. Children would first be shown photograph (a). Then they were shown a second photograph, in which an object was added to the scene (b), the perspective of the photograph was changed, or the objects or their parts were rearranged. (Michel Craig.)

ficult to discover general principles applicable to memory in all circumstances; principles may vary with the content to be remembered.

Developmental Changes in Memory. As children grow older, their ability to remember information improves. One factor that is bound to make remembering easier is that as children grow their knowledge base becomes greater. As a result, it is easier to code the information that has to be remembered. For example, it would be easier for you to remember, "bear, tree, woods" than to remember "plax, siret, emir" because you know the meaning of the first set of words. A child who does not know the meaning of a word or object may have difficulty registering it initially and therefore have trouble recalling it later.

Second, as children get older they are more likely to use **strategies** to help code and store information. Strategies useful in memory include *organization, rehearsal,* and *association.* Organization — grouping objects or bits of information to be remembered — makes the process of memory much simpler. For example, if asked to remember nine digits — say, 731246598 — older children will group the numbers into triplets (731 246 598) to make remembering easier. Younger children do not often spontaneously use the grouping strategy, but if it is done for them — that is, if the numbers are presented in triplets — they remember more of the numbers. Older children performed equally well no matter how the numbers were presented, because they had a natural tendency to use the grouping strategy (8).

The same conclusion was reached in an experiment involving children ranging from first- to sixth-graders. Each child was shown a set of 24 pictures of objects that belonged to one of four conceptual categories (transportation, animals, furniture, and clothing). The pictures were laid on a table randomly, and the children were told they would have 3 minutes to study them, during which time they were free to move them around or do anything else that might help them remember the pictures. None of the first-graders and only a few of the third-graders rearranged the pictures by category. However, beginning with the fourth-graders and continuing through the sixth-graders, there was an increasing tendency to rearrange the pictures into category groups and to recall pictures of the same category together (20).

Rehearsing the information to be remembered also aids memory, and older children are more likely to use this strategy than younger children. Even when younger children are able to say the names of objects to be remembered, they seem not to realize that rehearsing the names could help them remember. Older children, however, are more likely to use the "trick" of saying the names of the pictures to themselves in order to help them remember (6).

Elaboration or association, a third strategy, involves noting a relation among the items to be remembered. Remembering a list of words — such as house, glass, and spoon — is easier for the child if he or she makes up a story about "a boy who lived in a house and used the glass and spoon."

Finally, not only does the use of strategies involved in retrieving information improve with age, but the motivation to remember does, too. Younger children asked to remember a list of words may become bored and not care whether they remember the words; older children, on the other hand, are more concerned with their ability to recall all the requested information.

In one study an investigator worked with rural Costa Rican children. First, 8-year-old children's memory for words and objects was assessed. Then some of the children were taught certain strategies of organizing the material, rehearsing it, and making up associations to aid their memory. Another group of children was simply motivated to try harder; they were not taught any of the strategies for coding or rehearsal. After several such sessions of either teaching of strategies or motivation, all the children were tested again. Both the children who were taught strategies and those who were motivated showed improved memory, while those who merely saw the experimenter but were not motivated or taught strategies did not improve. The reason that the motivated children improved was that they began to invent strategies spontaneously (26).

While motivation and strategies involved in memory improve with age, environmental factors also play a role in the rate of development of memory. For example, among American children, there is usually a sharp increase around 7 years of age in the length of a string of numbers or words that can be recalled, probably due to the 7-year-old's unconscious use of strategies to aid memory. However, use of these strategies emerges later than age 7 in children growing up in rural, isolated settings where experiences are less varied and schooling is absent or of poor quality (13).

Such differences were evident in an experiment involving children from three different settings — the urban United States, an Indian town of 5000 people in the highlands of northwest Guatemala, and a more isolated and more traditional Guatemalan village of 900 people. Most of the 10- and 11-year-old American children could remember a series of 12 words or 12 pictures, while the children in the larger Guatemalan town could not remember 12 units until they were about 13 years old. And it was not until late adolescence that some children in the very isolated village could remember 12 words or pictures. But there was a steady rate of improvement across the period from 6 years through adolescence in all three settings (13). These data suggest that sometime between 5 years of age and adolescence, children begin spontaneously to use more efficient strategies to help memory, and these include coding, organization, and retrieval strategies. The timing of this development is, of course, affected by environmental experience.

**Process 3:
Reasoning**

If you encounter a new problem, what do you do? You try to figure it out, make inferences, and draw conclusions. Children are no different; they are continually making inferences. Suppose a 6-year-old boy sees his mother sobbing, and he cannot remember ever having seen her cry in the past. He will probably try to explain to himself why she is crying by generating hypotheses about possible solutions. Perhaps he will think of the conditions that make him cry, such as pain, fear, or loneliness. Then he will try, perhaps unconsciously, to decide if it is reasonable that one of these conditions could be making his mother cry. He may reject fear and loneliness as possibilities because he believes firmly that adults are never afraid and never lonely. However, he knows that adults can feel pain and decides that his mother must be crying because she is sad.

This simple example illustrates the three steps involved in the generation of any hypothesis. Children first search their knowledge for possible causes of events they do not immediately understand and generate possible explanations. Second, they check each explanation for consistency with older rules about the event (e.g., grownups are not afraid). Finally, if the explanation is inconsistent with an older rule that they believe more strongly, they will reject the new hypothesis. But if the explanation is consistent with other information and seems appropriate for the event, they will probably accept it as correct. Of course, younger children are not as systematic or sophisticated in their approach as an adolescent would be (see Chapter 12).

The Importance of Critical Attributes. The reasoning process is also used by children in categorizing new objects or ideas. Children have by age 6 learned a number of basic concepts. They know about animals, food, clothing, planes, cars, furniture, homes, money, women, and men, to name only a few. As noted earlier, an important part of being able to reason correctly is the ability to distinguish critical features. For example, when a child sees a new object — say, a helicopter — he or she will try to categorize that object by deciding what known object the helicopter most closely resembles. The child looks for a few special, or critical, points of similarity between the unknown object and a known category. Some qualities are simply irrelevant. For example, the color of the helicopter may be green and the color of a tree may be green, but this similarity does not help the child categorize the helicopter correctly, for the new object is clearly not a tree. The more critical features for classifying a helicopter are the propeller on top of the metal body and the capacity to fly. These characteristics are similar to those of an airplane, and a helicopter and airplane therefore share some of the same critical features — the helicopter must belong to the concept aircraft.

The child's judgment that two objects are similar is partly a function of the degree to which the two objects share the same critical features. But the critical features that distinguish one physical event from another depend on the problem the child is trying to solve. For example, to determine that a sound you hear is a car and not someone walking, you listen for certain features that distinguish the sound of a car from that of a person's footsteps. But to distinguish the sound of a car from that of a plane, you must listen for a different set of critical features.

However, a child does not always deal with concrete, physical events. Occasionally the child categorizes ideas like fairness or good or bad. The child must extract the essential defining components of these abstract ideas—that is, decide on the critical dimensions of the concepts. The typical American 10-year-old, if asked to define the word *good*, is likely to say, "Obey your parents, tell the truth, and be kind"—three different rules about behavior. Many psychologists assume that the child, like the adult, extracts an ideal or prototypic representation of each concept that represents the characteristics that are most often shared by all the members of the concept. And there is one best example of the category. For example, most birds in North America, but not all, are about 6 inches long, fly, have some coloring but not a great deal, sing, are absent in winter and return in the spring. One bird that comes very close to meeting all these criteria is the robin, and most North Americans regard the robin as the prototypic or ideal bird, as they might regard baseball as the prototypic sport or "taking a stranger in on a cold night" as a prototypic act of kindness.

The Concept of Creativity. Generating correct hypotheses is usually the purpose of the reasoning process. But sometimes being correct is not enough; one must also generate original and constructive hypotheses.

If a child has a high IQ score, does it naturally follow that the child is

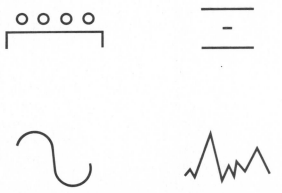

Figure 8.5 Drawings used to test creativity. (From M. A. Wallach & N. Kogan. *Modes of thinking in young children.* New York: Holt, Rinehart and Winston, 1965, figs. 2 and 3.)

creative? No—the fact that a child possesses a lot of knowledge does not guarantee that the child will use this knowledge in an original and constructive way. Generally, a child with a rich and varied storehouse of schemata, images, concepts, and rules is regarded as *intelligent*. But it is only the child who uses such units in an original and constructive way who is regarded as *creative*. Children range from being both highly intelligent and highly creative to having low intelligence and low creativity. In between, of course, are those who are high in intelligence but low in creativity or low in intelligence but high in creativity.

In one study, fifth-grade children were tested and classified in one of the four categories listed in Figure 8.5. Some interesting personality differences related to intelligence and creativity were found. In general, the creative child who was intelligent was willing to take a chance, to risk a "crazy" idea. He or she seemed to have a less severe attitude toward error. Girls who were both intelligent and creative seemed to be successful both in school and in their relationships with peers. Differences in creativity among boys, however, did not relate closely to their social behavior with their peers. But both boys and girls who were intelligent and creative seemed to be self-confident and free of anxiety over generating unconventional ideas (27).

To be creative, one must be willing to risk failure and criticism for having a strange idea. Children must have a permissive attitude toward their own errors.

Obstacles to Creativity. Sometimes children demonstrate creativity; at other times they do not. As with other cognitive skills, the emergence of creativity may depend on the specific problem, but there are at least five major obstacles to the generation of useful or creative solutions to problems.

Failure to understand the problem is one common obstacle to creativity. Children may be unable to solve a problem not because they are unable to perform a task but simply because they do not understand what to do because of the vocabulary or grammar used in the problem.

Second, memory is important in the reasoning process. If a child cannot remember the basic elements of a problem, how can he be expected to solve it? Particularly as problems get a bit more complicated, children may forget the facts given at the beginning of the problem.

But assume that a child both understands and remembers the problem. If the child lacks the appropriate knowledge—that is, the relevant concepts or rules—then she will not be able to solve the problem.

Sometimes a child may be blocked from solving a problem correctly because of a firm belief in a rule that contradicts the correct explanation. For example, a child who believes that ice is cold will have a hard time believing that dry ice can ''burn'' the skin.

A fifth obstacle to solving problems creatively is fear of making a mistake. The average school-age child not only is afraid of criticism from others for failure but also wants to avoid the feelings of self-doubt that result from failure. The easiest and most frequent reaction a child has to the possibility of failure is to withdraw, to refrain from offering any answer about which he is unsure. To be creative, one must be willing to risk failure and criticism for having a strange idea. Children must have a permissive attitude toward their own errors.

The five conditions that stifle creativity may be present at any age, but each is particularly dominant at a particular stage of development. For example, preschool children are most often hampered by a failure to comprehend or remember the problem or because they lack sufficient knowledge, while fear of failure is particularly dominant during middle childhood.

Generating hypotheses is only the third step involved in solving a problem. A fourth process is the evaluation of the quality of ideas and solutions.

**Process 4:
Reflection**

Ask a group of children to solve a problem and chances are that some of them will rush headlong into the situation and quickly volunteer a solution, while others will take a little more time to work out their solution. This difference in response time relates to a child's tendency to engage in reflection, or evaluation. Reflection refers to the process in which a child pauses to stop and consider the quality of his thinking. Unconsciously, the child may ask, "Am I perceiving the problem correctly? Have I remembered the facts accurately? Does this solution make sense?" A child who solves problems without much reflection is said to be **impulsive;** a child who spends a longer period of time evaluating the quality of his or her thinking is said to be **reflective.** This difference among children is evident as early as 5 or 6 years of age and seems to be relatively stable over time (11). That is, a child who at age 5 or 6 tends to be impulsive will probably also be impulsive as an adolescent.

This personality difference does not show up in all situations. If a problem is straightforward and the answer is obvious, or there are no alternatives, chances are that both kinds of children will probably give their answers quickly, though of course the children must comprehend the problem and feel they have some knowledge on which to base their answer. But in situations in which children know they are being evaluated and the correct solution is not immediately obvious, and they do have several alternatives to choose from, then some children pause to reflect on the best solution while others do not.

Which is "better"? Is it better to be impulsive and quick about solving problems, or is it better to take a little longer to reflect? Studies show that the reflective child is more accurate than the impulsive child.

For example, one of the tests used to assess the tendency of the child to be reflective or impulsive is called Matching Familiar Figures (see Figure 8.6). A child is asked to select from six variants one stimulus that is identical with the standard. The important variables are the time the child takes to select her hypothesis and the number of errors made. Among American children there is a dramatic decrease in errors and a corre-

Figure 8.6 Sample items from the Matching Familiar Figures test for reflection-impulsivity in the school-age child.

sponding increase in response time from 5 to 12 years of age. Moreover, the faster the child's decisions, the more mistakes the child makes.

But all is not lost for the impulsive child. Although, as mentioned earlier, the tendency to be impulsive or reflective is generally rather stable over time, through training a child's disposition to be reflective or impulsive can be modified. Sometimes simply telling the child to slow down during several training sessions can help the child be more reflective. Also, the impulsive child can be trained to be more reflective, more accurate, and more thoughtful through either reward and punishment or through merely watching other children or a teacher behave reflectively (5, 23).

The Basis for Reflection-Impulsiveness. Probably the primary reason for a child's being reflective is fear of making a mistake. Most American children become increasingly concerned with avoiding errors, and as a result they also tend to become more reflective with age. But a second, less obvious basis for reflection-impulsiveness may be inherent, for there is some reason to believe that some children are born with a disposition that makes it a little easier for them to become reflective or impulsive. Third, socialization practices influence a child's reflective tendencies. Japanese children are generally more reflective than American children, in part because Japanese children are socialized to avoid error earlier and more consistently than American children. In the United States, lower-class children are slightly more impulsive than middle-class children, which is partly because of different socialization practices regarding error on intellectual tasks (19).

We can now add one more basis for incorrect answers to problems. If children do not think about their hypothesis and fail to reflect upon their initial perception, comprehension (memory), or final answer (reasoning), then they are more likely to be wrong, even though they may understand the problem and have the knowledge to solve it.

For example, suppose a child is given the following problem: "A man gave $9 to each of his 8 sons. How much money did he give out?" A child may answer incorrectly for a number of reasons. First, he may perceive the problem incorrectly. Second, he may forget the elements of the problem (e.g., was it 8 or 9 sons?). Third, he may not know how to solve the problem; that is, he may not reason that the process called for in the problem is the multiplication of 9 by 8. A fourth reason for answering incorrectly may be that the child is too impulsive: he may know that 9×8 is 72 but may hurriedly say that 9×8 is 82, not pausing to reflect upon and check his answer. In fact, the tendency toward reflection is helpful in aiding accuracy of any of the three cognitive processes: perception, memory, or reasoning.

Helping an Impulsive Child to be More Reflective

Because an impulsive attitude can impair certain school performances, especially in arithmetic and early reading, it is sometimes useful to help an impulsive child become more reflective. This is not a difficult thing to do.

First one helps the child to realize the advantages of thinking about his answer before he gives it, of considering all the possible solutions to a problem before offering the first one he generated. Simple exercises help.

For example, a teacher working one-to-one with a child might say: "I'm going to ask you some questions. Don't answer at once. Wait for 10 seconds, and during that 10 seconds think about your answer. Try to improve it. Think about whether it is complete."

A second exercise involves tests like the matching familiar figures test (see Figure 8.6). Here the child must pause and consider all the alternatives, and the teacher can show the child how to examine all the possible solutions.

A third strategy is to ask the child to generate many answers to a problem—for example, to list all the ways a person might get involved in an automobile accident.

But perhaps the most effective teaching technique is to present the child with difficult problems where an impulsive approach is bound to be incorrect and to demonstrate the usefulness of reflecting on all possibilities and pausing to evaluate the quality of one's answer. The best kinds of tests involve perceptual analysis, as do the matching familiar figures test or the embedded figures test, where a familiar object is disguised in a set of randomly generated lines.

One of the simplest procedures one might use is to put a dozen objects from the home on a table and tell the child to look at the array, ask him to turn around, and then remove an object. When the child turns back to the array, ask him to name the object that was removed. Here an impulsive answer is likely to be wrong, and so the child will eventually learn that pausing to reflect helps him get more correct answers.

Process 5: The Generation of New Relationships

Now let us add a fifth cognitive process: the deduction of new relationships between two or more segments of knowledge.

Suppose a 10-year-old boy sees a large animal lying still by a tree. His initial assumption might be that it is sleeping. But if he watches it for a few minutes and sees no motion, he may think that perhaps the animal is dead. How can he decide which of his hypotheses is correct? One method may be for him to throw a rock at the animal. If the animal moves, it is not dead. At this point, the child has generated two hypotheses (the animal is alive or dead) and a way of gaining more information in order to prove one or the other of them false.

Often, in order to discover a new relationship, the child must actively work with the components of the problem, either mentally (as in an arithmetic problem) or physically, as in the above example. This cognitive process is called the deductive phase—the generation of new relationships between two or more segments of knowledge. Deductive ability shows a dramatic difference between preschool and school-age children. A younger child—say, a 5-year-old—does not systematically check alternative hypotheses in order to gain further information. Nor does the young child apply logical rules to select the most likely course of action. These mental processes are characteristic of children 9 to 12 years old who are entering Piaget's formal operational stage (see p. 345).

How can the child decide which of his hypotheses is correct? One method may be for him to throw a rock at the animal. If the animal moves, it is not dead.

Thus, as you can see, as children grow older, their cognitive capacities improve. Moreover, they improve in their implementation, or use, of these capacities when problems are presented. This leads to a very important principle. The number of problem situations in which a particular ability or skill will be implemented increases dramatically during the period from 5 to 12 years of age. Now the child who will rehearse when he or she is trying to memorize the multiplication tables will also use rehearsal when he or she is trying to remember some rules of geography. The child who pauses to check on the logic of a conclusion in arithmetic will also pause to check on the logic of an argument in social studies. There are other processes that are changing. Indeed, there is a whole set of processes called executive functions. Let us look briefly at these.

The Executive Functions

It is believed that a small set of cognitive functions that mature during the years prior to adolescence are responsible for the increased generality of cognitive activities during middle childhood. We call these **executive functions**—that is, they direct the functions of perception, memory, reasoning, reflection, and insight in much the same way that a company executive directs the staff workers. Among the executive functions are the following: (1) Recognizing the nature and difficulty of the problem and its requirements and adjusting one's effort to match the difficulty of the task;

(2) discarding inefficient solution hypotheses and searching systematically for better ones; (3) activating problem-solving strategies (for example, organization, rehearsal); (4) processing information more quickly; and (5) controlling of distraction and anxiety.

In addition to these five executive functions, two important attitudes develop during the years prior to adolescence. The first is faith in the usefulness of thought—the belief that when one is having difficulty solving a problem it is helpful to stop and think in the hope that one might generate a good idea or a correct solution. The second attitude refers to a desire to produce the best possible solution to a problem, along with an equally strong desire to avoid error.

Although these executive functions and attitudes toward problems develop eventually in all normal children, environmental conditions affect their rate of growth. Children growing up in modern, technical societies with good schools and challenging experiences develop these processes faster than children in other societies. Most of these executive functions develop between 5 and 10 years of age in children growing up in Europe and the United States, while they may not appear until adolescence in children growing up in rural, subsistence-farming communities that are common in other parts of the world (2).

Thus far we have described some of what we know about the major cognitive processes as well as the hypothetical cognitive units involved in these processes. However, we have still not presented a general theory of cognitive development to explain what happens during middle childhood. One such theory is that of Jean Piaget (22). We shall now present a brief summary and critique of his theory.

PIAGET'S THEORY OF INTELLECTUAL DEVELOPMENT

When we studied infants we noted that they were in the sensorimotor stage of development according to Piagetian theory. The preschool child was in Piaget's preoperational, or intuitive, stage. From about ages 7 to 12, children are in the Piagetian **stage of concrete operations.**

According to Piaget's theory, a child's progress from one stage to another is not automatic but depends on certain kinds of experiences that children normally have. Piaget assumes that reaching one stage depends on successful progression through previous stages — that is, that each new, more advanced stage is built upon an earlier one. Thus, there is always a relationship between the child's present ability and beliefs and those of the past. Piaget's theory of intellectual development is like the gradual establishment of the ability to do arithmetic and mathematics. Just as one must first learn to add, subtract, multiply, and divide before one can do algebra, similarly, a child must first learn to cope with the world on the sensorimotor level before progressing to an intuitive level.

Piaget's use of the term *intelligence* has a specific meaning. Intelligence is "the coordination of operations to aid adaptation." The **operation** is therefore the central cognitive unit in Piagetian theory. An operation has two important characteristics: It is an *internalized* action that is *reversible*. The concept of addition is a good example of an operation. One can *add* two apples to three apples, or perform the reverse operation of subtracting two apples from five apples. Addition has the reverse operation of subtraction.

Sometime between 6 and 8 years of age, most children pass into the stage of concrete operations. Children in isolated or undeveloped areas may enter the stage a few years later. In the following section, we shall examine the child in the stage of concrete operations.

The Stage of Concrete Operations

According to Piaget, children in the stage of concrete operations have developed a new set of rules, which have special logical qualities.

The first rule is a statement of equivalence: If A is equal to B in some attribute (say, length) and B is equal to C, then it must be true that A is equal to C. Given this information, one doesn't have to measure A and C to know that this fact is true.

A second is similar, being a statement of relation. That is, there are certain fixed relations among objects or qualities of objects. For example, if the red line is longer than the blue line and the blue line is longer than the yellow line, then it must be true that the red line is longer than the yellow line. Children in the stage of concrete operations know the validity of this conclusion even if they have not seen the colored lines.

A third rule concerns the relationships among categories—Piaget calls them *classes*. The concrete-operational child can appreciate that there is a hierarchy among certain classes. For example, children at this stage realize that all oranges belong to the class *fruits* and all fruits belong to the class *foods*.

Finally, the fourth rule the concrete operational child realizes is that specific attributes or objects can belong to more than one class or more than one relationship at one time. Consider the two classes natural foods and manufactured foods and the two classes sweet foods and nonsweet foods. Children in the concrete operational stage appreciate that bananas, for example, can belong simultaneously to the class of natural foods and the class of sweet foods, while bread belongs to the class of manufactured foods and the class of nonsweet foods.

Next, let's take a look at a series of experiments made famous by Piaget that point out the abilities of the concrete operational child.

Conservation. A child in the stage of concrete operations learns that shape does not determine quantity. For example, if a child is shown two balls of clay of equal mass and shape, and then one ball is flattened into a pancake shape, a 5-year-old child, who is in the preoperational stage, will say the ball has more clay. Typically, however, 2 years later the same child will insist that the ball and pancake have the same amount of clay because "the pancake is thinner but it is wider." She now understands the rule of **conservation of mass.**

Similarly, suppose a child is shown two groups of five buttons arranged in identical rows (see Figure 8.7). If one row is rearranged so that it is shorter than the other, a 5-year-old will say that the longer row has more buttons. The 7-year-old, however, will realize that the number of buttons remains the same regardless of the arrangement. This belief that buttons can be returned to their original arrangement is, in Piagetian terms, an operation. The child has learned that no matter how a particular number of pebbles, quantity of water, or amount of sand or clay appears or is arranged, the number, quantity, or amount remains the same. It is conserved.

This is an example of the principle of equivalence noted earlier. If the original two rows of buttons (a and b) had the same number ($a = b$) and all

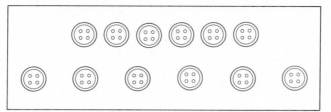

Figure 8.7 Children in the preoperational stage have difficulty conserving number and may insist that there are more buttons in the bottom row because the row extends over more space. As they develop and realize that number is invariant, they will be able to deal with arrangements of objects intellectually, through counting, rather than simply perceiving "a whole lot" of buttons.

one did was to rearrange the buttons in a to produce the arrangement called c, then $a = c$. If the child believes in the principle of equivalence, then he would know that b equals c.

Relational Terms. Children in the stage of concrete operations understand that many relative terms, such as taller, shorter, or darker, refer to a relation between events and not to an absolute quality. Preoperational children, on the other hand, have trouble understanding some relational terms. They tend to think absolutely; for example, they interpret *darker* as meaning very dark rather than darker than another object. If they are shown two light objects, one of which is slightly darker, and are asked to pick the darker one, they may not be able to answer. By age 7 or 8, the child realizes the relativity of brightness and can answer correctly.

Class Inclusion. According to Piaget, the concrete-operational child can reason simultaneously about the part and the whole. Thus, if an 8-year-old is shown eight yellow candies and four brown candies and is asked, "Are there more yellow candies or more candies?," the child will say there are more candies. However, a 5-year-old given the same problem is likely to say, "More yellow candies." Piaget believes the reply of the younger child means that she cannot reason about a part and the whole simultaneously. This concept of **class inclusion** is an example of Principle 3. According to Piaget, the child constructs an equation in which a (all of the candies) equals b (the yellow candies) plus c (the brown candies). He or she also realizes that b (the yellow candies) equals all the candies minus the brown candies.

Serialization. The concrete-operational child also has the ability to arrange objects in a sequence according to one dimension, such as weight or size. For example, the 8-year-old can arrange eight sticks of different length in a row according to their length. You can readily see that serialization ability is critical to understanding the relation of numbers to one another and therefore critical to the learning of arithmetic.

Evaluation of Piaget's Theory of the Stage of Concrete Operations

Central to Piaget's theory is the notion that the operation is the "work horse" in cognitive development. An operation, you will recall, is a special dynamic rule, derived from the child's actions with objects, that one can reverse a state of affairs in action or in thought.

For example, if a 5-year-old child is shown two identical glasses of equal shape filled to the same height with colored water, the child, when asked if the two glasses have the same amount of water or unequal amounts, will quickly acknowledge that they have the same amount. But if the water from one container is poured into a tall, thin glass so that the water level is higher in the new container, the 5-year-old says that the tall container has more water, while a 7-year-old will insist that both have the same amount of water.

Piaget's interpretation is that a child in the stage of concrete operations is able to give the correct answer because the child knows the action can be reversed. The older child will say, "They are the same because you can pour the water back to the other glass and then the height will be the same." Piaget's explanation of the ability of the operational child and the failure of the preoperational child to solve the problem correctly rests on whether the child has developed a rule for reversibility of the action. But there exist other explanations for one child's ability and another's failure. One possibility is that the child who could not solve the problem does not relate the original situation of the two containers of equal height with the final situation of two containers of unequal heights. Children may not realize that the water used in the transformation to make the final pair of containers was the same water they saw earlier (1).

Methodology may also affect the child's performance. There is a standard Piagetian experiment that tests children's ability to demonstrate conservation of number—that is, their ability to recognize that rearrangement of objects does not change the number of objects. When the conservation task was administered in the standard Piagetian manner, the children said that the number of objects had changed when the examiner pushed one row of objects together so that it appeared shorter. But when the children were told that there was a mischievous teddy bear who always "messed up their toys," and the examiner made the teddy bear move the objects in one row closer together, many of the children realized that the number of objects had not changed. Over 63 percent of the children showed conservation of number under the "teddy bear" condition in contrast to only 16 percent tested under standard conditions (18).

Just as methodology can affect the child's performance in an experiment, so can the wording of the questions used. If children do not understand the semantic elements of a question, they will obviously perform at an immature level. Although a 5-year-old child may have difficulty placing a food in two categories simultaneously (e.g., cake is of the class "manufactured" *and* of the class "sweet"), this does not mean the child is incapable of classifying *any* object in two categories simultaneously. The 5-year-old may readily admit that a dog is of the class "animal" and of the class "furry." These classifications may be clearer for the child than a word such as "manufactured." The child may not even know that cake is manufactured, not a natural food. Thus, the fact that a competence is lacking in one situation does *not* necessarily mean that the child does not possess the ability at all; as you will recall, the many competences of school-age children may appear in a few contexts in much younger children.

Another example of this sporadic display of a competence is seen in problems involving relative (comparative) dimensions such as darker or bigger. Piaget argues that preschool children who are not yet in the concrete operational stage cannot solve such problems. But children between 18 and 23 months were shown a small and a large piece of wood. The examiner said, "I have a baby and a daddy. Which one is the baby (or which one is the daddy)?" Most of the children correctly pointed to the smaller piece of wood for the baby and the larger piece of wood for the daddy. Then the examiner showed the child a new pair of wooden forms of different sizes. Still, a great many of the children could identify correctly the "daddy" and the "baby" of the second pair, even though in this case the "baby" had been the "daddy" in the first pair (12).

Thus it appears that children as young as 2 years old, long before they enter the stage of concrete operations, are to some extent capable of making inferences involving the relationship between objects, though they may do this only in a few specific problem contexts. It is likely that young children have some knowledge, too, of the other groupings characteristic of Piaget's stage of concrete operations; that is, 3- and 4-year-old children do seem to have some ability in serialization and class inclusion, but they will display this knowledge only in very specific and familiar problem situations.

We turn next to the subject of intelligence. Although Piaget uses the concept of intelligence, it has a special meaning in his theory. As noted earlier, intelligence, for Piaget, refers to the "coordination of operations to aid adaptation." This is not what most parents, teachers, or psychologists mean by the term, nor is it the meaning implied by a score on a standard intelligence test. What does the term *intelligence* mean? In the next section we shall explore this question. In addition, we shall examine the relation between intelligence and the IQ test, looking at the development of the IQ test and its use and application today.

THE CONCEPT OF INTELLIGENCE AND THE INTELLIGENCE TEST

Of ten people shipwrecked and adrift on a life raft, whom would you consider more intelligent—the person who can compose a poem on the beauty of the ocean, or the one who can catch and cook a fish? Within the confines of that situation, the people on the life raft would no doubt choose the fisherman as the more intelligent.

Although the above may be a rather extreme example, **intelligence** is a relative concept, and societies may differ in the skills and behaviors that

Child Prodigies

Although almost all children are potentially capable of learning to read, do arithmetic, play a simple melody on the piano, and draw a farm scene, there have been and are a few very exceptional children who show an unusually mature talent for language, mathematics, art, or music early in life. Mozart and John Stuart Mill, for example, both showed precocious development.

While these children typically come from families with intellectual or artistic interests and accomplishments, it is generally believed that they have inherited some very special intellectual talent for the area in which they excel. Typically they are not outstanding in areas outside their special skill: Albert Einstein, for example, had great difficulty learning to read, and some have speculated that had he been growing up in America today he would have been called dyslexic.

Tests for detecting musical talent exist, but aside from everyday behavior or performance in school, there are no special tests to diagnose a prodigy in poetry or graphic art. Before the Second World War, most American schools had special programs for these gifted children, some of which separated the child from his peers. During the 1950s and 1960s these programs were abandoned, in part because of the rising tide of egalitarianism and the suggestion that the recognition of unusual talent was elitist and therefore not democratic. Fortunately, this phase is passing and schools are again showing some concern for children with exceptional intellectual skills.

For example, Dr. J. C. Stanley of Johns Hopkins University has been working with junior-high-school boys who show an unusual aptitude for learning mathematics. Some gifted mathematical students are being allowed to take higher math courses or even to enroll in university-level courses. Similarly, children with exceptional language skills are being encouraged in their writing.

characterize an "intelligent" person. The specific talents that are celebrated will depend on the nature of the society. The !Kung San band in the Kalahari Desert in southern Africa, for example, prize superior hunting skills. South Pacific islanders value outstanding navigational skills. Even societies that value mental ability above other qualities—many do not—do not necessarily prize the same intellectual talents. The prerevolutionary Chinese valued mastery of the written form of language; ancient Greeks celebrated mastery of oratorical skill; and the Indians of modern Guatemala praise alertness to opportunity. For many complex reasons, modern America has come to emphasize the value of abstract intellectual abilities, especially language and mathematical skills.

You, along with most other Americans and Europeans, probably hold four assumptions about intelligence. The first is that intelligence is a generalized ability to learn new ideas and skills quickly and to solve different kinds of problems efficiently. Second, a person with high intelligence is likely to attain more wealth and status than one with less intelligence. A child with high intelligence will benefit from parental encouragement, good schooling, and environmental opportunity, and should succeed. Third, differences among children in intelligence are partly due to heredity. That is, because genes influence the anatomy and physiology of the nervous system, and the nervous system is intimately involved in intellectual processes, genetic differences among people probably contribute to differences in intelligence. Finally, IQ tests measure the intelligence described or implied in these three assumptions.

It is this last assumption, not the first three, that has created so much of the current controversy about the role of heredity and racial and social-class differences in intellectual ability. Therefore, let us look at the concept of intelligence as measured by scores on standardized IQ tests.

The Stanford-Binet Test

One of the best-known intelligence tests for children is the Stanford-Binet. In this test children are asked questions that evaluate their vocabulary level, ability to reason, and memory for symbolic materials. There are, of course, easier questions for younger children and more difficult ones for older children. The questions are given to large numbers of children at varying ages from 2 through adolescence in order to determine the expected performance of the average child of that age, as well as those children above and below average. Once this has been determined, a table of expected scores is prepared so that any particular child's score can be compared with that of the average child (see Table 8.1). The tables are constructed so that an IQ score of 100 represents the expected score of an average child of a particular age. Some children score above 100; some children score below. However, it is important to remember that a 10-year-old with an IQ score of 100 has much more knowledge and has answered more questions correctly than a child of 6 years who scores 100.

Table 8.1 THE MEANING OF VARIOUS IQs OBTAINED WITH THE REVISED STANFORD-BINET SCALE

THE CHILD WHOSE IQ IS:	EQUALS OR EXCEEDS	THE CHILD WHOSE IQ IS:	EQUALS OR EXCEEDS
136	99 percent	98	45 percent
135	98	97	43
134	98	96	40
133	98	95	38
132	97	94	36
131	97	93	34
130	97	92	31
129	96	91	29
128	96	90	27
127	95	89	25
126	94	88	23
125	94	87	21
124	93	86	20
123	92	85	18
122	91	84	16
121	90	83	15
120	89	82	14
119	88	81	12
118	86	80	11
117	85	79	10
116	84	78	9
115	82	77	8
114	80	76	8
113	79	75	6
112	77	74	6
111	75	73	5
110	73	72	4
109	71	71	4
108	69	70	3
107	66	69	3
106	64	68	3
105	62	67	2
104	60	66	2
103	57	65	2
102	55	64	1
101	52	63	1
100	50	62	1
99	48		
160		1 out of 10,000	
156		3 out of 10,000	
152		8 out of 10,000	
148		2 out of 1,000	
144		4 out of 1,000	
140		7 out of 1,000	

Source: From *Supplementary guide for the revised Stanford-Binet Scale* (Form L) by Rudolph Pinter, Anna Dragositz, & Rose Kushner. With permission of the Stanford University Press.

The original version of the Stanford-Binet intelligence test was developed in 1905 by two Frenchmen, Alfred Binet and Theophilus Simon. They wanted to develop tests by which they could identify students who were mentally retarded, so that these students could be given special instruction. The efficiency of the entire school system could then be improved. To this end, Binet and Simon picked tests they considered representative of the kinds of mental abilities that children used in performing school tasks — processes such as memory, perception, reasoning, and verbal ability. Test items that were not correlated with school success were eliminated; thus it is not surprising that IQ scores are fairly good predictors of academic performance.

Constancy of IQ

The IQ test score is useful because it remains fairly constant over time. Although tests given to infants under 2 years of age are called intelligence tests, they do not predict intelligence test scores when children are 6, 8, or 10 years of age. IQ test scores given to children over 3 years of age, however, are predictive. The correlations between scores vary with the ages being compared. For example, the child who has a low IQ score at age 10 will probably also have a low score at age 18, for the correlation between scores at age 10 and 18 is 0.70.

In general, after age 10, IQ scores remain fairly constant. However, this is *not* to say that in *all* cases a low score at 10 means a low score at 18. The correlation is only 0.70; it is not 1.00 (9). Shifts in IQ may be related to health, emotional stability, and marked environmental changes — either improvements or deterioration. There is also evidence that personality characteristics affect IQ scores and changes in these scores, though it is very difficult to specify the cause of change in any particular case.

The Usefulness of IQs

What do we actually know when a child obtains an IQ of, for example, 132 on the Stanford-Binet? At the very least, we know the child can do the items on this test better than 97 percent of the other children on whom the test was standardized. Even so, what does that mean in the everyday real world?

The fact of most significance is that intelligence test scores are good predictors of academic achievement. A child who does well on IQ tests will probably do well in school.

As we noted earlier, the high correlation between IQ and school grades is not surprising or difficult to explain. The test was designed to differentiate between good students and poor students. A second factor that helps explain the high correlation between IQ and school performance is related to the first. That is, the skills and knowledge that help a person do well on an IQ test — good vocabulary, knowledge of the standard language used in the test, for example — are the same ones that help a child do well in school. Even personality factors and motives are similar — self-

confidence, high motivation to succeed in intellectual tasks, and reflecting on answers to questions rather than answering impulsively, for example, are related to both high IQ scores and good grades in school.

In the next section we will look at some of the factors that affect performance on intelligence tests.

Factors That Affect Intelligence Test Performance

Because IQ scores, while somewhat variable, are among the most stable human qualities psychologists have discovered and because they predict school performance, it is important that we determine what factors result in high or low scores on intelligence tests. The most popular view is that environmental, personality, and genetic factors influence performance on intelligence tests. For example, certain personality factors and motives lead to good performances on intelligence tests: self-confidence, high motivation to succeed in intellectual tasks, and being reflective rather than impulsive. Being persistent, nonaggressive, and behaving responsibly are personality correlates of school success and thus also correlate positively with high IQ scores.

According to the data of one study, children whose IQ scores increased between the ages of 6 and 10 were more independent, more competitive, and more verbally aggressive than other children in the same study whose IQs did not increase. Additionally, those who gained in IQ worked harder in school, showed a strong desire to master intellectual problems, and were not likely to withdraw from difficult problem situations.

Current life experience sometimes — but not always — affects IQ scores. The difficulty in predicting IQ is illustrated below in several case studies. They show fluctuations in both directions as well as stability. All three children had similar IQ scores at age 4 (see Figure 8.8).

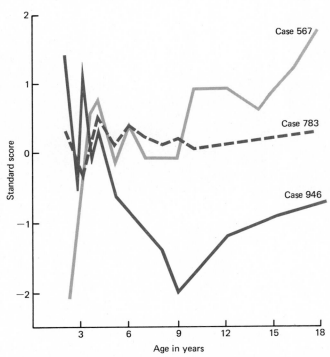

Figure 8.8 Records made by three children on successive mental tests. (From M. P. Honzik, J. W. Macfarlane, & L. Allen. The stability of mental test performance between two and eighteen years. *Journal of Experimental Education*, 1948, *17*, 454–455.)

Case 567 was sickly and shy as a young child, but after age 10 her social life expanded and she became much more interested in music and sports. These changes in her situation were reflected in improved intelligence test scores.

Case 783 had a poor health history, had difficulties in school, was insecure, and showed some symptoms of emotional disturbance. Nonetheless, his IQ test scores remained stable.

The scores of case 946 fluctuated from a high of 142 (preschool) to a low of 87 (age 9). She was the child of immigrant parents of grammar-school education, both unstable and fighting constantly, who were divorced when the girl was 7. She was acutely uneasy around her young stepfather for the first years of her mother's new marriage. The child's extreme scores may reflect the internal and external turmoil she experienced (9).

Relation of Social Class and IQ. Children from the middle class tend to achieve better scores on IQ tests than children from the lower social classes. The usual explanation of this fact is that, compared with middle-class parents, some lower-class families put less stress on the importance of intellectual mastery. Also, the child's cognitive and language experiences are likely to vary with social class. Compared with lower-class parents, those in the middle class consistently talk more and use richer language in responding to their children's questions and in teaching them how to solve problems. They also offer greater cognitive challenges and more opportunities for using language and for talking about their feelings. In contrast with lower-class mothers, middle-class mothers typically use sentences with much more complex grammar as well as more abstract concepts.

In addition, factors outside the home are different. Children from different social classes in the United States grow up in different neighborhoods and interact primarily with youngsters of their own class who share values about intellectual skills. Moreover, they attend schools with teachers who often have differential expectations for children from lower- and middle-class families. Thus the consistent differences in IQ between lower- and middle-class children of all ethnic groups may be due as much to factors outside the home as to direct parent-child interactions.

In America, IQ is believed to be the key to wealth and status. That is, IQ is seen as a good predictor of future occupation and level of educational attainment.

In America, IQ is believed to be the key to wealth and status. That is, IQ is seen as a good predictor of future occupation and level of educational attainment. However, it is not really necessary to know a child's IQ in order to predict his or her eventual occupational status; the child's social class, as measured by the father's education and occupation, is as good a predictor as the child's own IQ. In fact, it is slightly better. Early IQ scores (those during the first 5 to 7 years of life) are not highly predictive of later adult occupational and educational attainment. The correlation between IQ scores after the age of 7 and occupational and educational attainment is

Bias and Factors Influencing IQ Tests

Despite the fact that most parents probably believe that intelligence tests represent a broad evaluation of all the child's abilities, this is not true.

The two leading intelligence tests for children, the Stanford-Binet and the Wechsler Intelligence Scale for Children, evaluate primarily the richness of the child's vocabulary, her ability to reason with verbal propositions (for example, how are a lizard and a bird alike?), memory for numbers and words, and the ability to solve puzzles. There is no test of the child's ability to learn something new, no evaluation of the child's artistic or musical ability, and no evaluation of her self-confidence or her desire to master cognitive skills. Thus the score reflects only a sample of the child's intellectual talent.

There are three major sources of potential error in using the IQ test as an index of the child's basic intellectual ability. First, the language of the test and the words that are used are much more familiar to middle-class children than to lower-class children. Children are asked to define the word *shilling* but are not asked to define *smack* or *fuzz*.

A second source of bias in the test comes from the fact that the tests are timed and the child gains extra points by solving certain of the test items quickly. A child who was extremely cautious or not accustomed to working quickly with difficult problems would get a lower score.

Finally, anxiety and motivation are very important. Children who are anxious about the testing situation because they are asked questions from an unfamiliar person score lower than children who find such a situation more familiar. And of course the motivation, or the desire to perform as well as possible, influences test scores.

Our knowledge of the experiences and life style of middle-class children and of children from the lower classes or from certain ethnic minorities leads us to expect that middle-class children are more familiar with the language of the test, more confident about their ability to solve the novel test problems, and more highly motivated to do well. Thus the fact that the average middle-class child has a higher IQ score than many lower-class children is believed to be due in part to these extraintellectual factors and not only to differences in the ability to learn new ideas.

better—about 0.50. However, the education of the child's father, which is a reflection of the family's social class, was correlated 0.60 with the child's eventual occupation (17).

Social class also serves as a better predictor of IQ during the school years than the child's own psychological qualities during the first two years of life. Infant characteristics such as attentiveness, activity, and excitability were evaluated in an attempt to see if there would be any correlation with later IQ scores. However, none of these infant qualities predicted the child's IQ at age 10 after the effect of social class had been taken into account. Only the occupation and education of the family predicted

1839 Vocabulary Test

Most of the criticism of "culture bias" that is directed at standardized intelligence tests is aimed at the vocabulary subtest. Familiarity with particular words reflects the chances you have had to encounter them. Test yourself on this vocabulary list, taken from a nineteenth-century American school manual (Howland, 1839):

1 abba	1 A word used for father.
2 abluent	2 That which washes clean.
3 antipodes	3 Those people on the other side of the globe who have their feet opposite ours.
4 appal	4 To be frightened or grow faint.
5 besom	5 A broom.
6 clothier	6 One who finishes cloth.
7 cooper	7 One who makes barrels and tubs.
8 cordwainer	8 One who makes boots and shoes.
9 crier	9 One employed to proclaim things.
10 currier	10 One who blacks and dresses off leather.
11 draper	11 One who sells cloth.
12 gauger	12 One who measures vessels.
13 glazier	13 One who sets glass in windows.
14 haberdasher	14 One who sells small things.
15 mechanic	15 A person who has the knowledge of some art.
16 whitesmith	16 One who works in polished iron and makes tools and instruments.

the children's IQ scores (14). Even among small, rural, subsistence-farming villages in less developed countries such as Guatemala there is a positive correlation between the amount of land the family owns and the size of their house — good indexes of social class — and the children's scores on tests of cognitive ability (12).

All these facts suggest that factors related to the values and practices of the family, the quality of the schools children attend, the values of the peer group, opportunities for intellectually challenging experiences, and identification with parents who seem to have power in the environment may be as important in determining a child's future level of educational attainment and occupational role as intellectual ability during childhood.

Race and IQ. The title for this section could well be "social class and IQ," for race alone is not the reason for differences in IQ between white and nonwhite children. It is a fact that children from economically disadvantaged minority groups in both the United States and Europe — most of whom are nonwhite — obtain lower IQ scores than the average child in the same country.

The issue of race and IQ has generated considerable controversy. Most notably, Arthur Jensen, an educational psychologist at the University of California, concluded that heredity accounts for 80 percent of the variation in IQ scores and suggested further that the 10- to 15-point average difference in IQ between whites and blacks in the United States is the result of genetic factors (10). Like many other psychologists, we disagree with Jensen's interpretations of the data. The available evidence does not support the conclusion that one race is genetically inferior to another. Rather, black children have lower IQ scores because of experiences in their families and the events associated with economic disadvantage.

Support for this view comes from the fact that if black children are adopted by middle-class white families during the first 2 or 3 years of life, their IQ scores are significantly higher than that of the average black child (raised by his or her biological parents) in the United States. Also, the higher the educational level of the adoptive mother, the higher the adopted child's IQ. The improvements in the scores of the adopted children were due to improved social environment (25).

SUMMARY

1. During middle childhood the child continues to grow physically and makes steady progress in physical strength and motor skills.

2. The child's intellectual and cognitive skills also increase during middle childhood. A contributing factor to cognitive development is the changes in a child's conceptual thinking.

3. A child's competence in memory can be tested using either the recall

or the recognition method. Memory can be classified as sensory, short-term, or long-term, according to how long the information lasts.

4. There are cultural as well as individual differences in memory ability, and the results of testing for memory, as well as for other cognitive competences, may depend on the nature of the problem.

5. The memory capability of older children increases in part because their knowledge base becomes greater but also because they begin to use strategies to help code and store information. Strategies useful in memory include organization, rehearsal, and association.

6. A child's reasoning capability includes the ability to categorize objects or ideas, and the child must become increasingly sensitive to the critical attributes of an object or idea.

7. A child's reasoning capability also determines how creative he or she will be. Sometimes possessing knowledge is not enough; the child must be able to use knowledge in an original and constructive way.

8. Children who respond quickly to problems without pausing to reflect are called impulsive; those who pause to evaluate their solution are reflective.

9. During middle childhood children make great progress in the ability to generate new relationships between two or more segments of knowledge—called the deductive phase of cognition.

10. The emergence of executive functions is believed to account for the increased implementation or generality of perception, memory, reasoning, reflection, and deduction.

11. According to Piaget's theory of intellectual development, children from about ages 7 to 12 are in the stage of concrete operations. They have developed a new set of rules that have special logical qualities.

12. Intelligence is a relative concept, differing from culture to culture. Consequently, standardized tests of intelligence are subject to cultural bias. In addition, other factors such as life experience, certain personality factors, and motivation affect scores on intelligence tests.

Suggested Readings

Flavell, J. H. *Cognitive development.* Englewood Cliffs, N.J.: Prentice-Hall, 1977.

Furth, H. G., & H. Wachs. *Thinking goes to school: Piaget's theory in practice.* New York: Oxford University Press, 1974.

Piaget, J. *Six psychological studies.* New York: Random House, 1967.

Stanley, J. C. Intellectual precocity. In J. C. Stanley, D. P. Keating, and L. H. Fox (Eds.), *Mathematical talent: Discovery, description, and development.* Baltimore: Johns Hopkins University Press, 1974.

Chapter 9

Personality and Social Development: Socialization in the Family

FOR MOST children, the parents and the family remain the most significant factors in the development of personality during middle childhood. It is true that the child goes to school and his or her social world enlarges, and, as we will discuss in the next chapter, during middle childhood the child becomes more independent of the family and more subject to the influence of outside forces. Nonetheless, parent-child relationships, the family situation, and sibling interaction still play the major role in shaping the child's personality. Thus we shall examine the nature of parent-child relationships, the effects of having or not having brothers and sisters, and the effects of divorce of parents.

As we have seen, the child is changing during this period, developing motor capabilities, greater cognitive skills, and, in some areas, different patterns of behavior. It follows that parents must then change some of their patterns of **socialization.** Consequently, while some of the issues we look at in this chapter, such as **sex typing** and **aggression,** represent a continuation of areas of influence of the parents, the nature of the socialization may change as the child gets older.

We will also look at some new areas of concern, such as the development of the child's **self-concept.** And, as we look at the development of the personality and self-concept, we will consider some of the psychological problems of adjustment children may face during middle childhood. Finally, we will look at **conscience development** and **prosocial behavior** during middle childhood.

Most parents continue to treat boys and girls differently during the middle childhood years.

THE CONTINUING INFLUENCES OF THE FAMILY

As mentioned above, the process of socialization is continuous, and parents will be dealing with some of the same areas of influence while their child is anywhere between the ages of 2 and 20. But the child is more mature now, and consequently the nature of the issues concerning parents will shift, reflecting the greater age and the different life experiences of the child. While parents may still be concerned with socialization for aggression or sex typing, they will expect more mature behavior by this age.

Sex Typing

Most parents continue to treat boys and girls differently during the middle childhood years. Specifically, parents put greater emphasis on their sons' achievement, competition, independence, assumption of responsibility, and control of expression of emotion. With girls, there is less stress on achievement and more on being trustworthy and truthful. In addition, parental relationships with daughters tend to be warmer and closer than parent-son relationships. Girls are encouraged to "wonder and think about life," while boys presumably are encouraged to be curious and actively explore and experiment with life. Parents are more concerned with their sons' acquiring sex-appropriate behavior. With daughters, they worry more. They are more restrictive of their daughters' activities and supervise them more. However, they are more reluctant to punish them (3).

A recent trend, though, is that many parents are trying hard *not* to treat their sons and daughters differently, attempting to encourage in both the good qualities traditionally associated with either sex.

Changing American Family

During each historical period parents have some dim awareness of the psychological qualities that will be most adaptive in their society when their child reaches young adulthood, and they try to promote those qualities as best they can. Their awareness comes from the behavior of people around them, the books they read, and in modern times, television, movies, and magazines.

During colonial times in the United States the ideal adult was supposed to be obedient to authority, religious, a good Christian, and loyal to the family. After the Industrial Revolution and especially following the Civil War, when industry became organized in urban areas, young people left their families and had to deal with problems on their own in a competitive and individualistic atmosphere. Consequently, American parents began to promote a competitive attitude, a capacity for independence, and the willingness to stand up to authority much more than their colonial counterparts did.

Although these values are still strong in the United States, the growth of large bureaucratic industries and institutions—General Motors, AT&T, Chase National Bank—requires an ability to get along with others, to please authority rather than defy it, and to accommodate to the bureaucratic rules. And during the last 30 to 40 years, American parents have become more concerned with their child's ability to get along with others and to be popular—much more than their nineteenth-century counterparts were. Thus each segment of history places different demands on its citizens and therefore slightly different profiles of personality attributes and beliefs. Parents, sensing what the next generation will require, try as best they can to prepare their children for an unknown future.

Aggression

As with the area of sex typing, the focus of concern in socialization for aggression is slightly different from the preschool years. Parents of children of school age find themselves faced with a new set of aggressive behaviors, for within our culture, the forms of children's expression of aggression generally change with age. While nursery-school children are both physically and verbally aggressive toward others, school-age children insult, tease, and call each other names more than younger children do. For example, if a preschool child insults a classmate, the latter is likely to hit in response. Elementary-school children, on the other hand, are more likely to respond to an insult with another insult (6). Excluding a child from a group, club, or team is another way of expressing aggression that is more common among older children than among younger ones.

The parents' socialization for aggression during middle childhood is important, for what they do will have consequences later: Aggression appears to be a fairly stable characteristic, at least for males. Boys who are relatively more aggressive than most of their peers when they are 6 to 10 years old are more likely than others to become easily angered and manifest aggression when they become adults (10).

As before, the parents' most effective means for dealing with aggression is to apply techniques of "good parenting." That is, they should be firm and consistent, making reasonable demands on their children and explaining the reasons for their rules, and applying rewards and punishments consistently.

Parent-Child Relationships

Because the parent-child relationship is so influential in determining the personality and social development of the child, it is important to realize that there are many variations in parent-child relationships. Although it is impossible to measure accurately all the differences in these relationships, there are two dimensions along which they have been characterized. The first is **warmth-hostility;** the second is **restrictiveness-permissiveness** (2).

Warmth-Hostility. This dimension of parental behavior is defined at the warm end by such characteristics as accepting, approving, understanding, and child-centeredness. Warm parents are affectionate and respond positively to their child's dependency behavior. Warm parents also frequently use explanations, especially in disciplining, use physical punishment infrequently, and demonstrate a high use of praise in discipline. Hostile parents, on the other hand, generally show the opposite of these characteristics.

Restrictiveness-Permissiveness. This dimension is defined at the restrictive end by many restrictions and strict enforcement of demands in areas such as noise, obedience, and aggression (to siblings, peers, and parents). Restrictive parents are also concerned with neatness, table manners, care of household furniture, modesty behavior, and sex play (2). The permissive end of the spectrum, as you might expect, reflects the opposite of these qualities.

Suppose you can easily describe a parent you know as restrictive. Or suppose you know that another parent is warm, although you don't know whether the parent is restrictive or permissive. Do these one-dimensional descriptions reveal anything about the probable effect on the child of the parental relationship? Yes, there are some meaningful (though rather limited) generalizations that can be made based on one of these dimensions separately, without regard to variations in the other. For example, most studies suggest that the children of hostile parents show counterhostility and aggression, either in feelings or behavior. Similarly, children of restrictive parents tend to be inhibited, while children of permissive parents are less inhibited (2).

However, if we consider the interactions between these two dimensions, we can be more precise and make more meaningful generalizations about the effect of parents' behavior on children. For example, while the child of a hostile, permissive parent and the child of a hostile, restrictive parent may both have deep-seated feelings of hostility, they may differ greatly in the way they express that hostility. The child with permissive parents may express aggression directly against the parents, while the other child (who has restrictive parents) may suppress the aggression when with his parents but transfer those feelings of hostility to peers or even to the self (2).

In the following sections we shall look briefly at the probable effects upon the child of various combinations of parental warmth-hostility and restrictiveness-permissiveness.

The child with permissive parents may express aggression directly against the parents.

The Warm-Permissive Parent.
Children of parents who are both warm and permissive are likely to be rather active, outgoing, socially assertive, and independent (2). These children want to master their environment; therefore they try to learn adult ways of doing things. They also tend to be friendly, creative, and lacking in hostility toward others or themselves (10). (So far these kids sound perfect, don't they? Keep reading—there are a few points that parents might find difficult to handle.) They may also be somewhat aggressive and bossy and, on occasion, somewhat disobedient and disrespectful, particularly at home (1). But these aggressive actions do not reflect chronic anger and frustration or hostility; rather, they emerge because the child feels secure and because the parents have not severely punished such responses in the past. The responses appear to be easily turned on and off in response to reinforcing conditions.

The Warm-Restrictive Parent.
Children reared in warm-restrictive homes, as compared with those reared in warm-permissive homes, are likely to be more dependent, less friendly, and less creative. Interestingly, they are *either* very high *or* very low in persistence. They are likely to be submissive to parents, conforming, polite and neat, lacking in aggression and competitiveness with peers, and less oriented toward mastery in the assumption of autonomy and independence (10).

In general, it seems that the more extreme types of behavior disorders, such as neurotic disability or delinquency, are not so likely to occur when there is adequate parental warmth. However, there are significant differences depending on whether the warm parent is permissive or restrictive. The child with warm-permissive parents is more outgoing and independent; the child with warm-restrictive parents is less assertive and more conforming.

The Hostile-Restrictive Parent. Woe be unto the child with hostile-restrictive parents, for this parental behavior pattern is often found among neurotic children (11). The child is not allowed much freedom and is punished often for even small transgressions. Consequently, the child feels hostile toward the parent, yet is not allowed to express this hostility through behavior. Being unable to express this resentment, the child internalizes it, some of it being turned against the self and some of it producing inner turmoil and conflict (2). This can lead to self-punishment, suicidal tendencies, and accident-proneness (18). In addition, the child is likely to be shy, to have difficulties in relating to peers, and to show little confidence in or motivation toward adult role taking (10).

The Hostile-Permissive Parent. While hostile-restrictive parents produce internalized conflict in the child, hostile-permissive parents also produce counterhostility and resentment in the child, but in this case the child is more likely to express, or "act out," the hostility. In fact, juvenile delinquents frequently have parents who lack warmth and are either permissive or inconsistent in exercising discipline. Studies show, too, that highly aggressive children have parents who are highly permissive yet inflict high punishment.

Parent-Child Relationships and Self-Concept. Perhaps one of the most influential components of a child's personality is the self-concept. Self-esteem or self-concept (the terms are used interchangeably to refer to individuals' judgments about themselves relative to others) is central to good psychological adjustment, personal happiness, and effective functioning in children and in adults. Although many children are generally high in self-confidence in more than one area of functioning, many children may feel confident about some aspects of themselves but be unsure of themselves in other areas. For example, one girl may be a math whiz and have high self-confidence with respect to her performance in school but may lack self-confidence about her popularity with other children. Still others may have a negative self-concept for both school and popularity.

Children who have generally high self-concepts — that is, who esteem themselves highly in most areas — are self-confident and self-assured. Because they expect that they will be well received and successful, they are not afraid to express their ideas or to follow their own judgments. Moreover, their self-confidence allows them to veer from the mainstream and to consider novel ideas. Children who are generally lacking in self-confidence, on the other hand, prefer to fade into the woodwork. They tend to be apprehensive about voicing unpopular or unusual ideas and to avoid attracting attention, choosing to be alone rather than participate in social interchange or they are extremely aggressive and rebellious as a reaction to their lack of self-confidence (16).

Obviously, it is advantageous in many ways to have a good self-concept. And the source of a child's self-concept is to a large extent the child's experiences at home, as well as parental identification. Thus it is of interest to examine what kinds of parents produce children with high self-esteem.

"A child has a right to his own point of view and ought to be allowed to express it." Do you agree or disagree? Parental responses to this statement show a marked contrast, 93 percent of the parents of high self-esteem boys but only 9.7 percent of the parents of those low in self-esteem agreeing with it! Thus it seems highly possible that an element that contributes to a boy's high self-concept is that his parents respect his opinion.

This result was derived from a study of preadolescent boys and their parents (4). Each filled out a self-report test: The boys answered questions on how they felt about themselves, about school and their studies, and about their personal relationships, and their parents answered questions about their own personality characteristics, child-rearing practices, and marital happiness.

Boys who scored high in self-esteem had parents who were themselves high in self-esteem. The parents were emotionally stable, self-reliant, effective in their child-rearing practices, and compatible with each other. Furthermore, mothers of boys high in self-esteem were accepting and supportive and consistent in discipline. As pointed out earlier, parents of boys high in self-esteem respected the opinions of their children. Perhaps because their opinions were taken into account, these boys gained confidence in their own opinions, which they generalized to self-confidence in other situations.

In contrast, the parents of those lacking in self-confidence regarded their sons as burdens, were harsh and disrespectful in their treatment, and gave them little guidance. They were inconsistent in their discipline, sometimes acting unconcerned about the boy's misbehavior and sometimes punishing severely.

Although the above study centered on boys only, a 6-year longitudinal study (that is, the same group of children were studied for a period of 6 years) that included girls found similar results: Parental warmth and acceptance were related to high self-esteem 6 years later. Children were more likely to have high self-esteem if at least one of their parents displayed warmth and acceptance than if both parents were cold and unaccepting. Having a dominating father was associated with lowered self-esteem for boys but not for girls (19).

In discussing socialization in the family, we have typically referred to "the parents" as though all children are raised by both mothers and fathers. But what about the many children who are being raised in single-parent households? Let's look next at the effects of divorce.

Divorced Parents and Their Children

Because the divorce rate in America is currently at 40 percent and climbing, many of today's children are being raised in single-parent households. In many, though not all, cases, the children will be reared primarily by their mothers. In fact, over 10 million children in the United States live in fatherless homes, in most cases because the parents are divorced and the mothers have been granted custody of the children.

As with other psychological issues, the impact of divorce on a child is dependent on many variables. We must consider the total context of the divorce, including parental reactions to the divorce, the events leading up to it, and the many consequences—added stress and conflict, changed interactions within the family, and the difficulties of adjusting to a new way of life. We must also consider the effects of the divorce on the parents. If the parents maintain a friendly, nonhostile relationship, then the child is likely to suffer less from the trauma of his parents separating. Still the effects of the divorce may make life rather difficult for the mother. For example, single (divorced) mothers tend to encounter many more stresses than married ones: They have more child-rearing tasks to perform and more work in running the household; financial hardships; sexual frustrations; social isolation and thus lack of social and emotional support; loss of self-esteem; and feelings of loneliness, depression, and helplessness. In addition, single mothers frequently find it difficult to discipline their children, for many times children think of their fathers as having more power and authority and are more obedient with fathers than with mothers (7).

Positive Effects of Divorce

Other things being equal, a family with two parents is the most desirable environment for a growing child. This is so not only because it is still the most popular arrangement (and therefore the child feels he is more like everyone else), but also because stressful situations and crises can be shared by two adults rather than handled by one. In addition, a child with both a father and a mother has two role models and potential sources for nurturance. However, there are some situations in which one can imagine the separation or divorce to be psychologically helpful.

For example, if the parents are continually fighting and the child believes he is the cause of some of the friction, then a great deal of guilt can be generated. If a child feels excessive guilt, he is likely to become apathetic or, more seriously, act in an antisocial way in order to provoke punishment.

Moreover, there are those rare but dangerous situations where one parent is physically abusive to the child, generating extreme fear. Under these conditions the child's growth is helped if he is not living with that parent.

Another potential advantage of divorce is that a single parent is likely to be forced to give responsibilities to the preadolescent or adolescent child for the running of the household. Efficient implementation of these responsibilities cannot help but make the child feel more competent and grown up.

Finally, a divorced parent living alone with his or her children might become more concerned with spending time with the children than when he or she was married. As a result, the parent might provide happy experiences that he or she might not have created when both parents were living together. For example, a person whose habit it was to disappear into the living room with the spouse for drinks, excluding the children, may, after divorce, choose to wind down from the day by spending time with the children.

One area in which effects on children have been noted is that of cognitive abilities. On the average, children of single mothers, especially the sons, get poorer school grades and lower intelligence and achievement test scores than children from intact homes (20). Both boys and girls tend to show higher scores in verbal than in quantitative (mathematical) tests. It may be that the breakdown of discipline and communication that often occurs with a divorce results in children who are impulsive and unable (or unwilling) to concentrate and persist. The ability to concentrate attention is more critical in tasks involving reasoning (such as mathematical problem solving); thus the children who *lack* this ability are unlikely to do well on quantitative tests (7).

Fortunately, these harmful effects on cognitive functioning can be avoided. If divorced mothers are readily available, maintain firm and sensitive discipline, communicate with their children, and encourage independent mature behavior, their children are not as likely to show cognitive deficits.

In general, boys seem to suffer more than girls from divorce. Because of the many stresses and conflicts of divorced parents, parent-child, especially mother-son, relationships often deteriorate. Divorced mothers show fewer positive reactions to their sons' behavior and use more negative techniques (such as negative commands, prohibitions, and opposition to requests) in handling them. Also, boys separated from their fathers before the age of 5 are, on the average, less masculine in orientation and behavior. Outside the home, sons of single mothers are more antisocial and impulsive, less self-controlled, rebellious against adult authority, lacking in a sense of social responsibility, and less able to delay immediate gratification. In making moral judgments, these boys are primarily concerned with the probability of being detected or punished for what they do rather than with internalized standards. Also, the harmful effects of divorce on a preschool boy's personality and social behavior are considerably lessened in cases where fathers are well adjusted and maintain considerable contact with their sons (7).

In contrast, girls are much less likely to react to their parents' divorce in an "acting out," aggressive, and antisocial way; actually, few differences between the daughters of divorced and intact families have been found.

Although the influence of parents is of primary importance in shaping the child's development, let us not forget the influence of brothers and sisters. The pacts and perils shared by **siblings** also have a significant effect on the child's personality and social behavior.

The Influence of Siblings

Through interactions with siblings, a child may learn patterns of loyalty, helpfulness, and protection. "This is my little brother. Let's teach him how to play." "Here, Sis, let me help you." On the other hand, the interactions may take a different form: "She took my book." "He colored on my page." "She hit me." Through interactions such as these a child may learn patterns of conflict, domination, and competition. And most children do learn a little of both sets of patterns, as more than 80 percent of American children have brothers and/or sisters.

Birth Order

Although a child's birth order is far less important in development than how the parents treat him or her, social class, or the personality of his or her parents and the role models they provide, nonetheless it can have some influence.

In the United States, in middle-class families, first-borns, in comparison with later-borns, tend to get better grades in school and higher IQ scores and are generally more responsible and less rebellious. How can we interpret this interesting set of facts?

It is generally believed that the first-born identifies more strongly with his or her parents than the later-born and is therefore more likely to adopt the values that the parents promote. Since middle-class parents encourage good school performance and intellectual excellence, first-borns are disposed to adopt those values and to act on them.

The later-born, especially if the older child is of the same sex, is likely to assume that the older child has unfair privileges that are denied to the younger—the older child is allowed to stay up later, usually gets more expensive gifts, and is given more freedom. The younger child cannot help but feel less competent than the older child. Therefore the younger child feels rebellious toward the older sibling and toward authority in general.

These facts have led some to suggest that among eminent scientists, later-borns would be more likely to invent and support a theory that challenged a dominant belief held by the society. This turns out to be true. For example, Darwinian theory challenged the nineteenth-century biblical explanation of the origin of living things. Not only was Darwin a later-born, but the scientists who supported Darwin tended to be later-born. Similarly, those who supported Freudian theory in the early years of this century, when it was controversial, were more likely to be later-born than first-born.

It appears that sibling position is an important psychological variable because it duplicates many of the significant social interaction experiences of adolescence and adulthood. Because of sibling position, a child learns during early childhood what it's like to be first or second, to have great or little power, to side with authority or rebel against it, to feel guilt over hostility, or to be able to "place the blame."

Aside from the nature of the relationship a child has with brothers and sisters, the number of siblings he or she has and the child's birth order in the family (called ordinal position) may also affect what is learned in the home setting. Age, too, is a factor, for the influence of siblings on the child is probably felt most keenly when the child is between 2 and 10 years of age.

Sex of Sibling. In general, children with brothers have more "masculine" traits than children with sisters. The girls with brothers, as compared with the girls with sisters, are more ambitious and more aggressive and do better on tests of intellectual ability. Girls with older brothers have more "tomboyish" traits than girls with older sisters. Boys with older sisters are less aggressive and less daring than boys with older brothers. Children with an older brother are more likely to be classified as physically active than passive, while children with no older brother are more likely to be passive (see Figure 9.1) (15).

Such results are not unexpected, given what we know about identification and imitation. Children are more likely to identify with or imitate a powerful figure, and an older sibling certainly qualifies as "powerful" in the eyes of the younger. The older child is stronger, knows more, can stay up later, and eats adult foods. The younger sibling, therefore, will strive to become similar to the older by attempting to adopt the behaviors of the older brother or sister.

Girls with older brothers have more "tomboyish" traits than girls with older sisters.

Ordinal Position. Each position in the birth order—first, second, middle, last—has its own set of advantages and disadvantages. For example, oldest children at first have their parents all to themselves, so they are likely to get a great deal of attention and affection, to have their needs gratified quickly, and to receive help promptly when in distress. They readily learn to depend on and relate to adults. However, all this attention is not without its disadvantages. Oldest children may be overindulged and overprotected, and they may be handicapped by the relative inexperience of their parents. Being somewhat unaccustomed to children, the parents may treat their first child more like an adult than a child. They may expect too much and push the child hard to accomplish more than he can do.

Another disadvantage of being the oldest is coping with the arrival of other children in the family. While the arrival of a new sibling may

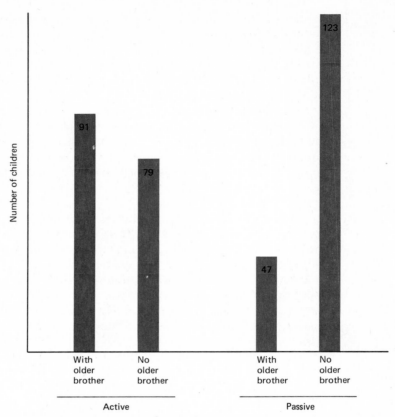

Figure 9.1 Teachers of kindergarten through sixth grade were asked to nominate the most physically active and most physically passive student of each sex. Of 170 pairs of children, physically active students were more likely to have an older brother than were physically passive students. (After L. E. Longstreth, G. V. Longstreth, C. Ramirez, & G. Fernandez. The ubiquity of big brother. *Child Development,* 1975, *46,* 769–772. Copyright 1975 by The Society for Research in Child Development, Inc.)

threaten any child's security — "Will my parents still love me?" — the oldest child alone must face the problem of losing "only child" status. The arrival of a new sibling is especially threatening if the child is between 3 and 6 years of age.

In middle-class families first-borns are generally more likely than later-born children to identify with their parents and to adopt parental (rather than peer) values and to maintain high standards for themselves. They are more strongly motivated toward achievement and more likely to achieve prestige in their professions. In addition, they are a conscientious group, respecting authority and social pressures, concerned with cooperation and responsibility, and prone to feelings of guilt. Finally, they are more inclined to enter occupations involving a parental role, such as teacher.

Later-born children encounter quite a different home situation from first-borns. Beginning very early in life, later-born children interact not only with their parents but also with their older siblings, who may serve as teachers, guides, and models for identification and imitation. But a disadvantage is that older siblings may be viewed as powerful competitors, having special privileges and status. The later-born child may feel a sense of inadequacy in comparison with an older sibling, particularly if the older sister or brother is between 2 and 4 years older. Later-born children are apt to regard themselves as less competent than their older siblings in some important ways. The older sibling makes being able to ride a bicycle look so easy; the younger child, who is simply not yet physiologically coordinated enough to ride a bike, may feel frustrated and incompetent.

Compared with first-borns, later-born children are a somewhat more "relaxed" group, not as strongly motivated toward achievement and success. They are less cautious in behavior — for instance, they tend to participate more in dangerous physical activities. Later-borns tend to be more realistic in self-evaluations, though they are also more likely to suffer from feelings of inadequacy. One benefit of being a later-born child is that these children learn important social skills. In their homes, later-born children learn to consider and to accommodate to the needs and wishes of others, including their siblings. These interpersonal skills tend to generalize to other situations, and consequently their interactions with peers tend to be successful, leading to greater popularity.

While there are some generalizations that can be made about personality development based on birth order, the effect of ordinal position is very dependent on the sex of the siblings and the spacing between them. When siblings are of the same sex and separated by less than 2 years, there are few differences between them. When the spacing increases to 4 years or the sibs are of the opposite sex, the behavioral differences between them are more marked. For example, a boy with a brother 4 years younger is less aggressive and more responsible than a boy with a sister 4 years younger than himself.

The psychological effects of birth order also depend on how children are treated by both parents. For example, in Japan and some other tradition-oriented societies, being a first-born male is an especially privileged status and entails more privileges and greater responsibilities. In contrast, in contemporary middle-class American families, there is often a conscious effort to try to treat children of both sexes as equally and fairly as possible.

PSYCHOLOGICAL PROBLEMS OF MIDDLE CHILDHOOD

Anxiety, frustration, and conflict are a part of the human condition, and all children will encounter some psychological problems at one time or another during childhood. A child who has lost a parent or even a pet will likely pass through a period of depression; a child who has been through a terrifying real-life experience, such as a car wreck, may understandably have many anxiety reactions, such as jumpiness, distractibility, irritability, and bad dreams. Other expressions of anxiety, however, are not always so easily understood: **phobias** (strong fears) that seem unrealistic or fantastic and appear to have no basis in actual experience; motor disturbances, such as **tics,** in which a child constantly and without apparent awareness blinks his or her eyes or shrugs his or her shoulders; obsessional, recurrent, apparently absurd thoughts that won't go away; compulsive behaviors, such as a need to wash one's hands constantly; and psychosomatic symptoms of various sorts. Sometimes it is quite difficult to understand why the child manifests these behavioral problems.

There is some evidence that psychological problems are more frequent at certain ages than at others. For example, referrals to psychiatric and psychological clinics tend to peak in the periods 4–7 years and 9–11 years, as well as 14–16 years. It may be that children pass through certain "natural" stages or transitions involving either accelerations in physical or cognitive development or rapid changes in what parents or society expect of them (for example, toilet training, beginning school).

What about sex differences? Are boys or girls more prone to psychological problems? Before puberty, boys have a much higher frequency of psychological problems. For example, during the first grade, boys are referred for clinical help *11 times* as frequently as girls for such problems as high rates of absenteeism, inability to concentrate or follow directions, shyness, and slow learning. Overall clinic referrals during middle childhood are several times higher for boys than girls for speech and reading difficulties, personality and behavioral problems, school failure, and delinquency.

There are also differences in the way boys and girls manifest their emotional difficulties: Girls will most often show symptoms of anxiety, fearfulness, and timidity; in contrast boys with emotional difficulties become aggressive and destructive and lack self-control.

What children are *least* likely to encounter severe emotional problems? First, if the child's neurophysiological functioning is normal, and if the child is not subjected to abnormally intense traumas, then he or she will be less likely to experience severe psychological problems. The second key factor is, as you might expect, the child's parents. Parents must provide good role models for the children. If the parents are characteristically warm and accepting, consistent though flexible in discipline, and not overly dominating, then in most cases, the child of such parents will develop into a self-reliant individual who has a strong conscience—that is, neither too lax nor too harsh. Finally, for the best psychological health, a child needs a social environment that values him or her as an individual, provides for basic needs, and offers an opportunity for development of his or her potential.

On the other hand, the child who is *most* likely to encounter more severe psychological problems is the child who has experienced an abnormal environment. A child who is constantly criticized or ridiculed may be anxious and uncertain in new situations and inclined to withdraw and avoid them. A child subjected to harsh or inconsistent discipline may not develop a strong conscience and may emerge as an angry, rebellious, and unmanageable child. A child whose parents are overly meticulous, compulsive, and overprotective may well end up being quite similar to his or her parents, that is, overly meticulous, cautious, and lacking in spontaneity.

Anxiety

We encounter numerous examples of anxiety in everyday life, and children during the middle years of childhood are subject to anxiety just like everyone else. A boy wants to jump on a trampoline and turn somersaults as his older brother does, but he is afraid. A girl wants to spend the night with her friend, but she has never stayed away from home all night by herself before.

A Case of a Phobia

An 11-year-old girl who was doing well in school and seemed well adjusted by her parents and teachers suddenly became very anxious. Her anxiety followed a Sunday picnic on which she had a slight choking episode on a piece of food. Several days later she told her parents she was going to die and she became very frightened. Apparently, the precipitating event for this anxiety was the choking episode.

The parents tried to reason with her but were unsuccessful. The child was taken to a psychologist, who learned the following facts from the child. Both parents were professionals and had to leave for work early each morning. They gave the responsibility of getting the two younger children ready for school to the 11-year-old girl. Since this was a reasonable request on the part of the parents, the girl could not refuse it, but unconsciously she felt resentment at this burden, which prevented her from attending to her own possible activities. Additionally, the family tended to suppress the expression of anger or resentment.

The psychologist decided that the girl's fear of dying was a reaction to the guilt she felt over her resentment of her parents. Since she had no right to be resentful, unconsciously she felt she should be punished. The presentiment of death was that punishment.

The psychologist explained his theory of the girl's guilt and resentment to the parents, and encouraged them to lighten her responsibilities and to get the child to talk about her resentment. They took his advice, and within 2 weeks the fear had disappeared.

Frequently, anxiety also involves guilt, in that the child's impulses conflict with his or her internal standards about what is right or wrong. For example, a 10-year-old girl may feel anxious because she would like very much to slap her younger brother, who teases her, but according to her conscience, it is wrong to do this.

There is no precise or generally accepted definition of anxiety, but commonly, the term refers to unpleasant states of tension, discomfort, or worry. This generalized apprehension may be caused by factors such as threats to well-being or self-esteem, conflicts, frustrations, and pressures to perform beyond one's capabilities. A small amount of anxiety may, and often does, serve constructive purposes, acting as a spur to creativity and problem solution. However, strong, continuing anxiety may be emotionally crippling, producing a deep sense of helplessness and inadequacy, rendering the child ineffectual and desperate.

However, if the child cannot deal with the anxiety adaptively, that is, attack its source and get rid of it, there are techniques of coping with it or defending against it. These are the so-called coping responses and defense mechanisms.

Defense Mechanisms

There are several kinds of defense mechanisms, and typically we are unaware that we are using them. Yet they help reduce anxiety and enable us to live more comfortably. However, when a defense is used, some aspect of reality is usually distorted. Some of the defense mechanisms discussed below are more likely to be used by children; others are seen just as frequently in adults.

In **repression,** the most basic underlying defense, the anxiety-producing thoughts are simply kept from conscious awareness. Repression is an unconscious defense mechanism — it is not a refusal to remember an event, nor is it a denial of its reality. Rather, the thought or event has been removed from consciousness by forces beyond the child's control. The total inability of a person to recall a particularly painful experience is one example of repression; not being able to recall the name of a person who dislikes you is another. Although clearly aware of these thoughts at one time, after repression the child is unaware of them, and direct questioning will not bring them to conscious awareness.

In **denial,** a closely related but more primitive defense, the child insists that an anxiety-arousing event or situation is not true and believes the denial is accurate. For example, a little girl who has been criticized and rejected by her father may deny that she is angry and insist that she is loved by her father and loves him. Some children who have been rejected by their families deny that these people are their real parents. Instead, they say that they are adopted, and that their true parents love them.

There is a subtle distinction between denial and repression. In repression the child has no awareness of the frightening or painful thought. For example, a girl cannot recall hearing a heated argument between her parents. This is repression. But in denial, the anxiety-arousing thought is denied, and the child actively denies having heard the argument.

Projection and **displacement** are defense mechanisms in which the unacceptable feeling or impulse is acknowledged, but it is attributed to other sources. Projection, for example, is attributing an undesirable thought or action to another person when in reality the thought or action applies to oneself. The plea, "She started the fight, Mother, not me," is one of the most common examples of projection in young children.

In displacement, the child has the appropriate emotional response but does not attribute it to the correct source. A boy's fear of his father, for example, may be too painful for him to acknowledge, but because he is afraid, he attributes the fear to an acceptable symbolic substitute for the father (e.g., lions).

Rationalization is a comforting defense that all of us — not only children — engage in. In rationalization, we find socially acceptable reasons for our behavior or attributes when the real reason is not acceptable, and would, if permitted into awareness, lead to painful anxiety and guilt. The father who harshly punishes his daughter because of his own intense anger toward the child but who then says he is doing it for her (i.e., the child's) own good is engaging in rationalization. The student who goes out on the night before an exam instead of studying and defends it by saying that everyone needs relaxation time is engaging in rationalization. Similarly, the extremely shy child who justifies his failure to interact socially and make friends by saying that none of the children at school are any fun is using rationalization.

Reaction formations are used as defense mechanisms when a person does not wish to acknowledge the truth. For example, a boy who is overly preoccupied with being spotlessly clean and tidy may actually be defending himself against strong and unacceptable wishes to be dirty and messy, either literally or symbolically (for example, sexually). It is as though the child were saying, "I can't have any desire to be messy or dirty, because look how preoccupied I am with being clean."

Withdrawal is one of the most frequently used defenses of preschool children; it is the direct avoidance of threatening situations or people. Children will hide their eyes or run to their own room when a stranger enters the house; they will refuse to approach a group of strange children despite their desire to play with them; they will shy away from a jungle gym if they doubt their ability to climb it successfully. Using withdrawal as a defense mechanism can be harmful to the child's development, for the tendency to withdraw becomes stronger each time the child practices this behavior, and so the child who refuses to cope with stressful situations may eventually become fearful of all problems and never learn to handle the crises that are inevitable in the course of development.

Regression is seen when a child reverts to a behavior that was characteristic of an earlier stage of development. Regression often occurs when a new baby is brought into the home. The older child may start thumbsucking or bed wetting in an attempt to withdraw from the current anxiety-arousing situation to the less anxious state of infancy. By adopting infantile behaviors, the child is attempting to gain attention and to retain the parents' love and nurturance.

While everyone uses defense mechanisms, the child who depends too heavily on these behaviors is not coping adequately with the real world. Particularly if the child's defensive structure is rigid and limited, the child's defensive reactions will usually not be appropriate to a particular situation. In such a case, using these mechanisms may interfere with more adaptive behavior (17).

Tics

Have you ever seen a child who is continually shaking her head slightly to one side or shrugging her shoulders? This type of motor response may be completely involuntary; that is, it may be a tic, one of the most commonly observed symptoms of psychological tension. You may have experienced a **tic** at some point in your life—a repeated, involuntary, seemingly purposeless motor response, usually of the face, neck, or head. The movement may be a blinking of the eyes, nose wrinkling, throat clearing, yawning, or the like. Tics are frequently symptoms of repressed needs and conflicts, and sometimes the nature of a tic serves as a clue to the underlying conflict. Could it be that the boy who is continually blinking his eyes is trying to blot out the memory of something unpleasant he saw? Or the girl who is always shaking her head is saying "no" to some unconscious wish? (11).

Tics are more common in tense children with fairly strict parents who put too much pressure on their child. The movement may be the child's involuntary reaction to stress. Because tics are involuntary, it is important that the child should not be scolded or corrected because of it, for this may only make the tic worse. An effort should be made to make the child's life at home as relaxed and agreeable as possible, with parents restraining their tendency to nag the child. The child's school and social life should be reasonably satisfying and not overstrenuous. If tics persist despite such efforts, it is important to seek psychological help in order to find out more about the specific nature of the tension and ameliorate it.

"Keep still!" Schoolteachers and parents often get annoyed with children who are fidgeting and restless. This general movement may be no more than a sign of diffuse anxiety, an effort to restore a feeling of ease, but it may also be related to tics in that it may serve as a defense against some other motor act that is forbidden, such as masturbation or aggressive behavior. As in the case of tics, generalized restlessness and fidgeting seem to be more common among children subject to strict parental restrictions (11).

Obsessions and Compulsions

Another reaction to unresolved anxiety is continually recurrent thoughts **(obsessions)**, acts or impulses to act **(compulsions)**, or a mixture of both. This defense is particularly useful in the case of conflicts between the child's needs and the demands of a strict conscience, for the child may not only ward off unacceptable impulses; he or she may also emphasize the opposite of the unacceptable impulse. For example, a child who has been told that masturbation is "dirty," yet wants to indulge in it, may develop compulsions to be extremely clean or to engage in repeated hand washing. It is as though the child were saying, "Look, I can't possibly have these impulses to engage in dirty behavior. See how concerned I am with being clean."

Mild obsessions and compulsions are common among children in the middle-childhood years, particularly around ages 8, 9, and 10 and are not necessarily a source of serious concern (11). On the other hand, when obsessions and compulsions are more severe, sustained, or unusual, it may be necessary to seek psychological or psychiatric help. Not unexpectedly, serious obsessive-compulsive neuroses are more frequent in the children of overly strict, fastidious, demanding parents. When parents place too much pressure for accomplishment on the child and allow little room for the expression of normal childhood impulses and desires, then the child is

likely to develop a psychological symptom such as an obsession or compulsion.

Fears and Phobias

Like the characters in *The Wizard of Oz*, many children are afraid of "lions and tigers and bears." Of course, children have some realistic fears, such as fear of being bitten by a dog or hit by a car. These fears are a function of direct experience or a product of parental warnings about certain objects. However, children also have many fears that are symbolic. About 20 percent of the fears held by children are unrealistic and deal with imaginary creatures, the dark, and being alone (9). In fact, children between 9 and 12 are only moderately afraid of immediate and possible dangers, such as getting hit by a car, but are strongly afraid of remote or impossible events, such as a lion attack or ghosts. These remote fears, which usually involve being seriously hurt or killed, may be symbolic of anticipated parental punishment or rejection. That is, the typical child learns during the first year of life that the pleasure of a misdemeanor is generally followed by some form of parental punishment. However, the child may suppress this fear of punishment, being unable to admit it directly.

For example, a 10-year-old who has strong, excessively unrealistic fears may be experiencing a large amount of guilt and conflict. In such a case, rationally pointing out to the child that ghosts do not exist is not likely to be successful in reducing the child's fear. After all, the ghosts in this case are merely a symbol for the child's unrecognized fear of the parent. Thus the best way to reduce the fear is to treat the actual source of the fear.

School Phobias. Sometimes children develop a fear, which may approach panic, of leaving home and going to school. All children occasionally are reluctant to go to school, but here we are talking about a persistent, serious fear. School phobias are more common among girls than boys, perhaps because of the greater social acceptability of fear and dependency in girls.

As with a strong fear of ghosts, a fear of school is a significant symptom; it indicates a dread of some aspect of the school situation, a fear of leaving home, or frequently, both. The most common problem indicated by school phobia involves separation anxiety, a fear of separation shared equally by parent and child. It seems that mothers of school-phobic children frequently are threatened by the thought of the child not being dependent on them. They may see the school as a cold, forbidding place and try to protect their child from it and all other painful facts of existence. Thus it is likely that the child will respond to the mother's wish to keep the child dependent.

Conduct Problems Psychological problems during middle childhood sometimes surface in conduct problems. Two of the more frequent problems, especially during early middle childhood, are lying and stealing. We are not talking here about children who "tell tales," that is, stretch the truth — rather imaginatively at times — simply because it would be more exciting. For example, a child may claim to have seen a great big bear in the backyard instead of just the neighbor's dog. But the kind of lying that is more symptomatic of a psychological problem is illustrated by, for example, a girl who claims to have made an A in school when in fact she has not. In cases such as this one, the child may be lying because of fear of failure to meet parental or social expectations. Thus it is important to determine whether these expectations are overly rigid and also whether the parents or other adults are overly demanding, punitive, and lacking in warmth or understanding.

But sometimes children lie without any obvious motivation. A child may say that she saw Mrs. Jones today and that Suzy Jones has the flu, when in fact she did *not* see Mrs. Jones, nor does Suzy have the flu. When such lying is unaccompanied by anxiety, the child may have a severe disturbance in conscience development or in the ability to distinguish reality from fantasy.

As in the case of lying, children may steal for different reasons, and thus the seriousness of the problem varies. Stealing may simply indicate a rather thoughtless giving in to an impulse of the moment or "going along with the crowd." It may, however, indicate a serious psychological disturbance, for a child may symbolically be trying to "steal" love and attention, particularly from parents. Stealing and getting caught may serve as an unconscious way for children to call attention to themselves and their problems and to ask for help. Or children may be expressing hostility toward parents by violating their standards or embarrassing them by getting caught. Then, too, getting caught may be the child's way of punishing himself for real or imagined wrongs. Many of these same motivations may be involved in other childhood conduct problems, such as vandalism, fire setting, and truancy.

DEVELOPMENT OF CONSCIENCE AND PROSOCIAL BEHAVIOR

In Europe, a woman was near death from cancer. There was one drug that the doctors thought might save her. It was a form of radium that a druggist in the same town had recently discovered. The drug was expensive to make, but the druggist was charging 10 times what the drug cost him to make. He paid $200 for the radium and charged $2000 for a small dose of the drug. The sick woman's husband, Heinz, went to everyone he knew to borrow the money, but he could get together only about $1000, which was half of what it cost. He told the druggist that his wife was dying, and asked him to sell it cheaper or let him pay later. But the druggist said, "No, I discovered the drug and I'm going to make money from it." Heinz became desperate and broke into the man's store to steal the drug for his wife (14, p. 98).

Should Heinz have stolen the drug? Why or why not?

A 5-year-old's answer to the question above will probably differ from a 12-year-old's answer. The 5-year-old is likely to adhere to strict, concrete principles of right and wrong, saying that stealing is wrong; therefore the man should not have broken into the store. A 12-year-old child, on the other hand, will weigh the factors involved in the case and might decide that saving a life is more important than anything else and that the man was right to steal the drug.

Children show considerable development in the area of conscience and prosocial behavior during middle childhood. One psychologist who has been particularly interested in the progressive development of conscience is Lawrence Kohlberg. Kohlberg and his associates have studied the development of moral thinking and reasoning in children by going directly to the children. Children read stories, or were told stories, containing moral dilemmas and were then asked to make judgments and give the reasons for their judgments. The story cited above of the man stealing a drug for his sick wife is an example of one such dilemma.

Children of different ages and different cultural backgrounds were given the stories and questions. Using their answers to the questions, Kohlberg formulated a scheme of three moral levels, each with two types

Table 9.1 KOHLBERG'S MORAL FORMULATION

I. Premoral	1. Orientation toward punishment and obedience	2. A naive kind of hedonism
II. Morality of Conventional Rule-Conformity	3. "Good boy-good girl" morality (trying to maintain the approval of others and good relations with them)	4. A reliance on the precepts of authority
III. Morality of Self-accepted Moral Principles	5. Morality-contractual obligations and democratically accepted law	6. Morality of individual principles of conscience

of moral reasoning. Table 9.1 shows the levels and types of moral reasoning.

The developmental process was clearly seen in the children's answers to the problems. Four-year-olds, for example, tended to judge an act as good or bad depending on whether it led to punishment or reward in the story — that is, in terms of its reinforcements rather than in terms of the rule governing the interaction. By the age of 5 to 7 years, children evaluated the act in terms of its moral quality — that is, whether the act itself was considered good or bad. They determined "goodness" or "badness" by the possibility of future punishment, so that they were essentially just changing the terms from short-range to long-range reinforcement. But by preadolescence, a majority of children made "disinterested" moral judgments — that is, they decided the goodness or badness of an act according to moral principles alone. Also, they had by this age formulated some concept of a morally good self, of a person who subscribes to moral ideas not because of fear of punishment but because of a moral belief (12).

In a study similar to Kohlberg's, children from kindergarten through college ages were asked, "What is a rule?" The younger children (kindergarten through second grade) tended to emphasize the "do not," or negative, aspect of a rule; that is, they defined a rule as a guideline prohibiting certain behaviors. For example, a young boy gave this response: "A rule is not to run around, not to hit anybody, not to break anything." Older children (from fourth to eighth grades) saw a rule as more neutral; it was a *prescription* for behavior. They defined a rule as "something to keep." Some of the older children also emphasized the beneficial (helpful) and rational (logical) aspects of a rule. That is, it makes sense for people to respect the property of others. If they didn't, there would be chaos. For example, an eighth-grade boy emphasized the prescriptive *and* beneficial/rational aspects: "Well, a rule is mainly something to keep, to make the place better" (22).

Interestingly, however, while most older children subscribe to high ideals of morality in principle, they do not use them as the basis for actual behavior. When asked, "Why do *you* (italics ours) follow rules?," the answers of many middle-school children and adolescents revealed that they, like the primary-school children, follow rules because they want to "avoid negative consequences." Only 7 percent of middle-school children and 22 percent of older adolescents gave reasons indicating that it was useful for society.

It is clear that conscience development requires a certain maturity of cognitive functions, as well as a number of complex psychological processes based on learning. For a time, a child is cognitively capable of handling only highly specific, concrete prohibitions; it is not until the child is capable of more abstract thinking that he or she can develop generalized standards (13). That is, higher cognitive functioning is required for moral reactions that require shifting from absolute, rigid standards that judge only the act itself to more flexible standards that take into account the intention behind the act.

In sum, there are many cognitive functions that play a role in conscience development. And as children develop a more articulated concept of time and the future, of values and ideals, they are better able to see how their actions affect others, and they begin to see logically that it is necessary for people to cooperate with one another in the interests of all (12).

A child's developing moral beliefs inevitably have some effects on his or her behavior. In the next section we will explore the extent of those effects as we look at the development of prosocial behavior.

Prosocial Behavior

As with many other aspects of behavior, the extent to which a child acts in accordance with his or her moral beliefs is influenced heavily by the child's parents. For example, the child's demonstration of prosocial behavior is affected by the nature of discipline used by the parents, the strength of the child's identification with the parent, and the type of example set by the parent. As noted earlier (Chapter 7), children are likely to develop strong identifications with their parents when their parents are warm and nurturing, and strong identifications lead children to adopt the behavior of the parents. It follows, then, that if the model (that is, the parent) displays prosocial behavior often, the child is likely to adopt that behavior. Thus we see that there are two requirements for the child to develop strong prosocial behavior: First, the parent must be a role model for the child, and second, the parent must be warm and nurturant in order for the child to develop a strong identification.

Parental disciplinary techniques are important. Parents who discipline through **power assertion** — that is, control by physical power or material resources, including threats and deprivation of privileges — have children who show little consideration for others. On the other hand, parents who use *induction* — that is, reasoning with the child and pointing out painful consequences of the child's behavior for others — have children who show higher levels of consideration for others (8).

What accounts for these differences? It may well be that induction evokes feelings of empathy in the child—that is, the ability to share the emotional responses of others. In using induction, parents train their children to consider the effects of their actions on others and to regulate their activities accordingly. This leads to an understanding of the feelings of others (empathy) and attempts to help others. But when parents use power-assertive techniques, they teach their children that they should act according to the will of authority. Subsequently, these children are likely to behave according to prescribed rules rather than to react on the basis of considering the possible effects of their actions on others (8).

Other influences on the frequency of a child's prosocial behavior in a laboratory include the child's sex, age, whether the child is emotionally aroused, and whether the child is alone or with other children. For example, in one experiment, the effect of the child's sex and emotional arousal on prosocial behavior was measured (5). Children were brought individually to a large unoccupied classroom for the experiment. Each child was told that the experimenter was interested in learning about children's imagination and was given a bag of 25 balloons for helping with the research. The children were told that they could share some of the balloons with children who could not participate in the experiment.

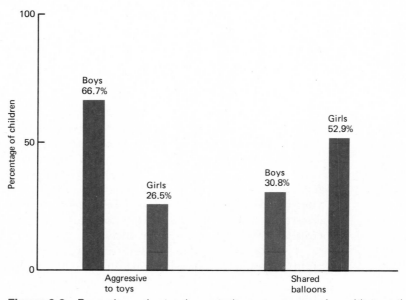

Figure 9.2 Boys showed a tendency to be more aggressive with toys than did girls, and girls showed a tendency to be more altruistic—that is, to share more balloons with the other children. (After M. B. Harris, & C. E. Siebel. Affect, aggression, and altriusm. *Developmental Psychology*, 1975, *11*, 623–627.)

The experimenter told the children in one group to mentally generate happy, sad, or angry thoughts. Children in the control group were asked to simply count very slowly. After each child had generated these thoughts (or counted), the experimenter said she was going to leave the room. The child was shown the box marked "Balloons for other children" and was also told that he or she could play with any of the toys in the room. The children could express aggression with some of the toys (for example, a large inflated Popeye doll could be punched), while other toys were more neutral (a truck, a puppet, and a yo-yo, for example).

In all conditions (happy, sad, angry, or control) the girls were more altruistic than the boys. The girls were more likely to leave balloons behind for the other children. Boys were more likely to be aggressive than girls (see Figure 9.2). Interestingly, the effect of the emotional arousal was to *increase* aggressive behavior in boys, while it *decreased* aggressive behavior in girls.

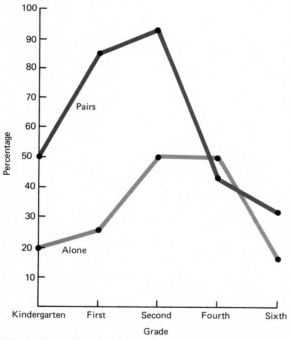

Figure 9.3 Prosocial behavior peaked at about the second grade, and children who were with another child helped more than those who were alone. (Adapted from E. Staub. A child in distress: the influence of age and number of witnesses on children's attempts to help. *Journal of Personality and Social Psychology*, 1970, *14*, 130–140. Copyright 1970 by the American Psychological Association. Reprinted by permission.)

A second experiment evaluated the effect of the child's age and whether the child was alone or with a friend on behavior reflecting concern for another. Children were brought alone or with a same-sex classmate to a room where they were going to draw color pictures (21). After entering the room the experimenter said she had forgotten the crayons, but before going to get them she said she had better check on the child in the next room. She returned and said that the child was all right, but hoped the child would not stand on the chair again. She then left to get the crayons. About a minute later the child alone or the pair of children heard a noise and a scream coming from the next room. The child or pair of children could help by going to the next room, by telling the experimenter when she returned, or they could do nothing.

Prosocial behavior increased from kindergarten to second grade and then declined. More important, children who were with another child were more likely to help than those who were alone (see Figure 9.3). Thus, the sex and age of the child as well as the specific social situation the child is in influence the likelihood of prosocial behavior. It is not possible to say that a particular child will be helpful or empathic in all situations.

SUMMARY

1. During middle childhood, parents continue the process of socialization, though by this age they expect more mature behavior of their children. In the areas of sex typing and aggression, the focus of concern in socialization is slightly different from the preschool years, but most parents continue to treat sons and daughters differently and discourage the expression of aggression.

2. The parent-child relationship, so important in determining the personality and social development of the child, can be characterized along two dimensions: warmth-hostility and restrictiveness-permissiveness.

3. Children's overall self-concepts are very much influenced by their relationship with their parents and other family members. Parental warmth and acceptance seem to foster high self-esteem.

4. Over 10 million children in the United States live in fatherless homes and are reared primarily by their mothers. On the average, these children, especially boys, have cognitive deficits that are reflected in poorer school grades and lower intelligence and achievement test scores.

5. Boys who are separated from their fathers before the age of 5 tend to be less masculine in behavior, more dependent, and less aggressive than boys from intact families. However, adverse effects of divorce on a young boy's personality and social behavior may be considerably re-

duced if the father is well adjusted and maintains contact with his son.

6. Relationships with brothers and sisters may also have significant effects on a child's personality and social behavior. First-borns generally identify with their parents, adopt parental values, and maintain high levels of achievement motivation. Later-born children are more likely to suffer from feelings of inadequacy but, at the same time, to acquire skills that lead to social success and popularity.

7. Psychological problems of middle childhood may be manifested in anxiety reactions, obsessions and compulsions, phobias, tics, or psychosomatic symptoms. Neurophysiological functioning, the parent-child relationship, and the child's social environment are all factors that influence the development of severe emotional problems.

8. Girls most often show symptoms of anxiety, fearfulness, and timidity; in contrast, boys with emotional difficulties become aggressive and destructive and lack self-control. In an attempt to cope with their anxiety, both boys and girls may turn to defense mechanisms such as repression, denial, projection, displacement, rationalization, reaction formations, withdrawal, and regression.

9. The middle-childhood years represent a critical period for conscience development, which is dependent on the level of cognitive maturation and also on parental and other influences to which the child is subjected.

10. The first signs of conscience development are related to prohibitions against specific acts. Gradually the child's conscience becomes more internalized, and more idealized standards are established.

11. Observation of parental models and identification with parents are of utmost importance in acquiring prosocial behaviors such as honesty, generosity, kindness, altruism, and consideration of the rights and welfare of others. Prosocial behavior is found more often in children whose parents use induction (that is, reasoning and pointing out painful consequences for others of the child's behavior) than in children of parents who discipline through power assertion (that is, control by physical power or material resources).

Suggested Readings

Bar-Tal, D. *Prosocial behavior.* New York: Wiley, 1976.

Hoffman, L. W., & Nye, F. I. *Working mothers.* San Francisco: Jossey Bass, 1974.

Lamb, M. E. *The role of the father in child development.* New York: Wiley, 1976.

Martin, B. Parent-child relations. In F. D. Horowitz (Ed.), *Review of child development research.* Chicago: University of Chicago Press, 1975.

Chapter 10

Socialization Outside the Family

$\mathcal{N}$OW THAT we have followed the development of the child within the family through the age of middle childhood, let's look at how the child is affected by the forces of the outside world. The child is influenced by peers, by school, and by the media, especially television. In this chapter we shall look at the effects of all these nonfamilial influences.

It is obvious that peers exert a powerful force on the developing child. Now the child is capable of comparing himself or herself with others, and children at this age become quite concerned with being liked by their peers. Many children in this age group seem to care more about their ranking with their peers than they do about their ranking in the family.

School, too, is a strong influence on the child. This is not surprising in light of the fact that the child spends more weekday waking hours at school than anywhere else except home. In looking at the influence of school, we will also examine the problem of school failure—its causes and what might be done to reduce the incidence of school failure.

Finally, we shall look at the effects of a fairly recent influence on children. Television is a phenomenon that has only in the last 25 years or so become a major agent of socialization, and as you well know, it is a powerful one.

PEER INFLUENCE

With the beginning of school, a child's peer group grows in size and influence. One reason behind this increasing influence is that the percentage of time the child spends in school and other activities increases steadily from kindergarten to high school (6). In fact, it may be said that children live in two worlds, that of their parents and other adults and that of their peers.

The world of peers is a subculture of its own, though it is influenced in many ways by the larger culture of which it is a part. It has its own history and its own social organization. It may even be said to have its own "folklore," which children pass on from one to another without benefit of the teachings of adults. It is as though there are always younger children ready and eager to take on the roles of older children, and thus much of the ritual of the childhood years is transmitted by peers, not by parents, even though the rituals themselves may have changed little over the years (28). For example, probably all children of all ages have played hide-and-seek at one time or another, even though their parents may never have taught it to them.

Peer interaction is unique. It offers the child what no adult-child relationship can—the opportunity to learn how to interact with age mates, how to relate to a leader, and how to deal with hostility and dominance. Especially in later childhood, peers may function in a kind of counseling role, helping the child to deal with personal problems and anxieties.

The influence of the child's peer group is significant: The values and attitudes of the child's peer group help to shape the developing child's personality. Peers also contribute directly and indirectly to the develop-

ment of the child's self-concept. We shall now look at these and other aspects of peer influence.

The Nature of Children's Groups

The structure, function, and membership of children's groups—and changes in these—tend to occur mostly independently of adult influence, with marked similarities from generation to generation. But while a child's world may be a world unto itself, a subculture in which no adults can dictate who is the leader, adults do have some influence on the initial makeup of the group. Parents, of course, determine where the child lives, and the suburban, middle-class white child or the urban, lower-middle-class black child may each have restricted opportunity for interaction with children of other cultural, ethnic, or socioeconomic backgrounds, often to the detriment of both. In addition, sometimes parents may restrict, even among available opportunities, the other children with whom they allow their children to associate.

The "Secret Society of 17th Street" may arbitrarily select or reject prospective members and may have elaborate rituals for conducting meetings.

During the early years of middle childhood—say, 6 to 9—children usually participate in informal groups. They refer to their group as "the gang," there are few formal rules, and membership in "the gang" is largely determined by convenience. If a child lives too far away to participate easily, for example, then it is unlikely that he or she will be considered part of "the gang." Later, however, between the ages of 10 and 14, there is a tendency for children's groups to become more highly structured (11). The "Secret Society of 17th Street" may arbitrarily select or reject prospective members and may have elaborate rituals for conducting meetings. Even so, membership may change frequently, and the group itself may not last long. There is also at this age, especially among middle-class children, a tendency to join formal organizations such as the Boys' Clubs or the Campfire Girls.

Peers as Socializers

Just how much power do peers exert on the attitudes and values of a developing child? This varies from culture to culture and from one historical era to another. Obviously, one factor that will affect the strength of peer influence is how much time a child spends with his or her peers. American children are strongly encouraged to interact with peers and are therefore inevitably influenced by them. But children in many other cultures—Chinese, French, and Mexicans in small villages—do not play with their friends as much as American children. And in general, European children are much less likely than Americans to rely on peers rather than on adults for opinions and advice (3). The exception is English children, who spend more time with peers and less with parents than children in other countries do. In addition, their activities with peers are relatively unstructured and freer of adult supervision or direction than those of many other children.

The Industrious Age

For Erik Erikson, in his "eight stages of man," the central task of the middle-childhood years is the development of a *sense of industry,* of industriousness. The child of 5 or 6 has "an enormous curiosity—a wish to learn, a wish to know." Faced with a new gadget, the child wants to know how it works. Armed with expanding cognitive skills, the child of this age is not content to observe how others do things— ride a bicycle, operate a typewriter, solve a puzzle. The child wants to prove to others and to the self that he or she can do it. In short, there is what Robert White calls a *striving for competence.*

Much of this striving initially has a playful quality to it—a carry-over from the preschool years. Increasingly, however, it has a serious purpose as well. The child senses that as he or she grows older, it will be necessary to be able to understand and to master the tasks and events with which he or she is confronted. The child who learns during these middle-childhood years that he or she is competent, can do things, and can do them well, will be far better prepared to deal confidently with the uncertainties of puberty and adolescence.

The danger of this period, in Erikson's view, is that the child will not develop these feelings of confidence and competence—that he or she will develop a *sense of inferiority.* There may, of course, be many reasons for this: excessive dependency on parents, inadequate prepa-ration for school-age tasks, being derogated, or put down, by teach-ers, parents, or peers. "The development of a sense of inferiority, the feeling that one will never be 'any good,' is a danger which can be minimized by a teacher who knows how to emphasize what a child *can* do." Most insidious, perhaps, the child's sense of excitement and adventure may be discouraged. The truly creative teacher or parent can help the child to understand that learning and doing can be both work—real work—and still fun.

Erik H. Erikson, *Identity: Youth and crisis.* New York: Norton, 1968.

Richard I. Evans. *Dialogue with Erik Erikson.* New York: Harper & Row, 1967.

Robert W. White. *Lives in progress.* New York: Dryden Press, 1952.

What exactly is the peer-group influence? Do peer group values tend to match those of the adult culture, or do children have different "rules"? Once again we find cultural variations. Children in the Soviet Union, for example, have peer group norms that are quite similar to those of adults, while children in the United States and England tend to endorse sets of rules that are different from those of adults.

Children from four countries—the United States, the Soviet Union, England, and Germany—were presented with a dilemma or conflict between the norms of adults and peer pressure. For example, one dilemma read, "You and some of your friends accidentally find a copy of a quiz that your class will be given the next day together with the correct answers to the quiz questions." In the story, some of the friends suggest that the child say nothing to the teacher about finding the quiz, so that all of them can get better grades. Other dilemmas involved playing tricks on the teacher, neglecting homework to join friends, or going to a movie recommended by friends but disapproved of by parents (4).

English children were the most susceptible to peer pressure, while Soviet children were most resistant. American children were willing to go along with peer suggestions to misbehave when they thought that only their peers, but not adults, would see their answers to the questionnaire. The answers of American children demonstrate that the norms of children and adults are different in the United States, and that American children do feel that they are living in two worlds. English children, on the other hand, subscribe more fully to the norms of the peer group, which are also different from those of adults. The peer group norms of Soviet children, however, differ little from those of adults.

Conformity to Peers

There are vast individual differences in children's tendencies to conform, and the tendency varies with age. Preschool children, for example, show little evidence of conformity to group norms, but during the middle childhood years conformity behavior increases. However, while children tend to conform *more* on social issues, such as how to behave or what to wear as the latest fad, as they get older, their tendency to conform on concrete, cognitive judgments *decreases* during middle childhood, although even on cognitive issues, conformity is still a powerful force.

In one experiment, children were shown a single, black line (called the standard). Then they were shown three black lines of different lengths and asked to choose which of the three lines was equal in length to the standard line (10). When tested alone, most children were accurate in their judgments. But when placed with peers—all of whom were "stooges" who had been instructed ahead of time to report the wrong answer—all children showed an increased tendency to go along with the majority and report the wrong answer. The young children (ages 7 to 10) were more influenced by the incorrect majority than the older children (ages 10 to 13).

In a second experiment, a teacher served as the "stooge." Children were still influenced, though to a lesser extent, by the teacher's wrong answer. Again, younger children were much more influenced than the older children.

In most situations, girls have been found to be more conforming to peer-group pressures than boys (19), perhaps because girls are more oriented toward others and feel a greater need for social approval. Individual personality factors also influence a child's conforming tendencies. Conforming children tend to be more dependent and anxious (15, 31), lower in self-esteem, and higher in social sensitivity (13).

Peers as Teachers

Peers function as agents of socialization, sometimes reinforcing the values of their parents, sometimes counteracting these values, but often dealing with a completely different category of behaviors. As agents of socialization, peers really teach one another how to act in various social situations. They do this in the same ways that parents do—through rewards, punishment, and modeling—that is, they reinforce certain responses and punish others, and serve as models for each other. If Ray sees Andy being helpful to a younger child, then Ray may adopt that same behavior the next time he is around a younger child.

In addition, the peer group provides an opportunity to learn how to interact with age mates, how to relate to a leader, and how to deal with hostility and dominance. Peers can also help one another deal with personal problems and anxieties. Sharing problems, conflicts, and complex feelings with peers may be very reassuring for a child. For instance, discovering that other children are also angry at their parents or concerned with masturbation may relieve tension and guilt somewhat.

Clearly, a child can be influenced by the values and attitudes of his or her peer group. The attitudes of peers toward education may strongly affect the child's feelings about school as well as his or her academic interests, aims, and aspirations. If getting high grades in school is not looked upon with respect by the peer group, then a child may not be motivated to try for higher grades.

A child's self-concept—that is, the child's overall feelings about himself or herself—is also subject to both direct and indirect influence from the peer group. A boy who is accepted by the peer group will feel better about himself than he would if he were rejected by the peer group, for example. In addition, peer groups can provide children with information about themselves—sometimes realistic, sometimes distorted—and this information is taken into account in the formation of the self-concept. Of course, children can be cruel—deliberately or unintentionally. They can tell a slightly overweight child she is fat and make her terribly self-conscious about her weight; they can call another child a "sissy," poking fun at him because his mother insists that he wear galoshes over his sneakers.

The peer group is also a valuable source of comparison for children, and they are constantly comparing themselves with others in their peer group. If in the child's own view, he or she ranks high relative to peers on characteristics such as attractiveness, intelligence, and popularity, the self-concept will be enhanced; if he or she ranks lower than most peers on these characteristics, the self-concept may be diminished.

The personality characteristics of children who are most likely to be accepted — that is, are most popular during middle childhood — vary with social-class background (22). Among middle-class children, the qualities of friendliness, cooperativeness, and helpfulness are valued. Children who are aggressive, untrustworthy, and/or uncooperative are unpopular. Lower-class boys tend to respect two types of peers: the aggressive, belligerent youngster who has earned the respect of peers because he is tough and strong, and the boy who is outgoing and sociable but not overly aggressive. Lower-class boys tend to be highly suspicious of the "teacher's pet." In contrast, lower-class girls are more willing than their male peers to respect the friendly, neat, and studious girl who is not necessarily a leader. Thus the lower-class girl, like the middle-class girl, can be a good student without alienating her friends.

Peers as Socializers of Aggression

If it were not for peers, many children might be less aggressive. Children express aggression about 3 times as much during free play in school or on the playground as they do at home. Thus children, particularly boys, learn effective aggression skills from peers—how to hit in order to defend oneself and how to make another person angry.

Children learn aggression from other peers through reinforcement and imitation. First, aggressive acts may be reinforced in that other children yield to aggression. Then, less aggressive children, learning to counterattack and gaining power through aggression, may initiate aggressive actions themselves. Second, peers serve as models for aggression. Children can readily observe and imitate the responses of an aggressive child.

Fortunately for parents, however, peer groups also often act to control these aggressive acts. Consequently, parents in every society rely on the child's peers to help in socializing the expression of aggression and learning aggression controls, such as how to resist the temptation to attack someone else. In interactions with peers, children may find that it is better to try to reason with another child in order to get one's way than it is to hit the other child and then to be shunned by the peer group (12).

Peer Influences on Sex Typing

Most children's peer groups, as a rule, seem to be fairly traditional in their definitions of sex-appropriate behavior. Thus, in most cases they support and extend the parents' efforts in socializing children to behave in ways the society considers sex-appropriate. In fact, through their peer group, children may learn more sex-appropriate responses—that is, sex-typed activities, interests, and attitudes that may not have been acquired at home. For example, a girl whose mother does not sew may learn to sew at a friend's house.

During middle childhood, peer groups are usually segregated by sex—boys play with boys, and girls play with girls (13). Because these peer groups tend to be traditionally sex-typed, sometimes peer influence may counteract the effects of training and identification in the home. For example, a young boy who is highly identified with his mother—perhaps because she is the parent who is seen as more nurturant, powerful, or competent—may have many characteristics that are generally considered feminine, but after associating with other boys in school, he may behave in a more masculine manner. Then, too, some parents are consciously trying to break through customary sex-role stereotypes and rear children of both sexes to adopt desirable characteristics (for example, expressiveness,

nurturance, assertiveness, and sociability) even if they have not traditionally been considered appropriate for the sex of their child. For example, a boy's parents may try to foster expressiveness and nurturance by permitting him to play with dolls if he wants to. But if he plays with dolls outside the home, he may find that other boys are quick to call him "sissy" or punish him in other ways when he does these things. Thus, as he is deprived of one outlet for his self-expressive and nurturant responses, these behaviors may diminish, and the parents may find their efforts undermined by the child's peers, who pressure him to act in more sex-stereotyped ways.

Peer Models and Prosocial Behavior

Since peers are highly effective models of aggression and sex-typed behavior, it seems only natural that they can also be effective models of constructive and cooperative — prosocial — behavior. Children are likely to imitate what they observe their peers doing, including donating to charity, expressing sympathy, or helping someone in distress (5). Peer models can also help reduce children's timidity or fear responses and promote greater participation in social activities.

SOCIALIZATION IN THE SCHOOL

From kindergarten onward, school remains for more than a decade the center of the child's world outside his or her home, occupying almost half the waking hours of each weekday. Since a major share of the child's interactions with peers occurs in the school setting, our discussion of peers as socializers, in a sense, has dealt with the school, but in this section we will look at the more direct forces of socialization in the school — that is, the teacher's role in socialization and the school itself as a molder of personality and social behavior.

The Teacher's Role

The teacher is generally the first adult outside the immediate family who plays a major role in the youngster's life and, in many instances, acts as a parent substitute. Some teachers help children to overcome handicaps and make the most of their talents and interests, while others, who are basically ill suited to working with children — or with a particular child or group of children — may have serious detrimental effects on their pupils. This may be especially true of teachers working with socioeconomically disadvantaged or minority-group children, as we shall see. Like other agents of socialization, teachers make their influences felt by modeling, by encouraging (reinforcing) certain responses, and by discouraging others.

Sex Typing in the School. Since almost all teachers in kindergarten and the primary grades are women, at least in the United States, schools tend to reinforce traditionally feminine behaviors (being quiet, obedient, compliant, passive) in both boys and girls. Traditional masculine responses such as assertiveness, aggression, competitiveness, and rough play are ignored, discouraged, or actively suppressed at school. However, because of peer pressures and reinforcement, at home and with friends, "boys will be boys"; that is, they are likely to maintain the masculine patterns of behavior they acquire at home and in interactions with other boys.

Because feminine behavior is encouraged and masculine behavior is discouraged at school, it is not surprising that many boys think of school and academic activities as essentially feminine, of a smart boy as a "sissy." This undoubtedly accounts in part for the fact that boys have more adjustment problems in school and, in the early grades, don't care as much about school and do not perform as well as girls. For example, reading problems are 3 to 6 times as frequent among boys as among girls in the United States (2).

When there are male teachers in the early grades, boys become more attached to them than to women teachers. Interestingly, in Japan, where there are many male teachers in the lower grades, difficulties in reading are no more common among boys than among girls, and, in America, boys taught by males do better in reading than those taught by females (23).

Teacher Characteristics. Does a teacher's personality make a difference in the classroom? Apparently, the answer is yes. Teachers' personal characteristics are reflected in the way they discipline and deal with their pupils, and this in turn affects the pupils' attitudes toward learning. One study clearly showed this. Dogmatic people who are intolerant of complexity or uncertainty were rigid, authoritarian, and punitive teachers. In contrast, people who were flexible and independent-minded, more democratic, and interested in novelty were warmer and more relaxed teachers who, in their classes, encouraged pupil participation and freer expression of feelings.

Pupils of the more authoritarian teachers were less helpful, less cooperative, and more aggressive.

As you might expect, children reacted differently to the two types of teachers. Compared with the pupils of the authoritarian teachers, those who had more flexible teachers became more interested and involved in classroom activities. They volunteered for more tasks, acted more independently, and expressed feelings more freely. They achieved more academically and showed more creativity. Pupils of the more authoritarian teachers were less helpful, less cooperative, and more aggressive.

Teachers as Therapists. Obviously, teachers have some influence on their pupils' personality and social behavior. They are important agents of socialization. Often their influence is unintentional, but teachers can also be powerful agents of a deliberate program of **behavior modification,** and such a program can have a marked impact on socialization. This has been dramatically demonstrated in experiments in which teachers act as behavior-modification therapists, intentionally manipulating rewards and punishments in order to alter children's behavior—for instance, to help them to reduce aggression and increase cooperation and to find better substitutes for behaviors that antagonize others or interfere with learning.

Behavior modification, as you may know, is a kind of therapy based on learning principles, with the therapist using conditioning and reinforcement to modify and shape a child's behavior. In one study, teachers gave their students points and tokens for desirable responses, such as a high score on a quiz, being quiet during rest period, and completing assignments. The points and tokens could be exchanged for prizes such as candy and toys. The use of this program had positive effects on school attendance and academic performance (21). Among other results, one was that the pupils displayed much less undesirable and disruptive behavior in the classroom.

But like almost any other program that involves human behavior, behavior modification is not a magical, fail-safe strategy; the effectiveness of behavior therapy is related to the pupils' attitudes toward the teachers who are serving as therapists. If the students like and respect the teacher, then they will be far more interested in receiving rewards, for rewards from a teacher who is disliked may not be highly valued. Moreover, many psychologists believe that the *child* holds the key to success for any behavior-modification program. They have found that a program can be successful only if the child wants it to work—that is, if he or she is ready to make behavioral changes. The children retain the privilege of choice and ultimately are not governed by the teacher's program of rewards and punishments; rather they decide whether they wish to go along with such a program. They may, like one first-grader, sometimes choose the punishment. Before leaving for school on the morning of the classroom mothers' tea, the boy told his mother, "I think I'll lose a token today, so I'll have to stay after school. Then I'll already be in the room when you come for tea."

Nonetheless, it is still true that some students may feel that the rewards that they earn (more recess time, greater freedom to do creative things) make it worthwhile to conform to the school rules. In time they become more convinced of the advantages of hard work and obedience and the rewards are no longer necessary.

Teachers as Models. In the course of growing up, no doubt you have encountered some teachers who influenced you profoundly. Young children,

From Up the Down Staircase

There was one heady moment when I was able to excite the class by an idea: I had put on the blackboard Browning's "A man's reach should exceed his grasp, or what's a heaven for?" and we got involved in a spirited discussion of aspiration vs. reality. Is it wise, I asked, to aim higher than one's capacity? Does it not doom one to failure? No, no, some said, that's ambition and progress! No, no, others cried, that's frustration and defeat! What about hope? What about despair? — You've got to be practical! — You've got to have a dream! They said this in their own words, you understand, startled into discovery. To the young, clichés seem freshly minted. Hitch your wagon to a star! Shoemaker, stick to your last! And when the dismissal bell rang, they paid me the highest compliment: they groaned! They crowded in the doorway, chirping like agitated sparrows, pecking at the seeds I had strewn — when who should appear but [the administrative assistant to the principal].

"What is the meaning of this noise?"

"It's the sound of thinking, Mr. McHabe," I said.

In my letter box that afternoon was a note from him, with copies to my principal and chairman (and — who knows — perhaps a sealed indictment dispatched to the Board?) which read:

"I have observed that in your class the class entering your room is held up because the pupils exiting from your room are exiting in a disorganized fashion, blocking the doorway unnecessarily and *talking*. An orderly flow of traffic is the responsibility of the teacher whose class is exiting from the room."

The cardinal sin, strange as it may seem in an institution of learning, is talking.

From the book *Up the Down Staircase* by Bel Kaufman. © 1964 by Bel Kaufman. Published by Prentice-Hall, Inc., Englewood Cliffs, New Jersey 07632.

too, may imitate the behavior of their teachers, especially if the teacher is attractive and is a positive figure in the child's life.

Through modeling a teacher can exert significant influence on the child's tempo — that is, the tendency to be impulsive or reflective. Students work and move at different paces. Some are quick and impulsive; others are more reflective and slower in reacting. First-grade children, especially impulsive ones, tend to become more reflective, more careful, more orderly, and slower in their own responses if they are taught by experienced, reflective teachers, and the modeling effect is more marked for boys than for girls (34).

This information could be put to good use in school reading programs. Reading is harder for boys than for girls, in part because boys are more impulsive (16). If extremely impulsive boys were placed with a teacher who was temperamentally reflective, they might slow down enough to improve their reading skills.

School Size

Even the size of the school the child attends may influence his or her social development. Teachers in large schools with large classes tend to be more formal in their approach. They discipline using control, restraint, and direct guidance. In contrast, in the freer and more intimate atmosphere of many small schools with smaller classes, teachers interact more with their students and are less likely to impose restrictions on behavior (10).

Like large schools, small ones can offer many and varied opportunities to participate in extracurricular activities, such as athletics, music, journalism, student government, and other organizations and clubs. The difference is that small schools are more intimate and have fewer students available for each activity. Consequently, students in such schools are much more likely to participate actively in extracurricular activities than students in large schools. According to the data of one study, the proportion of students participating in various activities was 3 to 20 times greater in small than in large institutions.

Textbooks

Classic characters in readers used in the primary grades tend to be happy, middle-class, suburban children, and the stories are about a world of friendly, good, smiling people, who are ready and eager to help. These stories are not of much relevance to all first-graders; the poor urban child is not living in a sunny Caucasian middle-class suburban world, and poor children are not likely to be highly motivated to read textbooks that present what is for them an unrealistic world. In recent years, educators have recognized special educational needs of poor and minority children. Reading problems are very common among these children, especially among the boys. Unfortunately, even the few readers for primary grades that attempt to focus on the working class and racially mixed urban neighborhoods rarely do so. Instead, they present the same basic middle-class themes, only they substitute a different cast of characters in a different setting. Moreover, it seems that even children who do live in neighborhoods that are relatively comfortable may find the "Pollyanna" themes of these readers boring. When children choose their own books in libraries, they prefer stories about real-life events, folk tales, and nature rather than the "Dick and Jane" middle-class themes.

There is another major shortcoming in the elementary-school texts: Most of them present a very narrow, stereotyped picture of sex roles and sex-appropriate behavior. Boys and men are the important characters in these stories. Boys work and play actively and aggressively; they are competent and capable of solving problems. Girls, on the other hand, are portrayed as inactive and lacking in ambition and creativity; they are sociable, outgoing, kind, timid, easily frightened, conforming, and prone to fantasy, all qualities traditionally associated with girls and women. Adult men are generally involved in constructive and productive activities, usually working outdoors or in business. On the other hand, most textbooks still promote the idea that "a woman's place is in the home." Women are portrayed as conforming, and their work activities are ordinarily in the home or schools.

It is unfortunate for both boys and girls that they are presented with such rigid, stereotyped views of sex-appropriate behavior. Both may suffer negative self-concepts and unnecessary restriction of personality development. For example, boys who followed the patterns of masculine behavior prescribed in the textbooks would be unwilling to express their emotions or to be nurturant and warm; girls would not be assertive or creative. Girls would be convinced that their future roles were restricted to being mothers, secretaries, teachers, nurses, or store clerks, and that only males become doctors, engineers, reporters, scientists, taxi drivers, and letter carriers.

School Failure and the Disadvantaged Child

School failure is a common experience for disadvantaged children. By the time they are in third grade, they are approximately a year behind middle-class children academically; by the sixth grade, 2 years behind; and by the end of junior high school, they may be as much as 3 years below grade level.

There are many factors that account for these findings. In the first place, poor and some minority children start out at a great disadvantage. Compared with their middle-class peers, lower-class children are much less prepared for school because they do not have as many cognitive skills before they enter kindergarten. School is essentially a middle-class institution: Most of the teachers are middle-class, as are the values stressed. Middle-class parents encourage and reward academic progress, whereas lower-class parents place more stress on obedience to rigid regulations (14). In introducing their children to a school situation, lower-class parents stress disciplinary demands, while middle-class parents stress the cognitive, teaching function of the school and give explanations for school rules. Moreover, most lower-class parents typically have a limited educational background, and therefore cannot serve as models of educational achievement or help their children with their homework. Nor does the lower-class child have peers who can be models of academic success. In fact, while middle-class children gain "points" (prestige and status) from school success, lower-class children are likely to be rejected by their peers if they do well in school. In brief, a lower-class child does not usually find much outside support from friends or family for doing well in school.

Another disadvantage suffered by poor or minority children is that the schools they attend are often physically deteriorated (sometimes posing real dangers to health and safety) and are deficient in essential physical facilities such as playgrounds, cafeterias, or even adequate lavatories. The most basic kinds of equipment are frequently absent — teaching aids and books, for example (17). Even worse, many schools across the nation are plagued with violence and vandalism.

The schools are often overcrowded and understaffed, and even the teachers they do have tend to favor the middle-class children in their classes. Sometimes it seems as though the teachers fail to understand the differences in background, experience, and values of lower-class children, and they *expect* these children to fail in school. This can become a self-fulfilling prophecy, as they devote more of their teaching time to the middle-class students, acting more as disciplinarians with their lower-class pupils.

But providing poor children with decent physical surroundings, educational facilities, and dedicated skillful teachers is not the complete solution to their problems. These children must also be motivated — their own interests must be used as a basis for teaching programs. The particular assets and aptitudes of lower-class children should be taken into account in planning the curriculum. For example, a child from a rural area of the mountains in West Virginia may know little about poetry but may possess complete knowledge about, say, the fine art of cutting and collecting wood and building a steady, warm fire. Thus, assigning a composition to be written on how to build a fire would be a much more meaningful assignment for this child than an assignment to discuss the meaning of a short poem. To be sure, at some point it might be good to introduce the child to poetry, but the initial task of getting the child interested in school will be more likely to be accomplished if, as one educator has said, schools "meet the child in his home territory and then take him for the ride" (24). That is, instructors must start the teaching process by using the knowledge and abilities the child already possesses and take it from there. Teachers cannot expect a lower-class child without the knowledge and abilities of a middle-class child to begin with the same traditional program.

Too Many "Frills"?

Recent studies indicate that many children emerge from elementary school — or even high school — unable to read, write, or do arithmetic well enough to handle even such problems of daily living as figuring out the cost per pound of grocery store items, understanding the manual for a driver's license, or reading a statement from the bank. Disturbed by these findings, parents and school boards in many areas are proclaiming the need for a "return to basics" and the elimination of "frills."

The goal itself is a laudable one — all children in our society need these basic skills, and a primary function of the schools is to help students to acquire them. There is, however, a danger of oversimplifying the issues and of throwing out the baby with the bath water.

In the first place, teachers and administrators are not solely responsible for their students' poor performance. Other factors also play a part: poor preschool preparation, lack of parental concern, poverty, peer values, inadequate facilities, discouragement, and low self-esteem, among others. Nevertheless, there seems little doubt that many schools could be doing a better job. But is this best done by an exclusive emphasis on reading, writing, and arithmetic, with little recognition of the needs of individual children? What are really "frills"?

Though too many schools include courses in the curricula that are trivial, irrelevant to the student's basic needs, and unchallenging, are art, music, literature, history, and science among them, as some school boards seem to believe? What about the needs of the individual child? Helping the child who is anxious and fearful to become more secure, the child who is withdrawn to become more outgoing, or the impulsive child to become more deliberate may make as much difference in the child's academic — as well as psychological and social — development as greater emphasis on the acquisition of basic skills, which are also essential. So may counseling and treatment provisions for reading disabilities or other problems, now being dropped from many schools as budgets shrink.

Learning to read, write, and do arithmetic is essential, but it can only be accomplished successfully by considering the whole child and his or her needs. The truly gifted teacher knows this, and given proper facilities and support, such a teacher can make an enormous difference.

For example, an economically disadvantaged 11-year-old black boy was doing poorly in school despite above-average intelligence; he was shy and unhappy and stuttered under stress. Working with a group of actors, musicians, and writers in a dramatic-arts workshop, the teacher helped the boy, who had a fine natural singing voice, to obtain the lead in a musical play written by the students themselves. Although the boy's parents worried about his stuttering, the play and his performance went so well that many in the audience had tears in their eyes. Not only did the boy not stutter during the performance, but he has not stuttered since. He now has a scholarship in a competitive private school, is receiving musical training, and finds his life and schoolwork exciting and rewarding. This teacher knew the whole child and had the opportunity to do something about it.

Most important, schools need to provide an atmosphere that makes learning a rewarding and relevant experience. How can a child possibly succeed when faced with so many setbacks in a traditional program—no family or peer support for academic achievement, disadvantages in background, and teachers who expect failure? And failure in school certainly will contribute to a low self-concept. By providing an environment in which the poor or minority student can learn, the school can contribute to the development of self-confidence, self-respect, and a sense of cultural identity.

These improved programs need to be introduced early in the child's experience, preferably at the preschool level or earlier, and to continue throughout the entire educational career (1). Finally, if school programs for poor and minority children are to work, they must gain the confidence and involvement of parents and the community (9).

These noble ideals may sound good on paper, you may well say, but show me a successful program in operation. Some schools are in fact succeeding, in spite of the difficulties. One such school is the John H. Finley elementary school in Harlem, which has a student body that is "89 percent black, 10 percent Puerto Rican, and 1 percent 'other,' i.e., white" (24, p.99). Virtually all the entering students at this school in a recent survey scored below the national median in reading readiness; however, by the end of the second grade more than three-fourths of these same students scored above the national median. Moreover, these children *continue* to score above the national average; their scores do not drop later, as is the case with students in most ghetto schools.

How are such results achieved? Several factors appear to play a major role. In general, an atmosphere of warmth and kindness prevails; there is more freedom, and disruptive behavior is handled more gently and more positively. Teachers believe in their students' ability to learn, and they use innovative, flexible approaches to the development of reading and other skills. Teachers take advantage of every opportunity to enhance the child's self-esteem and pride in his or her cultural identity, and they try to involve the parents in their children's education.

It is imperative that more schools follow these guidelines for helping disadvantaged children learn. Otherwise millions of children will enter adulthood unprepared to lead reasonably happy, self-sustaining, and productive lives.

Explaining School Failure

School failure is not limited to economically disadvantaged children. There are many middle-class children as well who do poorly in school.

What about that small group of children who learn more slowly than the rest of the class? In most schools they read more slowly and are less proficient in mathematics and are typically called either *academically retarded* or **learning-disabled.**

There are many different reasons why children have difficulty learning to read, write, spell, or do arithmetic. A small number have poor vision or hearing, and a few have had a serious injury to the central nervous system. But these are only a small part of those who are learning-disabled; the majority see and hear well and do not have obvious neurological disorders, and it is more difficult to specify the cause of their learning problem.

Most of these children have their greatest difficulty with reading, and the problem usually begins in the primary grades (30). Again, there are a variety of reasons for this difficulty with reading. Children from minority groups often come from homes where standard English is not spoken; hence they have difficulty learning to read the language in their primers. Others come to school hungry, tired, or anxious; still others are not highly motivated. But there is also a group of middle-class children who have trouble reading and do not suffer any of the disadvantages mentioned above. Their problem with reading is often attributed to biological factors. For example, some psychologists believe that a very small group of these children with at least average intelligence have inherited the difficulty in learning to read, since in some cases their parents also had difficulty in reading and spelling when they were in school. Thus there may be some genetically transmitted biological factor (as yet unspecified) that interferes with learning to read. This special group is often called **dyslexic** (30).

Another potential explanation, also biologically based, concerns the two halves of the brain. The brain is composed of two nearly identical hemispheres, and normally the left one is dominant over the right one in language skills. It may be that children who are slow to develop this pattern of dominance have difficulty learning to read. However, proving this hypothesis experimentally is difficult: Some studies have supported this conclusion; others have not (29).

The most popular explanation of why children have difficulty learning to read is that they have suffered some subtle brain damage — they are said to have **minimal brain dysfunction** (32). The majority of these children show no obvious signs of brain damage. That is, they do not display any of the *hard signs* of brain damage, such as severe motor tremors or paralysis or serious irregularities in brain wave patterns. Instead, they show what some have called *soft signs* — hyperactivity, impulsiveness, inattentiveness, and motor clumsiness, though no brain damage can be detected with existing medical techniques.

There are several problems with the notion of minimal brain damage based on soft signs. One is that brain damage normally occurs during or soon after birth, and neurologists believe that most infants recover from minimal damage to the brain. Moreover, *most* academically retarded children show no hard *or* soft signs of brain damage at all. Finally, academically retarded children, some of whom are presumed to have minimal brain dysfunction, have a puzzling set of results on various tests. Most perform better on tests requiring complex, cognitive processes than they do on tests that require only knowledge of simple facts or words. One would not expect that a child with brain damage would do better on reasoning than on tests of simple knowledge, such as vocabulary or general information.

One fact that does point to a biological basis for difficulty with reading is that some of these children show a significant deficit in recall memory. That is, they may have trouble remembering more than four unrelated words or numbers, whereas a normal child can remember five or six. This specific cognitive deficit may be due to abnormal functioning of parts of the central nervous system, but so far the evidence is not firm, and so this idea, too, is only a hypothesis.

In summary, there is some evidence that a small proportion of children who have serious trouble learning to read, write, and do arithmetic are different from other children. The structure or functioning of their brains may be different, but it has been difficult to prove any of these hypotheses conclusively. Moreover, it may well be that the soft signs (hyperactivity, clumsiness, and inattentiveness) are due to *psychological* rather than biological factors. In a number of instances, child clinical psychologists have found that apparent indications of brain dysfunction, such as perceptual difficulties, disappear when a child's emotional difficulties — anxiety or low self-esteem, for example — are resolved. As a result, many psychologists, educators, and pediatricians believe that, for the present, the concept of minimal brain damage is not a satisfactory explanation of most reading failures.

Motivational Factors. Other explanations for academic failure are not biologically based. Not all children want to do well in school. Some simply lack any positive motivation, others have low standards, and some have anxiety and conflict or hostility. In the early grades, children often want to do well to gain praise from the teacher. Children differ in the degree to which they want or seek that praise, and these differences in motivation affect their efforts to do well on school tasks.

Identification with a model is also important for school success, and a child who perceives similarity to a teacher who is admired (not necessarily physical similarity; it may be psychological similarity) will want to adopt the teacher's actions and values and, therefore, will be motivated to do well in school. However, a child who perceives no similarity to the teacher will be less motivated to do well on school tasks.

In addition, children sometimes feel hostile toward their parents, and since failure in school often disappoints parents and teachers who want the child to do well, the child may express his or her hostility by *not* doing well in school. Interestingly, hostility toward peers can sometimes have the opposite effect. That is, children who are angry because they have been rejected by their classmates may develop *superior* skills in school and thus generate a feeling of envy among their peers. This often happens among boys and girls who are unpopular because they have not acquired the traditional sex-role characteristics, such as athletic talent for the boys and attractiveness or social skills among the girls.

Importance of Expectations of Success. If you were asked to try to scale a vertical cliff, and you had no experience in rock climbing, chances are that you probably would not try very hard, because you would know that you probably would not succeed. Similarly, children have a relatively good idea of how well or poorly they will perform on a particular school task, and their expectancy of success or failure influences the amount of effort they will put forth and consequently how well they will perform. Some children may have a strong motive to master school tasks, such as reading, but do not expect to succeed. Therefore, they are unlikely to make the effort necessary to learn the skill and will behave as if they do not care about schoolwork. Furthermore, children who are extremely anxious about their ability to do well may not be able to learn because the anxiety interferes with their ability to concentrate.

Although children from economically disadvantaged homes do less well in school, they do not perform less well than middle-class children on all cognitive tasks. Indeed, when there is less emphasis on quality and more on quantity, they may do better than middle-class children. For example, when asked, "How many things can you do with a spoon?" or "How many ways can you change a tin can?," the economically disadvantaged children offer more answers than middle-class children, even though some are not of high quality. Apparently, they have lower standards for evaluating the quality of their own answers than middle-class children and so are more productive.

Additionally, the child's willingness to take a risk depends on the nature of the problem presented. The middle-class children were more willing than the lower-class children to try to read sentences that the children knew would be difficult. But the lower-class children were more willing than the middle-class children to attempt feats of physical skill. For example, they were more likely to attempt walking a narrow tape while balancing some objects. Thus, each child's history leads to a different pattern of skills and expectations of success and failure (33).

TELEVISION AS SOCIALIZER

The average American child spends more time watching television than in any other single activity except sleep. By the time the child reaches adolescence, he or she has watched television for a total of over 15,000 hours (25). Consequently, it is inevitable that the child will be affected by television, whether it is in good or harmful ways.

Television as Socializer

By the time an individual graduates from high school today, he or she will have spent more time in front of the television—17,000 hours on the average—than in the classroom (approximately 10,000 hours). From earliest childhood through age 18, the average American spends more time viewing television than in any other activity except sleeping. About 70 percent of the programs children watch contain at least one incidence of violence, and violent events are portrayed at an average rate of eight per hour. No wonder the public is worried about the impact of television on children's social and personality development.

Data from numerous investigations show that exposure to aggressive models in television programs may evoke aggressive behavior from children. For example, in one experiment, nursery-school children participated in 11 sessions during which they viewed cartoons involving considerable interpersonal aggression and destruction of objects. These children were significantly more aggressive to others during play periods than children in a control group who saw only nonaggressive cartoons, and the differences between the experimental and the control groups became more marked with increased exposure to the cartoons.

Violent television programs elicit higher levels of aggression, both physical and verbal, from adolescents, too. The effects are more marked for boys than for girls, and for those who are highly aggressive than for those who are habitually less aggressive. Furthermore, heavy viewers of violence not only behave more aggressively but have more positive attitudes toward aggression, which they regard as an effective way of dealing with conflicts. One authority on the subject summarizes the findings this way: "While there is indeed no *scientific* evidence that excessive viewing of televised violence can or does provoke violent crime in any one individual, it is clear that the bulk of the studies show that if large groups watch a great deal of televised violence, they will be more prone to behave aggressively than similar groups of children who do not watch such TV aggression" (E. Rubinstein, Television and the young viewer, *The American Scientist,* November 1978, p. 190).

Since viewing TV violence can induce aggressive behavior, is it not likely that TV programs that stress altruism, helping, and sharing will stimulate the viewer's prosocial actions? Again, a considerable body of evidence suggests that this is the case: Children are likely to imitate the prosocial responses they see on the television screen. After being exposed to programs containing many instances of pro-social behavior, children manifest more cooperation, generosity, nurturance, and sympathy than they had previously, and these were lasting effects.

Because of the predominance of aggressive programs on television today, the adverse effects of television viewing on children may be greater than the beneficial ones. But this does not lessen the *potential* of television to enhance constructive, prosocial behavior and thus to contribute to the improvement of social relationships. However, that potential can be fulfilled only if the nature of programming is changed radically.

Critics of television argue that its influence has been predominantly harmful. Many of the studies reviewed here suggest that they may be right. That is, much of the past and present fare on television may have harmful effects. Since children cannot avoid learning from television, it is undeniably true that television has the potential to contribute to the *improvement* of human behavior and society.

Television Viewing and Aggression

A large cat sees a tiny mouse approaching. He prepares to pounce on the mouse. A large group of mice gather behind the cat, toss a net over him, and beat him senseless.

Police officers trying to capture a wanted criminal kill two members of his gang; one police officer is shot.

The fictitious plots sketched above are not atypical. From cartoons to police stories, violence abounds on television. About 70 percent of the programs surveyed over a 6-year period contained at least one incident of violence, and the average rate of violent events per hour was *eight*. To make matters worse, aggressive acts are often presented as successful means of handling conflicts. No wonder that in 1977 an adolescent murderer in Florida maintained as part of his defense for the crime that long hours of viewing violence on television had "mentally unbalanced" him and thus inspired his crime.

The issue of the effects of television on social behavior is of importance because television is such a pervasive force, and its effects, whatever they may be, will inevitably be widespread. Aware of these far-reaching effects, in 1970 the Surgeon General of the United States appointed a scientific advisory committee to study the relationship between television and social behavior, particularly violence and aggression. In addition, a number of scientists are studying the socialization impact of television. What many are finding is that exposure to aggressive models in television programs does in fact lead to increased aggressive behavior in young children. Girls tend to watch violent television less than boys do, and they are less aggressive, but they, too, are likely to imitate aggressive models. And it is not necessary for the models to be human: Do not underestimate the power of violence in cartoons, for many young children watch cartoons more than any other type of program, and they are significantly affected by these cartoons (27).

Young children are relatively uninhibited about expressing aggression; therefore the effects of watching violent television programs are perhaps less complex than with older children. By the elementary-school years, however, many children have acquired internal prohibitions against expressing aggression, and, consequently, they may become anxious while they are watching television programs that are violent. Studies show that the children who become the most anxious when frustrated or while watching violence on television are the *least* likely to become more aggressive later (18). However, the more children are exposed to violent shows, the less likely they are to have anxiety reactions while watching violence (7). These findings suggest that, as critics have long maintained, children become hardened to violence after seeing a great deal of it. Therefore we cannot expect the child's anxieties to keep him or her from becoming aggressive after repeated viewing of violence on television.

"A fight is the best way to get what you want." Children who got a heavy dose of violence on television tended to agree with the above statement more than their peers who did not watch as much violence. They also agreed more with statements such as "Anybody who says bad things about me is looking for a punch in the nose" and "A fight is the best way to settle an argument once and for all" (8). Heavy viewers of violence regard aggression as an effective way of dealing with conflicts (20). Thus we see that not only does aggressive behavior increase after repeated exposure to violence, but aggressive attitudes also become stronger.

Many have raised the point that it may be that children who are more violent *choose* to watch the more violent programs, that the tendency to be violent exists *first*, rather than being a *result* of watching violence. However, findings from a group of students who were studied for 10 years (from third grade through college) indicate that the reverse is true—that watching violence on television does in fact lead to more aggressive behavior later.

In this study it was found that the third-grade boys who were more aggressive showed a slight (though significant) tendency to watch more violence on television than their less aggressive peers. But a more significant correlation was found for boys when they reached college age. The boys who had watched the most violence on television were the most aggres-

In addition to increased aggression, viewing violence on television also reduces the frequency of behaviors such as self-control, tolerance for frustration, cooperation, helping, sharing, and friendly social interaction.

sive in behavior during college (26). In fact, it may be that television violence has an accumulative long-term effect that shows up more clearly over time than it does when aggression is measured immediately after viewing violence.

What of the other harmful effects of viewing violence on television? In addition to increased aggression, viewing violence on television also reduces the frequency of behaviors such as self-control, tolerance for frustration, cooperation, helping, sharing, and friendly social interaction.

However, while most of the studies of television effects are consistent in showing that exposure to television violence is likely to lead to increased aggression and other undesirable behavior by child viewers, we must be cautious about blaming television for the high levels of violence in our society. Though it seems safe to conclude that television violence is not uplifting or beneficial to child viewers, most of the data are from laboratory studies conducted in contrived settings quite different from the settings in which children ordinarily watch television. For example, in some experiments children may watch a program with many other children in a room containing little more than chairs and a television set.

It is possible that the effects of watching a program in such a setting may be stronger than if the child were to watch the same program at home alone in a room with many distracting stimuli. Furthermore, the aggressive aftereffects immediately after the showing may be high simply because the children are in contact with each other and feelings are high after the viewing. The results could be quite different if the children were alone during and after the film. Also, other studies have given surprising results. For example, an unexpected result of one study showed that some children actually showed increased *prosocial* behavior after exposure to aggressive programs. These children, who habitually watched fewer aggressive programs than their peers, were apparently stimulated by the fast-moving, noisy, aggressive programs to greater social activity, and this was reflected in increased prosocial behavior.

In our opinion, there is still an urgent need for better data on the effects of television violence on children's behavior in real-life situations.

Television and Prosocial Behavior

If television can be such a powerful force in influencing aggressive behavior and attitudes, then it seems logical to infer that it could be equally useful in promoting desirable behavior. According to the evidence, it is true that television characters can serve as models of helping behavior, nurturance, sympathy, and other prosocial actions, although the data on the helpful aspects of television are nowhere near as extensive as the evidence on the harmful aspects of television. Nonetheless, there are some studies that show that exposure to prosocial programs can produce lasting positive changes in children's behavior.

Several of the studies presented below were conducted with nursery-school children of ages 3 to 5. Still, we can infer from the results from these younger children that similar effects would result with children during middle childhood. After all, the amount of time spent daily in watching television increases gradually between age 3 and the beginning of adolescence.

Even 2 weeks after viewing prosocial programs, nursery-school children showed greater persistence in tasks and an increase in their ability to tolerate delays, as well as more obedience to school rules. Lower-class children gained in cooperation, nurturance, and sympathy, and they talked more about their own and others' feelings than they had previously (26).

In another study, kindergarten children were shown television programs stressing helping, sharing, and understanding others (26). In addition, some of them were given training in role playing (acting out scenes with puppets) and/or verbal labeling training—that is, they participated in group discussions of the altruistic, or prosocial, events shown in the film, and labeled the feelings brought out by the events. As expected, exposure to the prosocial programs had positive results. Children who saw these programs were much more helpful even in a situation far different from those modeled on television. Furthermore, both kinds of additional training, verbal labeling and role playing, enhanced these positive effects.

In still another experiment, first-grade children also responded positively to prosocial films. After they saw television episodes in which a boy risked his life to save a dog, first-grade children gave substantially more help to puppies in a distressed situation than did children who were exposed to other kinds of programs. Finally, children exposed to generous models in TV episodes donated more of the prizes they had won in a game to needy children than did peers who had witnessed television characters who were stingy (26).

SUMMARY

1. A number of people outside the family—for example, peers, teachers, and characters portrayed on television—participate in significant ways in the process of socializing the child.

2. With the beginning of school a child's peer group grows in size and influence. The influence of the peer group appears stronger in the United States than in some other societies where children live more in the family and less in the peer society.

3. In general, conformity behavior increases in the middle-childhood years, but there are wide individual variations in the strength of the tendency to conform. Girls are more likely to conform to peer group suggestions than boys, and dependent, anxious, children are more conforming than their independent, nonanxious peers.

4. Peers have significant influences on behavior, usually supporting and extending parental efforts in socializing children to behave in ways that society considers appropriate, in the areas of sex-appropriate behavior, expression of aggression, and prosocial behavior.

5. Beginning with kindergarten, the school becomes the center of the child's life outside the family, occupying about half the waking hours of each day. The kinds of teachers children have, the teaching methods they encounter, and the types of textbooks they are exposed to will have strong impacts not only on academic progress but also on general adjustment, personality, and self-esteem.

6. The size of the school attended may also affect the student's social and personality development. Students in small schools tend to participate in more activities than those in large schools.

7. Many elementary-school textbooks present a very narrow view of life, with most being set in middle-class suburbia. Sex roles portrayed in the text also tend to be narrow and stereotyped.

8. Since the school is primarily a middle-class institution, it is not surprising to find that poor and minority children are at a great disadvantage and soon fall behind in their studies. Poor children need to be motivated in school by having their own interests engaged and used as a basis for teaching programs.

9. Some students who experience school failure are not from disadvantaged homes. It is thought that there may be a biological basis for some of these difficulties in learning; other students may lack any positive motivation to do well in school.

10. Another significant effect on children's behavior is television. Depending on what is portrayed and what behavior is modeled, the effects can be positive, enhancing prosocial behavior, or negative, promoting aggressive behavior.

Suggested Readings

Chess, Stella, & Whitbread, Jane. *How to help your child get the most out of school.* New York: Dell, 1976.

Farnham-Diggory, Sylvia. *Learning disabilities.* Cambridge, Mass.: Harvard University Press, 1978.

Hartup, William W. Peer interaction and social organization. In P. H. Mussen (Ed.), *Carmichael's manual of child psychology* (3rd ed.), Vol 2. New York: Wiley, 1970.

Kohl, Herbert. *36 Children.* New York: Signet Books, 1968.

Murrow, Casey, & Murrow, Liza. *Children come first.* New York: Harper & Row (Perennial Library), 1971.

Silberman, Charles E. *Crisis in the classroom: The remaking of American education.* New York: Random House, 1970.

Part Five

Adolescence

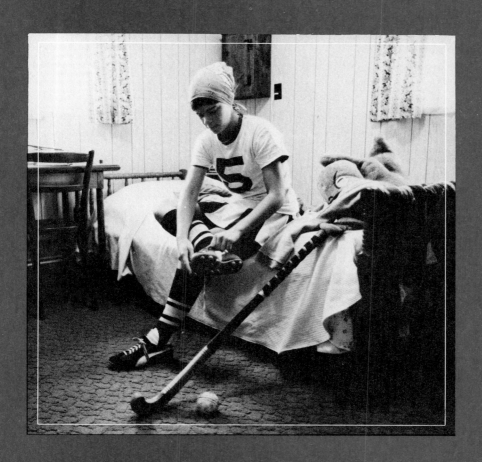

Chapter II

Adolescence: Physical Change, Sex, and Social Development

*A*DOLESCENCE IS a time of great changes for the developing boy or girl. It has also been viewed by many writers and psychotherapists—including G. Stanley Hall, the father of the scientific study of adolescence in the early twentieth century—as a period of great "storm and stress" (24). The notion that adolescence is a difficult period in development, both for adolescents and their parents, is by no means a recent idea. More than 300 years before the birth of Christ, Aristotle and Plato warned of the difficulties of dealing with adolescents, who, as Aristotle said, were "passionate, irascible, and apt to be carried away by their impulses" (2). Plato complained that they were prone to argue for the sake of argument (46). But for a long time adults concentrated on trying to "tame" adolescents, to control their "unruly impulses."

It is only since the end of the nineteenth century that the period of adolescence has been recognized as a psychologically complex stage of development, worthy of scientific study. Contributing to this emergence of adolescence as a topic of attention was the increasing age segregation of young people in schools and, for many, the delayed entrance into the work force that went along with the shift to an industrialized, technological society. A teenager on a nineteenth-century farm may have been troublesome at times, but neither the adolescent nor the parents had the time to dwell on problems such as identity. Although some recent investigations of typical adolescents indicate that the extent of adolescent and parental turmoil during this period has been exaggerated, there is still general agreement that adolescence is a period of psychological highs and lows—a difficult stage in the young person's struggle toward maturity.

Why is this so? The first and most obvious answer is that the individual is dealing with many changes—physical, sexual, psychological, and cognitive ones as well as changes in social demands. It is ironic that so many changing social demands—for independence, changing relationships with peers and adults, sexual adjustment, educational and vocational preparation—are made at a time in the individual's life when he or she is also adjusting to a significant number of physical changes.

In this chapter and the next, we shall explore the many transformations adolescents go through. First we shall deal with the basic physical changes that are happening and how the adolescent deals with these changes. We shall then look at the behavior of adolescents with respect to some of the developmental tasks of adolescence, such as establishing independence and becoming a sexual being. And finally, we shall look at the social behavior of adolescents—how they relate to their peers. In the final chapter (Chapter 12), we will look more closely at the identity problems that adolescents go through in their efforts to answer the age-old question "Who am I and where am I going?" Related to the question of identity is the process of choosing a vocation, for certainly much of the future identity of adolescents as adults will depend on their vocations. Finally, we shall consider those adolescents who failed to master the tasks of adolescence successfully and shall look at how problems of adjustment are manifested.

One point we wish to make clear is that although adolescents share a number of experiences and problems, there is no standard adolescent. To be sure, all undergo the physiological and physical changes of puberty and later adolescent growth, and all face the need for establishing a sense of who they are and for preparing to make their own way as independent members of society. But adolescents clearly are not all alike and do not all face the same environmental demands. A poor youth coming from a broken home in an urban ghetto faces a different set of problems from those of a middle-class adolescent growing up in a loving and protective suburban family. Young people growing up in the early 1980s face problems different from those who grew up during the "silent decade" of the 1950s or the social chaos of the 1960s and early 1970s. Consequently, the responses of young people in different situations will vary significantly.

The physical changes that come with adolescence are inevitable—rapid acceleration of physical growth, changing body dimensions, sexual changes, and further growth and development of cognitive ability. All adolescents must deal with these changes.

The physical changes that come with adolescence are inevitable—rapid acceleration of physical growth, changing body dimensions, sexual changes, and further growth and development of cognitive ability. All adolescents must deal with these changes. But cultural attitudes toward adolescence may differ widely. Culture will determine whether the period of adolescence is long or short and whether its social demands represent an abrupt change or only a gradual transition from earlier stages of development. Indeed, it may be said that adolescence begins in biology and ends in culture. That is, adolescence begins with the physical changes called **puberty** and ends when society requires that the individual take on the responsibilities of an adult. Let's look first at the basic physical changes.

PHYSICAL DEVELOPMENT IN ADOLESCENCE

The culture may facilitate or hinder the young person's adjustment to the physical and physiological changes of puberty, and it may influence whether these changes become a source of pride or of anxiety and confusion. But it cannot change the fact that these changes will occur, and that in one way or another the adolescent must cope with them.

The word **puberty** refers to the first phase of adolescence when sexual maturation becomes evident. In clinical practice and research, puberty is often dated from the beginning of breast development in girls and the emergence of pubic hair in boys (55). The onset of sexual maturation is accompanied by a "growth spurt" in height and weight that usually lasts about 2 years.

Hormonal Factors in Development

Both the physical and physiological changes of puberty are initiated by an increased output of certain activating hormones released by a gland called the **pituitary gland,** located immediately below the base of the brain. These hormones, in turn, stimulate the production and release of other hormones, such as growth-related and sex-related hormones. Sex-related hormones include **androgens** (masculinizing hormones) and **estrogens** (feminizing hormones) (44). The hormones of both sexes are present in both men and women. Thus, the hormonal difference between sexes is one of proportion—a male has more androgens and a female has more estrogens. These and other hormones interact with one another in complex ways to stimulate the orderly progression of the many physical and physiological developments of puberty and adolescence.

Adolescent Growth Spurt

Suit jackets outgrown in less than a year, dresses that are too short after only one season's wearing, shoes that are too small before they are worn out—these are the laments of parents of adolescents as they attempt to provide clothing for their teenaged sons and daughters going through the growth spurt.

The term **adolescent growth spurt** refers to the accelerated rate of increase in height and weight that occurs with the onset of adolescence. The age of onset and the duration of the spurt vary from one child to another, even among perfectly normal children—a fact often poorly understood by adolescents and their parents, and, consequently, often a source of needless concern.

In normal boys, the growth spurt may begin as early as $10\frac{1}{2}$ years or as late as 16 years (56). For the average boy, however, rapid acceleration in growth begins at about 13 years, reaching a peak rate of growth at about 14 years and declining by around $15\frac{1}{2}$. Further slow growth may continue for several years thereafter (see Figure 11.1). Girls, on the other hand, may begin their adolescent growth spurt as early as $7\frac{1}{2}$ years of age or as late as $11\frac{1}{2}$ (56). For the average girl, rapid acceleration in growth begins about age 11, reaches a peak at about 12 years, and then decreases rapidly to pre–growth-spurt rates by about age 13, with slow continued growth for several additional years.

The age of onset and the duration of the growth spurt vary from one child to another, even among perfectly normal children —a fact often poorly understood by adolescents and their parents.

One of the matters likely to concern both adolescents and their parents is that of ultimate height, particularly when they subscribe to persisting masculine and feminine stereotypes and worry that a boy will be "too short" or a girl will be "too tall." But much of this needless concern results from a peculiar combination of developmental relationships. That is, individuals who are already tall at preadolescence tend to begin the adolescent growth spurt early (31), and thus for a time it may seem to the tall youngsters that they will surely end up as giants, while the short boys and girls may think that they will never attain any semblance of normal height. However, once both the tall and the short individuals have passed the

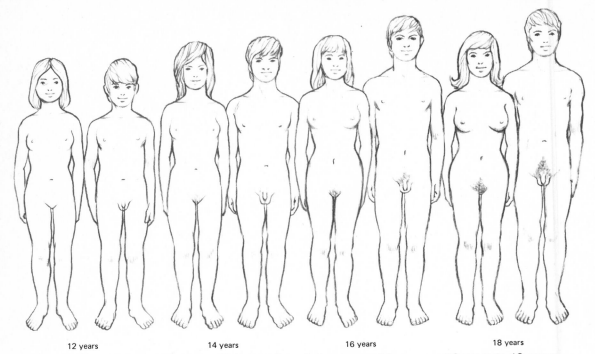

12 years   14 years   16 years   18 years

Figure 11.1   Body growth and development from ages 10 years to 18 years.

period of rapid adolescent growth, they will probably find that their relative standings in height are about the same as they were before their peers started growing.

Along with the increases in height and weight during this period, less obvious physical changes are occurring, too. In both boys and girls, muscular development proceeds rapidly, though boys show a greater gain in muscle tissue and therefore in physical strength (56). Greater strength in boys is also due partly to a number of other related developmental factors: larger hearts and lungs, a higher systolic blood pressure, a greater capacity for carrying oxygen in the blood, and a lower heart rate while at rest. Both boys and girls show a decline in the rate of development of fat during the adolescent growth spurt, although the decline is greater for boys. And the size of one organ stays nearly the same—the brain, which, by the beginning of adolescence, has already attained 95 percent of its total adult weight (56).

Sexual Maturation   As in the case of the growth spurt in height and weight, there are marked individual differences in the age of onset of puberty. But physical development during puberty and adolescence generally follows a rather orderly progression, and so some predictions can be made. For example, both boys and girls who are tall will probably have an early growth spurt and early sexual maturation (51). Thus, a boy who has an early growth spurt is also likely to develop pubic hair and other aspects of sexual maturation early; the girl who has an early growth spurt is likely to show early breast development and early **menarche** (onset of menstruation) (56).

Sexual Development in Boys. The first outward indication of impending sexual maturity in boys is usually an increase in the rate of growth of the testes and scrotum (the baglike structure enclosing the testes). There may also be beginning, perhaps slowly, growth of pubic hair at about the same time or shortly thereafter. Approximately a year later, an acceleration in growth of the penis accompanies the beginning of the growth spurt in height. Body hair and facial hair usually make their first appearance about 2 years after the beginning of pubic hair growth, although some boys get body hair before pubic hair (15).

One of the most obvious — and sometimes embarrassing — aspects of development in adolescent boys is a definite lowering of the voice, usually very late in puberty. In some boys, this voice change is rather abrupt and dramatic, whereas in others it occurs so gradually that it is hardly perceptible. During this process, the larynx (or Adam's apple) enlarges significantly, and the vocal cords (which it contains) approximately double in length. This lengthening of the vocal cords results in a drop in pitch of about an octave.

Sexual Development in Girls. In girls, the beginning elevation of the breast (the so-called bud stage of breast development) is usually the first external sign of sexual maturity, although in about one-third of girls, the initial appearance of pubic hair may precede breast development (50). Growth of the uterus and vagina occurs simultaneously with breast development, and the female genitals — the labia and clitoris — also enlarge. The menarche (i.e., age of beginning menstruation) occurs relatively late in the developmental sequence and almost invariably after the growth spurt has begun to slow down (56).

Differential Development Is Normal. It should be emphasized that the average developmental sequences for boys and girls discussed here are just that — *average*. Among perfectly normal boys and girls, there are wide variations in the age of onset of the developmental sequence. For example, while maturation of the penis may be complete in some boys by 13½, for others it may not be complete until as late as 17 or even older. Pubic-hair development may vary even more (49). The bud stage of breast development may occur as early as age 8 in some girls or as late as 13 in others (50), and the age of menarche may vary from about age 10 to 16½.

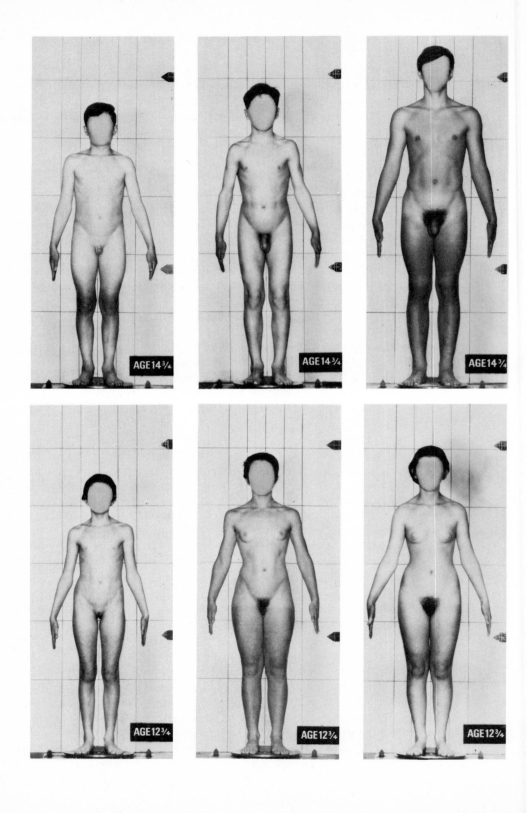

It is important for young people and their parents to realize that on any measure of maturation, almost 50 percent of girls and boys mature before and 50 percent after the age cited as average. The great differences that occur among normal boys and girls in their rates of development are dramatically illustrated in Figure 11.2, which shows the differing degrees of pubertal maturity among three normal boys, all aged 14¾ years, and three normal girls, all aged 12¾ years.

PSYCHOLOGICAL ASPECTS OF ADOLESCENT GROWTH AND DEVELOPMENT

While adults may be amused when they look back on those sometimes painful years of adolescence, they should remember that for the adolescent, the traumas are real. No matter how we may be tempted to minimize a teenager's problems once we gain some perspective in such matters as the relative insignificance of a male's bicep size or a female's breast size, such worries and concerns often seem of great importance to an adolescent. The average adolescent is acutely aware of the entire growth process, and all these physical and physiological changes are not without their psychological effects. These physical and physiological developments naturally have an unsettling effect on his or her feelings of self-consistency, and it takes time for the adolescent to integrate these changes into a slowly emerging sense of a positive, self-confident, individual identity. Faced with the task of developing a sense of self-identity, the adolescent is trying to answer the question "Who am I?" and yet must deal with many changes and inconsistencies in him- or herself.

One of the factors that may confound an adolescent's ability to form a clearly defined sense of self is that there is a heavy emphasis at this age on conformity to the peer group—not only in social behavior but in appearance and physical skills as well. Although today's youth seem to be a bit more tolerant of diversity, being different from the norm in physical appearance and rate of development can still be an agonizing experience for many young people. Adolescents who are markedly different from currently accepted standards of physical appearance, skills, and interests—standards that conform largely to the culture's stereotypes and masculinity and femininity—may not be well accepted by their peers and consequently may think poorly of themselves.

In addition, the adolescent's perception of his or her own body may be distorted because of prior experiences that have led the young person to

Figure 11.2 Different degrees of pubertal development at the same chronological age. Upper row: three boys, all aged 14¾ years. Lower row: three girls, all aged 12¾ years. (From J. M. Tanner. Growth and endocrinology of the adolescent. In L. J. Gardner, Ed., *Endocrine and genetic diseases of childhood*. Philadelphia: Saunders, 1969.)

view himself or herself as attractive or unattractive, strong or weak, or masculine or feminine, regardless of his or her actual physical appearance and capabilities. For example, a boy who is physically of average size and strength may view himself as smaller and weaker than he is because he generally feels inadequate in many areas. A girl who is really quite beautiful may view herself as unattractive because she has been told for years that she "looks just like" a parent or other relative who is not well liked by others (11).

In the following section we shall consider the psychological effects of various aspects of maturation.

Attitudes Toward Menstruation

A teenage girl's attitude toward menstruation is important, for menstruation is much more than just a simple physiological readjustment. It is a symbol of womanhood, of sexual maturity. Because a girl's reactions to menstruation may generalize to other aspects of being a woman, it is important that her initial experience with it be as favorable as possible.

The effects of socialization by family and peers may heavily influence a girl's attitude. If her parents and friends act as though she deserves sympathy for her "plight," the girl herself is likely to adopt similar attitudes.

Maturation in Boys

Although there may be some individual— and perfectly normal— variations in the sequence of events leading to physical and sexual maturity in boys, the following sequence is typical:

1. Testes and scrotum begin to increase in size.
2. Pubic hair begins to appear.
3. Adolescent growth spurt starts; the penis begins to enlarge.
4. Voice deepens as the larynx grows.
5. Hair begins to appear under the arms and on the upper lip.
6. Sperm production increases, and nocturnal emission (ejaculation of semen during sleep) may occur.
7. Growth spurt reaches peak rate; pubic hair becomes pigmented.
8. Prostate gland enlarges.
9. Sperm production becomes sufficient for fertility; growth rate decreases.
10. Physical strength reaches a peak.

And many girls do perceive the effects of menstruation as negative—61 percent did so in a recent survey (52).

Sometimes a negative reaction to menstruation is fostered by physical discomfort, including headaches, backaches, cramps, and abdominal pain (29), but these symptoms generally either disappear or are greatly reduced as puberty progresses. Another side effect that may be associated with a girl's menstrual period is some increase in negative feelings such as anxiety and depression and greater irritability. But for most girls such fluctuations are simply variations in the normal range, possibly related to changing hormone levels but certainly not extreme or incapacitating, as some popular myths suggest.

It seems that girls' attitudes toward menstruation often are influenced by the negative attitudes of others. It is as though they are led to believe that menstruation is an uncomfortable and unsettling time. They tend to complain about their menstrual period, though ironically most believe that other girls experience more menstrual-related symptoms than they themselves do (52).

Maturation in Girls

Although, as in the case of boys, there may be normal variations in the sequence of physical and sexual maturation in girls, a typical sequence of events is:

1. Adolescent growth spurt begins.
2. Elevation of the breast (the so-called bud stage of development) and rounding of the hips begin.
3. Downy (nonpigmented) pubic hair makes its initial appearance.
4. The uterus and vagina, as well as labia and clitoris, increase in size.
5. Pigmented pubic hair is well developed; there are moderate amounts of body hair.
6. Breasts develop further; nipple pigmentation begins; areola increases in size.
7. Growth spurt reaches peak rate and then declines.
8. Menarche, or onset of menstruation (almost always *after* the peak rate of growth in height has occurred).
9. Further maturation of breasts and growth of axillary hair occurs.
10. Period of "adolescent sterility" ends, and girl becomes capable of conception (usually about a year or so after menarche).

Parental reactions can have a significant effect on their daughter's reactions to menstruation. They can help by explaining to her the naturalness of the phenomenon and showing pride and pleasure in her greater maturity. One father, for example, presented his daughter with flowers on the occasion of her first menstrual period, celebrating the fact of her new young womanhood. In the case of physical difficulties, parents can see that their daughter gets adequate medical care. When parents make the onset of menstruation a rewarding rather than a feared or hated event, ultimately their daughter will assume her future sexual and social roles more readily.

Erection, Ejaculation, and Nocturnal Emission

Just as the onset of menstruation may cause concern to the girl, uncontrolled erection and initial ejaculation may surprise and worry some adolescent boys. During puberty, the penis becomes erect very readily, and while they may be proud of their emerging virility, boys may be worried or embarrassed by an apparent inability to control this response. They may become apprehensive about dancing with a girl or even having to stand up in a school classroom to give a report. They may wonder if other boys show a similar apparent lack of control.

Initial ejaculation of seminal fluid may also be a source of concern. The adolescent boy's first ejaculation is likely to occur within a year of the onset of the growth spurt (around age 14, although it may occur as early as 11 or as late as 16) (11). First ejaculation may occur as a result of masturbation or **nocturnal emission** (ejaculation of seminal fluid during sleep, often accompanied by erotic dreams). A boy who has previously masturbated, with accompanying pleasant sensations but without ejaculation, may wonder if the ejaculation of seminal fluid is harmful or an indication that something is physically wrong with him.

Fortunately it seems that contemporary adolescents are better informed and less likely to be concerned about such developmental events as menstruation or nocturnal emission than those of earlier generations. Nevertheless, many boys and girls, especially in the early years of adolescence, do not have proper information from parents, schools, or peers, and torture themselves with unnecessary fears (47).

Early Versus Late Maturation

As we have already seen clearly, maturational rates vary widely among normal adolescents. The effects of early and late maturation on the psychological (personality) development of adolescents are different for boys and girls.

For boys, in general, early maturation is an advantage. Early-maturing boys are more self-assured and confident than late-maturing boys, who tend to be more tense and higher in anxiety and less self-controlled (33). Early-maturing boys are generally more popular than late maturers, who are rated by their peers as less attractive in physique. The problems of late-maturing boys seem to persist; even at age 33, late maturers were still less self-controlled, less responsible and dominant, and more inclined to turn to others for help and support (32). However, many of the potential problems of late-maturing boys can be helped considerably by appropriate guidance and counseling (20).

It seems that the differences between the psychological development of early- and late-maturing girls are not as significant as they are for boys, and they vary with time. For example, in the sixth grade, being more mature than the other girls is usually a disadvantage, for the girls rated most highly in prestige-enhancing personality traits by their peers were those who had not yet reached puberty. By the eighth and ninth grades, however, the girls who had reached puberty were rated somewhat more highly; that is, as possessing many positive personality traits, such as being friendly, being a good leader, enthusiastic, and having a sense of humor (22). However, there is not much evidence to show that early-maturing girls are significantly better "adjusted" than later-maturing girls (22).

Why the sex differences in the effects of early and late maturation? One theory is that the cultural stereotype for feminine behavior is not as closely tied to physical attributes as the stereotype for males. Thus, because early-maturing boys tend to show greater strength and physical prowess—and, eventually, early active sexual behavior—they conform early to the traditional cultural stereotype of masculine behavior and are regarded as closer to the "ideal." But it is not clear whether early sexual maturity for girls is a help or a hindrance. Society often gives girls mixed messages on these matters, as do peers. It is less important for girls to have physical strength, and certainly it is not clear whether sexual activity at an earlier age than peers is desirable. There is a good chance that a girl who is sexually attractive at an early age may date older boys, and then she may fail to develop mature relationships with other girls her own age or fail to develop as an individual in her own right. Also, it may be difficult adjusting to the complex feelings aroused by menstruation when most of her peers are still more like "little girls."

COGNITIVE DEVELOPMENT IN ADOLESCENCE

The dramatic gains of adolescents in their physical development are accompanied by equally impressive, if less obvious, gains in cognitive ability. The average 14- or 15-year-old can handle easily and efficiently many kinds of intellectual tasks or problems that the average 10-year-old would find either impossible or very difficult to master. Although parents may sometimes express consternation about their adolescents' apparent inability to follow seemingly simple instructions about straightening up a bedroom, taking out the garbage, or putting the cap back on the toothpaste, the fact is that adolescents are clearly more advanced cognitively than their younger brothers and sisters.

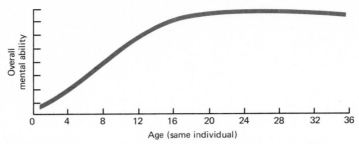

Figure 11.3 Curve of the growth of intelligence based on repeated examination of the same individuals over the years. (After N. Bayley. Development of mental abilities. In P. H. Mussen, Ed., *Carmichael's manual of child psychology*, Vol. 1. New York: Wiley, 1970. P. 1176, fig. 3. Reprinted by permission of John Wiley & Sons, Inc.)

The years between puberty and adulthood are very important ones for the young person's intellectual or cognitive development. It is in this period that much of a person's capacity to acquire and utilize knowledge approaches its peak efficiency. If considerable progress in mental ability is not made during these formative years, it is unlikely that it will be made up later. This is not to say, however, that many people do not continue to develop their mental abilities as adults (see Figure 11.3). This is particularly true of people in good health who lead intellectually stimulating lives.

It should also be noted that not all mental abilities develop — or decline — at the same rate. Abilities that appear most directly to reflect "pure" biological capability, such as speed of perception and intellectual flexibility, develop more rapidly during childhood and adolescence, and decline somewhat earlier and more rapidly during the adult years, than those that are more likely to be influenced by experience, such as word fluency (30).

Sex Differences in Intelligence

Although adolescent boys and girls show no consistent difference in *overall* intelligence, there are some differences in specific competences. Beginning about 10 or 11 years of age, girls tend to outscore boys on tests of *verbal ability*, while boys score higher on *visual-spatial* tasks (for example, conceptualizing how an object in space would look from a different angle; seeing how a set of gears works; or solving mazes). Also, beginning about age 12 or 13, boys score somewhat higher in *mathematical ability*. It is not yet clear, however, how much these differences are due to genetic influences and how much they are the result of sexual stereotypes in our society that encourage boys to develop mathematical and mechanical skills and girls to develop verbal and language skills (39).

Piaget's Stage of Formal Operations

Traditional intelligence tests tell us that the mental ability of the average adolescent is superior to that of the younger child, that the adolescent can perform with relative ease a wide variety of intellectual tasks that the younger child can perform only slowly, inefficiently, and with great difficulty, if at all. What intelligence tests do not tell us, however, is *why* this is so. In other words, they do not tell us much about the kinds of qualitative changes that take place between childhood and adolescence in the basic processes underlying the adolescent's intellectual performance.

What is the nature of these changes? As we have seen, the cognitive development of children during middle childhood — what Piaget calls the stage of concrete operations (see pp. 252–256) — is still rather limited when compared to that of adolescents or adults. However around the age of 12, but with marked individual variations, young people enter Piaget's fourth major stage — the **stage** of **formal operations.** During this stage, the adolescent gains a number of important capabilities not generally present in the middle-childhood years. Probably the most basic of these involves a shift of emphasis in his or her thinking from the *real* to the *possible*, from what merely is to what might be. Furthermore, unlike the concrete-operational child, the adolescent is able to consider various possibilities in a more thorough, objective fashion. Thus, he or she can consider not merely one possible answer to a problem or explanation of a situation, but many possible alternatives. The adolescent is not limited to solutions that occur spontaneously; he or she can logically exhaust all possible alternatives. While a concrete-operational system enables the child to distinguish between reality and appearance, between how things look and how they really are, formal operational thought enables the young person to judge hypotheses against the available evidence, to distinguish between what is true and what is false (28).

Adolescent thought also becomes more abstract (more general and more divorced from immediate experience) than that of the younger child. Thus in defining *time*, the younger child is likely to say that it is "something that the watch tells," or "time means the clock." A 15-year-old, on the other hand, may say that "time is sort of like an interval of space." Similarly, when asked what is the purpose of laws, a typical 12-year-old in one study replied, "If we had no laws, people would go around killing people." In contrast, one 16-year-old answered, "To insure safety and enforce government." Another commented, "They are basically guidelines for people. I mean like this is wrong and this is right and to help them understand" (1). While the younger child's thinking is concrete, the adolescent can deal readily with metaphors. For example, studies have shown that it is not until around ages 12 to 14 that children can go beyond a literal meaning of a political cartoon to its metaphorical meaning.

Not surprisingly, the development of formal operational thought is related not only to age but also to overall intelligence; it develops earlier in adolescents with higher IQs. Furthermore, some adolescents and adults may never develop true formal operational thinking, because of either limited ability or cultural limitations. Finally, formal operational thought is not an all-or-none affair. The really gifted adolescent girl or boy is likely to display greater imagination, greater flexibility, and more precision in the exercise of formal operational thinking than less gifted peers, although the basic processes involved are similar (11).

Mental Growth and Personality Development

It would be hard to overestimate the importance of the changes in mental ability that take place during adolescence, particularly the shift in the direction of formal operational thinking. Without these changes, the young person would be unable to deal adequately with many of the intellectual demands made upon him or her during these years — mastering ever more difficult academic skills, preparing for a vocation, and gaining necessary factual information about how to deal with an increasingly complex world. For example, it would be virtually impossible to understand the use of metaphors in poetry or the reasoning involved in calculus without a fairly high level of abstract thinking.

Perhaps less obvious, however, is the fact that many other aspects of adolescent development also depend on the cognitive advances occurring during this period, including changes in the nature of parent-child relationships, emerging personality characteristics, and mounting concerns with social, political, and personal values. As we have noted, one of the most important aspects of the emergence of formal operational thought is the ability to entertain hypotheses that do not stem directly from immediately observable events. In contrast to the child who is preoccupied, for the most part, with learning how to function in the world of "here and now," the adolescent is able "not only to grasp the immediate state of things but also the possible state they might or could assume" (11, p. 152). The implications of this change alone are enormous.

For example, the adolescent's new-found and frequently wearing talents for discovering his or her previously idealized parents' feet of clay — for questioning their values, for comparing them with other "more understanding" or less "square" parents, and for accusing them of "hypocritical" inconsistencies between professed values and behavior — all depend, at least partly, on the adolescent's changes in cognitive ability. As David Elkind, an expert on adolescent cognitive development, comments, "The awareness of the discrepancy between the actual and the possible also helps to make the adolescent a rebel. He is always comparing the possible with the actual and discovering that the actual is frequently wanting" (19, p. 152).

The relentless criticism by many adolescents of existing social, political, and religious systems, and their preoccupation with devising elabo-

Many adolescents voice their strong devotion to humanitarian causes but then do little to implement them.

rate or highly theoretical alternative systems, also depends to a considerable extent on the young person's emerging capacity for formal operational thought. However, a good deal of an adolescent's apparently passionate concern with the deficiencies of parents and the social order often turns out to be primarily verbal—more a matter of word than deed. This is probably at least partly a reflection of the fact that this stage of development is still relatively new and has not yet been fully integrated into the adolescent's total adaptation to life. Many adolescents voice their strong devotion to humanitarian causes but then do little to implement them.

At the same time, it is important to recognize the positive aspects of the young person's newly acquired ability to conceptualize and reason abstractly about hypothetical possibilities and instant convictions. Not only is the exercise of this ability a pleasure in itself; it also provides valuable and necessary practice in the development of reasoning skills and critical abilities the young person will need throughout life (45, p. 15).

Adolescent cognitive development is also reflected in the young person's attitudes toward himself or herself and in the personality characteristics likely to become prominent during this period. Many adolescents at this stage become more *introspective* and *analytical*. They may also appear **egocentric** and self-conscious in their thought and behavior. Young people at this stage are able to realize that other people are capable of thinking processes similar to their own. But at least initially, they are not likely to differentiate clearly between the content of their own thoughts and those of others. Consequently, because young people's concerns at this age are likely to be focused on themselves, they are likely to conclude that other people, including their peers, are equally obsessed with their behavior and appearance (18).

Thus, the adolescent who feels self-conscious, concerned about some supposedly unattractive physical feature, or ashamed about something is likely to feel that all eyes will be riveted upon his or her particular defect—real or imagined. By the same token, when the young person is in a happy, self-admiring mood, he or she may project these feelings onto peers or adults. The younger adolescent boy who stands before the mirror flexing his muscles and admiring his profile, or the girl who spends hours applying her makeup or trying one hair style or one dress after another, may be dreaming of the dramatic impression that he or she will make on a date or at a party that evening. One of the minor tragedies of adolescent life is that when these young people actually meet, each is likely to be more preoccupied with himself or herself than with observing others (18).

Even the quality of adolescent love reflects to some degree the cognitive changes of adolescence. Many young people fall in love, not so much with the reality of the other person as with a carefully constructed fantasy, based on all kinds of untested assumptions, many of which may have little

basis in fact. "The girl of my dreams" extolled in popular songs is often just that.

The adolescent's cognitive development also plays an important role in the emergence of a well-defined sense of identity. The ability to consider the possible as well as what currently is, to try out alternative solutions to problems, to look further into the future, all help the young person to address the central questions "Who am I?," "Who do I want to be?," and "What are my chances of getting there?" The adolescent can try out many different roles, seeking to find those that seem personally most comfortable, rewarding, or challenging and that appear realistic or unrealistic in the light of his or her talents, skills, and opportunities. Indeed, just being aware that there is a part of the self that can reason, formulate and modify assumptions, consider alternatives, and arrive at conclusions, however tentative, helps to foster a sense of identity.

The expanded cognitive development that takes place in adolescence can make it a time of great creativity, challenge, and intellectual adventure. It is unfortunate that rather than encouraging these possibilities, we so often pour cold water on them, urging the young person instead to be "practical" or "realistic" (by which we tend to mean giving up dreams and lowering expectations of what it is possible to achieve). Many adolescent dreams may never be fulfilled, but just having had them can make the remainder of the person's life fuller, richer, and more meaningful.

DEVELOPMENTAL TASKS OF ADOLESCENCE

If an adolescent is to become truly adult and not just physically mature, he or she must accomplish a number of basic developmental tasks. In Western society these include adjusting to the physical changes of puberty, developing independence from parents or other caretakers, taking on new sexual and social roles, and establishing effective relationships with peers. Throughout all these processes, the adolescent must also develop a sense of identity and some sort of philosophy of life (11). Each of these tasks is a critical and indispensable part of adolescent development. In today's changing world, accomplishing these tasks may be more complex than it was in the past, and, as we shall see in Chapter 12, a number of adolescents do not succeed. Still, the majority of adolescents are managing to grow and develop successfully. Let's look at the processes involved in mastering these tasks.

The Development of Adolescent Independence

One of the most basic tasks faced by the adolescent is establishing his or her independence. If the adolescent fails to do this, then the other tasks of forming successful peer relationships, preparing for a vocation, and forming a sense of identity will be more difficult as well.

Most of the time it is not easy to establish true independence from parents. The process may be a kind of push-pull situation—children are likely to be rewarded both for independence *and* for continued dependence on the family.

Parents may want their children to become independent, but they may also have difficulty in realizing that their little girl or boy is no longer a child and that rules and regulations that may have been appropriate when their children were younger are appropriate no longer. Adolescents, too, are likely to have mixed feelings about dependence and independence. They look forward to the prospect of greater freedom to run their own lives, free from parental constraints. But the prospect of independence and its responsibilities can also be a bit frightening. How, the young person may wonder, am I going to go about running my own life when I don't yet know who I am, what I can do, and what I *really* want? Who will be there to straighten things out if I run into trouble? Is it any wonder that the behavior of adolescents often fluctuates between dependence and independence? However, there are several factors that will affect the degree of difficulty that the adolescent will encounter in establishing independence.

First, there is the general attitude of the society at large toward the independence training of adolescents. Second, there are the child-rearing practices and models of behavior provided by the adolescent's parents. Third, there are the interactions with peers and their support of independent behavior. The interaction of these three factors can be seen in the cultural examples discussed below. There are wide variations in patterns of independence training, both from one culture to another and from one set of parents to another.

For example, among the Mixtecan Indians of Mexico, socialization for independence is a gradual and informal process (43). Mixtecan children gradually learn to take on increasing responsibility and begin performing the tasks they will assume as adults. Girls around the age of 6 or 7 begin caring for younger siblings, going to market, helping to serve food and wash the dishes, and perhaps caring for small domestic animals. At about the same age, boys begin gathering produce or fodder in the fields and caring for large animals such as goats or burros. Parents assume that their children will learn to do such fundamental jobs adequately, and there is no demand or expectation for achievement beyond this. There is little anxiety on the part of either parents or children, aggression is not a part of the process, and nurturance plays a strong role among these people.

In contrast, the Mundugumor adolescents of the South Seas have a much more difficult period of socialization for independence. From birth they are raised in an essentially hostile environment—all members of the same sex are hostile toward each other, including mothers against daughters and fathers against sons (42). In addition, relations between husbands and wives are usually hostile. Because of this lack of nurturance, Mundugumor children develop a hardy independence early and thus are somewhat prepared for the demands they must face as adolescents. But even the advantage of early independence can be of only a little help in their assumption of the extreme independence required in their society.

Parent-Child Relationships and the Development of Independence. Obviously, establishing independence from the parents will be strongly affected by the nature of the relationship between parent and child, and one important factor involves the parents' position along the dimension of love and caring versus hostility and rejection.

The need for parents who are loving and caring is vital. Research has shown that without strong and clear manifestations of parental love, children and adolescents have little chance of developing self-esteem, constructive and rewarding relationships with others, and a confident sense of their own identity. Parental hostility, rejection, or neglect occur more frequently than acceptance, love, and trust in the backgrounds of children with a wide variety of problems, ranging from academic difficulties and impaired relationships with others to neurotic disorders, psychosomatic disorders, and conduct problems, such as delinquency (11).

Control Versus Freedom. Perhaps less obvious but equally important is the parents' position on the question of control versus freedom. We are living in a turbulent era of social change, in which there are few clearly defined social and moral guidelines and in which the shape of the future is uncertain. To cope effectively with today's and tomorrow's world, adolescents need discipline (ultimately self-discipline), but they also need independence, self-reliance, adaptability, and a strong sense of their own values.

Research has shown that these qualities are fostered best by parents who show respect for their children, involve them in family affairs and decision making, and encourage the development of age-appropriate independence but who also confidently retain ultimate responsibility — parents who are, in the words of psychologist Diana Baumrind, **authoritative** without being **authoritarian** (3). Such parents value both autonomous self-will *and* disciplined behavior. They encourage verbal give-and-take, and when they exercise parental authority, in the form of demands or prohibitions, they explain their reasons for doing so. Studies in several countries have shown that such parents are most likely to be perceived as fair and as valuing their children; they are also most likely to have children who, as adolescents, are self-confident, high in self-esteem, and independent (17, 35). In the words of one 16-year-old girl: "I guess the thing I think is great about my parents, compared to those of a lot of kids, is that they really listen. And they realize that eventually I'm going to have to live my own life — what I'm going to do with it. A lot of the time when I explain what I want to do, they'll go along with it. Sometimes, they'll warn me of the consequences I'll have to face if I'm wrong or just give me advice. And sometimes, they just plain tell me no. But when they do, they explain why, and that makes it easier to take" (12).

Authoritarian Parents. In contrast to the authoritative parent is the authoritarian (or in more extreme form, autocratic) parent, who just tells the child or adolescent what to do and feels no obligation to explain why. Such parents favor obedience as an absolute virtue and are likely to deal with any attempts at protest with punitive, forceful measures. Any sort of free discussion or two-way interaction between the parent and child is discouraged, in the conviction that the young person should unquestioningly accept the parent's word for what is right. Some parents may take this stance out of feelings of hostility or because they can't be bothered; others, however, may be doing so because they think that this is the way to develop "respect for authority." A mistake they make is that while they may suppress dissent, they don't usually get rid of it and may just encourage resentment. As one 14-year-old girl remarked about her mother, "She says, 'I just don't want to hear anymore; go back to your room.' And I think, as a human being, she shouldn't be able to say that to me without

getting my response back; I just don't feel that's right. And I'm going to be sure to give my kids that right" (38, p. 67).

This girl was able to retain her own values and adopt an identity of her own. However, many children of autocratic or authoritarian parents—because they aren't given a chance to test out their own ideas or take independent responsibility and because their opinions aren't treated as worthy of consideration—emerge from adolescence lacking in self-confidence and self-esteem and unable to be self-reliant, act independently, and think for themselves. As adolescents, the children of authoritarian and autocratic parents are far more likely than the children of authoritative parents to say they felt unwanted by both fathers and mothers (16).

"Doing Your Own Thing": Laissez-Faire and Equalitarian Parents. Parents who are **laissez-faire,** or who assume a false and exaggerated **"equalitarianism,"** also don't provide the kind of support that their adolescent young need in today's world. In several recent studies of middle-class adolescents, high-risk drug use and other forms of socially deviant behavior occurred most frequently among adolescents with parents who, while outwardly expressing for themselves and their children such values as individuality, self-understanding, and the need for equalitarianism within the family, are actually using these proclaimed values to avoid assuming parental responsibility. They may be doing this because of uncertainties about their own convictions, indecision about how to handle their children, needs to be liked or feel useful, or, as often appeared to be the case, their own unresolved childhood antagonism toward authority—parental or social (4).

Children and adolescents, no matter how much they may protest at times, don't really want their parents to be equals; they want and *need* them to be *parents*—friendly, understanding parents but parents nonetheless. The father or mother who tries to act "with it"—to adopt adolescent values, fashions, or behavior—both confuses and embarrasses the young person. Furthermore, such a parent deprives the adolescent of what he or she needs most in a parent in addition to love, guidance, and caring: a model of successful, independent, problem-solving *adult* behavior.

It appears that parents in contemporary society face the problem of steering a delicate course between authoritarianism, on the one hand, and overpermissiveness, "equalitarianism," or neglect on the other. But for parents who are able to achieve the right balance, the results can be rewarding to both parent and child. As an 18-year-old Chicano girl said of her mother: "She's given me confidence in myself, and sometimes she tries to make me understand her point of view. Then when she says something and it's right even though it hurts me, I kind of listen to her even though I pretend I'm not listening, I turn my face, and she makes me believe in myself, even when I'm down" (38, p. 65). Or this from a 16-year-old black boy: "My dad's kind of special, I guess. Like he takes me camping, and he sits down and talks to me about trouble at school. He wants to know what I'm doing, where I'm going. He helps me to learn things, and I admire him for being smart and strong and able to handle problems."

A second developmental task of adolescence has to do with coping with the new issue of sexuality. Like the development of independence, how an adolescent develops sexually depends on many factors.

ADOLESCENT SEXUALITY

No doubt you can remember the excitement of your first serious kiss. Indeed, the emergence of a sex drive is a dramatic and challenging event, and integrating sexuality meaningfully with other aspects of the self-concept is a major developmental task for all adolescents.

However, the way in which an adolescent deals with sexuality depends on many factors, both psychological and cultural, as well as on the young person's sex. Boys, for example, find it difficult to deny the physically obvious signs of sexual arousal, which, as noted earlier, may appear frequently and sometimes uncontrollably. Among girls, however, sexual drive is likely to be less urgent and to produce more diffuse and vague feelings. As adolescence proceeds, girls become more aware of sexual impulses, but, even then, for many girls sexual gratification is likely to remain secondary to, or at least closely related to, the fulfillment of other

needs such as self-esteem, reassurance, affection, and love (13). Boys engage in more sexual activity in general, and masturbation in particular, than girls, although the amount of girls' sexual activity has increased in recent years (6). Furthermore, girls typically display more conservative attitudes than boys toward sexual matters such as premarital intercourse or pornography (60). Why do these sex differences in sexual behavior and attitudes exist? A number of theories have been advanced — some primarily physiological in nature, others primarily cultural.

Some physiological theories hold that a woman's sex drive is lower than a man's and that her capacity for arousal is lower (5). However, the view held by a two-thirds majority of today's adolescent girls is that "women enjoy sex as much as men" (27, p. 96), and only 1 in 10 adolescent girls believes that a woman's capacity for sexual pleasure is lower than a man's. Their opinion that women can enjoy sex as much as men is backed up by William Masters and Virginia Johnson, the gynecologist-psychologist team of investigators, who were the first scientists to study human sexual responses comprehensively and objectively. They hold that a woman's basic physiological capacity to respond sexually is actually greater than a man's (41).

Another argument has been that boys are more easily aroused than girls by a wider variety of external "psychosexual stimuli," such as provocative behavior, erotic art, films, and literature (40). The truth is that the actual current differences are smaller than originally supposed (60). In fact, in some situations, females are more aroused than some males by such stimuli (for example, younger, more sexually "liberated" women versus older, more conservative males) (57).

Sexuality appears to be more intimately bound up with other personality factors in the case of girls, and thus the conditions necessary for their arousal — or for acknowledging their arousal — may be more complex than those that arouse boys. A girl may be "turned off" by stimulation if it is threatening, conflicts with existing values, is impersonal, or is aesthetically offensive, whereas her male peer may not require as complex a set of conditions for arousal (6).

The fact that adolescent males generally are more sexually aggressive than adolescent females may be related, at least in part, to vastly greater increases in testosterone levels among males at puberty. It has been demonstrated that this hormone increases sexual and aggressive behavior in both sexes under experimental conditions (5).

Cultural Influences on Sexual Attitudes and Behavior

Regardless of the ultimate significance of these and other factors, the lesser sexual activity of female adolescents and the differences between male and female sexual behavior may be at least partially attributed to our culture's more restrictive attitudes toward sexual gratification for girls (41). Learning plays a significant role in determining how people respond to and satisfy their sexual drives (5). Consequently there are wide variations in sexual attitudes and behavior from one culture to another. Some cultures, for example, restrict sexual activity throughout childhood, adolescence, and even to some extent in adulthood. Among the Cuna of the coast of Panama, children are told nothing about sex until the last stages of the marriage ceremony (23). The Ashanti of Africa have a puberty ceremony for girls, and they believe that sexual intercourse with a girl who has not undergone the puberty ceremony is so harmful to the community that the offense is punishable by death for both partners (23).

Other cultures are thoroughly permissive at all ages. The Chewa of Africa believe that unless children begin to engage in sexual activity early in life, they will never beget offspring, and so their children freely engage in sexual intercourse before marriage. Similarly, the Lepcha of India believe that early sexual intercourse is necessary in order for girls to mature, and early sex play leads to regular intercourse for girls by the time they are 11 or 12 years old (23).

Still other cultures are highly restrictive during childhood and adolescence and then suddenly become much more permissive about sexual activity in adulthood. In our own society, children are frequently taught to inhibit and control sexual behavior until marriage. Many children are still taught, consciously or unconsciously, to be anxious about sex, yet they are expected to be able to respond without inhibition or anxiety once they are married.

Effects of Changing Values on Sexual Behavior

America has supposedly undergone a recent "sexual revolution." How are these changes reflected in the behavior of contemporary adolescents? Table 11.1 contains the percentage figures, but let's see just what these figures indicate.

If we look at the percentage of boys who have masturbated by age 19,

Table 11.1 PERCENTAGES OF ADOLESCENTS PARTICIPATING IN SEXUAL BEHAVIOR

	1940s		1970s	
MASTURBATION	AGE 13	AGE 19	AGE 13	AGE 19
Girls	<16	30	33	42
Boys	45	86–90	65	85–90
PREMARITAL INTERCOURSE	AGE 16	AGE 19	AGE 16	AGE 19
Girls	3	<20	30	57
Boys	39	72	44	72

Sources: J. J. Conger Sexual attitudes and behavior of contemporary adolescents. In J. J. Conger (Ed.), Contemporary issues in adolescent development. New York: Harper & Row, 1975. Pp. 221–230.
M. Hunt, *Sexual behavior in the 1970s.* Chicago: Playboy Press, 1974.

things haven't changed much in the rates of masturbation since the time of their fathers' adolescence. But differences show up when we look at boys of younger ages, for today many boys begin masturbation earlier than boys during the 1940s. Among girls, recent data indicate that there has been an increase in masturbation at all ages since their mothers' generation.

The increase in masturbation is probably due largely to more tolerant social attitudes and a decline in myths about the harmful effects of masturbation (it will not make your hair or teeth fall out) (10). Masturbation is a normal developmental phenomenon and becomes a problem only when it serves as a substitute for social relationships and activities in which the young person feels inadequate. But in such instances, masturbation is not primarily a cause of the individual's problems but rather a response to them.

Petting among adolescents has increased somewhat in the past few decades, and it tends to occur slightly earlier (54). The major changes, however, have probably been in frequency of petting, degree of intimacy of techniques involved, the frequency with which petting leads to erotic arousal or orgasm, and, certainly, frankness about this activity (53).

A topic of much interest is the incidence of premarital intercourse among adolescents today. Clearly, there has been an increase (see Table 11.1), particularly among females. To understand the reasons for this increase, we must look more closely at the makeup of the groups that have changed.

Diversity of Sexual Attitudes and Behavior

Not all adolescents hold the same sexual attitudes and values. For example, younger adolescents are more conservative about sexual matters than older adolescents; girls are more conservative than boys, and boys engage more in all forms of intimate sexual behavior than girls. Also, more girls than boys believe that partners in advanced forms of petting or intercourse should be in love, engaged, or married (54). Politically conservative and religiously oriented youth are more conservative in sexual attitudes and behavior than their liberal or religiously inactive counterparts (58), and black adolescents are more active sexually than whites of the same age (6).

In the last 30 or 40 years, the greatest changes in sexual behavior have occurred among economically privileged, more highly educated youth, especially girls. As a rule, these young people tend to be less conservative than their peers who are less economically favored, and this tendency has been true with regard to sexual matters, although the differences currently appear to be decreasing (10).

Serial Monogamists and Sexual Adventurers. Although more adolescents are having sexual intercourse now than in the past, the great majority are not promiscuous. In fact, over 48 percent of all adolescents have never had intercourse by age 19, and only 15 percent of all adolescents can be classified as **sexual adventurers,** that is, those who "sleep around" with no obligation of faithfulness to any one sex partner (54). Most of the remaining 37 percent of adolescents can be classified as **serial monogamists,** that is, they generally have a strong, affectionate relationship with only one partner for a period of time and have intercourse only with that partner during that time. The term "serial" is used because one such relationship is often succeeded by another (54).

Not surprisingly, serial monogamists and sexual adventurers vary significantly in attitudes as well as in behavior. Basically, monogamists believe that sexual involvement is "okay as long as you're in love," and stress openness and honesty, while adventurers do not believe that love is a necessary part of sexual relationships. Some adventurers believe that sex is a "good way to get acquainted." Adventurers feel no particular personal responsibility for their partners, although neither do they believe in hurting others.

As a group, monogamists tended to be more satisfied with themselves and life in general, to get along better with parents, and to be more conventional in social, political, and religious beliefs than sexual adventurers. Monogamists also express greater satisfaction with their sex lives, reporting a greater frequency of orgasm than adventurers.

Certainly there are positive aspects to the "new morality" found among contemporary adolescents—a greater emphasis on openness and honesty, mutual respect and lack of exploitation, and a more "natural" and better-informed approach to sex. And many experienced adolescents, particularly older ones, appear able to handle their sexual involvement and state that sex makes their lives more meaningful (10). But others—girls more than boys—report feelings of conflict and guilt, especially after the first experience of intercourse. There are obviously dangers in assuming that sexual activity is "okay as long as you're in love." Encouraged by such a philosophy among peers, youngsters may become more deeply involved emotionally than they can handle responsibly at a particular stage of maturity (11).

Pregnancy and Contraception

Although you would think that with the "new morality" there would be a new awareness of the responsibility for preventing unwanted pregnancies, such is not the case. A disturbingly high percentage—between 55 and 75 percent—of unmarried girls having intercourse have used no contraceptive whatever, at least in their first experience, and only a minority consistently use such a device thereafter. Less than a third have used the contraceptive pill to prevent pregnancy (21), and even among monogamists, only two-thirds reported always using contraceptive devices (54).

As a result, every year over 1 million 15- to 19-year-old girls in the

United States (10 percent of this entire age group) are becoming pregnant, with two-thirds of these pregnancies being conceived out of wedlock (59). In addition, some 30,000 girls *under* the age of 15 are becoming pregnant annually (21). The consequences of this "epidemic" of adolescent pregnancies are serious indeed. Among the 15- to 19-year-olds, more than a quarter are terminated by induced abortion; 21 percent result in births to unmarried mothers; and 14 percent lead to miscarriages. The remainder were already married or subsequently got married prior to the birth of the child.

Pregnant adolescents, whether married or unmarried, face serious problems. Aside from the increased psychological and social difficulties of adolescent motherhood, adolescent pregnancies are far more likely to endanger the physical health of both mother and child (see Chapter 2).

Why, then, don't these adolescents use contraceptives? According to the reports of adolescent girls and young women, either contraceptives were not available when they needed them, or they thought they could not become pregnant because of time of month, age, or infrequency of intercourse. Only 1 in 11 adolescents indicated they wouldn't mind getting

Problems Faced by Teenage Mothers

Aside from the greater physical risks they and their infants face, teenage mothers are likely to encounter a host of other problems. Some facts:

- Eight out of 10 young mothers under 17 are unmarried at the time of their child's birth, and 79 percent have had no prior job experience.
- Twice as many teenage mothers drop out of school and do not return as those who do not give birth till after age 20. Indeed, for girls, pregnancy is the most common cause of school dropout.
- Teenage mothers face a far greater risk of unemployment and becoming dependent on welfare. Among those 15 to 17, the welfare rate is 4.5 times that for mothers in their early twenties.
- Teenage marriages are 2 to 3 times as likely to break up as those of couples married in their early twenties. Three out of every 5 pregnant teenage brides are divorced within 6 years.

11 Million Teenagers. New York: The Alan Guttmacher Institute, Planned Parenthood Federation of America, Inc., 1976.

pregnant, and only 1 in 15 pregnant adolescents stated that they did not use contraceptives because they were trying to have a baby. Obviously, better education and more adequate service programs are needed. Currently only 1 in 3 high schools teaches about birth-control methods, despite the fact that 8 out of 10 Americans old enough to have children of junior-high or high-school age favor such teaching.

Of those adolescents who are either seeking or not trying to avoid pregnancy, a common theme is that of emotional deprivation. In the words of one pregnant 15-year-old: "I guess for once in my life, I wanted to have something I could call my own, that I could love and that would love me." Other related motivations may include being accepted as an adult, getting back at one's parents, "holding" a boyfriend, gaining attention from peers, escaping from school, or just looking for some change in an unrewarding existence (37).

Of all the lasting effects of the youth culture of the 1960s, greater sexual freedom appears to be the most enduring (11). However, we must hope that the adolescents who do enter sexual relationships can be helped to become informed and concerned enough about the welfare of others to handle sex responsibly. In this way the inevitable "casualties" of the sexual revolution can be kept to a minimum and sex as a vital part of human relationships can promote, rather than hinder, growth toward maturity and emotional fulfillment.

ADOLESCENTS AND THEIR PEERS

Possibly one of the most common images associated with adolescence is that of a group of teenagers "hanging out" together, whether on the corner, in a pizza parlor, or at a community center. The peer group plays a vital role in the psychological development of most adolescents, just as it did for children. Adolescents also learn to interact socially with age mates, to develop skills and interests appropriate for their age group, and to share similar problems and feelings (25). But peers become important for other reasons during adolescence.

First of all, because the adolescent's relations with both same-sex and opposite-sex peers are closer to those of adults, adolescents who have good relationships with their peers are learning good adult relationships. Second, adolescents' ties with their families are weakening, and thus they may become more dependent on their peers. On some issues, adolescents may be at odds with their parents and may find that age mates understand their problems better. Finally, adolescents need the companionship and support of others who are going through the same life stage they are. No matter how understanding adults try to be, they are in different positions

from adolescents: Adolescents are still struggling to reach adult status; adults are already there. Adolescents find comfort in being with others who are experiencing the same physiological and psychological changes they are. Being accepted by peers and having one or two close friends can help an adolescent through this period of changes.

Conformity to Peer Culture

Along with the image of a group of teenagers "hanging out" is the idea that all teenagers are alike. Indeed, they often *look* alike—dressed almost identically in the prevailing fashion. And often they seem to act alike—all listening to the same music, all following the same fads. The commonly held stereotype of teenagers is that they all conform rigidly to the norms of the peer group and that the norms of the peer group do *not* conform to those of the adult culture around them. Let's see how much of this stereotype is true.

There is, in fact, increased conformity to the values, customs, and fads of peer culture during adolescence (see Figure 11.4), no doubt because the peer group increases in importance during this period. There appears to be a rather rapid rise in conformity needs and behavior during the preadolescent and early adolescent years, followed by a gradual but steady decline from middle through late adolescence (7). But the answer to the question of whether adolescent norms differ from those of their parents may be surprising, as you will see in the next section.

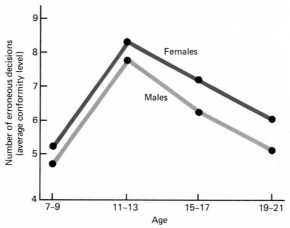

Figure 11.4 Graph summarizing the results of children's conformity to the judgments of a peer group. The results for both females and males show that susceptibility to peer influences increases with age until early adolescence and then gradually declines. Such data are but one indicator of the importance of peer influences in later childhood. (After P. R. Costanzo & M. E. Shaw. Conformity as a function of age level. *Child Development*, 1966, *37*, 967–975.)

Parental and Peer Influences—Same or Different? In general, teenagers (adolescents) listen to different music, wear different clothes, and follow different fads from their parents. These differences are conspicuous but rather superficial; in actuality, the values of most adolescents do not ordinarily differ drastically from those of their parents.

Since the adolescent's parents and peers have similar cultural backgrounds, there is usually considerable overlap between their values. Consequently, peers may actually serve to reinforce parental values, particularly in the case of moral and social values and understanding of the adult world (9). While peer influence is, as mentioned before, usually predominant in such matters as tastes in music and entertainment, fashions in clothing and language, and patterns of social interactions, on other issues, the relative influence of parents or the peer group varies with the issue and the individual. An adolescent who is neglected at home may be more influenced by the peer group than by parents (8), while an adolescent whose parents are interested in him or her, and who are understanding, and willing to be helpful, will be more likely to follow the basic values of the parents. Such an adolescent is also less likely to feel a need to differentiate between the influence of the parents and his or her best friend. In addition, adolescents who are more self-confident and autonomous can relate to both parents and peers without feeling as though they must be strongly dependent on either (48).

The Changing Nature of Adolescent Peer Groups As with so many other areas of experience, there is a change in the nature of the peer groups that are important to the adolescent. During middle childhood and preadolescence boys and girls play separately. Boys tend to be more involved with "gangs" than girls, who tend to remain somewhat closer to parents and to have more intimate, "best friend" relationships with peers. During adolescence there is a swing toward more interactions with friends of the opposite sex, and there are also changes in the size and function of the peer groups. The circle of friends and casual acquaintances widens: there is the broad "crowd," the smaller, more intimate group known as the **clique,** and individual friendships.

Cliques and Crowds. Should hair be long or short, straight or curly? Are flannel shirts or crew-neck sweaters in fashion? The adolescent finds answers to these and other such questions in the clique. The clique permits the adolescent to keep up to date on current fads and fashions in clothes, personal grooming, music, language, popular topics of conversation, and the like. At a deeper level, cliques can serve as a testing ground for the young person's developing social beliefs and values. Moreover, cliques plan the activities of the larger crowd, the crowd being the center of larger and more organized social activities, such as parties, which provide for interaction between the sexes (14).

In early adolescence, same-sex cliques predominate; when these young teenagers interact with the opposite sex, it is usually within the larger, safer, crowd setting. Gradually, small heterosexual cliques begin to emerge, although same-sex cliques also continue, and the crowd is still important. In late adolescence, loosely associated groups of couples are frequent; same-sex friendships continue but become more stable; and the importance of the crowd lessens as the need for conformity to peers decreases and the adolescent begins to feel that he or she wants to develop his or her own individual identity (7).

Friendships and Identity Development. Friendships may help the adolescent in several ways. Friends can confide or "let off steam" to one another; they may be surprised and happy to find that others have feelings similar to theirs. Because close friends may feel free to criticize one another, an adolescent may learn to change his or her behavior, tastes, or ideas within the safe confines of the friendship instead of facing the painful experience of being rejected by the larger group (13). In addition, an adolescent's self-confidence may be bolstered by having a friend who "really understands," who genuinely knows, likes, and values him or her.

A disadvantage of adolescent friendships is that their paths are often perilous; that is, perhaps because they are so intense, they may end bitterly—unlike most adult friendships, in which generally less is invested *and* less is gained.

Adolescent Popularity

What determines which adolescents will be popular? There are many factors—some predictable, such as being physically attractive and lively and having a sense of humor. Adolescents who are tolerant, who like other people, who are flexible and sympathetic, cheerful and good-natured, are generally accepted by their peers (25). Further, adolescents usually like peers who make *them* feel accepted and involved, who actively promote and plan enjoyable group interactions and activities (36).

Given the personality characteristics and social behaviors typical of popular adolescents, it is fairly easy to predict what characteristics are least admired, for they are in many ways the opposite of those leading to acceptance and popularity. For example, an adolescent who is ill at ease and lacking in self-confidence, rather than being a planner of group activities, is likely to be neglected by peers. Likewise, the adolescent who goes overboard in the other direction—that is, who reacts to insecurity by demanding attention or becoming overaggressive—is not accepted by the peer group either. In fact, rather than being simply neglected, this kind of person may be actively disliked and rejected. Similarly, a person who is so self-centered that he or she does not respond to the needs of others, and the sarcastic and inconsiderate person who contributes little to group effort are not likely to be accepted by the peer group (11).

There are, of course, many other factors that affect popularity. Despite the stereotyped notion that adolescents regard intelligence as unimportant, it seems that intelligence tends to be positively correlated with acceptance among both boys and girls. Special talents, too, can affect an adolescent's acceptance by the peer group. After all, it's always fun to have a ventriloquist or a guitar player around.

What Is a Friend?

Over 1000 adolescent girls were interviewed about their feelings toward friends. Two themes stood out clearly with respect to the desirable qualities they searched for in friends.

1. A friend is someone you can *trust*, who does not speak ill of you behind your back, who can keep secrets, and who is available when you need him or her.

2. Friends must be able to listen, to understand on a feeling level.

For example, one adolescent said,

I think [a friend is] somebody that is loyal. Somebody that would stay on your side no matter what anybody—well, if somebody started a rumor and everyone believed it, somebody that wouldn't believe it. Or somebody that, if they knew you did it, they wouldn't say, "Aw, you did it" just to be like everybody else.

(14, *White, rural*)

Another said that

[A friend is] someone who . . . when you really need them, they will come. Someone who sticks close and is truthful and, y'know, I won't really have to worry about them goin' out and tellin' your business or somethin' like that.

(15, *Black, urban*)

Another adolescent girl defined a friend in terms of trust:

A friend don't talk behind your back. If they are a true friend they help you get out of trouble and they will always be right behind you and they help you through stuff. And they never snitch on you. That's what a friend is.

(14, *Black, urban*)

G. Konopka, *Young girls: A portrait of adolescence.* Englewood Cliffs, N.J.: Prentice-Hall, 1976. Pp. 84–85.

Belonging to the culturally dominant majority is also a factor that contributes to popularity. Consequently, many high-school social groups tend to be predominantly segregated. Unfortunately, this restriction limits those peers with whom the adolescent can be friends, although there may be persons with compatible personal characteristics and shared interests,

What "Turns On" or "Turns Off" a Member of the Opposite Sex

In a recent national survey, adolescent American girls, aged 16 to 21, were asked what qualities in boys "turned them on"—or off. Rated as most important (90 percent or more) were: good personality, kindness, good manners, and a sense of humor; these were followed by compassion, good looks, and charm (over 70 percent). In contrast, the following emerged as the most frequent "turn-offs": heavy drinking, inability to communicate feelings, profanity, and drug use (all over 70 percent), followed by indecisiveness, "super-jock," and "don't kiss goodnight" (40 percent or more). Apparently, these young women wanted boys to be somewhat "androgynous"—sensitive and compassionate but also reasonably assertive and decisive.

In another recent survey of boys of the same ages, a number of traditional myths did not hold up too well. When asked if a girl asking them for a date was a "turn-on," was a "turn-off," or it "doesn't matter," the largest number (44 percent) said it would be a "turn-on"; about the same number (43 percent) said it didn't matter, and only 13 percent considered it a turn-off. A similar pattern of responses was found when boys were asked about a girl taking the lead in making out. Similarly, a majority of boys were turned off by a girl's refusing a goodnight kiss on the first date. In contrast, only a small minority (11 to 13 percent) were turned off by a girl's refusing a drink or marijuana, and less than 3 percent were turned on by profanity. Both boys and girls were attracted by intelligence (contrary to a popular myth), as well as by a sense of humor and good looks. A prominent reason for not wanting to date a second time was "boredom."

Gilbert Youth Research, *Seventeen*, April 1979 and March 1978.

outlooks, and goals in other cultural groups. It would be fortunate if adolescents could develop confidence and pride in their cultural identity *and* in themselves as individual human beings so that they would be less defensive about cultural groups and freer to select friends from any group.

Not all adolescents have the support of a clique or crowd. Some individuals, either through choice or, more frequently, through rejection by peers, are isolates (26). Although some of today's adolescents seem more tolerant and understanding than previous generations, there are still many adolescents who can be indifferent or even cruel toward other adolescents who do not fit in (11).

Few adolescents (or adults) are unaffected by neglect or rejection (34). And unpopular adolescents are caught in a vicious circle. First, they may not be accepted initially by their peers because they are lacking in self-confidence. Then, because they are aware of rejection by their peers, they become even less self-confident, and their sense of social isolation increases.

SUMMARY

1. Adolescence is a challenging and sometimes difficult period, for the young person must adjust to many rapid physical, sexual, psychological, cognitive, and social changes. However, it should be remembered that no two adolescents are identical; moreover, their experiences may differ because of family or social experience or because of the culture in which they live.

2. Puberty refers to the first phase of adolescence when sexual maturation becomes evident. At this time adolescents also have a "growth spurt" in height and weight. There are wide variations in the onset of puberty and the rate of development.

3. Early maturation and late maturation have different effects on the personality development of adolescent boys and girls. Early maturation is, in general, an advantage for boys, while it is not a significant advantage for girls.

4. Cognitive development continues during adolescence; young people enter Piaget's stage of formal operations. During this stage the adolescent shifts the emphasis in his or her thinking from the *real* to the *possible*. That is, the child is able to think abstractly and generate and consider many possible solutions to a problem.

5. An adolescent must develop a sense of independence, and parents and the culture in which the adolescent lives may aid or hinder this process. Authoritative parents—that is, those who are neither authoritarian and arbitrary nor overly permissive and laissez-faire, but who are reasonable and consistent and who explain the reasons behind

their rules and standards of behavior—foster a healthy sense of independence in their children.

6. Sex differences in sexual arousal and behavior, when they exist, may have a biological component, but are also clearly related to cultural influences. Cultural influences also significantly affect sexual behavior in general. For example, American attitudes toward sex are much more tolerant now than they were 50 years ago, and sexual behavior has increased since that time.

7. Although sexual activity has increased in recent years, almost half of all adolescents have still never had intercourse by age 19. Of those who do have intercourse, 15 percent can be classified as sexual adventurers and 37 percent as serial monogamists.

8. Over 1 million 15- to 19-year-old girls become pregnant each year; thus it is obvious that better education and more adequate service programs for birth control are needed.

9. The peer group plays a vital role in the development of most adolescents. Though there is a tendency toward increased conformity, in most cases there is considerable overlap between peer group and parental values.

10. During adolescence peer groups widen to include members of both sexes. The size of the peer group also increases, and most teenagers are members of a broad crowd and a smaller clique, as well as having individual friendships.

11. Many factors influence adolescent popularity, including intelligence, physical appearance and skills, social status, and special talents.

Suggested Readings

Chilman, Catherine S. *Adolescent sexuality.* Washington, D.C.: U.S. Government Printing Office, 1978.

Conger, John Janeway. *Adolescence and youth: Psychological development in a changing world* (2nd ed.). New York: Harper & Row, 1977.

Kandel, Denise B., & Lesser, Gerald S. *Youth in two worlds.* San Francisco: Jossey-Bass, 1972.

Konopka, Gisela. *Young girls: A portrait of adolescence.* Englewood Cliffs, N.J.: Prentice-Hall, 1976.

Sorensen, Robert C. *Adolescent sexuality in contemporary America: Personal values and sexual behavior, ages 13–19.* New York: World Publishing, 1973.

Film

Conger, John Janeway (with Jerome Kagan). *Adolescence: The winds of change.* New York: Harper & Row Media, 1976.

Chapter 12

Adolescence: Identity, Values, and Problems of Adjustment

CENTRAL task of adolescence, and one that encompasses many other developmental tasks, is that of establishing a clear sense of identity — of finding some kind of workable answer to the age-old question "Who am I?"

As Erik Erikson observes, before adolescents can successfully abandon the security of childhood dependence on others, they must have some idea of who they are, where they are going, and what the possibilities are of getting there (19). In the process of finding answers to these questions, adolescents must begin to decide what their values and moral convictions should be, what it means to be a man or woman in today's world, and what they want to do with their lives.

In this chapter, we shall examine the problems confronting young people generally in developing a system of values and a sense of ego identity and choosing a vocation. We will look as well at the special problems of those who for one reason or another — social, psychological, economic, or ideological — find themselves outside the mainstream of adolescent culture in America.

THE QUESTION OF IDENTITY

In order to have a strong sense of **identity,** an adolescent or adult needs to see himself or herself as a distinctive individual, even though many values and interests may be shared with others. Closely related is the need for self-consistency, for a feeling of wholeness — a workable integration of one's needs, motives, and goals. Finally, in order for the adolescent to have a clear sense of identity, there has to be a perception of the self as stable over time; that is, we need to perceive the person that we are today as, if not the same person we were yesterday, at least similar to and having consistent links with the person we were yesterday and will be tomorrow.

If we stop and think for a minute about these requirements for a strong sense of identity, it is easy to see why the problem of identity formation is a central problem of adolescence. Confronted by all the rapid physical and physiological changes taking place within himself or herself, as well as the many changing societal demands we have discussed, the young person finds it difficult to maintain a feeling of stability of the self over time. Even at a particular moment, new and sometimes strange thoughts, impulses, and feelings may threaten the young person's effort to achieve a feeling of self-consistency. Given all these rapid changes, the adolescent needs a period of time to integrate them into a slowly emerging sense of identity.

An amusing but informative example of the problem of identity development in adolescence involved a young adolescent girl who had three distinctly different handwriting styles. When asked why she didn't have just one style, she replied, "How can I have just one style till I know who I am?" (17). Many adolescents have similar feelings. Not only do they find themselves playing roles that shift from one situation, or one time, to another and worry about "which, if any, is the *real* me," but they also self-consciously try out different roles in the hope of finding one that seems to fit.

Some adolescents seem to develop a strong sense of identity early; for others, the process is long and perhaps never really resolved. While the current popular opinion is that the typical adolescent goes through an intense period of identity confusion — an **"identity crisis"** — before establishing a stable identity, there is increasing evidence that there has been a tendency to exaggerate the frequency and especially the extent of serious identity crises among young people (15).

Nonetheless, it is true that adolescence is a time of identity formation, and there are certain factors that can make this process harder or easier. One such factor is the culture.

Identity in Other Cultures

In a simple primitive society, where there is only a limited number of possible adult roles, the process of identity formation is quicker and easier than in a rapidly changing, complex society like our own, where there is so much choice (25). With American adolescents, there is generally a somewhat greater emphasis on self-reliance and independence than there is in other cultures. In China and Japan, for example, there is greater emphasis on achieving one's identity and sense of worth through close relationships with others and through sharing in the group identity of an established social order. However, even in cultures that place a relatively heavy emphasis on group identity, as compared with individual identity, there is still a need to develop a sense of self as a distinct person, to develop both individual and group identity.

Parent-Child Relationships and Identity Formation

The establishment of a firm sense of identity is made easier by a number of factors. A rewarding, nurturant relationship between the child or adolescent and *both* parents is important. It is good, too, for the same-sex parent to provide a personally and socially effective role model with which the child finds it rewarding to identify. In addition, it is helpful for the opposite-sex parent to be an effective individual also and to approve of the model provided by the same-sex parent (40, 57). The children of such parents tend to see themselves as having greater role consistency. That is, if they have a sense of themselves as relaxed or formal or warm or indifferent in one situation, they believe they will respond in a similar fashion in another situation (26).

The Cognitive Influence on Identity Formation

Achieving a well-defined sense of individual identity is also influenced by the cognitive capacity of the adolescent. That is, to establish a sense of identity, the adolescent must be able to view himself or herself objectively, at times almost like a spectator. This ability to consider one's own thoughts objectively is part of Piaget's stage of formal operations (see pp. 345–346). But while in one sense the capacity to engage in formal operational thinking aids the adolescent's search for identity, in another sense, the adolescent's emerging cognitive powers also increase the difficulty of the search, for the adolescent becomes capable of imagining all sorts of possibilities for his or her identity, yet must narrow the choices down in order to form a consistent sense of self-identity.

Sex Typing and Sexual Identity

Sexual identity begins early in life and is an important component of one's overall sense of personal identity.

Sex-typed behavior and **sexual identity** are terms that are frequently confused and refer to two different concepts, and it is important to distinguish between them. As you may remember from previous discussions of socialization, *sex-typed behavior* is appropriate behavior as a man or woman, although such behavior need not (and, as we shall see, in many instances probably should not) mean rigid conformity to sex-role stereotypes. For example, it is entirely appropriate for a woman to be assertive or a man to be nurturant, although these behaviors may have traditionally been linked to the opposite sex. *Sexual (or sex-role) identity* refers to an awareness and emotional acceptance of one's basic biological nature as a man or woman. For example, a woman with a female sexual identity accepts the fact that she is a woman, although she may or may not choose to be a wife and mother or manifest other sex-typed behaviors.

Sexual identity begins early in life and is an important component of one's overall sense of personal identity. Therefore, conflicts in sexual identity are likely to create significant problems in the development of a confident, rewarding sense of ego identity.

Parent-Child Relationship and Sexual Identity

In general, a positive, conflict-free sexual identity, like overall identity, is fostered by a rewarding identification with the same-sex parent, an identification that is also supported by the opposite-sex parent (9, 15). Once more, however, it should be stressed that achieving a clear sense of sexual identity is *not* dependent on adopting traditionally sex-typed behavior. A girl who is identified with a traditionally very feminine mother *and* another girl who is identified with a socially assertive, intellectual, highly independent mother may *both* achieve a relatively conflict-free adjustment and a strong sense of ego identity, even though the latter girl would be likely to score low on a stereotyped measure of "femininity." But establishing a stable, secure identity — sexual as well as otherwise — may be difficult for the daughter of a nonnurturant mother or of a mother who rejects her basic biological identity (15).

As for sex typing, children of parents who represent extremely exaggerated sex-role stereotypes, or who reverse their sex roles, are more likely to have difficulty establishing a sense of identity, including sexual identity. Children of parents who provide relatively traditional sex-role models and those who are somewhat more flexible and less stereotyped may both achieve relatively conflict-free identities, so long as the parents are authoritative — showing an active concern for their children's development and setting appropriate standards (see Chapter 11, pp. 349–353). However, sons and daughters of the parents who are more flexible and less stereotyped in their own sex roles are somewhat more secure and relaxed in the development of their personal identity (9).

The Trend Toward Androgyny

Androgynous individuals are those who combine traditionally masculine ("andro" from the Greek) and feminine ("gyne") attitudes and behaviors. Recent trends in sex-role stereotyping seem to be toward less rigid sex typing. For example, in a couple of recent studies of high-school and college students, from one-third to one-half of the students were classified as androgynous based on their answers to questionnaires about their own personality characteristics. (The "masculinity" or "femininity" of various traits was determined in an earlier study in which students rated traits as masculine or feminine.) About the same percentage (one-third to one-half) of the students were classified as traditionally sex-typed. The remainder were classified as either cross-sex-typed or, in one study, as undifferentiated — that is, they did not score high on either the masculine or the feminine scale.

In the opinion of many, there are advantages to being somewhat androgynous rather than rigidly conforming to traditional sexual stereotypes. For example, traditional femininity is not often associated with the qualities of being self-reliant, assertive, and independent in judgments, but one needs such qualities in order to function in our modern complex society. Similarly, traditional masculinity is not generally associated with being sensitive to the needs of others or depending on them for emotional support, but these, too, are qualities that are needed for successful, healthy functioning in our world. Androgyny allows both males and females to incorporate both sets of qualities, thus enabling them to cope with a wide range of situations (7).

However, while there are some advantages to androgyny, we would hope that the trend toward androgyny will be tempered with flexibility. It is important to avoid the danger of imposing new sets of stereotypes — even some "ideal" androgynous balance — on all boys and girls, men and women. It is more important in the process of socialization to permit each adolescent to develop his or her *unique* potential as a human being, consistent with the rights of others.

VOCATIONAL CHOICE

Certainly working out a sexual identity is important for the adolescent, but just as essential to defining one's identity is choosing a vocation. In fact, the problem of deciding on and preparing for a vocation represents one of the major developmental tasks of adolescence. Yet this process is not one on which the adolescent gets much help or guidance. Our society does little to provide adolescents with experiences that will help them make the transition to work. However, there have been some efforts to provide adolescents with work experience. For example, in one high school in Chicago, formerly characterized by a high delinquency rate, students spend half of each day studying academic subjects at their own pace, earning credits when they complete a prescribed amount of work. During the other half of the day, they work in business-funded training projects, such as renovating buildings in the community, earning a small salary for their work. A high rate of attendance and elimination of vandalism have been two of the results (52). But such training programs are not common. Moreover, little is done to provide beginning employment for adolescents once they enter the labor market.

The unemployment rate among teenagers seeking work has consistently averaged 2½ times that of adults—in good years and bad (see Figure 12.1). Among black and other minority youth, the situation is even worse (see Figure 12.2).

Most adolescents begin thinking about their career plans early in adolescence and get progressively more realistic as the time to begin working gets closer. That is, at first they just think about what their interests are, and choose a career on that basis. For example, a young girl may be fascinated by outer space and want to be an astronaut. In the next stage they consider their capacity for performing the jobs that interest them. That is, the girl in our example may start to assess her skills in science or math, since astronauts must be capable of operating highly sophisticated technical equipment. Still later, they attempt to integrate their interests and capacities with their value system. The girl may begin to wonder if she really believes in the government spending billions of dollars on a space program while there still exist some deplorable social and environmental conditions on this planet.

After this stage, adolescents are ready for the transition to the period of realistic choice, somewhere around age 17 or 18. It is usually about this time that an adolescent will evaluate his or her aspirational level and motivation and the requirements of the job desired, and then pursue that ob-

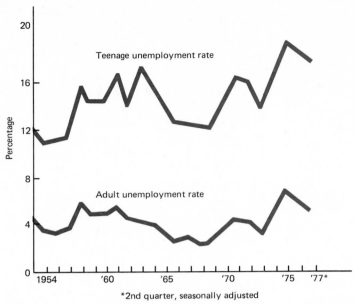

Figure 12.1 Comparison of teenage and adult unemployment rates, 1954–1977. (From U.S. Department of Labor, Bureau of Labor Statistics, 1978.)

jective by educational and vocational planning. The vocational interests of most adolescents are more stable by this age, though some go through a period of uncertainty and exploring in the first few years after high school. By age 25, about 75 percent have achieved vocational stability, although the remainder still lack clearly developed vocational goals (49).

Psychological Aspects of Career Choice

Psychological factors may also influence an adolescent's choice of vocation. If a person has motives that are not fully gratified in other ways, then a particular vocation may offer a socially approved way to satisfy these motives directly or indirectly. Thus, motives such as dominance over others, aggression, nurturance, and occasionally, sexual curiosity may play a part in leading the young person to one or another occupation, such as police officer, social worker, business executive, physician, or nurse.

Vocational Problems of Contemporary Adolescents

It used to be that the number of possible vocations was relatively small, and adolescents were familiar with most of these jobs either through observation or by actually helping with the job. Once they had selected a career, chances were that at an early age they could become an apprentice and learn the trade. In today's society, however, life is more complicated.

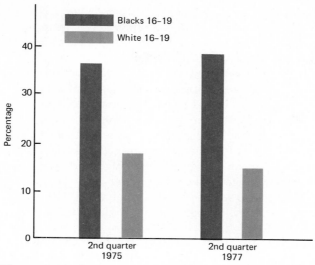

Figure 12.2 Changes in unemployment rates among black and white youth, 1975–1977. (From U.S. Department of Labor, Bureau of Labor Statistics, 1978.)

There are many different kinds of specialized jobs available, but most adolescents typically have only a vague idea of the nature of many of these possible jobs. Most young people are directly exposed to only a few and hear about only a small fraction more, and thus their vocational choice is likely to be based on only a limited range of possibilities. An adolescent from a small town, for example, may have just the right abilities and interests to be an excellent traffic engineer, planning ways to handle rush-hour traffic in a metropolitan area, but may be unaware that such a job exists. Similarly, other adolescents do not know what they would be able to do successfully and would enjoy doing, the training required for a specific job, or the present or future demands for workers in various occupations. The problem is not getting any easier, either, as society grows more complex, more specialized, and more technologically oriented. Consequently, the young person's vocational interests are guided by such influences as parental desires and experience, suggestions of school counselors (who are frequently poorly informed), accidental contact with various occupations, and the kinds of jobs friends are going into.

Influence of Social Class on Vocational Choice

An adolescent's social class influences his or her vocational goals in a variety of ways. It helps to determine the kinds of occupations with which the young person will be familiar and thus be likely to consider. In addition, an adolescent's social class influences the social acceptability of various

jobs. For example, becoming a truck driver, a clerk in a grocery store, or an automobile mechanic may be considered an appropriate choice in a lower-middle-class group but not in an upper-class group. The individual who deviates from choosing jobs normally associated with his or her social class may be subjected to disapproval from peers, particularly if the deviation is in the direction of lower-class status.

There are several possible explanations for social-class differences in vocational goals. One is that differences in the values assigned to various occupations by adolescents of different social classes largely account for social-class differences in vocational goals (13). For example, it may be that working on an oil rig is rated high in value among lower-class youth, though it is rated low among upper-class youth. Thus a lower-class adolescent boy who wants to work on an oil rig may feel fine about the level of his aspiration, though an upper-class boy might feel that it is beneath him.

Other theorists, however, have argued that differences in goals stem *not* primarily from values but from what these adolescents see as realistic goals (47). For example, a lower-class girl whose parents are unable to help or uninterested in helping her go to college is less likely to aspire to be a doctor than one whose parents encourage such a vocational choice and who are in a position to help her. Similarly, a boy whose parents expect him to go to work upon completion of the ninth grade is not likely to spend much time contemplating the idea of becoming an engineer (48).

Becoming a truck driver, a clerk in a grocery store, or an automobile mechanic may be considered an appropriate choice in a lower-middle-class group but not in an upper-class group.

Sex Differences in Vocational Goals

Gone are the days when it could be said without a doubt that "a woman's place is in the home." Significant changes are taking place in the working habits of women. More young women are working prior to marriage,

Table 12.1 PERCENTAGE OF WOMEN WORKERS IN THE LABOR FORCE

	1950	1960	1970	1973	1974	1975	1976	1978
All women	33.9%	37.1%	42.8%	44.2%	45.1%	45.8%	46.8%	48.0%
All married women, husband present	23.8	30.5	39.2	42.2	43.0	44.4	45.0	46.6
With children under 6 years	11.9	18.6	28.2	32.7	34.4	36.6	37.4	39.3
With children 6–17 years only	28.3	39.0	47.1	50.1	51.2	52.4	53.7	55.6
With no children under 18 years	30.3	34.7	44.6	42.8	43.0	43.9	43.8	44.9

Note: One piece of evidence of the changing role of American women is the increasing proportion who work; even those with small children have moved heavily into the labor force. Over two-fifths of all married women are in the labor force, and 70 percent of all employed women work full time, although less than half of them work year-round.
Source: Bureau of Labor Statistics, 1979.

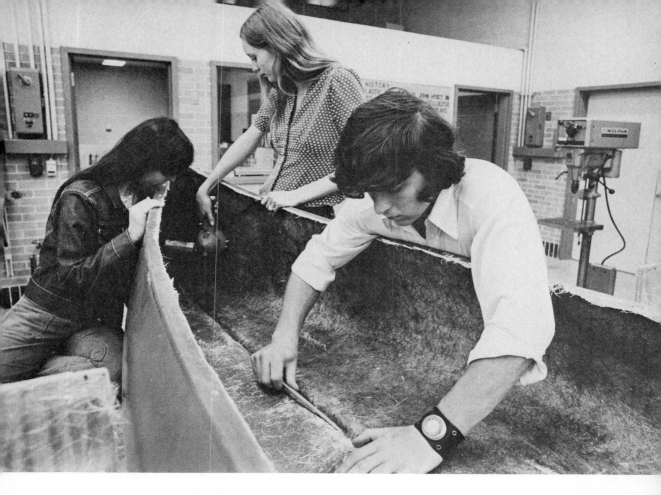

delaying marriage longer, and returning to work sooner and in greater numbers following the birth of children. Table 12.1 shows how the percentage of women working has shifted since 1950. These changes are occurring as a consequence of many other changing factors, such as changes in the nature of male-female relationships, in the family as an institution, and in society generally. Attitudes are changing; prices are higher and two incomes often are needed to support a family; divorces are more frequent —we could go on and on.

Not only is there a change in the number of women working; there are also changes in the kind of work women are seeking. More young women are entering jobs (both professional and nonprofessional) that previously were largely limited to men. Moreover, women are insisting on equal pay for equal work and registering effective protests when such demands are denied. The number of women in medical and law schools has increased dramatically in recent years, and they have also made substantial headway in the marketplace—in banking, investment, advertising, and business management. Nonetheless, among the nation's 13- to 18-year-olds as a

Not only is there a change in the number of women working; there are also changes in the kind of work women are seeking.

whole, traditional sex roles still appear to influence career choices, although the picture is changing somewhat. In 1977 the three top vocational goals among boys were skilled worker (mechanic, carpenter, electrician, etc.), engineer, and lawyer; among girls they were secretary, teacher, and nurse (20). In 1979, boys' top choices were skilled worker, doctor, dentist, and lawyer; girls favored secretary, medicine, fine arts (musician, artist, writer), and nurse—teaching had dropped to fifth place (22). Furthermore, although two-thirds of all girls currently prefer a two-career marriage (45), they tend to be less strongly committed to career goals.

With all the changes mentioned earlier, why is it that many girls are still setting lower career goals than boys and have less commitment to them (36)? There are several factors that contribute to this: At present, boys remain more likely than girls to have to go to work for the greater portion of their lives, although the difference is much smaller than it was even a decade ago. And the fact still remains that a family's standard of living, its place in the community, and its financial security usually depend more on the job and earning capacity of the husband. Also, for a *majority* of women identification with an adult role still involves primarily assuming successfully the roles of wife and mother and only secondarily that of breadwinner (5).

Affiliation Versus Aggression—A Fear of Success? According to a 1964 study, some women have a "fear of success"—a concern that striving for success is not "feminine" and that the woman who does so is likely to be socially rejected and not be able to form or maintain close relationships, especially with men (28). But more recent studies indicate that the concerns linked with "fear of success" are found *only* in *some* women in *some* fields. For example, such concerns are most likely to be aroused among women in vocational fields that have been traditionally viewed as masculine and that involve aggressive competition with others, particularly men. They may be much less common in fields that are viewed as "feminine," such as nurse, secretary, or teacher; fields that are not sex-stereotyped, such as psychologist, social worker, or writer; or in fields that involve meeting one's own standards of achievement more than victory over others, such as scientist, skilled craft worker, artist, musician, or other practitioner in fine arts. Further, many of these concerns are related to sex-role stereotypes, which are changing as more women work.

But times are changing rapidly, and as the percentage of women employed (and the number of adult years spent working) increases, and as women's perceptions of the meaning of work change, a significant number of women may find that their lack of concern with vocational goals was a mistake. In the world of tomorrow, they may wish that they had chosen a more meaningful career rather than adopting without question the traditional vocational views of parents, peers, and guidance counselors.

Parental Influences on Vocational Choice

Parents who encourage and support educational and vocational achievement are quite likely to have children who set high vocational goals. Even adolescents from working-class families are likely to seek higher education and to set occupational goals higher than those usually associated with their social class if their parents urge them to (46). They are less likely to do so if parents do not exert pressure in this direction.

Parental influence works in other ways as well. Many otherwise tolerant and reasonably flexible upper- and middle-class parents react strongly to the announcement that their adolescent daughter intends to raise vegetables and make clothes on a communal farm or that their son intends to take part-time laboring jobs in order to devote as much time as possible to writing poetry. These parents may fear that such choices will lead to social disapproval of their child and, indirectly, of themselves.

The father's occupation exerts a significant influence on the career choice of sons, though not generally on that of daughters (60). Probably this is because the son is more familiar with the father's occupation than with others and may have easier access to such a job. Also, there may be strong parental motivation—and sometimes pressure—for the son to enter that occupation, as well as the influence of identification with the parent, encouraging the development of similar interests, values, and goals.

Effects of Maternal Employment. In like manner, having an employed mother can influence a young person's attitudes toward women working outside the home. But not surprisingly, the kind of influence exerted by an employed mother depends on the mother's attitude toward her employment—whether she feels satisfied and fulfilled, for instance, and whether she successfully combines the roles of employee, mother, and wife (6).

In general, however, young women whose mothers are employed outside the home are more likely to view outside work as something they will want to do if and when they themselves become mothers (27). They also tend to view women as more competent than do daughters of nonemployed full-time homemakers. There are also indications that daughters of employed mothers tend to be somewhat more autonomous and active (27), and somewhat more likely to consider their mothers as people they admire and want to be like (6).

Peer Group and School Influences

Peers and the school environment can have a significant effect on adolescents' career choices. For example, a boy from a lower-class home is more likely to have upwardly mobile educational and vocational aspirations if he attends a largely middle-class school than if he attends one whose students come primarily from a lower-class background (10). In general, however, parental influence has a greater effect on career aspirations than peer influence (46).

Vocational Values and Social Change

For many years, the traditional work ethic consisted of the beliefs that hard work leads to "success and wealth" and that these goals are worth striving for (24). Then during the 1960s a significant minority of young people became disenchanted with the vocational world. Some criticized it for exploiting its workers and the public while remaining indifferent to the ills of society. Others thought there was too much restriction of personal freedom and individual expression (14). Even though it may have seemed during the sixties that most young people were endorsing a totally different set of values, there was still a solid majority of youth who subscribed to the traditional ideas about hard work and success.

What has happened to vocational values since the 1960s? Are there any lasting effects of the youth movement? To discuss this question meaningfully, it is necessary to consider college (or college-bound) young people and the noncollege majority separately.

College Youth. On the one hand, there have been some changes since the 1960s that indicate a concern with matters more pragmatic (practical) than idealistic. For example, college students today are increasingly interested in preparing for careers during their college years instead of seeing college as a time for "finding themselves," as a period of self-discovery and change (61) (see Figure 12.3).

Moreover, during the late 1960s only one-third of all college students rated economic security and the amount of money they could earn as very important job criteria. But by 1973 around 60 percent felt that making money was very important. There have also been changes in college majors since that time: In 1976 significantly more students majored in such

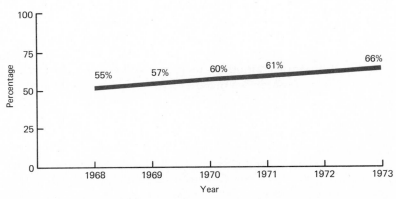

Figure 12.3 Size of the "career-minded" group (college youth). (From D. Yankelovich. *The new morality: A profile of American youth in the 70's.* Copyright 1974. Used with permission of McGraw-Hill Book Company.)

specific career fields as agriculture, business, and the health professions than in 1968; significantly fewer chose such areas as teaching, humanities, and the fine arts (3).

But though the economic attitudes of young people have changed since the 1960s, college students of today have retained some of the values celebrated in the late sixties. Values such as self-expression, personal growth, and the right to a private life of one's own remain strong (61). Today's college students are significantly more optimistic than their predecessors in the 1950s or early 1960s about their chances for finding self-fulfillment *and* economic security in a conventional career. In other words, they believe that it's possible to be happy doing what they get paid to do (61).

The Noncollege Majority. The noncollege majority have also begun to adopt certain values of college youth of the late 1960s, including a genuine desire for self-fulfillment and for individual expression in work and in their lives as a whole. They still want good pay and economic security, but they also want their work to be interesting and rewarding. However, the noncollege majority is apparently less optimistic and more skeptical about the future, perhaps because they are less likely than their more privileged peers to find jobs that combine good pay and personal fulfillment.

MORAL DEVELOPMENT AND VALUES

Like work, the development of a consistent set of morals and other values is integrally related to the development of a sense of personal identity. At no other time in life is the individual as likely to be as concerned about moral values and standards as during adolescence, for it is at this stage that cognitive abilities increase, leading to both a greater awareness of moral questions and values and a greater capacity for dealing with them. Also, the demands placed on the adolescent by society are changing rapidly, and so the adolescent must continually reappraise his or her moral values and beliefs — particularly in a society as filled with conflicting pressures and values as our own. As Erikson says, without some idea of what one believes in and stands for, it is impossible to develop and maintain a stable sense of self or identity.

For example, suppose an adolescent is in a crowd of peers and someone suggests an act of vandalism, such as throwing cherry bombs through open windows "just for kicks." In such a situation the adolescent will probably begin to think about his or her values and whether such an act is right. Or an adolescent may have an opportunity to take a stand on racial matters. How the adolescent reacts in such situations will be affected by his or her values. The young person who does not have any basic values, who drifts with the influences of the moment, cannot have clear convictions about his or her own identity.

Cognitive Growth and Moral Development

It should come as no surprise that there is a relationship between cognitive growth and moral development. After all, moral development requires that one "think" about moral issues, and consequently it is only with the onset of adolescence and the further development of formal operational thought that the young person is likely to reach the **postconventional stages** of moral development, characterized by more abstract moral principles. That is, as the adolescent becomes capable of more abstract thought, he or she is likely to adhere to more abstract moral principles and not to be as tied to norms of any particular social group. The preadolescent reaches the level of conventional moral thinking — that is, believes that behavior should conform to the prevailing social order — and eventually becomes interested in maintaining and justifying this order (35). Adolescents, however, are more independent in their moral thinking and may no longer be able to adopt without questioning the social order and political beliefs of their parents; they may begin to formulate their own moral principles. Although most adolescents do begin to think more for themselves on moral issues, many do not proceed beyond this stage. However, some do go on to develop clear rational or universal principles, achieving what has been classified by Kohlberg (see pp. 293–295) as the highest stage of moral reasoning. An illustration of an abstract, universal principle is a belief in the sacredness of human life, a universal value of respect for the individual. For example, in response to the moral dilemma in which a husband steals a drug for his sick wife because the druggist has priced it so high that he can't afford to buy it, Steve, age 16, said, "By the law of society he was wrong but by the law of nature or of God the druggist was wrong and the husband was justified. Human life is above financial gain. Regardless of who was dying, if it was a total stranger, man has a duty to save him from dying" (34, p. 244).

Our main emphasis thus far has been on factors that sensitize the adolescent to moral values and influence his or her ability to conceptualize these values in a sophisticated, thoughtful way. But there is another side to the issue of moral development. A person may be able to think of moral issues with considerable sophistication and to draw up the proper moral course to take but may not always act in accordance with this formulation. In other words, an adolescent's behavior does not always conform to his or her moral beliefs and values. Some may be rather firm about sticking to their moral beliefs; others may yield rather quickly to temptation or to group pressure. Still others appear to be guided almost solely by the threat of external punishment rather than by internalized standards.

Whether moral standards will be internalized and serve as strong guides to behavior depends largely on the nature of the parent-child relationship. If parents are warm and loving, provide good models of ethical behavior for their child, reason with the child, and provide explanations of their rules and standards, rather than imposing arbitrary discipline, then their child will probably have more mature moral development; he or she will internalize the parents' moral standards and behave in accordance with them. Such parents point out the practical realities of a situation to the child or explain how inappropriate behavior may be harmful to the child or others. They may also appeal to the child's pride and strivings for maturity. In short, these parents are authoritative, rather than authoritarian, laissez-faire, permissive, or neglectful (see pp. 349–353).

Adolescent Values

In contrast to younger children, adolescents must make many more important choices. How are they going to earn a living? What sort of person do they eventually want to marry if, in fact, they want to marry at all? Such choices are affected by the adolescent's moral beliefs and personal values. For example, in the area of vocational choice, if the young person places a high value on helping others, then he or she is likely to make a different career choice than if a high value is placed on material success. A young person who believes in freedom and autonomy will be likely to choose a career different from that of a person who is primarily concerned with security.

Religious Beliefs. Religious beliefs are likely to change significantly during adolescence. Some of the changes reflect the adolescent's increased cognitive development; for example, religious beliefs are likely to become more abstract and less literal between the ages of 12 and 18 (15). God comes to be seen more frequently as an abstract power and less frequently as a fatherly human being.

Other changes reflect shifts in cultural values. For example, while most young people still express a general belief in God or a universal spirit (21), there has been a steady decline of interest in formal religion during the past decade (61). At least part of this decrease seems clearly related to changing values among young people and their perception that, like other social institutions, institutionalized religion is failing to reflect these changes, particularly in areas such as sex, birth control, and women's rights (8).

However, while there has been a decline in interest in formal religion, there is some indication that today's adolescents are placing more emphasis than previous generations on personal rather than institutionalized religion (8, 24). Again, this change reflects the trend throughout contemporary culture to emphasize personal values and relationships instead of relying on traditional social beliefs and institutions.

A still minor though apparently growing development among young people is the emergence of a number of new religious sects, such as the Children of God, Hare Krishna, and Sun Myung Moon's Unification Church. Some of these sects are loosely structured; others are highly authoritarian. It may be that the young people who join these movements have found more traditional approaches spiritually empty and are turning to a more comfortable, secure, conventional mode of thought. Some do this after a period of rootlessness and identity confusion, while others, particularly in less authoritarian movements, may join simply because the movement seems to express simple, straightforward values in an otherwise chaotic society. Finally, for at least some young people, joining a particular movement may be merely another fad and a way to confuse their conventional middle-class parents.

Current Trends in Adolescent Values. Before we discuss what is happening in the world of young people today, let's step back and see what happened during the sixties and early seventies. Much was made of a so-called revolution in the values of young people, who were said to be developing a "counterculture." It is true that there were changes in values, and many of these changes were significant ones, but most observers tended to exaggerate the extent of these changes—both the number of young people involved and the degree of change. The truth is that the most radical changes were confined to a highly visible, often highly articulate *minority* of young people. Certainly the majority were not living in communes, dropping out to become hippies, taking drugs, or engaging in "revolutionary" political protest movements.

If the extent of revolutionary ideas was exaggerated during the sixties, the reverse seems to have happened in the seventies. Because there has been a decline in political and social activism, many commentators have assumed, a countertrend in other areas as well—a return to traditional attitudes and beliefs. Once again, however, the observers have tended to simplify matters, for closer examination of the youth of the late seventies reveals that current trends in adolescent values are much more complicated than some observers would have us believe. There are many variations in adolescent values, and it is not possible to summarize the values of all adolescents with a couple of catchy phrases.

There are differences between the value systems of college or college-bound young people and the majority of their "working-class," blue- and white-collar peers—although current differences between these groups appear significantly smaller now than during the late 1960s.

College and College-Bound Youth. Contrary to some current observations, the college youth of today have not rejected all of the "new values" that emerged during the 1960s. Love and friendship, which came to be the two most important values in the late 1960s, remain so today for 9 out of 10 students (61). Other values, such as self-expression and self-fulfillment, and treating people with dignity regardless of their race, sex, or social origins, have also been retained. So have greater sexual freedom and skepticism regarding the wisdom, altruism, and, sometimes, even honesty of social institutions, such as government, big business, big labor, and the military.

College students are more interested in pursuing their own personal goals and values now, and privacy as a personal value has steadily increased in importance since the 1960s. In fact, it is somewhat discouraging to note that a slight majority of contemporary college youth expressed the view "I'm more concerned with myself than with the world," and only one in four considers "changing society" to be a very important personal value.

The Blue-Collar "Revolution." During the 1960s, the noncollege majority was far more conservative than their college peers in many areas, ranging from attitudes toward sexual freedom, drug use, the Vietnam War, business and government, and "law and order." However, it is interesting to see what happened to the values of noncollege adolescents and youth between 1969 and 1973. In a period of only 4 years, most of the moral norms and social values held by college youth in 1969 were adopted by a majority of the noncollege, working-class youth (61). They became less likely to view religion as a very important value, less sure that hard work always pays off, more tolerant of premarital relations, more skeptical about social institutions, and more concerned with self-fulfillment and self-expression.

This transfer of values poses a potential problem. These noncollege youth are now concerned with finding work that is "more than just a job," but there are not enough opportunities for this kind of work. A major challenge of our era is to find work for youth generally that offers some opportunity for self-fulfillment and personal growth, as well as for adequate pay and economic security.

Fortunately, although there is the potential for dissatisfaction with society and life in general among both college and noncollege youth, three-quarters feel that "my own life is going well." That is, the majority seem to be fairly well adjusted. But for a significant minority, life is not going well.

PROBLEMS OF ADJUSTMENT

Apparently, a significant minority (note: minority, *not* majority) of today's young people do not successfully master the developmental tasks of adolescence, or do so only with considerable difficulty. This is indicated by rapidly rising rates of juvenile delinquency among both boys and girls, of adolescent suicide (nearly a threefold increase in the past 25 years), of adolescent pregnancies (currently 10 percent annually of all girls in the United States aged 15–19), of alcohol and drug use, of school problems, of adolescent runaways, and of psychiatric problems.

Alienation

Alienation is a term that was overused during the 1960s to explain everything from student demonstrations and inner-city riots to increased use of drugs and the rise of the hippie movement (43). But the term by itself explains nothing: It merely implies that something is missing in a relationship—one's relationship with other people, with society, or with oneself. In the following section, we shall see why some adolescents feel alienated.

Alienation of Minorities and the Poor. For adolescents in disadvantaged groups such as lower-class minorities and poor whites, alienation is to a large extent imposed by society. These young people are not able, whether because of their economic situation or because of ethnic discrimination, to participate fully in the affluent society that they see all around them and on the television screen. We have already discussed the fact that disadvantaged youth often go to inferior schools; this, coupled with inadequate preparation for school, means these children may have academic difficulties and may drop out as soon as they can. Few jobs are likely to be available at their low level of skills, and they may find themselves discriminated against even in jobs for which they are qualified. The unemployment rate for minority youth in recent years has been a staggering 40 percent, and for those living in the disorganized, dilapidated ghettos of many of our largest cities, unemployment is almost total. No wonder that many poor and minority youth feel alienated; for them, the idea of the American dream becomes a nightmare. Still worse, some of these young people may feel alienated not only from the predominant American culture but also from themselves and their own cultural roots. Having accepted some of the attitudes, values, and beliefs of the dominant majority in society, and being excluded from the mainstream of society, they may experience a loss of self-esteem, a negative identity, and an alienation from the self (19). Although the recent rise of racial and ethnic pride, particularly among young people, appears to have helped to increase self-esteem, one wonders how long the truly disenfranchised can persevere in the face of continued societal rejection and indifference (15).

No wonder that many poor and minority youth feel alienated; for them, the idea of the American dream becomes a nightmare.

Social Dropouts. The hippie movement of the late 1960s—with its disapproval of status seeking, aggressive competition, and material success and its highly publicized emphasis on "love," personal freedom, self-expression ("doing your own thing"), and mystical sensory experience (typically aided by hallucinogenic drugs)—has largely disappeared from the social scene. This does not mean, however, that the kinds of young people to which the hippie culture appealed no longer exist, although their numbers are reduced, especially within the middle class.

Approximately half a million young people under 17 run away from home each year, and the same number between 17 and 21 years of age leave home as well (2). For many of these young people, their flight is temporary. They return to the nest without being permanently alienated from parents and society. For others, the break from their previous way of life is

serious and may be permanent. Some of these become "street people," living on the fringes of university towns and in urban ghettos (39). These young people are even more powerless and vulnerable than their middle-class "hippie" predecessors, for many are truly poor and there is no hippie culture, in its original sense, to support them. As a result, thousands of adolescent runaways, male and female, have recently become involved in prostitution, including homosexual prostitution, and in pornographic

Where Have All the Flowers Gone?

What has happened to the original hippies—the flower children of the 1967 "summer of love in San Francisco"—who are now young adults? Some, of course, have returned to the mainstream of society and the life they once renounced. Some have become permanent casualties of a once hopeful revolution—victims of drug abuse, freaked-out, drifting endlessly from one bleak "scene" to another; a few are in jail. Many, however, appear to occupy a middle ground, working at part-time jobs, using fewer hallucinogens but more alcohol, establishing more enduring heterosexual relationships, but still indifferent to the political and social system.

What differentiated those who were able to rejoin the mainstream of society from those who remained partly or wholly outside of it? In a recent analysis of a large sample of hippies followed since 1967, subjects were divided into three broad groups: a *reentry* group (those who had ceased all drug use, were back in school or regularly employed, were not transient, and had a stable relationship with another person, usually of the opposite sex, for at least 6 months); a *nonreentry* group (regular users of more serious drugs, no regular job, unstable relationships, etc.); and an intermediate *semireentry* group. Of particular interest were the differences in family background that emerged between these groups. Reentry group members reported more family cohesiveness and happiness, participation in shared family activities in childhood, openness of communication, and, most dramatically, a sense of family belongingness and acceptance. In addition, those who had appeared least disturbed, emotionally and cognitively, at the time of the initial assessment, were most likely to have found their way into the reentry group.

S. M. Pittel & H. Miller. *Dropping down: The hippie then and now.* Berkeley, Calif.: Haight Ashbury Research Project, Wright Institute, 1976.

films and magazines, especially in big-city areas such as Los Angeles and New York. Many runaways are robbed, physically assaulted, underfed, or lured into drug use and small-time pushing. Their need for adequate human services — health care, shelter, protection, and counseling — is often desperate (15, 53).

ADOLESCENTS AND DRUGS

Runaways are by no means the only adolescents involved with drugs. The use of drugs among teenagers in general is widespread. To some extent, this reflects the fact that for some years our society has been steadily moving in the direction of becoming a "drug culture." The use of tranquilizers, for example, has more than doubled in the last 10 years. And the use of alcohol, barbiturates, and pep and diet pills is also high. Among young people, use of marijuana, alcohol, and tobacco is widespread, and smaller numbers use such "counterculture" drugs as LSD, "uppers" **(amphetamines),** and "downers" (barbiturates), as well as **heroin,** cocaine, **phencyclidine (PCP, or "angel dust"), Quaaludes,** and the like.

Alcohol. Despite the 1960s fears that adolescents everywhere would be tripping or otherwise spacing out on **hallucinogens** forever, this has not turned out to be true, and alcohol remains the drug of choice for more adolescents than any other drug. By twelfth grade, 93 percent of adolescents have tried alcohol — more than have tried marijuana or any other drug (1, 41). But alcohol should certainly not be regarded as a "safe" drug. It is just as much a **psychoactive** drug as marijuana, and its dangers have been more clearly established (55, 56).

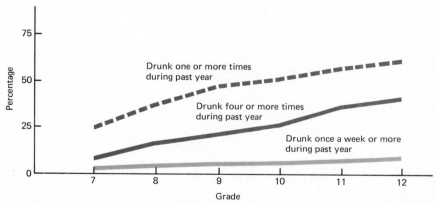

Figure 12.4 Percentage of teenage drinkers who report getting drunk by frequency and school grade, 1974. (From *Alcohol and health: New knowledge.* Second special report to the U.S. Congress, National Institute on Alcohol Abuse and Alcoholism, U.S. Department of Health, Education, and Welfare. Washington, D.C.: U.S. Government Printing Office, June 1974. No. 1724-00399.)

Although most adolescents who drink do so moderately, the number of problem drinkers is increasing. Even now, at least 5 percent of students in grades 7–12 get drunk once a week or more (see Figure 12.4) and can thus be termed "problem drinkers." Generally, these adolescents have other problems along with their drinking problem and engage in more deviant behavior than the nonproblem drinkers. Many of the problem drinkers, for example, are involved in multiple drug use.

Marijuana. By ages 18–21, nearly 60 percent of all young people have at least experimented with marijuana, and the rate is continuing to rise (1), with the largest percentage of marijuana users falling into the category of experimenters or occasional users and the smallest percentage into the category of heavy users (32). Adolescents who use marijuana only occasionally or moderately tend to be slightly different from their peers in personality and life style. For example, they are less conventional, more impulsive, and more open to experience (54). More serious differences are found among chronic heavy users, who show significant psychological and social maladjustment, being often hostile and adjusting poorly in social and work situations. But this is not to say that heavy marijuana use alone causes these problems. First of all, chronic heavy users often use other drugs in addition to marijuana. Second, heavy drug use is often a result of psychological problems rather than their cause, although clearly once such drug use is begun, a "vicious circle" may be established (15). A boy or girl who is chronically using marijuana (or any other drug, including alcohol) to escape life's stresses and problems will find it harder to adjust to problems later because he or she is not learning how to deal effectively with frustration and daily problems.

Other Drugs. While alcohol, marijuana, and tobacco are the drugs most used by adolescents, smaller percentages have been involved with other drugs. By the end of the senior year in high school, about a quarter of young people have at least tried some other psychoactive drug (1), ranging from a high of 23 percent for stimulants to a low of 1.8 percent for heroin. Use (including one-time use) of hallucinogens (like LSD), cocaine, inhalants (like amyl nitrate), and opiates other than heroin varies between 10 and 14 percent, although current use is lower (see Figure 12.5). A number of these drugs are either addictive, highly toxic, or both.

Why Do Adolescents Use Drugs?

In a recent national survey (1977), American adolescents were asked why young people were using alcohol and drugs. The most frequent replies were peer pressure and conformity, escape from the pressures of life and society, having a good time or to feel good, and "kicks." Other reasons were problems at home with family, showing off, "acting grown up," boredom, rebellion, and parental indifference (21). One 15-year-old girl

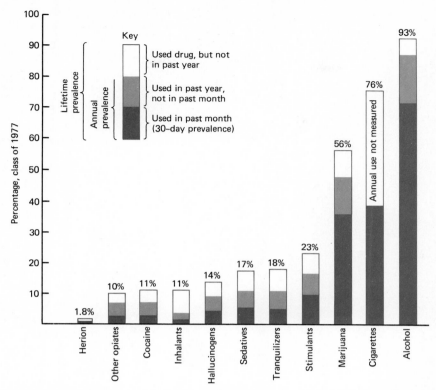

Figure 12.5 Lifetime, annual, and 30-day prevalence of use (and recency of use) for eleven types of drugs, class of 1977. (From *Drug use among American high school students 1975–1977*. U.S. Department of Health, Education, and Welfare; Alcohol, Drug Abuse, and Mental Health Administration. Washington, D.C.: Government Printing Office, 1977.)

said, "People my age sometimes follow the group so they won't be out-casts. They try to enjoy themselves but then things get out of hand." A high-school boy replied, "Alcohol and drugs are an escape from school and family problems and they let the world drift away" (21).

Other young people — particularly those who use several different drugs — may rely on drugs because of emotional disturbances, an inability to find a meaningful personal identity, or an inability to cope with the demands of living. Some drug users have even acknowledged that they have never known any other way to cope with problems or to have fun.

DELINQUENCY   Delinquency is not a new problem. Six thousand years ago an Egyptian priest carved on a stone, "Our earth is degenerate. . . . Children no longer obey their parents" (31, p. 840). In our times the increased concern with

delinquency is well justified: Since 1948 the number of youth under 18 committing offenses has risen substantially, although there has recently been a slight decline (see Figure 12.6). These offenses include illegal acts ranging from curfew violations, truancy, running away, underage drinking, and similar activities to robbery, assault, rape, or homicide (16). Since 1960 the incidence of more serious offenses among young people has been rising at a faster rate than delinquency in general and twice as fast as comparable adult crimes (11). For example, in 1976 in Chicago, one-third of all murders were committed by people aged 20 or younger, a 29 percent increase over the previous year (50)! Nationwide, in 1977, one-third of all serious crimes were committed by young people under 18, and nearly two-thirds by those under 24 (51).

Sexual Differences in Delinquency

Boys have traditionally been "more delinquent" than girls. For many years, boys were apprehended for more active and aggressive behaviors, such as joyriding, burglary, auto theft, and robbery. In contrast, girls were more likely to be reported for such offenses as running away from home, being "uncontrollable," and illicit sexual behavior.

Boys are still responsible for most of the more serious and aggressive delinquent acts; for example, in 1977, 81 percent of all juveniles arrested for violent crimes were male (51). However, the arrest rate of girls has been increasing in recent years, and the ratio of boys' to girls' offenses is now about 3.5 to 1, instead of 4 or 5 to 1 as it was for many years. Also, the seriousness of offenses committed by girls has increased. One explanation for the recent rise in girls' delinquency is that girls are becoming more aggressive and more independent in their day-to-day activities. Unfortunately, some of this behavior has resulted in more girls running away from home and in increasing drug use, both of which require money and thus may necessitate other crime-related activities, such as shoplifting, robbery, and prostitution.

Social Change, Deprivation, and Delinquency

If children have been considered delinquent for thousands of years, why now has there been a sudden *increase* in the rate of delinquency? One of the factors that seems to have contributed to the rise of delinquency is the increased mobility of people today. No longer are people as likely to stay in the same community or neighborhood for most of their lives. Indeed, almost half of all families in the United States move every 5 years. This increased mobility means that the whole structure of society is changing,

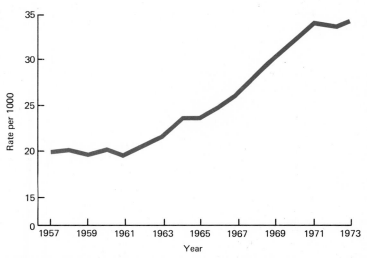

Figure 12.6 Rate of delinquency cases disposed of by juvenile courts involving children 10 through 17 years of age. (From U. Bronfenbrenner. The challenge of social change to public policy and developmental research. Paper presented at the biennial meeting of the Society for Research in Child Development, Denver, April 2, 1975. Source: U.S. Office of Human Development and U.S. Office of Youth Development, *Juvenile Court Statistics*, annual.)

and increases in delinquency are most likely to occur where the sense of community and family ties have been most disrupted—for example, in urban ghettos and some of the more affluent suburban "commuter" communities. They are least likely to occur where these ties have been preserved—for example, in some small, traditional, relatively isolated towns and cities (14).

Delinquency is still highest in rundown urban ghettos, where delinquency is often an approved tradition and there are many opportunities for learning antisocial behavior from delinquent peers (30). Delinquency is higher among children and adolescents from broken homes and economically substandard (poor) homes (58), probably because these families are more likely to live in deteriorated urban neighborhoods where the children can learn delinquent practices from their peers (16).

Many lower-class youth in urban ghettos join delinquent gangs (37). In recent years, these gangs have become quite violent and socially destructive. In five major cities alone—New York, Chicago, Los Angeles, Philadelphia, and San Francisco—525 gang-related murders were recorded in a recent 2-year period (38). And while 60 percent of gang-violence victims are themselves gang members, 40 percent are not. The nongang victims include teachers, elderly citizens, and nongang youth (37).

Of course, even in areas of high delinquency, such as urban ghettos, not all adolescents become delinquent, whereas some adolescents from economically sound and unbroken homes do become delinquent. In fact, although the absolute delinquency rate is highest in urban areas, the greatest *increases* recently in delinquency have been in the suburbs—more than double the urban increase. Thus although poverty and the environment contribute to delinquency, other factors play a role. Let's look at the personality differences between delinquents and nondelinquents that remain when the effects of social class, residence area, and the like have been controlled for, and at the relationships between delinquents and their parents.

Personality and Delinquency

Many juvenile delinquents do not like themselves. They often see themselves as "lazy," "bad," "sad," and "ignorant" and feel inadequate, emotionally rejected, and frustrated in their needs for self-expression. Not surprisingly, these feelings and poor self-concepts are reflected in various defensive personality traits, such as defiance, resentfulness, suspiciousness, hostility, and destructiveness. They are also ambivalent in their attitudes toward authority, lacking in achievement motivation, impulsive, and deficient in self-control (23). Moreover, the differences between nondelinquents and future delinquents in social behavior and personality characteristics tend to appear early—in one study they showed up as early as the third grade.

Although other influences, such as peer group pressure and a generally adverse social environment, obviously play a part in delinquency, the role of parents appears crucial (4, 18). With remarkable consistency, research studies indicate that "the early disciplinary techniques to which delinquents have been subjected are likely to be lax, erratic, or overly strict, and to involve physical punishment, rather than reasoning with the child about misconduct" (15). Among delinquents, relations between parent and child are likely to be characterized by mutual hostility, lack of family cohesiveness, and parental rejection, indifference, dissension, or apathy.

Fathers of delinquents are more likely to be rated by independent observers as cruel, neglecting, and inclined to ridicule their children (particularly sons) and less likely to be rated as warm and affectionate. In turn, their delinquent young, especially sons, are likely to have few close ties to their fathers and to consider them wholly unacceptable as models for their conduct. Mothers of delinquents are more likely to be rated as careless or inadequate in child supervision and as hostile or indifferent; they are less likely to be rated as loving and responsible. Many delinquents also come from broken homes. However, the likelihood of adolescent delinquency is far higher in nonbroken homes characterized by mutual hostility and indifference or apathy than it is in single-parent homes (usually mother only) that are unified and offer mutual affection and support.

Prevention and Treatment of Delinquency

Unfortunately, the rapidly rising rate of delinquency has not been significantly reduced by most treatment programs, even though many kinds have been tried.

Training schools or other "correctional" institutions are usually not effective in rehabilitating juvenile delinquents; in fact, young people often leave these schools knowing more about how to commit their next crime. Probation, where possible, produces fewer repeating offenders than imprisonment. However, it should be noted that most approaches—even those attempting to use a combination of possible solutions—have mostly been a matter of "too little too late." That is, they have concentrated largely on young people with already serious problems, and their efforts have not been comprehensive enough or lasted long enough.

One of the most promising new treatments of delinquency is the use of small, community-based, group homes in which skilled professionals work with the adolescents in a warm, intimate, homelike atmosphere. Here a significant variable is the quality of the caretakers; their warmth and understanding can significantly affect the success of the program (42).

The real formula for success in treating the problem of delinquency is to improve the social conditions that foster it—poverty, urban decay, discrimination, the breakdown of a sense of community among all classes of citizens, and increasing paralysis of our fundamental social institutions, including the family. Unless we, as a society, make a real commitment to attacking these problems vigorously, the rate of delinquency appears destined to increase still further.

PSYCHOLOGICAL AND PSYCHO-PHYSIOLOGICAL DISTURBANCES

Psychological and **psychophysiological** ("psychosomatic") disturbances are more likely to develop during periods of rapid change, such as school entrance or the transition to adolescence. In early adolescence particularly, the young person is faced both with increasing social demands and a virtual biological revolution within himself or herself, as a result of the onset of puberty, and some temporary disruption of the individual's equilibrium is inevitable. Although in most young people this does not lead to serious psychological problems, it may increase the vulnerability of already susceptible adolescents and may help to determine the form that their problems take. Here we will look briefly at a few of the most significant forms of adolescent disturbances, together with some observations about the special treatment needs of adolescents.

Anxiety Reactions

An adolescent with an acute anxiety reaction may experience a sudden fearfulness, becoming agitated and restless, and display physical symptoms such as dizziness, headache, or nausea. Sleep disturbances are also common (44).

While the adolescent may attribute the cause of his or her anxiety to a variety of external sources, it is often the case that deeper, more fundamental factors are involved—such as disturbed parent-child relationships, concerns about the demands of growing up, or fear and guilt over increased sexual or aggressive impulses. Because the adolescent may not be consciously aware of these problems, it is important to seek professional help if the anxiety attacks are frequent and prolonged. Early therapy while the causes of the anxiety are still present and can be determined is important before anxiety becomes a way of life for the individual.

Adolescent Depression

Adolescents may also encounter feelings of depression to varying degrees, though they may mask these feelings with restlessness, boredom, hypochondriacal complaints, or "acting-out" behavior, such as delinquent acts, excessive alcohol or drug use, or sexual activities (33).

Adolescent depression is most likely to take one of two forms. In the first the adolescent may complain of a lack of feeling and a sense of emptiness. It is as though his or her childhood self has been left behind but no growing adult self has replaced it. This vacuum can engender sadness and a high level of anxiety. In such a case it is not that the adolescent really has no feelings but that he or she does not know how to express them. Consequently, with adequate therapy, this kind of depression can usually be treated successfully.

A second form of depression, however, is more difficult to resolve. This depression has its basis in repeated experiences of defeat over a long period of time (29). These adolescents may feel that they can never solve their problems; too many times they have tried and failed to achieve their goals or solve their problems. Many—probably a majority—of adolescent suicidal attempts are a result not of one critical event but of a long series of unsuccessful attempts to find alternative solutions to difficulties. Frequently, the final straw in this type of depression is the loss of a meaningful relationship, whether with a parent, friend, or someone the adolescent was in love with.

Suicide

Certainly it is tragic when adolescents respond to their psychological problems by attempting suicide, and even more tragic when they succeed (see Figure 12.7). What causes these troubled adolescents to consider death as the only solution to their problems? While there is often an immediate event that leads to a suicide attempt, usually these young people have had a history of psychological difficulties. For example, many come from unstable families where they feel alienated from their parents and cannot communicate with them or turn to them for support (29). Frequently, these

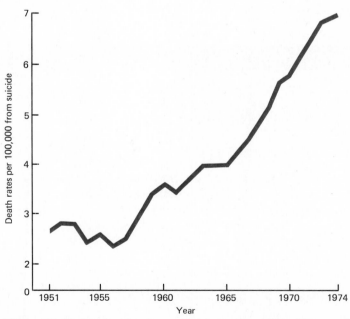

Figure 12.7 Death rates from suicide among 15- to 19-year-olds, 1951–1973. (From U. Bronfenbrenner. The challenge of social change to public policy and developmental research. Paper presented at the biennial meeting of the Society for Research in Child Development, Denver, April 2, 1975. Source: U.S. National Center for Health Statistics, *Vital Statistics of the United States*, annual.)

young people have struggled to achieve closeness with and emotional support from other people only to have these relationships also collapse for one reason or another, leading to a progressive sense of isolation and helplessness (59).

Hypochondriacs　Sometimes adolescents may channel their anxiety into a preoccupation with the functioning of their body. They may be concerned that something is wrong with their heartbeat, breathing, or digestion when these are perfectly normal; or they may exaggerate the significance of minor ailments, such as a slightly stuffy nose, a minor stomach upset, or a muscle cramp (59). These adolescents are **hypochondriacal**—that is, they imagine or exaggerate certain physical symptoms and are preoccupied with them.

Sometimes there is some realistic basis for the adolescent's complaint but not one serious enough to warrant as much concern as he or she devotes to it. Adolescents who develop hypochondriacal symptoms frequently come from families that are preoccupied with health and illness. Hypochondriacal symptoms may serve as a face-saving way of avoiding certain activities, such as sports or dancing, in which they feel inadequate (33).

A certain amount of preoccupation with the body may be considered

Clues to Suicidal Risk

1. A persistently depressed or despairing mood.
2. Eating and sleeping disturbances.
3. Declining school performance.
4. Gradual social withdrawal and increasing isolation from others.
5. Breakdown in communication with parents or other important persons in the young person's life.
6. A history of previous suicide attempts or involvement in accidents.
7. Seemingly reckless, self-destructive, and uncharacteristic behavior, such as serious drug or alcohol use, reckless driving.
8. Statements such as ''I wish I were dead'' or ''What is there to live for?''
9. Inquiries about the lethal properties of drugs, poisons, or weapons.
10. Unusually stressful events in the young person's life, such as school failure, breakup of a love affair, loss of a loved one.

normal in an adolescent, for the rapid physical and sexual changes of puberty inevitably focus the adolescent's attention on the physical self. But an adolescent whose hypochondriacal symptoms persist or go beyond normal adolescent bodily concerns needs psychological help. Fortunately, adolescents usually respond well to such help and their symptoms disappear much more readily than those of adult hypochondriacs (33).

Psychophysio-logical Disturbances

Sometimes psychological problems may lead to actual disturbances of physiological functioning. Sometimes these are temporary, as with the typical complaints of stomachaches or headaches as a result of psychological stress. At other times, continued stress may lead to clearly defined psychosomatic disorders—such as peptic ulcer, ulcerative colitis, and some eating disorders.

Eating Disorders. Many adolescents go through weight fluctuations either upward or downward from what they would normally be expected to weigh. This is not surprising given the many rapid physical and physiological changes that follow the onset of puberty. Most adolescents, however, will correct their weight through regulation of their diet once growth has stabilized (12). A minority, however, will not. Some get seriously obese (overweight); others refuse to eat and become seriously underweight. The latter condition is called **anorexia nervosa** and is far more common among girls than boys.

Both obese and anorexic young people are likely to lack a clear sense of individual identity, a feeling of being in control of themselves and their lives. Anorexia is a particularly puzzling condition because the adolescent has such a distorted perception of her bodily image. Though she may look to be little more than skin and bones, she may still worry about putting on too much weight. There is still much to learn about this condition, but it seems to be increasing, especially among affluent (rather than disadvantaged) youth.

Biological factors may play some role, but psychological factors appear to be more important. Anorexic adolescents were usually "good" children; in fact, sometimes they seemed almost "too good"—quiet, obedient, always dependable, eager to please. Most have been good students. However, these adolescents seem to feel that they have been oppressed that they have not been allowed control over their own lives. They seem to react by maintaining this firm, obsessional control over their bodies. They may also fear growing up and meeting the demands of sexual maturity, and severe undereating, which retards growth, may appear, at least unconsciously, to be a way of delaying or avoiding growing up.

Treatment for anorexia nervosa or obesity must necessarily include specialized medical care. But psychological treatment, including family therapy—that is, therapy involving the adolescent's whole family—is also required, since parent-child relationships play an important role in the development of this illness.

Psychological Treatment of Adolescents

Adolescents are particularly skilled at spotting phoniness, and thus a successful psychological treatment program must necessarily include a therapist who genuinely likes adolescents. The therapist must be warm and open, confident and skilled. Above all, the effective adolescent psychotherapist must be flexible, prepared to move from listening to questioning, to reassurance, to interpretation—even to arguing—and, when necessary, to setting limits (15). As a result, the young person will usually develop a feeling of trust and respect, though he or she may still feel a need to make it clear that he or she isn't awed by "shrinks." At the same time, the therapist must guard against the adolescent's becoming too dependent on the therapist instead of going through the necessary struggle toward ultimate independence and self-reliance.

In short, the effective therapist shares a number of essential qualities with the effective parent. Both need to be worthy of the adolescent's trust and respect, and, in turn, both need to trust and respect the adolescent as a unique human being. In addition, both need to be authoritative, without being either authoritarian or autocratic, on the one hand, or laissez-faire, equalitarian, or neglectful on the other. Both need to be capable of setting limits when necessary with confidence but without hostility, while also recognizing the adolescent's critical need for developing independence. Neither job is an easy one, but each will be less difficult for those who genuinely like adolescents.

SUMMARY

1. Identity formation is a central problem of adolescence, and the rapid physical and physiological changes, as well as the changing demands of society, make this task a difficult one, for the adolescent often lacks a feeling of self-consistency. The establishment of a strong sense of identity will be facilitated by rewarding relationships with parents who provide personally and socially effective role models.

2. Sexual identity—that is, awareness and emotional acceptance of one's basic biological nature as a man or woman—is an important part of one's overall sense of personal identity. Having a firm sense of sexual identity, however, does *not* mean that one needs to rigidly conform to sex-role stereotypes—in personality characteristics, interests, or career choices.

3. Recent research indicates that individuals who are androgynous—that is, those who combine within themselves such positive "feminine" characteristics as nurturance, gentleness, and interpersonal sensitivity and such positive "masculine" characteristics as independence and appropriate assertiveness, are better equipped to function successfully in our modern, complex society.

4. Deciding on and preparing for a vocation is still another major developmental task and one that is more difficult in our complex industrialized society. An adolescent's vocational choice may be influenced by social-class membership, peer group and school influences, and the adolescent's sex.

5. Significant changes are currently taking place in the vocational orientation of girls and young women. More women are employed, and more are entering occupations that were previously largely restricted to males. Young women with mothers who are employed outside the home are not likely to want to do so themselves.

6. Today's college youth are more "career-minded" than their counterparts of the 1960s, but they place strong emphasis on challenging

work, the ability to express oneself, and free time for outside interests. Noncollege youth have adopted many of the values of college youth of the 1960s, including a desire for self-fulfillment and individual expression in work and in their lives.

7. Concerns about moral values and standards become especially important during adolescence and are vital to the development of a strong sense of identity. An adolescent's cognitive growth influences the course of his or her moral development. Religious and other values may also change during adolescence.

8. Despite a decline in political and social activism, adolescents today retain a number of values of the "youth culture" of the late 1960s, including an emphasis on the importance of love, friendship, privacy, self-expression, self-fulfillment, and a greater tolerance of others.

9. A significant minority of adolescents suffer from problems of adjustment. These problems are manifested in symptoms such as feelings of alienation, drug and alcohol use, and delinquency.

10. Among the psychological and psychophysiological disorders encountered in adolescence are anxiety reactions, depression (and sometimes suicide), hypochondriasis (concern with imagined physical symptoms), psychosomatic disorders (such as peptic ulcer), and eating disorders (including obesity and anorexia nervosa).

Suggested Readings

Conger, John Janeway. *Adolescence and youth: Psychological development in a changing world* (2nd ed.). New York: Harper & Row, 1977.

Conger, John Janeway. *Contemporary issues in adolescent development*. New York: Harper & Row, 1975.

Cottle, Thomas J. *Time's children: Impressions of youth*. Boston: Little, Brown, 1971.

Douvan, Elizabeth, & Adelson, Joseph. *The adolescent experience*. New York: Wiley, 1966.

Erikson, Erik H. *Youth: Identity and crisis*. New York: Norton, 1968.

Kagan, Jerome, & Coles, Robert (Eds.) *12 to 16: Early adolescence*. New York: Norton, 1971.

Larrick, Nancy, & Merriam, Eve. *Male and female under 18*. New York: Avon, 1973.

Glossary

accommodation

The disposition to change one's schema or concepts to fit new qualities or events that do not match acquired knowledge.

achievement motivation

The desire to accomplish something of value, to meet standards of excellence in what one does, to reach a position of high status.

actualize

To develop a potential competence. When a child begins to speak we say he actualizes his potential ability to master language.

adolescent egocentrism

The common belief among adolescents that others' thoughts and reasoning processes are similar to their own. For example, an adolescent who is preoccupied with his or her behavior or appearance is likely to believe that others share this concern.

adolescent growth spurt

The period of rapid acceleration of growth rate in height and weight during adolescence. It usually begins about age 12½ in boys and reaches a peak about age 14; in girls, these events typically occur about 2 years earlier.

affective disorder

Disturbance of mood or feeling, such as depression or manic state.

aggression

Responses that are intended to harm others.

alienation

A feeling of being separated from, or having lost, a previously important relationship. The relationship may have involved a set of beliefs, a society or segment of society, or even oneself.

altruism

Self-sacrificing behavior on behalf of others, without direct reward to the actor.

amnion

The protective membrane enclosing the fetus during prenatal development.

amniotic sac

Sac filled with watery fluid that surrounds and protects the fetus.

amphetamines

Stimulant drugs ("uppers," "pep pills") such as Benzedrine, Dexedrine, Methedrine. Though not physiologically addictive, they may be psychologically habituating and very dangerous.

anal stage

In psychoanalytic theory, the second stage of development (second or third year of life), during which the child experiences major gratification through elimination and stimulation of the anal area.

androgen

Masculinizing hormone (also found in lesser amounts in women).

androgyny
(adj.: androgynous)
Combining in one person in flexible fashion both traditionally "masculine" and traditionally "feminine" personality traits. The emphasis is usually on the more positive characteristics of each sex (e.g., sensitivity, assertiveness, compassion), rather than the more negative (e.g., excessive dependency or hostility).

anorexia nervosa
Severe, sometimes life-threatening weight loss due to pathologically prolonged and extreme dieting. Most common among adolescent girls (especially those who have been almost "too good and compliant"), it is thought to reflect psychological problems relating to identity formation and sexual and social maturation, among others.

anoxia
Damaging loss of oxygen to the tissues of the body, including the brain.

anxiety
Anticipation of danger or of an unpleasant event, feeling, or reaction; anxiety is free-floating, as distinguished from fear, which generally is a specific response to a particular real danger.

assimilation
A tendency to interpret a new object or event in terms of existing knowledge.

attachment
The emotional bond an infant and young child establish toward an adult, typically the caretaker.

authoritarian parent
A parent who is highly controlling and uses power freely in interactions with the child.

authoritative parent
A parent who is supportive and affectionate and at the same time maintains firm, clearly defined standards of behavior for the child.

autism
A severe mental disorder of young children characterized by absorption in fantasy to the exclusion of interest in reality and by the inability to use language for communication.

autonomy
The sense of being independent and free to make one's own decisions and choices.

autosome
Chromosome other than sex chromosome.

behavior modification
The systematic use of rewards, or rewards and punishments, to change behavior.

body cells
Cells making up the bones, nerves, muscles, and organs of the body; all cells except the germ cells from which sperm and ova are derived.

cerebral palsy
A disability resulting from damage to the motor areas of the brain before or during birth; outwardly manifested by muscular incoordination and speech disturbances.

chorion
Protective membrane enclosing the fetus during prenatal development.

chromosomes
Rod-shaped particles containing the genes, the transmitters of heredity.

class inclusion
A Piagetian concept that refers to the child's ability to recognize that one class of objects can be part of another class—for example, dogs belong to the class of pets.

classical conditioning	The procedure by which an association is established between an originally neutral stimulus and an unconditioned response. This is accomplished by repeatedly pairing the two, so that the conditioned stimulus eventually elicits the previously unconditioned response.
clique	An exclusive circle or group of peers; smaller than a crowd and larger than a two-person friendship.
cognition **(adj.: cognitive)**	The mental processes—including perception, memory, reasoning, and problem solving—by which the individual gains knowledge of the world.
competence	Behavior that is adaptive, self-reliant, and self-controlled.
compulsion	The need to repeat a stereotyped action (e.g., constant hand washing).
concept	A cognitive unit that stands for, or represents, a common set of attributes among a group of schemata, images, or symbols.
concrete operations	In Piaget's theory, the stage of mental development during middle childhood, characterized by the beginnings of understanding of reversible transformations of concrete objects and events.
conscience development	The development of the child's moral beliefs and behavior. See also SUPEREGO.
conservation	A Piagetian concept having to do with a child's knowledge that the mass, weight, or number of a set of objects remains the same despite physical changes in their appearance.
contour	An outline of the boundary between adjacent areas; a black line on a white background is said to be a contour.
cross-cultural study	A study in which the behavior, rules, and practices of individuals from different cultures are compared.
cross-sectional study	A study in which groups of individuals of different ages are observed, tested, and rated at a single point in time.
denial	A mechanism of defense in which a child insists that an anxiety-arousing event or situation is not true.
dependency	Reliance on others for comfort, nurturance, or assistance in accomplishing tasks or fulfilling needs.
dependent variable	The variable that changes as a result of changes in the independent variable.
depression	A psychological disturbance, ranging from mild to severe, characterized by sadness, inactivity, feeling of dejection, and at times by difficulty in thinking or concentrating.
discrepancy	An event that varies or is different from an acquired schema. We say that a stranger's face is discrepant from the child's scheme for his parent's face.

discrimination

Learning to respond differentially to different stimuli; making one response to one stimulus and a different response to another stimulus.

dishabituation

Attending again, or responding again, to a stimulus after a period of diminished interest (the loss of habituation).

displacement

A tendency to attribute a psychological quality to someone or some object other than the true source.

DNA (deoxyribonucleic acid)

Critically important chemical component of genes that carries the genetic code transmitting heredity.

Down's syndrome (mongolism)

A form of mental retardation, characterized by an Oriental cast to the facial appearance, which results from the presence of an extra autosomal chromosome.

dyslexia (adj.: dyslexic)

Impaired ability to read at the level of the individual's intellectual ability.

ectoderm

The outermost layer of the embryonic cell mass; source of the outer layer of the skin (epidermis), hair, nails, part of the teeth, skin glands, sensory cells, and the nervous system.

ego

A psychoanalytic term for the part of the personality that integrates and directs behavior, mediating between the impulsive demands of the id and the constraints of superego and reality.

egocentrism (adj.: egocentric)

See ADOLESCENT EGOCENTRISM.

embryo

The developing human individual from the time of implantation to the end of the eighth week after conception.

endoderm

The innermost layer of the embryonic cell mass; source of the lining of the entire digestive tract, bronchia, eustachian tube, liver, lungs, pancreas, salivary glands, thymus gland, thyroid gland, and trachea.

equalitarian parent

A parent who allows the child to share equally with the parent in making decisions about the child's behavior.

equilibration

The process by which a child resolves the complementary processes of assimilation and accommodation.

estrogen

Feminizing hormone (also found in lesser amounts in males).

evaluation

Consideration of alternative solutions in a problem situation.

executive functions

Psychological processes that are responsible for the improvement of cognitive functioning, including the ability to recognize the nature of a problem, the ability to discard inefficient solutions, the use of strategies, and control of distraction and anxiety.

extinction

Weakening or elimination of a response as a result of presenting a conditioned stimulus without the usual reinforcement.

extraversion

The tendency to focus on and derive satisfaction from people and events in the outside world.

fear	Anticipation of danger or an unpleasant event, feeling, or reaction; a specific emotion in response to real danger.
fetal alcohol syndrome	Prenatal developmental defects caused by mother's drinking during pregnancy. Symptoms may include severely retarded growth, prematurity, mental retardation, microcephaly (an abnormally small head), as well as auditory, visual, and heart defects.
fetal distress	Disturbed functioning of respiratory and other systems in the fetus.
fetus	The developing human being from the end of the second prenatal month until birth.
fixation	In psychoanalysis, arrested development or failure to progress to a more mature stage of development or more mature object of attachment.
formal operations	In Piaget's theory, the last of the major stages of the development of intelligence. It begins in adolescence, when the individual begins to deal with abstractions, verbal propositions, and formal logic.
fraternal twins	Twins derived from two separate fertilized ova.
frustration	An emotional or feeling state resulting from interference with attainment of a desired goal.
frustration-aggression hypothesis	The notion that being blocked from attaining a desired goal produces feelings of anger and hostility.
generalization	The principle that a learned response associated with a particular stimulus will be evoked by similar stimuli.
genes	Tiny particles (containing DNA), carried by chromosomes, that are the basic units of hereditary transmission.
genital stage	In classical psychoanalysis, the final stage of psychosexual development, beginning in adolescence, during which the individual chooses mature love objects and the mature genitals are the primary source of pleasure.
germ cell	An ovum or sperm cell or one of the cells from which they are derived.
gestation	The period of prenatal development in the uterus.
grasping reflex	The infant's tendency to close his or her hand around an object placed in it.
habituation	Diminished physiological and psychological responsiveness or attention to a stimulus after repeated presentations, as when a baby is no longer excited by a stimulus to which it is accustomed.
hallucinogens	Any of a variety of psychoactive drugs, such as LSD or mescaline, capable of producing visual, auditory, or other kinds of hallucinations.
hereditary	Determined by genetic factors.
heroin	A semisynthetic physiologically addictive drug derived from opium.

	Initially, it can produce feelings of physical warmth, peacefulness, and increased self-confidence. Withdrawal symptoms can be painful and severe; overdoses may lead to convulsions and death.
hostility	An attitude of anger or resentment toward another person.
hypochondriasis (adj.: hypochondriacal)	Imagined or exaggerated physical symptomatology reflecting an excessive preoccupation with the functioning of the body.
id	In psychoanalytic theory, the source of instinctual energy; the part of the personality that includes sexual and aggressive impulses seeking immediate expression and gratification.
identical twins	Twins derived from the same fertilized ovum, thus having the same heredity.
identification	The child's belief that he or she is similar to another person and shares vicariously in the emotions of that person.
identity	In psychology, the sense of knowing who one is as a person, and where one is going. The individual with a strong sense of identity sees himself or herself as a unique, well-integrated individual, whose personality and behavior show a reasonable degree of consistency over time.
identity crisis	The struggle that adolescents may undergo in attempting to achieve a confident sense of their own identity.
image	A cognitive unit that is a detailed, elaborate, and conscious representation created from the more abstract schema.
impulsive	Acting quickly, without reflecting about the relative accuracy of alternative solutions or answers.
independent variable	The variable selected and manipulated by the investigator to determine its effects on the DEPENDENT VARIABLE.
inflection	An ending to a word stem that expresses grammatical relation—for example, -s (plural) or -ed (past tense).
insight	The perception of new relationships between two or more events that leads to solving problems.
institutionalized	Referring to rearing of a young child in a group-care setting such as an orphanage, a day-care center, or a mental hospital.
intelligence	A term used to refer to the ability of a child to deal with problems and to learn new skills easily; also, a score on a standardized test designed to measure general mental ability.
intelligence tests	Tests of information, vocabulary, and problem solving. The results of the test are generally expressed as an IQ, or intelligence quotient, which is the ratio of mental to chronological age. $IQ = MA/CA \times 100$
intermittent	Not continuous. A tone that goes on and off would be called an intermittent tone.

intonation — The pattern of pitch changes a speaker produces in speaking a phrase or sentence.

introversion — Tendency to be predominantly concerned with and interested in one's own inner life.

Klinefelter's syndrome — A condition resulting from an excessive number of X (female) chromosomes in males, which prevents the development of male secondary sex characteristics at puberty unless treated; it may be accompanied by behavioral problems and retarded intellectual development.

laissez-faire parent — A parent who leaves the child or adolescent free either to subscribe to or to disregard parental wishes.

learning disability — Inability to learn at a level commensurate with the student's intellectual ability. Learning disabilities may result from a variety of causes, ranging from perceptual difficulties to psychological conflicts or cultural problems.

libido — According to psychoanalytic theory, the biologically determined sexual energy that governs basic pleasure-seeking drives.

longitudinal study — A developmental study in which the same individuals are observed, tested, and rated repeatedly over an extended period of time.

maturation — The inevitable emergence of skills, abilities, and capacities that develop as a part of the innate potential of the organism.

mediating response — See VERBAL MEDIATION.

memory — The storage and retrieval of information.

menarche — The onset of menstruation.

mesoderm — The middle layer of the embryonic cell mass; source of the inner skin layer (dermis), muscles, skeleton, and circulatory and excretory organs.

minimal brain dysfunction (MBD) — A disturbance in cognitive or behavioral functioning presumably due to some impairment in the central nervous system, though clear neurological signs are generally absent. Symptoms may include hyperactivity, excitability, learning problems, and impulsive behavior.

model (modeling) — In observational learning, the individual whose actions are observed and imitated by the observer. Modeling is the process by which the individual learns by observing the behavior of others.

mongolism — See DOWN'S SYNDROME.

Moro reflex — A reflex typically seen in the first 2 or 3 months of life. When the child's head is moved, his or her arms move out to both sides and then come together again in the midline.

myelinization — The development of the fatty sheaths surrounding certain nerve fibers.

nature — The effects of genes and physiological factors on development. See also NURTURE.

nocturnal emission   Ejaculation of seminal fluid (which contains sperm) during sleep, often accompanied by erotic dreams.

nurturance   Warm, caring, concerned, and responsive behavior.
(adj.: nurturant)

nurture   The effects of learning and environmental experience on the growing child. See also NATURE.

nutritional   Pertaining to the body's need for carbohydrates, fats, protein, minerals, and vitamins; malnutrition is an inadequate supply of these substances.

object permanence   In Piagetian theory, the child's belief that objects continue to exist even if they are out of sight.

observational learning   Process of learning by observing the responses of a model and then imitating the behavior observed.

obsession   Preoccupation with a stereotyped thought.

operant (instrumental)   A type of conditioning in which a new association between a stimulus
conditioning   and a learned response is formed through reinforcement.

operation   A special kind of mental routine that transforms information for some purpose and is reversible.

oral stage   According to psychoanalytic theory, the first stage of development in the first year of life, during which the mouth and activities associated with feeding are invested with libidinal energy and provide gratification.

ossification   The normal developmental process in which the bones forming the body's skeletal structure become hard.

overextension   Using a word for a category of objects larger than the adult's category labeled by that word—for example, *doggie* to refer to both horses and dogs.

ovum   Egg; the female sex cell.

PCP (phencyclidine,   A tranquilizer used to obtain a "high"; may produce disoriented, irra-
or "angel dust")   tional, life-endangering behavior.

perception   The detection of events in the environment and the organization and initial interpretation of them.

permissiveness   The opposite of restrictiveness. An attitude on the part of the caretaker that allows the child autonomy and freedom.

personal tempo   An individual's characteristic rate of responding in various situations (e.g., a person's "natural" rate of tapping); variations in rate appear to be influenced by genetic factors.

phallic stage   According to psychoanalytic theory, the stage between approximately ages 3 and 5, when the genitals become the primary source of gratification and pleasure.

phobias	Very strong fears, for example, of dogs, lightning, and the dark.
pituitary gland	Endocrine gland located immediately below the brain, which plays a major role in stimulating physical growth and sexual maturation.
PKU (phenylketonuria)	A genetic disorder that may result in damage to the nervous system and mental deterioration unless treated. Children with this disorder lack an enzyme that is necessary to rid the body of a toxic chemical (phenylalanine) common in many foods.
placenta	Vascular organ that unites the fetus and the mother's uterus; it conveys food, oxygen, and various chemicals to the fetus and carries away waste materials.
polygenic	A characteristic or condition of the individual that is collectively controlled by a group of genes rather than by a single gene.
postconventional stage	Advanced stage in the development of moral reasoning, according to Kohlberg, in which the individual becomes capable of thinking in terms of abstract moral principles and general rules of conduct, rather than simply adopting the beliefs and practices of parents or a particular social group.
postmaturity (postterm)	Delayed birth beyond the normal gestational period.
postnatal	Following birth.
power assertion	Control of others by physical power or material resources.
prematurity	Birth prior to the end of the normal gestational period.
prenatal	Prior to birth.
preoperational stage	According to Piaget's theory, the second period of the development of intelligence, between the ages of 2 and 7, when the child perceives and records experiences symbolically and tends to think in terms of classes, numbers, and relationships.
projection	The tendency to attribute some undesirable thought or action of one's own to another person.
prosocial behavior	Actions that show concern with the welfare and rights of others.
psychoactive drug	A drug capable of producing psychological effects, such as euphoria, tranquillity, depression, stimulation, or agitation.
psychoanalysis	The theory and psychotherapeutic procedures developed by Freud to uncover and resolve unconscious emotional conflicts underlying neurotic symptoms and to explain normal and abnormal behavior.
psycholinguistics	The study of the psychological aspects of language.
psychophysiological (psychosomatic) disturbances	Psychological disturbance manifested by actual disturbances in physiological functioning, either acute (as in temporary gastrointestinal complaints or muscle-tension headaches) or chronic (as in peptic ulcer).
puberty	Period of sexual maturation.

Quaaludes ("Ludes")	A sedative, similar to barbiturates, except users claim to feel euphoria without drowsiness. Withdrawal symptoms similar to those for barbiturates.
rationalization	A defense mechanism characterized by the individual giving socially acceptable reasons for behavior based on less acceptable reasons.
reaction formation	A tendency to think and behave in a way that is the opposite of one's basic unconscious motivation.
reasoning	The use of knowledge to make inferences and draw conclusions.
recall	Perception of an event as having been experienced in the past.
recognition	Remembering events experienced in the past, indicated by the individual's ability to recognize such events.
reflection	The evaluation of the quality of ideas and solutions.
reflective	Tending to inhibit an initial response and to consider various alternatives to problem situations. Children are reflective when they take some time to evaluate a problem before answering.
reflex (or reflex response)	A relatively simple, unlearned, and involuntary response elicited by a specific stimulus and occurring rather mechanically. For example, the infant's sucking in response to stimulation of the lips is a reflex.
regression	A tendency to revert to a behavior characteristic of a younger child.
repression	An unconscious mechanism of defense in which the person is unable to remember an unpleasant or anxiety-arousing event.
restrictiveness	An attitude or behavior on the part of a parent or caretaker toward a child involving the limiting of the child's freedom and autonomy.
Rh factor	Any of one or more genetically determined substances present in the red blood cells of most people, capable of inducing the formation of antigens. When an Rh-positive man is married to an Rh-negative woman (about 1 chance in 9), there can sometimes be serious consequences for their offspring, because antibodies from the mother may cross the placenta and attack the unborn infant's red blood cells, leading to anemia, retardation, or even death.
rubella ("German measles")	A contagious viral disease that can be extremely serious if contracted prenatally—particulary in the first 3 months—leading to mental retardation, heart malformations, deafness, blindness, or other birth defects.
rule	A unit of cognitive processing. Essentially a rule is a statement about a concept.
schema (plural: schemata)	An abstract representation of an event in the environment.
schizophrenia	The most common form of severe mental illness (psychosis), characterized by marked defects in logical thinking and emotional responsiveness.

self-concept	A child's beliefs about the psychological qualities that characterize himself or herself.
semantics	The study of word meaning.
sensorimotor	In Piaget's theory, the earliest phase of the development of intelligence, in which knowledge is derived from motor actions and sensory perceptions.
separation anxiety	The crying and distress a child shows when her mother leaves her or when her mother or caretaker leaves her alone in an unfamiliar place or with an unfamiliar person.
serialization	A Piagetian concept that refers to the child's ability to arrange objects in a sequence according to one dimension, such as weight or size.
serial monogamist	An individual who generally has a love relationship and sexual intercourse with only one partner at a time, although such a relationship may soon be followed by another, rather than involving a long-term commitment.
sex chromosomes	The one pair of chromosomes that determines the sex of the individual. Girls and women have two female chromosomes (XX). Males have one female and one male chromosome (XY).
sex-typed behavior	Behavior primarily associated with, or viewed by society as associated with, one sex, either male or female.
sex typing	Adoption of personality traits, beliefs, attitudes, and behaviors that the culture defines as appropriate for the individual's sex.
sexual adventurer	An adolescent who moves freely from one sex partner to the next and feels no obligation to be faithful to any particular individual.
sexual (or sex-role) identity	Awareness and psychological acceptance of one's basic biological nature as male or female.
siblings	Brothers and sisters.
socialization	The process by which an individual acquires behaviors approved by the culture and society; the result of the individual's social experiences that affect personality, motives, values, and behavior.
sperm	Male sex cell (which unites with ovum to produce a new individual).
stage	A period of development when there is a special or unique organization of the qualities of the child.
stranger anxiety	The fearfulness and inhibition an infant shows when approached by an unfamiliar person.
strategies	Mental operations used to aid memory, perception, and reasoning; they include rehearsal, elaboration, and association.
superego	In psychoanalytic theory, the part of the personality that corresponds to

conscience, prohibitions, restraints, and moral prescriptions of the culture, internalized through identification.

symbol — A cognitive unit; an arbitrary way of representing concrete events, characteristics, or qualities of objects and actions.

symbolic — Pertaining to a mental representation of an object or event that has an agreed-upon or obvious relationship to its physical qualities; a red light is symbolic of "stopping."

telegraphic sentences — Speech of the young child in which some words such as articles and prepositions are omitted.

tic — An involuntary motor response that seems to be the result of excessive psychological tension.

toxemia — An abnormal condition associated with the presence of toxic substances in the blood. Toxemia of pregnancy is a disorder of unknown origin that affects about 5 percent of pregnant women; its effects may range from mild (increased blood pressure, weight gain, retention of fluid) to severe (convulsions, or even death). It may lead to retardation in the unborn infant.

Turner's syndrome — A condition usually resulting from the absence of one X chromosome in girls and characterized by a failure to develop secondary sex characteristics at puberty. With treatment, feminine body characteristics will develop, though the girl remains sterile; intelligence and sex identity remain unaffected.

umbilical cord — Cord, arising from the navel, that connects the fetus with the mother's placenta.

uncertainty — A state produced by an unfamiliar event, inability to predict the future, or potential danger.

underextension — Use of a word for a category smaller than the adult category named by that word; for example, when the child restricts the use of the word *dog* to her own pet. See also OVEREXTENSION.

verbal mediation — Internal, verbal responses of labeling and coding stimuli that facilitate children's thinking, reasoning, and problem solving.

visually directed reaching — The infant's tendency to move his or her hand directly toward an object that he or she sees.

warmth — In a parent-child relationship, the expression of love and affection.

withdrawal — The avoidance of threatening situations or people.

X chromosome — Female sex chromosome.

Y chromosome — Male sex chromosome.

References

CHAPTER 1

1. Freud, S. *Introductory lectures on psychoanalysis* (standard ed.), Vols. 15, 16. London: Hogarth, 1963.
2. Hilgard, E. R. *Theories of learning.* New York: Harper & Row, 1954.
3. Mead, M. *Coming of age in Samoa.* New York: Morrow, 1928.
4. Miller, N. E., & Dollard, J. *Social learning and imitation.* New Haven: Yale University Press, 1941.
5. Piaget, J. *The origins of intelligence in children.* New York: International Universities Press, 1952.

CHAPTER 2

1. Apgar, V., & Beck, J. *Is my baby all right?* New York: Pocket Books, 1974.
2. Bell, R. Q.; Weller, G. M.; & Waldrop, M. F. New born and preschooler: Organization of behavior and relations between periods. *Monographs of the Society for Research in Child Development*, 1971, *36* (1, 2).
3. Brackbill, Y. Longterm effects of obstetric medication. Paper delivered at the biennial meeting of the Society for Research in Child Development, San Francisco, March 15–18, 1979.
4. Corah, N. L.; Anthony, E. J.; Painter, P.; Stern, J. A.; & Thurston, D. Effects of perinatal anoxia after 7 years. *Psychological Monographs*, 1965, *79*, 1–34.
5. DeFries, J. C., & Plomin, R. Behavioral genetics. In M. R. Rosenzweig & L. W. Porter (Eds.), *Annual review of psychology*, 1978, *29*, 473–515. Palo Alto, Calif: Annual Reviews.
6. Drillien, C. M., & Ellis, R. W. B. *The growth and development of the prematurely born infant.* Baltimore: Williams & Wilkins, 1964.
7. *11 million teenagers: What can be done about the epidemic of adolescent pregnancies in the United States.* New York: Alan Guttmacher Institute (Planned Parenthood Federation of America), 1976.
8. Ernhart, C. B.; Graham, F. K.; & Thurston, D. Relationship of neonatal apnea to development at three years. *Archives of Neurology*, 1960, *2*, 504–510.
9. Fawcett, J. Biochemical and neuropharmacological research in the affective disorders. In E. J. Anthony & T. Benedek (Eds.), *Depression and human existence.* Boston: Little, Brown, 1975. Pp. 21–52.
10. Freedman, D. An ethological approach to the genetic study of human behavior. In S. G. Vandenberg (Ed.), *Methods and goals in human behavior genetics.* New York: Academic Press, 1965. Pp. 141–161.
11. Freedman, D. G., & Freedman, N. C. Behavioral differences between Chinese-American and European-American newborns. *Nature*, 1969, *224*(5225), 1227.

12. Gesell, A, & Amatruda, C. S. *Developmental diagnosis: Normal and abnormal child development.* New York: Hoeber, 1941.
13. Gottesman, I. I. Personality and natural selection. In S. G. Vandenberg (Ed.), *Methods and goals in human behavior genetics.* New York: Academic Press, 1965. Pp. 63–74.
14. Illingworth, R. S. *The development of the infant and young child: Normal and abnormal.* Edinburgh: Churchill Livingstone, 1975.
15. Jones, K. L., & Smith, D. W. Recognition of the fetal alcohol syndrome in early infancy. *Lancet,* 1973, *2,* 999.
16. Kessler, S. Psychiatric genetics, In D. A. Hamburg, H. Keith, & H. Brodie (Eds.), *American handbook of psychiatry,* Vol. 6: *New psychiatric frontiers.* New York: Basic Books, 1975. Pp. 352–384.
17. Klein, R. Malnutrition and human behavior. Paper presented at Conference on Malnutrition and Behavior, Cornell University, 1975.
18. Lubchenco, L. O. *The high risk infant.* Philadelphia: Saunders, 1976.
19. Mendels, J. Biological aspects of affective illness. In S. Arieti & E. B. Brody (Eds.), *American handbook of psychiatry,* Vol. 3 (2nd ed.). New York: Basic Books, 1974. Pp. 491–523.
20. Munsinger, H. The adopted child's IQ: A critical review. *Psychological Bulletin,* 1975, *82,* 623–659.
21. *New York Times,* May 31, 1977.
22. Noble, E. P. *Alcohol and health.* Third Special Report to the U.S. Congress from the Secretary of Health, Education, and Welfare, June 1978.
23. Reed, E. W. Genetic anomalies in development. In F. D. Horowitz (Ed.), *Review of child development research,* Vol. 4. Chicago: University of Chicago Press, 1975. Pp. 59–100.
24. Singer, J. E.; Westphal, M.; & Niswander, K. R. Sex differences in the incidence of neonatal abnormalities and abnormal performance in early childhood. *Child Development,* 1968, *39,* 103–112.
25. Sontag, L. W. The significance of fetal environmental differences. *American Journal of Obstetrics and Gynecology,* 1941, *42,* 996–1003.
26. Stern, C. *Principles of human genetics* (3rd ed.). San Francisco: Freeman, 1973.
27. Usher, R. H. The special problems of the premature infant. In M. E. Avery (Ed.), *Neonatology.* Philadelphia: Lippincott, 1975. Pp. 157–188.
28. Wagner, M. G., & Arndt, R. Postmaturity as an etiological factor in 124 cases of neurologically handicapped children. *Clinics in Developmental Medicine,* 1968, No. 27. P. 89.
29. Whaley, L. F. Understanding inherited disorders. St. Louis: Mosby, 1974.
30. Windle, W. F. Neuropathology of certain forms of mental retardation. *Science,* 1963, *140,* 1186–1189.

CHAPTER 3

1. Acheson, R. M. Maturation of the skeleton. In F. Falkner (Ed.), *Human development.* Philadelphia: Saunders, 1966. Pp. 465–502.
2. Ames, L. B. The sequential patterning of prone progression in the human infant. *Genetic Psychology Monographs,* 1937, *19,* 409–460.
3. Bakwin, H., & Bakwin, R. M. Growth of thirty-two external dimensions during the first year of life. *Journal of Pediatrics,* 1936, *8,* 177–183.
4. Campos, J. J.; Langer, A.; & Krawitz, A. Cardiac responses on the visual cliff in prelocomotor human infants. *Science,* 1970, 196–197.

5. Charlesworth, W. Development of the object concept. Paper presented at the Meeting of the American Psychological Association, New York City, 1966.

6. Crook, L. K., & Lipsitt, L. P. Neonatal nutritive sucking. *Child Development*, 1976, *47*, 518.

7. Dennis, W. Infant development under conditions of restricted practice and of minimum social stimulation. *Genetic Psychology Monographs*, 1941, *23*, 143–191.

8. Fantz, R. L., & Fagan, J. F. Visual attention to size and number of pattern details by term and preterm infants during the first 6 months. *Child Development*, 1975, *46*, 3–18.

9. Garn, S. M. Fat, body size, and growth in the newborn. *Human Biology*, 1958, *30*, 265–280.

10. Garn, S. M., & Rohmann, C. G. Variability in the order of ossification of the bony centers of the hand and wrist. *American Journal of Physical Anthropology*, 1960, *18*, 219–229.

11. Gesell, A., & Amatruda, C. S. *Developmental diagnosis: Normal and abnormal child development*. New York: Hoeber, 1941.

12. Gesell, A.; Halverson, H. M.; Thompson, H.; Ilg, F. L.; Costner, B. M.; Ames, L. B.; & Amatruda, C. S. *The first five years of life: A guide to the study of the preschool child*. New York: Harper & Row, 1940.

13. Gibson, E. J., & Walk, R. R. The "visual cliff." *Scientific American*, 1960, *202*, 2–9.

14. Haith, M. M. The response of the human newborn to visual movement. *Journal of Experimental Child Psychology*, 1966, *3*, 235–243.

15. Haith, M. M. Visual competence in early infancy. In R. Held, H. Liebowitz, & H. R. Teuber (Eds.), *Handbook of sensory physiology*, Vol. 8. Berlin: Springer-Verlag (in press).

16. Kagan, J.; Kearsley, R.; & Zelazo, P. *Infancy: Its place in human development*. Cambridge, Mass.: Harvard University Press, 1978.

17. Kagan, J., & Klein, R. E. Crosscultural perspectives on early development. *American Psychologist*, 1973, *28*, 947–961.

18. Kinney, D. K., & Kagan, J. Infant attentiveness to auditory discrepancy. *Child Development*, 1976, *47*, 155–164.

19. Lapidus, D.; Kagan, J.; & Moore, M. Continuity in development over the first ten years of life. Unpublished manuscript, 1977.

20. Lipsitt, L. P. The study of sensory and learning processes of the newborn. In *Symposium on Neonatal Neurology, Clinics in Perinatology*, 1977, *4*(1), 163–186.

21. Piaget, J. *The construction of reality in the child*. New York: Basic Books, 1954.

22. Ross, G. R. Concept categorization in 1 to 2 year olds. Ph.D. dissertation, Harvard University, 1977.

23. Ruff, H. A., & Birch, H. G. Infant visual fixation: The effect of concentricity, curvilinearity and number of directions. *Journal of Experimental Child Psychology*, 1974, *17*, 460–473.

24. Tulkin, S. R., & Kagan, J. Mother-child interaction in the first year of life. *Child Development*, 1972, *43*, 31–42.

25. White, B. L., & Held, R. Plasticity of sensory motor development. In J. F. Rosenblith & W. Allinsmith (Eds.), *Readings in child development and educational psychology* (2nd ed.). Boston: Allyn & Bacon, 1966.

26. Wickelgren, L. W. The ocular response of human newborns to intermittent visual movement. *Journal of Experimental Child Psychology*, 1969, *8*, 469–482.

27. Wolff, P. H. Observations on newborn infants. *Psychosomatic Medicine*, 1959, *21*, 110–118.
28. Zelazo, N. A.; Zelazo, P. R.; & Kolb, S. Walking in the newborn. *Science*, 1972, *176*, 314–315.

CHAPTER 4

1. Ainsworth, M. D. S. Attachment and dependency: A comparison. In J. Gewirtz (Ed.), *Attachment and dependency*. Washington, D.C.: Winston, 1972.
2. Ainsworth, M. D. S. The development of infant-mother attachment. In B. M. Caldwell & H. N. Ricciuti (Eds.), *Review of child development*, Vol. 3. Chicago: University of Chicago Press, 1974.
3. Brackbill, Y. *Research and clinical work with children*. Washington, D.C.: American Psychological Association, 1962.
4. Caudill, W., & Weinstein, H. Maternal care and infant behavior in Japanese and American urban middle-class families. In R. Konig & R. Hill (Eds.), *Yearbook of the International Sociological Association*, 1966.
5. Dennis, W. *Children of the creche*. Englewood Cliffs, N.J.: Prentice-Hall, 1973.
6. Dennis, W., & Najarian, P. Infant development under environmental handicap. *Psychological Monographs*, 1957, *71* (Whole No. 436).
7. Harlow, H. F., & Harlow, M. K. Learning to love. *American Scientist*, 1966, *54*(3), 244–272.
8. Kagan, J. *Change and continuity in infancy*. New York: Wiley, 1971.
9. Kagan, J.; Kearsley, R.; & Zelazo, P. *Infancy: Its place in human development*. Cambridge, Mass.: Harvard University Press, 1978.
10. Kagan, J., & Moss, H. A. *Birth to maturity*. New York: Wiley, 1962.
11. Kessen, W. (Ed.). *Childhood in China*. New Haven: Yale University Press, 1975.
12. Peaslee, M. J. The development of competency in 2-year-old infants in day care and home reared environments. Ph.D. dissertation, Florida State University, 1976.
13. Provence, S., & Lipton, R. C. *Infants in institutions*. New York: International Universities Press, 1962.
14. Rheingold, H. L. The modification of social responsiveness in institutional babies. *Monographs of the Society for Research in Child Development*, 1956, 2(2, Serial No. 63).
15. Rheingold, H. L., & Eckerman, C. O. The infant separates himself from his mother. *Science*, 1970, *168*, 78–90.
16. Ross, G.; Kagan, J.; Zelazo, P.; & Kotelchuck, M. Separation protest in infants in home and laboratory. *Developmental Psychology*, 1975, *11*, 256–257.
17. Sander, L. W. Comments on regulation and organization in the early infant-caretakers system. In R. J. Robinson (Ed.), *Brain and early behavior*. New York: Academic Press, 1969.
18. Winick, M.; Meyer, K. K.; & Harris, P. C. Malnutrition and environmental enrichment by early adoption. *Science*, 1975, *190*, 1173–1175.

CHAPTER 5

1. Arsenian, J. M. Young children in an insecure situation. *Journal of Abnormal Social Psychology*, 1943, *38*, 225–249.
2. Braine, M. D. S. The ontogeny of English phrase structures: The first phase. *Language*, 1963, *39*, 1–13.
3. Bronfenbrenner, U. Socialization and social class through time and space. In E.

E. Maccoby, T. M. Newcomb, & E. L. Hartley (Eds.), *Readings in social psychology* (3rd ed.). New York: Holt, Rinehart and Winston, 1958. Pp. 400–425.

4. Clark, H. H., & Clark, E. V. *Psychology and language: An introduction to psycholinguistics.* New York: Harcourt Brace Jovanovich, 1977.

5. Dennis, W. Causes of retardation among institutional children: Iran. *Journal of Genetic Psychology,* 1960, *96,* 47–59.

6. Dollard, J., & Miller, N. E. *Personality and psychotherapy.* New York: McGraw-Hill, 1950.

7. Erikson, E. H. *Childhood and society.* New York: Norton, 1950.

8. Flavell, J. H. *The developmental psychology of Jean Piaget.* Princeton, N.J.: Van Nostrand, 1963.

9. Freud, A., & Burlingham, D. T. *Infants without families.* New York: International Universities Press, 1944.

10. Gesell, A., & Thompson, H. Learning and growth in identical infant twins: An experimental study of co-twin control. *Genetic Psychology Monograph,* 1929, *6,* 1–124.

11. Goodenough, F. L. Anger in young children. *Institute for Child Welfare Monograph.* Minneapolis: University of Minnesota Press, 1931.

12. Hindley, C. B.; Filliozat, A. M.; Klackenberg, G.; Nicolet-Meister, D.; & Sand, E. A. Some differences in infant feeding and elimination training in five European longitudinal samples. *Journal of Child Psychology and Psychiatry,* 1965, *6,* 179–201.

13. Huschka, M. The child's response to coercive bowel training. *Psychosomatic Medicine,* 1942, *4,* 301–308.

14. Jersild, A. T., & Holmes, F. B. Children's fears. *Child Development Monograph,* 1935, No. 20, 358.

15. Meredith, H. V. Change in the stature and body weight of North American boys during the last 80 years. In L. Lipsitt & C. Spiker (Eds.), *Advances in child development and behavior,* Vol. 1. New York: Academic Press, 1963, 69–114.

16. Nelson, K. Structures and strategy in learning to talk. *Monographs of the Society for Research in Child Development,* 1973, *38,* No. 149.

17. Peatman, J. G., & Higgons, R. A. Relation of infants' weight and body build to locomotor development. *American Journal of Orthopsychiatry,* 1942, *12,* 234–240.

18. Piaget, J. *The origins of intelligence in children.* New York: Norton, 1963.

19. Sears, R. R.; Maccoby, E. E.; & Levin, H. *Patterns of child-rearing.* New York: Harper & Row, 1957.

20. Slobin, D. I. *Psycholinguistics.* Glenview, Ill.: Scott, Foresman, 1971.

21. Slobin, D. I. Cognitive prerequisites for the development of grammar. In C. A. Ferguson & D. I. Slobin (Eds.), *Studies of child language development.* New York: Holt, Rinehart and Winston, 1973. Pp. 175–208.

22. Thompson, H. Physical growth. In L. Carmichael (Ed.), *Manual of child psychology* (2nd ed.). New York: Wiley, 1954. Pp. 292–334.

23. Watson, E. H., & Lowrey, G. H. *Growth and development of children* (3rd ed.). Chicago: Year Book Publishers, 1958.

24. White, R. W. Motivation reconsidered: The concept of competence. *Psychological Review,* 1959, *66,* 297–333.

CHAPTER 6

1. Anglin, J. M. *Word, object, and conceptual development.* New York: Norton, 1977.

2. Bellugi, U. Learning the language. *Psychology Today,* 1970, *4,* 32–35, 66.

3. Bloom, L. M. *One word at a time: The use of single word utterances before syntax.* The Hague: Mouton, 1973.

4. Bowerman, M. F. Semantic factors in the acquisition of rules for word use and sentence construction. In D. M. Morehead & A. E. Morehead (Eds.), *Normal and deficient language.* Baltimore: University Park Press, 1976. Pp. 89–179.

5. Brown, R. How shall a thing be called? *Psychological Review,* 1958, *65,* 14–21.

6. Brown, R. *A first language: The early stages.* Cambridge, Mass.: Harvard University Press, 1973.

7. Carey, S. The child as word learner. In M. Halle, J. Bresnan, & G. A. Miller (Eds.), *Linguistic theory and psychological reality.* Cambridge, Mass.: MIT Press, 1977.

8. Chomsky, C. *The acquisition of syntax in children from 5 to 10.* Cambridge, Mass.: MIT Press, 1969.

9. Clark, E. V. On the acquisition of the meaning of *before* and *after. Journal of Verbal Learning and Verbal Behavior,* 1971, *10,* 266–275.

10. Clark, E. V. What's in a word? On the child's acquisition of semantics in his first language. In T. E. Moore (Ed.), *Cognitive development and the acquisition of language.* New York: Academic Press, 1973. Pp. 65–110.

11. De Villiers, J. G., & de Villiers, P. A. *Language acquisition.* Cambridge, Mass.: Harvard University Press, 1978.

12. Flavell, J. H. *Cognitive development.* Englewood Cliffs, N.J.: Prentice-Hall, 1977.

13. Furth, H. G. Research with the deaf: Implications for language and cognition. *Psychological Bulletin,* 1964, *62,* 145–164.

14. Garber, H. L., & Heber, F. R. The Milwaukee Project: Indications of the effectiveness of early intervention to prevent mental retardation. Paper presented at the meeting of the International Association for the Scientific Study of Mental Deficiency, Fourth International Congress, Washington, D.C., August, 1976.

15. Gesell, A.; Halverson, H. M.; Thompson, H.; Ilg, F. L.; Castner, B. M.; Ames, L. B.; & Amatruda, C. S. *The first five years of life: A guide to the study of the preschool child.* New York: Harper & Row, 1940.

16. Gray, S. W., & Klaus, R. A. An experimental preschool program for culturally deprived children. *Child Development,* 1965, *36*(4), 887–898.

17. Heber, R.; Garber, H.; Harrington, S.; & Hoffman, C. Rehabilitation of families at risk for mental retardation. Unpublished progress reports, Research and Training Center, University of Wisconsin, Madison, Wis., (a) October, 1971; (b) December, 1972.

18. Klaus, R. A., & Gray, S. The early training project for disadvantaged children: A report after five years. *Monographs of the Society for Research in Child Development,* 1968, *33*(4).

19. Kagan, J., & Klein, R. E. Cross-cultural perspectives on early development. *American Psychologist,* 1973, *28,* 947--961.

20. Kessel, F. S. The role of syntax in children's comprehension from ages six to twelve. *Monographs of the Society for Research in Child Development,* 1970, *35*(6, Whole No. 139).

21. Knobloch, H., & Pasamanick, B. Exogenous factors in infant intelligence. *Pediatrics,* 1960, *26,* 210–218.

22. Kosslyn, S. M. Using imagery to retrieve semantic information. *Child Development,* 1976, *47,* 434–444.

23. Leonard, L. B. *Meaning in child language.* New York: Grune & Stratton, 1976.

24. Miller, L. B., & Dyer, J. L. Four preschool programs, their dimensions and effects. *Monographs of the Society for Research in Child Development,* 1975, *40*(5 & 6).

25. Newcombe, N.; Rogoff, B.; & Kagan, J. Developmental changes in recognition memory for pictures of objects and scenes. *Developmental Psychology,* 1977, *13,* 336–341.

26. Ninio, A., & Bruner, J. The achievement and antecedents of labelling. Unpublished paper, Hebrew University, Jerusalem, 1976.

27. Piaget, J. *Play, dreams, and imitation in childhood.* New York: Norton, 1951.

28. Sinclair-de-Zwart, H. Developmental psycholinguistics. In D. Elkind & J. H. Flavell (Eds.), *Studies in Cognitive Development.* New York: Oxford University Press, 1969.

29. Thompson, H. Physical growth. In L. Carmichael (Ed.), *Manual of child psychology* (2nd ed.). New York: Wiley, 1954. Pp. 292–334.

CHAPTER 7

1. Baumrind, D. Child care practices anteceding three patterns of preschool behavior. *Genetic Psychology Monographs,* 1967, *75,* 43–88.

2. Becker, W. C. Consequences of different kinds of parental discipline. In M. L. Hoffman & L. W. Hoffman (Eds.), *Review of child development research,* Vol. 1. New York: Russell Sage Foundation, 1964.

3. Block, J. H. Another look at sex differentiation in the socialization behavior of mothers and fathers. In F. Denmark & J. Sherman (Eds.), *Psychology of women: Future directions of research.* New York: Psychological Dimension, Inc., in press.

4. Carlsmith, L. Effect of early father absence on scholastic aptitude. *Harvard Educational Review,* 1964, *34,* 3–21.

5. Erikson, E. H. Toys and reason. In M. R. Haworth (Ed.), *Child Psychotherapy: Practice and theory.* New York: Basic Books, 1964. Pp. 3–11.

6. Feshbach, S. Aggression. In P. H. Mussen (Ed.), *Carmichael's manual of child psychology,* Vol. 2. (3rd ed.). New York: Wiley, 1970. Pp. 159–259.

7. Hagman, R. R. A study of fears of children of preschool age. *Journal of Experimental Education,* 1932, *1,* 110–130.

8. Holmes, F. B. An experimental investigation of a method of overcoming children's fears. *Child Development,* 1936, *7,* 6–30.

9. Jersild, A. T., & Holmes, F. B. Some factors in the development of children's fears. *Journal of Experimental Education,* 1935, *4,* 133–141.

10. Jersild, A. T., & Markey, F. V. Conflicts between preschool children. *Child Development Monographs,* 1935, No. 21.

11. Kessler, J. W. *Psychopathology of childhood.* Englewood Cliffs, N.J.: Prentice-Hall, 1966.

12. Kohlberg, L. A. A cognitive-developmental analysis of children's sex-role concepts and attitudes. In E. E. Maccoby (Ed.), *The development of sex differences.* Stanford, Calif.: Stanford University Press, 1966. Pp. 82–173.

13. Lynn, D. *The father: His role in child development.* Monterey, Calif.: Brooks/Cole, 1974.

14. Mead, M. *Sex and temperament in three primitive societies.* New York: Morrow, 1939.

15. Parke, R. D., & Collmer, C. W. Child abuse: An interdisciplinary approach. In

E. M. Hetherington (Ed.), *Review of child development research*, Vol. 5. Chicago: University of Chicago Press, 1975.

16. Patterson, G. R. The aggressive child: Victim and architect of a coercive system. In L. A. Hamerlynck, L. C. Handy, & E. J. Mash (Eds.), *Behavior modification and families*. Vol. 1: *Theory and research*. New York: Brunner/Mazell, 1976.

17. Ruebush, B. K. Anxiety. In H. W. Stevenson (Ed.), *Child Psychology* (62nd Yearbook of the National Society for the Study of Education). Chicago: University of Chicago Press, 1963. Pp. 460–516.

18. Rutherford, E., and Mussen, P. Generosity in nursery school boys. *Child Development*, 1968, *39*, 755–765.

19. Sears, R. R.; Maccoby, E. E.; & Levin, H. *Patterns of child rearing*. New York: Harper & Row, 1957.

20. Steele, B. F., & Pollock, D. A psychiatric study of patients who abuse infants and small children. In R. E. Helfer & C. H. Kempe (Eds.), *The battered child*. Chicago: University of Chicago Press, 1968.

21. Wright, M. E. The influence of frustration upon the social relationships of young children. Ph.D. dissertation, State University of Iowa, 1940.

22. Yarrow, M. R.; Scott, P.; & Waxler, C. Z. Learning concern for others. *Developmental Psychology*, 1973, *8*, 240–260.

CHAPTER 8

1. Block, S. C. Is the child a scientist with false theories of the world? Ph.D. dissertation, Harvard University, 1972.

2. Cole, M., & Scribner, S. Cross-cultural studies of memory and cognition. In R. V. Kail, & J. W. Hagen (Eds.), *Perspectives on the development of memory and cognition*. Hillsdale, N.J.: L. Erlbaum, 1977. Pp. 239–271.

3. Diagram Group. *Child's body: A parent's manual*. New York: Paddington Press, 1978.

4. Flavell, J. H. Concept development. In P. H. Mussen (Ed.) *A Handbook of child psychology*. New York: Wiley, 1970. Pp. 983–1060.

5. Flavell, J. H. Developmental studies of mediated memory. In H. P. Reese and L. P. Lipsitt (Eds.), *Advances in child development and behavior*, Vol. 5. New York: Academic Press, 1970. Pp. 182–211.

6. Flavell, J. H.; Beach, D. R.; & Chinsky, J. M. Spontaneous verbal rehearsal in a memory task as a function of age. *Child Development*, 1966, *37*, 284–299.

7. Hamill, P. V. V.; Drizd, T. A.; Johnson, C. L.; Reed, R. A.; & Roche, A. F. *NCHS growth charts, 1976*. Monthly Vital Statistics Report. Washington, D.C.: U.S. Department of Health, Education, and Welfare, 1976.

8. Harris, G. J., & Burke, D. The effects of grouping on short term serial recall of digits by children: Developmental trends. *Child Development*, 1972, *43*, 710–716.

9. Honzik, M. P.; Macfarlane, J. W.; & Allen, L. The stability of mental test performance between two and eighteen years. *Journal of Experimental Education*, 1948, *17*, 309–324.

10. Jensen, A. R. How much can we boost IQ and scholastic achievement? *Harvard Educational Review*, 1969, *39*, 449–483.

11. Kagan, J. Generality and dynamics of conceptual tempo. *Journal of Abnormal Psychology*, 1966, *71*, 17–24.

12. Kagan, J.; Kearsley, R. B.; & Zelazo, P. R. *Infancy: Its place in human development*. Cambridge, Mass.: Harvard University Press, 1978.

13. Kagan, J.; Klein, R. E.; Finley, G. E.; Rogoff, B.; & Nolan, E. Cross-cultural study of cognitive development. *Monographs of Society Research Child Development,* 1979, *44,* No. 5.
14. Kagan, J,; Lapidus, D.; & Moore, M. Infant antecedents of cognitive functioning. *Child Development,* 1978, *49,* 1005–1023.
15. Lowrey, G. H. *Growth and development of children* (7th ed). Chicago: Yar Book Medical Publishers, 1978.
16. Maccoby, E. E. Selective and auditory attention in children. In L. P. Lipsitt & C. C. Spiker (Eds.), *Advances in child development and behavior.* New York: Academic Press, 1967. Pp. 99–124.
17. McCall, R. B. Children's IQ as predictors of adult educational and occupational status. *Science,* 1977, *197,* 482–483.
18. McGarrigle, J., & Donaldson, M. Conservation accidents. *Cognition,* 1974–5, *3,* 341–350.
19. Messer, S. B. Reflection-impulsivity: A review. *Psychological Bulletin,* 1976, *83,* 1026–1052.
20. Neimark, E. D.; Slotnick, N. S.; & Ulrich, T. The development of memorization strategies. *Developmental Psychology,* 1971, *5,* 427–432.
21. Newcombe, N.; Rogoff, B.; & Kagan, J. Developmental changes in recognition memory for pictures of objects and scenes. *Developmental Psychology,* 1977, *13,* 336–341.
22. Piaget, J. Piaget's theory. In P. H. Mussen (Ed.), *Carmichael's manual of child psychology* (3rd ed.). New York: Wiley, 1970. Pp. 703–732.
23. Ridberg, E. H.; Parke, R. D.; & Hetherington, E. M. Modification of impulsive and reflective cognitive styles through observation of film mediated models. *Developmental Psychology,* 1971, *5,* 369–377.
24. Rogoff, B. A portrait of memory in cultural context. Ph.D. dissertation. Harvard University, 1977.
25. Scarr, S., & Weinberg, R. A. I.Q. test performance of black children adopted by white families. *American Psychologist,* 1976, *31,* 726–739.
26. Sellers, M. J. Cross-cultural study of memory. Ph.D. dissertation, Harvard University, 1979.
27. Wallach, M. A., & Kogan, N. *Modes of thinking in young children.* New York: Holt, Rinehart, and Winston, 1965.

CHAPTER 9

1. Baldwin, A. L. The effect of home environment on nursery school behavior. *Child Development,* 1949, *20,* 49–61.
2. Becker, W. C. Consequences of different kinds of parental discipline. In M. L. Hoffman and L. W. Hoffman (Eds.), *Review of child development,* Vol. 1. New York: Russell Sage Foundation, 1964.
3. Block, J. H. Conceptions of sex role: Some cross-cultural and longitudinal perspectives. *American Psychologist,* 1973, *28,* 512–529.
4. Coopersmith, S. *The antecedents of self-esteem.* San Francisco: Freeman, 1967.
5. Harris, M. B., & Siebel, C. E. Affect, aggression, and altruism. *Developmental Psychology,* 1975, *11,* 623–627.
6. Hartup, W. W. Aggression in childhood; Developmental perspectives. *American Psychologist,* 1974, *29,* 336–341.
7. Hetherington, E. M.; Cox, M.; & Cox, R. The development of children in

mother-headed families. Paper presented at the Families in Contemporary America Conference, George Washington University, June 1977.

8. Hoffman, M. L. Altruistic behavior and the parent-child relationship. *Journal of Personality and Social Psychology*, 1975, *31*, 937–943.

9. Jersild, A. T., & Markey, F. V. Conflicts between preschool children. *Child development Monographs*, 1935, No. 21.

10. Kagan, J., & Moss, H. A. *Birth to maturity*. New York: Wiley, 1962.

11. Kessler, J. W. *Psychopathology of childhood*. Englewood Cliffs, N. J.: Prentice-Hall, 1966.

12. Kohlberg, L. The development of children's orientations toward a moral order: I. Sequence in the development of moral thought. *Vita Humana*, 1963, *6*, 11–33.

13. Kohlberg, L. Development of moral character and moral ideology. In M. L. Hoffman & L. W. Hoffman (Eds.), *Review of child development research*, Vol. 1. New York: Russell Sage Foundation, 1964. Pp. 383–431.

14. Kohlberg, L. Children's perceptions of contemporary value systems. In N. B. Talbot (Ed.), *Raising children in modern America*. Boston: Little, Brown, 1974. Pp. 98–118.

15. Longstreth, L. E.; Longstreth, G. V.; Ramirez, C.; & Fernandez, G. The ubiquity of big brother. *Child Development*, 1975, *46*, 769–772.

16. Patterson, G. R. The aggressive child: Victim and architect of a coercive system. In L. A. Hamerlynck, L. C. Handy, & E. J. Mash (Eds.), *Behavior modification and families*, Vol. 1: *Theory and research*. New York: Brunner/Mazell, 1976.

17. Sarason, S. B.; Davidson, K. S.; Lighthall, F.; Waite, R. R.; & Ruebush, B. K. *Anxiety in elementary school children*. New York: Wiley, 1960.

18. Sears, R. R. The relation of early socialization experiences to aggression in middle childhood. *Journal of Abnormal Social Psychology*, 1961, *63*, 466–492.

19. Sears, R. R. Relation of early socialization experience to self-concepts and gender role in middle childhood. *Child Development*, 1970, *41*, 267–290.

20. Shinn, M. Father absence and children's cognitive development. *Psychological Bulletin*, 1978, *85*, 295–324.

21. Staub, E. A. A child in distress: The influence of age and number of witnesses on children's attempts to help. *Journal of Personality and Social Psychology*, 1970, *14*, 130–140.

22. Tapp, J. L., & Levine, F. J. Compliance from kindergarten to college: A speculative research note. *Journal of Youth and Adolescence*, 1972, *1*, 233–249.

CHAPTER 10

1. Bachman, J. G.; Kahn, R. L.; Mednick, M. T.; Davidson, T. N.; & Johnston, L. D. *Youth in transition*, Vol. 1: *Blueprint for a longitudinal study of adolescent boys*. Ann Arbor: Institute for Social Research, University of Michigan, 1967.

2. Bentzen, F. Sex ratios in learning and behavior disorders. *American Journal of Orthopsychiatry*, 1963, *33*, 92–98.

3. Boehm, L. The development of independence: A comparative study. *Child Development*, 1957, *28*, 85–92.

4. Bronfenbrenner, U. Response to pressure from peers versus adults among Soviet and American school children. *International Journal of Psychology*, 1967, *2*, 199–207.

5. Bryan, J. H., & Walbek, N. The impact of words and deeds concerning altruism upon children. *Child Development*, 1970, *41*, 747–759.

6. Campbell, J. D. Peer relations in childhood. In M. L. Hoffman & L. W. Hoffman (Eds.), *Review of child development research*, Vol. 1. New York: Russell Sage Foundation, 1964. Pp. 289–322.

7. Cline, V. B.; Croft, R. G.; & Currier, S. Desensitization of children to television violence. *Journal of Personality and Social Psychology*, 1973, *27*, 360–365.

8. Dominick, J. R., & Greenberg, B. S. Attitudes toward violence: The interaction of television exposure, family attitudes, and social class. In G. A. Comstock & E. A. Rubinstein (Eds.), *Television and social behavior*, Vol. 3: *Television and adolescent aggressiveness*. Washington, D.C.: Government Printing Office, 1972.

9. Gordon, E. W., & Wilkerson, D. A. (Eds.). *Compensatory education for the disadvantaged: Programs and practices, Preschool through college*. New York: College Entrance Examination Board, 1966.

10. Gump, P. V. *Big schools, small schools*. Moravia, N.Y.: Chronicle Guidance Publications, 1966.

11. Hartup, W. W. Peer interaction and social organization. In P. H. Mussen (Ed.), *Carmichael's manual of child psychology* (3rd ed.), Vol. 2. New York: Wiley, 1970. Pp. 457–558.

12. Hartup, W. W. Peer relations: Developmental implications and interaction in same- or cross-age situations. Address to seminar on "Children in Groups," Organisation Modiale pour l'Education Prescholaire, January 1976.

13. Hartup, W. W. Peer interaction and the behavioral development of the individual child. In E. Scholpler, *Proceedings of the First International Leo Kanner Colloquium on Child Development, Deviations, and Treatment*. New York: Plenum, 1977.

14. Hess, R. D., & Shipman, V. C. Early experience and the socialization of cognitive modes in children. *Child Development*, 1965, *36*(4), 869–886.

15. Jakubczak, L. F., & Walters, R. H. Suggestibility as dependency behavior. *Journal of Abnormal and Social Psychology*, 1959, *59*, 102–107.

16. Kagan, J. Reflection-impulsivity: The generality and dynamics of conceptual tempo. *Journal of Abnormal Psychology*, 1966, *71*, 17–24.

17. Kerber, A., & Bommarito, G. (Eds.). *The schools and the urban crises*. New York: Holt, Rinehart and Winston, 1966.

18. Liebert, R. M., & Baron, R. A. Some immediate effects of televised violence on children's behavior. *Developmental Psychology*, 1972, *6*, 469–475.

19. Maccoby, E. E., & Masters, J. C. Attachment and dependency. In P. H. Mussen (Ed.), *Carmichael's manual of child psychology* (3rd ed.), Vol. 2. New York: Wiley, 1970.

20. McLeod, J. M.; Atkin, C. K.; & Chaffee, S. H. Adolescents, parents, and television use: Adolescent self-report measures from Maryland and Wisconsin sample. In G. A. Comstock & E. A. Rubinstein (Eds.), *Television and social behavior*, Vol. 3: *Television and adolescent aggressiveness*. Washington, D.C.: Government Printing Office, 1972.

21. O'Leary, K. D.; Becker, W. C.; Evans, M. B.; & Saudargas, R. A. A token reinforcement program in a public school: A replication and systematic analysis. *Journal of Applied Behavior Analysis*, 1969, *2*, 3–13.

22. Pope, B. Socioeconomic contrasts in children's prestige values. *Genetic Psychology Monographs*, 1950, *42*, 81–158.

23. Shinedling, M. M., & Pederson, D. M. Effects of sex of teacher and student on

children's gains in quantitative and verbal performance. *Journal of Psychology,* 1970, *76,* 79–84.

24. Silberman, C. E. *Crisis in the classroom: The remaking of American education.* New York: Random House, 1970.

25. Stein, A. H., & Friedrich, L. K. Television content and young children's behavior. In J. P. Murray, E. A. Rubinstein, & G. A. Comstock (Eds.), *Television and social behavior,* Vol. 2: *Television and social learning.* Washington, D.C.: Government Printing Office, 1972.

26. Stein, A. H., & Friedrich, L. K. The impact of television on children and youth. In E. Hetherington (Ed.), *Review of child development research,* Vol. 5. Chicago: University of Chicago Press, 1975.

27. Stein, A. H.; Friedrich, L. K; Deutsch, F.; & Nydegger, C. The effects of aggressive and prosocial television on the social interaction of preschool children. Paper presented at the meeting of the Midwestern Psychological Association, Chicago, May, 1973.

28. Stone, L. J., & Church, J. *Childhood and adolescence* (2nd ed.). New York: Random House, 1968.

29. Vellutino, F. R. Alternative conceptualizations of dyslexia. *Harvard Educational Review,* 1977, *47,* 334–354.

30. Vernon, M. D. *Reading and its difficulties.* New York: Cambridge University Press, 1971.

31. Walters, R. H.; Marshall, W. E.; & Shooter, J. R. Anxiety, isolation, and susceptibility to social influence. *Journal of Personality,* 1960, *28,* 518–529.

32. Wender, P. H. *Minimal brain dysfunction in children.* New York: Wiley, 1971.

33. Yando, R. Problem solving in unconventional tasks. Unpublished manuscript, Department of Psychology and Social Relations, Harvard University, 1978.

34. Yando, R. M., & Kagan, J. The effects of teacher tempo on the child. *Child Development,* 1968, *39,* 27–34.

CHAPTER 11

1. Adelson, J. The political imagination of the young adolescent. Daedalus, Fall 1971, 1013–1050.

2. Aristotle. *Ethica Nicomachea* (W. D. Ross, trans.). In R. McKeon (Ed.), *The basic works of Aristotle.* New York: Random House, 1941.

3. Baumrind, D. Authoritarian vs. authoritative control. *Adolescence,* 1968, *3,* 255–272.

4. Blum, R. H., et al. *Horatio Alger's children.* San Francisco: Jossey-Bass, 1972.

5. Brecher, E. M. *The sex researchers.* New York: American Library, 1971.

6. Chilman, C. S. *Social and psychological aspects of adolescent sexuality: An analytic overview of research and theory.* Milwaukee: Center for Advanced Studies in Human Sciences, School of Social Welfare, University of Wisconsin, 1977.

7. Coleman, J. C. *Relationships in adolescence.* London: Routledge & Kegan Paul, 1974.

8. Condry, J., & Siman, M. L. Characteristics of peer- and adult-oriented children. *Journal of Marriage and the Family,* 1974, *36,* 543–554.

9. Conger, J. J. A world they never knew: The family and social change. *Daedalus,* Fall 1971, 1105–1138.

10. Conger, J. J. Sexual attitudes and behavior of contemporary adolescents. In J. J. Conger (Ed.), *Contemporary issues in adolescent development.* New York: Harper & Row, 1975. Pp. 221–230.

11. Conger, J. J. *Adolescence and youth: Psychological development in a changing world* (2nd ed.). New York: Harper & Row, 1977.

12. Conger, J. J., & Kagan, J. *Adolescence: The winds of change* (film). New York: Harper & Row, 1976.

13. Douvan, E., & Adelson, J. *The adolescent experience*. New York: Wiley, 1966.

14. Dunphy, D. C. The social structure of urban adolescent peer groups. *Sociometry*, 1963, *26*, 230–246.

15. Eichorn, D. H. Asynchronizations in adolescent development. In S. E. Dragastin & G. H. Elder, Jr. (Eds.), *Adolescence in the life cycle: Psychological change and social context*. New York: Wiley, 1975. Pp. 81–96.

16. Elder, G. H., Jr. Structural variations in the child-rearing relationship. *Sociometry*, 1962, *25*, 241–262.

17. Elder, G. H., Jr. *Adolescent socialization and personality development*. Skokie, Ill.: Rand McNally, 1971.

18. Elkind, D. Egocentrism in adolescence. *Child Development*, 1967, *38*, 1025–1034.

19. Elkind, D. Cognitive development in adolescence. In J. F. Adams (Ed.), *Understanding adolescence*. Boston: Allyn & Bacon, 1968. Pp. 128–158.

20. Ehrhardt, A. A., & Meyer-Bahlburg, H. F. L. Psychological correlates of abnormal pubertal development. *Clinics in Endocrinology and Metabolism*, 1975, *4*, 207–222.

21. *11 million teenagers: What can be done about the epidemic of adolescent pregnancies in the United States*. New York: Alan Guttmacher Institute, Planned Parenthood Federation of America, 1977.

22. Faust, M. S. Developmental maturity as a determinant in prestige of adolescent girls. *Child Development*, 1960, *31*, 173–184.

23. Ford, C. S., & Beach, F. A. *Patterns of sexual behavior*. New York: Harper & Row (Hoeber), 1951.

24. Hall, G. S. *Adolescence: Its psychology and its relations to physiology, anthropology, sociology, sex, crime, religion, and education*, Vol. 1. Englewood Cliffs, N.J.: Prentice-Hall, 1904, 1905.

25. Hartup, W. W. Peer interaction and social organization. In P. H. Mussen (Ed.), *Carmichael's manual of child psychology* (3rd ed.), Vol. 1. New York: Wiley, 1970. Pp. 361–456.

26. Horrocks, J. W., & Benimoff, M. Isolation from the peer group during adolescence. *Adolescence*, 1967, *2*, 41–52.

27. Hunt, M. Special sex educational survey. *Seventeen*, July 1970, 94 ff.

28. Inhelder, B., & Piaget, J. *The growth of logical thinking from childhood to adolescence*. New York: Basic Books, 1958.

29. Israel, S. L. Normal puberty and adolescence. *Annals of the New York Academy of Science*, 1967, *142*, 773–778.

30. Jarvik, L. F. Discussion: Patterns of intellectual functioning in the later years. In L. F. Jarvik, C. Eisdorfer, & J. E. Blum (Eds.), *Intellectual functioning in adults*. New York: Springer Verlag, 1973.

31. Jersild, A. T. *The psychology of adolescence* (2nd ed.). New York: Macmillan, 1965.

32. Jones, M. C. The later careers of boys who were early or late maturing. *Child Development*, 1957, *28*, 113–128.

33. Jones, M. C. A study of socialization patterns at the high school level. *Journal of Genetic Psychology*, 1958, *92*, 87–111.

34. Kagan, J., & Kogan, N. Individual variation in cognitive processes. In P. H. Mussen (Ed.), *Carmichael's manual of child psychology*, Vol. 1. New York: Wiley, 1970. Pp. 1273–1365.

35. Kandel, D. B., & Lesser, G. S. *Youth in two worlds*. San Francisco: Jossey-Bass, 1972.

36. Keislar, E. R. Experimental development of "like" and "dislike" of others among adolescent girls. *Child Development*, 1961, *32*, 59–66.

37. Klerman, L. V., & Jekel, J. F. *School-age mothers: Problems, programs, and policy.* Hamden, Conn.: Shoe String Press, 1973.

38. Konopka, G. *Young girls: A portrait of adolescence*. Englewood Cliffs, N.J.: Prentice-Hall, 1976.

39. Maccoby, E. E. (Ed.). *The development of sex differences*. Stanford, Calif.: Stanford University Press, 1966.

40. Masters, W. H., & Johnson, V. E. *Human sexual response*. Boston: Little, Brown, 1966.

41. Masters, W. H., & Johnson, V. E. *Human sexual inadequacy*. Boston: Little, Brown, 1970.

42. Mead, M. *From the South Seas, Part 3: Sex and temperament in three primitive societies*. New York: Morrow, 1939.

43. Minturn, L., & Lambert, W. W., et al. *Mothers of six cultures: Antecedent of child rearing*. New York: Wiley, 1964.

44. Money, J., & Ehrhardt, A. A. *Man and woman, boy and girl: The differentiation and dimorphism of gender identity from conception to maturity*. Baltimore: Johns Hopkins University Press, 1972.

45. Osterrieth, P. A. Adolescence: Some psychological aspects. In G. Caplan & S. Lebovici (Eds.), *Adolescence: Psychosocial perspectives*. New York: Basic Books, 1969.

46. Plato. Laws. In *The dialogues of Plato* (4th ed.) (B. Jewett, trans.), Vol. 4. Oxford: Clarendon Press, 1953.

47. Pomeroy, W. B. *Boys and sex*. New York: Dell (Delacorte), 1968.

48. Purnell, R. F. Socioeconomic status and sex differences in adolescent reference-group orientation. *Journal of Genetic Psychology*, 1970, *116*, 233–239.

49. Reevy, W. R. Adolescent sexuality. In A. Ellis & A. Abarbanel (Eds.). *The encyclopedia of sexual behavior*, Vol. 1. New York: Hawthorn Books, 1961.

50. Reynolds, E. L., & Wines, J. V. Individual differences in physical changes associated with adolescence in girls. *American Journal of Diseases of Children*, 1948, *75*, 329–350.

51. Roche, A. F. *Skeletal maturity of youths 12–19 years, United States*. Vital and health statistics: Series 11, No. 160, DHEW publication no. (HRA) 77-1642. Washington, D.C.: Government Printing Office, 1976.

52. Ruble, D. N., & Brooks, J. Attitudes about menstruation. Paper presented at the biennial Meeting of the Society for Research in Child Development, New Orleans, March 17–20, 1977.

53. Simon, W., & Gagnon, J. H. Psychosexual development. In W. Simon & J. H. Gagnon (Eds.), *The sexual scene*. Chicago: Trans-action Books, 1970. Pp. 23–41.

54. Sorensen, R. C. *Adolescent sexuality in contemporary America: Personal values and sexual behavior, ages 13–19*. New York: Abrams, 1973.

55. Tanner, J. M. *Growth at adolescence* (2nd ed.). Oxford: Blackwell Scientific Publications, 1962. Philadelphia: Davis, 1962.

56. Tanner, J. M. Physical growth. In P. H. Mussen (Ed.), *Carmichael's manual of child psychology* (3rd ed.), Vol. 2. New York: Wiley, 1970.

57. Wilson, W. C. (Ed.). *Technical report of the Commission on Obscenity and Pornography*, Vol. 6: *National survey*. Washington, D.C.: Government Printing Office, 1971.

58. Yankelovich, D. *The new morality: A profile of American youth in the 1970s*. New York: McGraw-Hill, 1974.

59. Zelnik, M., & Kantner, J. F. Survey of female adolescent behavior conducted for the Commission on Population. Washington, D. C., 1972.

60. Zubin, J., & Money, J. (Eds.). *Contemporary sexual behavior: Critical issues in the 1970s*. Baltimore: Johns Hopkins University Press, 1973.

CHAPTER 12

1. Abelson, H. I.; Fishburne, P. M.; & Cisin, I. *National survey on drug abuse: 1977*. Washington, D.C.: Government Printing Office, 1977.

2. Ambrosino, L. *Runaways*. Boston: Beacon Press, 1971.

3. Astin, A. W. The new realists. *Psychology Today*, September 1977, *11*(4), 50ff.

4. Bachman, J. G. *Youth in transition*, Vol. II: *The impact of family background and intelligence on tenth-grade boys*. Ann Arbor: Institute for Social Research, University of Michigan, 1970.

5. Bardwick, J. M. *Psychology of women: A study of bio-cultural conflicts*. New York: Harper & Row, 1971.

6. Baruch, G. K. Maternal influences upon college women's attitudes toward women and work. *Developmental Psychology*, 1972, *6*, 32–37.

7. Bem, S. L. Androgyny vs. the tight little lives of fluffy women and chesty men. *Psychology Today*, September 1975, 58–62.

8. Bengston, V. L., & Starr, J. M. Contrast and consensus: A generational analysis of youth in the 1970s. In R. I. Havighurst & P. H. Dreyer (Eds.), *Youth: The seventy-fourth yearbook of the National Society for the Study of Education*, Part 1. Chicago: University of Chicago Press, 1975. Pp. 224–266.

9. Block, J. H. Conceptions of sex role. Some cross-cultural and longitudinal perspectives. *American Psychologist*, 1973, *28*, 512–526.

10. Boyle, R. P. The effect of the high school on students' aspirations. *American Journal of Sociology*, 1966, *71*, 628–639.

11. Bronfenbrenner, U. The origins of alienation. *Scientific American*, August 1974, *231*, 53–61.

12. Bruch, H. *Eating disorders*. New York: Basic Books, 1973.

13. Caro, F. G. Social class and attitudes of youth relevant for the realization of adult goals. *Social Forces*, 1966, *44*, 492–498.

14. Conger, J. J. A world they never knew: The family and social change. *Daedalus*, Fall 1971, 1105–1138.

15. Conger, J. J. *Adolescence and youth: Psychological development in a changing world* (2nd ed.). New York: Harper & Row, 1977.

16. Conger, J. J., & Miller, W. C. *Personality, social class, and delinquency*. New York: Wiley, 1966.

17. Douvan E., & Adelson, J. *The adolescent experience*. New York: Wiley, 1966.

18. Duncan, P. Parental attitudes and interactions in delinquency. *Child Development*, 1971, *42*, 1751–1765.

19. Erikson, E. H. *Identity: Youth and crisis*. New York: Norton, 1968.

20. Gallup, G. Gallup youth survey. *Denver Post*, May 29, 1977.

21. Gallup, G. Gallup youth survey, *Denver Post*, October 9, 1977.

22. Gallup, G. Gallup Youth Survey. *Denver Post*, April 15, 1979.

23. Gold, M., & Mann, D. Delinquency as defense. *American Journal of Orthopsychiatry*, 1972, *42*, 463–479.

24. Harris, L. Change, yes — upheaval, no. *Life*, January 8, 1971, 22–27.

25. Hauser, S. T. Self-image complexity and identity formation in adolescence, *Journal of Youth and Adolescence*, 1976, *5*, 161–178.

26. Heilbrun, A. B., Jr. Identification and behavioral ineffectiveness during late adolescence. In E. D. Evans (Ed.), *Adolescents: Readings in behavior and development*. New York: Holt, Rinehart and Winston, 1970.

27. Hoffman, L. W. Effects of maternal employment on the child: A review of the research. *Developmental Psychology*, 1974, *10*, 204–228.

28. Horner, M. S. Femininity and successful achievement: A basic inconsistency. In J. M. Bardwick et al., *Feminine personality and conflict*. Monterey, Calif.: Brooks/Cole, 1970. Pp. 45–73.

29. Jacobs, J. *Adolescent suicide*. New York: Wiley, 1971.

30. Jensen, G. F. Parents, peers, and delinquent action: A test of the differential association perspective. *American Journal of Sociology*, 1973, *78*, 262–275.

31. Johnson, A. M. Juvenile delinquency. In S. Arieti (Ed.), *American handbook of psychiatry*. New York: Basic Books, 1959. Pp. 840–856.

32. Johnston, L., & Bachman, J. *Monitoring the future: A continuing study of the life styles and values of youth*. Ann Arbor, Mich.: Institute for Social Research, 1975.

33. Josselyn, I. M. *Adolescence*. New York: Harper & Row, 1971.

34. Kohlberg, L. Moral education in the schools: A developmental view. In R. E. Grinder (Ed.), *Studies in adolescence: A book of readings in adolescent development*. New York: Macmillan, 1969. Pp. 237–258.

35. Kohlberg, L., & Gilligan, C. The adolescent as a philosopher: The discovery of the self in a postconventional world. *Daedalus*, Fall 1971, 1051–1086.

36. Maccoby, E. E., & Jacklin, C. *The psychology of sex differences*. Stanford, Calif.: Stanford University Press, 1974.

37. Miller, W. B. *Report to the Law Enforcement Assistance Administration*. Department of Justice, May 1, 1976.

38. Miller, W. B. The rumble this time. *Psychology Today*. May 1977, *10* (12), 52 ff.

39. Miller, J., & Baumohl, J. *Down and out in Berkeley: An overview of a study of street people*. Berkeley: University of California School of Social Welfare, 1974.

40. Mussen, P. H.; Young, H. B.; Gaddini, R.; & Morante, L. The influence of father-son relationships on adolescent personality and attitudes. *Journal of Child Psychology and Psychiatry*, 1963, *4*, 3–16.

41. Noble, E. P. *Alcohol and health*. Third Special Report to the U.S. Congress from the Secretary of HEW, June 1978.

42. Phillips, E. L.; Phillips, E. A.; Fixsen, D. L.; & Wolf, M. M. Achievement place: Behavior shaping works for delinquents. *Psychology Today*, 1973, *7*, 75–79.

43. Schacht, R. *Alienation*. Garden City, N.Y.: Doubleday, 1971.

44. Senn, M. J. E., & Solnit, A. J. *Problems in child behavior and development*. Philadelphia: Lea & Febiger, 1968.

45. *Seventeen*, March 1979, p. 137.

46. Simpson, R. L. Parental influence, anticipatory socialization, and social mobility. *American Sociological Review*, 1962, *27*, 517–522.

47. Stephenson, R. Mobility orientation and gratification of 1,000 ninth graders. *American Sociological Review, 1957, 22, 203–212.*

48. Stevic, R., & Uhlig, G. Occupational aspirations of selected Appalachian youth. *Personnel and Guidance Journal, 1967, 45, 435–439.*

49. Super, D. E., & Hall, D. T. Career development: Exploration and planning. In M. R. Rosenzweig & L. W. Porter (Eds.), *Annual review of psychology, 1978, 29,* 333–372.

50. The youth crime plague. *Time,* July 11, 1977, 18–28.

51. U.S. Bureau of the Census. *Statistical abstract of the U.S. 9* (1978) (99th ed.). Washington, D.C.: Government Printing Office, 1978.

52. *U.S. News and World Report.* September 6, 1976, 52–53.

53. Van Houten, T., & Golembiewski, G, *Adolescent life stress as a predictor of alcohol abuse and/or runaway behavior.* Washington, D.C.: National Youth Alternative Project, 1978.

54. Victor, H. R.; Grossman, J. C.; & Eisenman, R. Openness to experience and marijuana use in high school students. *Journal of Consulting and Clinical Psychology, 1973, 41, 78–85.*

55. Wallgren, H., & Barry, H., III. *Actions of alcohol,* Vol. 2: *Chronic and clinical aspects.* Amsterdam: Elsevier, 1970.

56. Wallgren, H., & Barry, H., III. *Actions of alcohol,* Vol. 1: *Biochemical, physiological, and psychological aspects.* Amsterdam: Elsevier, 1970.

57. Walters, J., & Stinnett, N. Parent-child relationships: A decade review of research. *Journal of Marriage and the Family, 1971, 33, 70–110.*

58. Wax, D. F. Social class, race, and juvenile delinquency: A review of the literature. *Child Psychiatry and Human Development, 1972, 3, 36–49.*

59. Weiner, I. B., & Elkind, D. *Child development: A core approach.* New York: Wiley, 1972.

60. Werts, C. E. Paternal influence on career choice. *Journal of Counseling Psychology, 1968, 15, 48–52.*

61. Yankelovich, D. *The new morality: A profile of American youth in the 1970s.* New York: McGraw-Hill, 1974.

Name Index

Subject Index